D0804644

BACCHUS
AND
CIVIC ORDER

Studies in Early Modern German History

H. C. Erik Midelfort, Editor

BACCHUS
AND
CIVIC ORDER

*The Culture of Drink
in Early
Modern Germany*

B. Ann Tlusty

University Press of Virginia

Charlottesville and London

The University Press of Virginia
© 2001 by the Rector and Visitors of the University of Virginia
All rights reserved
Printed in the United States of America
First published 2001

♾ The paper used in this publication meets the minimum requirements of the American National Standard for Information Sciences—
Permanence of Paper for Printed Library Materials, ANSI Z39.48-1984.

Library of Congress Cataloging-in-Publication Data
Tlusty, B. Ann, 1954–
Bacchus and civic order : the culture of drink in early modern Germany
/ B. Ann Tlusty.
p. cm. — (Studies in early modern German history)
Includes bibliographical references and index.
ISBN 0-8139-2044-2 (cloth : alk. paper) — ISBN 0-8139-2045-0 (pbk. : alk. paper)
1. Drinking customs—Germany—Augsburg—History. 2. Drinking of
alcoholic beverages—Germany—Augsburg—Social aspects. 3. Taverns
(Inns)—Germany—Augsburg—History. 4. Augsburg (Germany)—
Social life and customs. I. Title. II. Series.
GT2883.G3 T58 2001
394.1'2'0943375—dc21

00-013133

To my parents
for teaching me how to question
before they taught me how to read

Contents

Contents

Illustrations

Acknowledgments

THIS WORK would not have been possible without the help of many friends, colleagues, and institutions, all of whom I thank most gratefully. I am also thankful to the project itself for leading me to make the acquaintance of many fascinating people. Here it is possible to acknowledge only a few of them.

The years I spent sifting through the documents of the Stadtarchiv Augsburg, which I count among the most exciting and pleasant of my life, would not have been nearly as positive an experience without the friendly and helpful archive staff. Equally deserving of praise and gratitude are the staff members at the Staats- und Stadtbibliothek Augsburg, where I always received professional and personal attention. My research in Augsburg was supported by grants from the Institut für Europäische Kulturgeschichte of the University of Augsburg, the German Academic Exchange Service (DAAD), and Bucknell University.

The spirit of scholarly cooperation and team effort that I found among my colleagues in Augsburg's archives and libraries was a constant source of both professional and personal support. For intellectual camaraderie, unflagging research support, and the comic relief that kept things in perspective, I am particularly indebted to Hans-Jörg Künast, Beth Plummer, Kathy Stuart, and Michele Zelinsky. Especially conducive to our collective success was the Thursday night Archivstammtisch, at which even diverse research topics found common ground for discussion and comparison. I am grateful for the opportunity to share ideas, chapters, and Augsburg's beer gardens and cafes with Mitch Hammond, Christine Johnson, David Lederer, Wolfgang Mayer, Erik Midelfort, Benedikt Mauer, Lyndal Roper, Lee Palmer Wandel, Merry Wiesner-Hanks, and all of the other friends and colleagues whose research paths crossed mine. Each of them has contributed in some way to the shaping of this book.

For suggestions and support on this side of the Atlantic, I wish to thank Susan Karant-Nunn and Richard Waller. I also received feedback and encouragement at earlier stages of this project from Tom Brennan, Johannes

Acknowledgments

Burkhardt, Werner Dieminger, Maureen Flynn, John Kirkland, William Meinecke, Max Strobel, Donald Sutherland, Sabine Ullmann, and the collective members of the Alcohol and History Temperance Group. A special note of thanks goes to Susan Speaker, who provided both editorial suggestions and general moral support.

Finally, I am deeply grateful to Helmut Graser for his tireless efforts as editor, language consultant, critic, and intellectual companion. It was his faith in my work that finally got it off my desk.

To all of the above, thank you, and Prost!

Portions of chapter 8 have been published in the following articles:

"Gender and Alcohol Use" originally appeared in Social *History/Histoire Sociale* 27 (November 1994): 241–59. Copyright Les publications Histoire sociale–Social History, Inc., The University of Ottawa. Reprinted in *The Changing Face of Drink: Substance, Imagery, and Behaviour,* edited by Jack Blocker, Jr., and Cheryl Krasnick Warsh, 21–42. Copyright Les publications Histoire sociale–Social History, Inc., Ottawa, 1997. Reprinted by permission of Histoire sociale–Social History, Inc.

"Crossing Gender Boundaries: Women as Drunkards in Early Modern Germany" originally appeared in *Ehrkonzepte in der Frühen Neuzeit: Identitäten und Abgrenzungen,* edited by Sibylle Backmann, Hans-Jörg Künast, B. Ann Tlusty, and Sabine Ullmann, 185–98. Copyright Akademie Verlag, Berlin, 1998. Reprinted by permission of Akademie Verlag.

A Note on Quotations and Translations

ENGLISH TRANSLATIONS of quotations from the sources are my own unless otherwise noted. Key phrases and terms that are included in the text (in parentheses after the translations) are wherever possible adapted to reflect standard modern German. Quotations in the footnotes appear in their original Early New High German form with the following variations: superscript vowels are either converted to modern umlauts or omitted; word endings abbreviated in the original text are expanded in brackets; and punctuation is modified only where necessary for clarity.

Introduction

WHEN THE DAY LABORER Lienhart Strobel was accused by the Augsburg city council in 1542 of allowing his daughter to practice prostitution in his house and accepting rounds of drinks from her customers in return for his compliance, he defended his honor by asserting that "he had always paid his round."[1] Half a century later, the alms recipient Georg Albrecht traded his livelihood for the right to brag about buying rounds for his fellows, and the clock-maker Hainrich Frey spent eight weeks locked in the tower rather than give up the right to drink with his customers. Georg Vetter, the son of one of Augsburg's leading families, stabbed a fellow patrician's son in 1519 for refusing to join him in rounds of toasting. Refusing a glass offered in fellowship was an affront to honor that could move men at all levels of German society to draw their swords, sometimes with fatal consequences.[2]

Drinking bouts, tavern brawls, and convivial toasts may seem an unusual starting point for examining urban history; yet as these examples show, social drinking held a significance for early modern Germans that went far deeper than merely enjoying the taste or effect of wine and beer. A closer look at drinking rituals and their layered meanings can tell us a great deal about how early modern folk defined their lives and relations with one another. Strobel's claim that he had always paid his round, for instance, suggests not only that he was willing to pay for his own drinks but also that he was financially able to do so, and therefore he had no need to resort to dishonorable means to provide drinks for himself and his company. The statement was more than just a denial of accepting drinks on someone else's tab. It was both an expression of his masculine honor and a general denial of participation in any kind of disreputable behavior. Paying for rounds of drinks was a public display of the largess that lay at the heart of early modern notions of honor and status—for Strobel, a "metaphor for right living."[3]

Right living for the early modern German townsman was intertwined in multiple ways with the city's taverns and the drinking rituals that took place therein. Business was conducted, identities were formed and confirmed, stages of life were celebrated, and notions of honor were tested and validated at the tables of urban taverns. At the same time, drinking and tavern going provided a potential source of disorder. Drinking could lead to drunkenness; tests of honor could end in violence; and tavern meetings could develop into rebellious challenges to authority. The early modern tavern, like the wine that was served there, could be a metaphor either for celebration and communal values or for disorder and despair.

The definition of order versus disorder in the use of drink was a highly gendered construct. The lines drawn between honor and deviance, business and leisure, drunkenness and sobriety, and fellowship and debauchery, nebulous in any case, shifted in accordance with prevailing conceptions of gender difference. Thus although most of the actors in this book are men, it is throughout also about women and the boundaries that defined their physical and social identities. As early modern philosophers knew, without a construct of the feminine as complement, masculinity could not exist.

For Peter Burke, the tavern stood at the crux of the cultural stand-off between learned and traditional popular culture. Burke found visual representation of this stand-off in the common theme of a mock battle between Carnival (the metaphor for popular culture, represented by the tavern) and Lent (learned culture, represented by the church); according to Burke, it was Lent that ultimately triumphed.[4] Peter Clark saw a similar role for the alehouse in early modern English society, where it served as a focus of traditional values in conflict with the social attitudes of the middling and upper orders.[5] The role of the church as a social and cultural institution has been the focus of much historical scholarship on early modern Europe. Considering its position at the heart of early modern urban culture and its importance to the lives of early modern townspeople, the tavern has come up extremely short in comparison. This work is an attempt to correct this imbalance.

A Drunken Century?

The Germans were known throughout Europe during the early modern period for their extravagant drinking bouts. "All of the Germans haue one National vice of drunckenness in such excesse . . . as it staynes all theire nationalle vertues," wrote Fynes Moryson, an Englishman who traveled in Germany between 1591 and 1597.[6] His observation was not a new one, for men of the Germanic race had had a reputation for attachment to alcohol at least since Tacitus advanced the opinion in the second century A.D. that inviting German men to drink to their hearts' content would do more to bring them down than could be accomplished in battle.

Both Tacitus and Moryson noted with apparent surprise that it was in no way considered disgraceful or shameful among their hosts to drink oneself into a stupor. On the contrary, German men were more likely to feign drunkenness or use some other trick to avoid keeping pace with their companions than to admit to wishing to stay sober. This phenomenon is described in colorful detail in Vincentius Opsopaeus's *The Art of Drinking* (*De Arte Bibendi Libri tres*), first published in 1536. Opsopaeus advocated leaving the table frequently to urinate or bribing the servant to water the wine in order not to sacrifice honor by failing to keep up with one's drinking companions.

Opsopaeus's description belongs to a genre of literature that became popular during the sixteenth century as the drink literature (*Trinkliteratur*). Travelers to Germany, including Moryson, Michel de Montaigne, Desiderius Erasmus, and many others, made much of the German "national vice" of drunkenness. The accounts of travelers who wrote of the "great German thirst" may well have been exaggerated; but whether or not drunkenness actually proliferated during this period, literature addressing the problem certainly did. The topic concerned the Germans even more than it did their visitors. German drunkenness was a theme explored repeatedly by Martin Luther, Sebastian Franck, Johannes von Schwarzenberg, Hans Sachs, and many other moralists and theologians. German preachers preached against it; urban and rural authorities published ordinances against it; and satirists extolled it.[7] The period thus has earned the reputation of a "drunken century."[8]

How do historians explain this preponderance of literature addressing drinking during the sixteenth century? Until recently, most have taken it at face value as "evidence of a fantastic excess hardly ever approached at any other time or by any other nation,"[9] presuming that only a serious rise in alcohol abuse could lead to such a propagation in moral, religious, and legal tracts addressing drunkenness. Accepting uncritically the drink-as-despair theory of alcohol use, which holds that excessive alcohol consumption within a society can normally be explained by the existence of social problems, many historians assumed that this apparent rise in alcohol abuse was a result of the insecurities brought about by social and religious upheaval.[10]

The Culture of Drink in the Early Modern German City

This picture of an insecure, drunken popular society goes hand in hand with the reputation of the preindustrial working classes as generally disorderly. According to this classic view, the laboring classes of early modern Europe were spontaneous, unrestrained, and undisciplined—their toleration of disorder coming into conflict with the orderly, prudent, and sober ethic of the reformers. This disorderly nature, according to some historians of the period of industrialization, was not brought into check successfully until the laboring classes were forced into the time and space restraints of factory labor. Only with the imposition of established working hours did the common laborer develop an internal sense of regulation and self-control. Frustrated by the loss of traditional patterns of life, the industrial worker turned to drink as an outlet for his disorderly nature and a means to drown his insecurities, while the immoderate drinking that resulted threatened to undermine the assimilation of the industrial values of routine, punctuality, and perseverance.[11]

Historians such as Keith Thomas and Fernand Braudel have thus attempted to explain the preponderance of literature addressing drink during the sixteenth century as a response to a rise in alcohol consumption. The popular classes, according to these and other historians, turned to alcohol as a narcotic to provide comfort in the face of social pressure and poverty.[12] This position is based on the assumption that drunkenness was the goal of all social drinking. Another version of the drunkenness explanation is suggested by Aldo Legnaro, who characterized the transition from medieval to modern drinking forms as a change from unbridled, unashamed drunkenness as an acceptable goal in itself to the pursuit of drunkenness for the purpose of relaxing inhibitions. In both cases, drunkenness was the "desired goal of drinking."[13] The basis for the sixteenth-century sobriety movement could thereby be found in a shift of attitude toward drunkenness, which had to be identified as socially unacceptable before it could be attacked.

Hasso Spode claimed that although the movement had only a limited effect on behavior, it nonetheless affected the way the elite classes viewed drinking bouts. With the gradual institutionalization of notions of civility and self constraint identified by Norbert Elias, extreme drunkenness ceased to be acceptable and began to cause feelings of embarrassment or distaste. According to Spode, these new values were at the root of the campaign against drunkenness; with time, they became the norm in polite society. Yet this development was limited to social elites, primarily the nobility.[14]

The change in upper-class drinking norms suggested by Spode would explain the greater gap between elite and popular culture, and particularly the rise in elite concern over popular drinking habits, that some historians have identified in later periods.[15] The sixteenth-century sobriety movement thus might be seen as the starting point for efforts during the eighteenth and nineteenth centuries to enforce tighter controls on drinking among the laboring classes, rather than a movement that simply failed. Nonetheless, locating the movement within a wider attempt by the elites of the sixteenth century to discipline the populace is anachronistic. During the sixteenth and seventeenth centuries, the gap between the norms of the elites and those of the common classes was, at least on the issue of drink, scarcely discernible. Proponents of the social discipline model who describe this sobriety movement as directed at the underclass contradict their own argument by explaining its cessation by changes in elite norms of behavior. A reaction to drunkenness among commoners thus ends as a result of the sobering up of the elites.[16]

Michael Stolleis's view of the sobriety movement of the sixteenth century as part of the wider attack on luxury and excess documented in sumptuary laws is similarly problematic.[17] The movement did have its roots in the ascetic and spiritualist movements of the late Middle Ages and the rebirth of the ideals of stoicism and moderation that found favor among the Renaissance humanists. Among the most influential of the earlier writers in this genre were Sebastian Franck, a spiritualist monk, and the ascetic Sebastian Brant.[18] The aim of these moderates, however, was hardly an attempt to discipline the disorderly laboring classes. Their objective was to reform the excessive behavior of the elites. Ordinances formulated during the period of moral fervor accompanying the Reformation and its aftermath consistently targeted the elite custom of pledging healths, a form of competitive social drinking that found its most dedicated followers at court and courthouse, although it was mirrored by similar popular drinking customs in public taverns. The controls later in the sixteenth-century, which were increasingly intended for commoners, were rooted primarily in specific economic concerns rather than aimed at general luxury.

Early modern critics of excess knew why these ordinances had so little effect—the issuers of the ordinances were the worst offenders. Not only did city council members and territorial lords set a bad example for their subjects by continuing their immoderate drinking habits, they capitalized on the profits by collecting excise taxes on alcohol and building breweries and distilleries.[19] It is tempting to assume that elites' continued abuses can be explained by the fact that laws against excessive drinking did not apply to elite society, but commoners had little more to fear from laws against drunkenness than did their social superiors. Nor can we explain the failure of the sobriety movement simply by noting the poor example the elites set and their exploitation of alcohol sales or by assuming that they were unable to enforce norms in the face of demand.[20] The problem was not that drunkenness laws were not enforceable but that they were not enforced. Those responsible for law enforcement recognized alcohol as a necessary part of social and professional life. The drunkenness that resulted was not viewed as debauchery or sin but as acceptable behavior for male citizens.

By focusing on drunkenness rather than drinking, these historians also ignored the social functions served by the process of drinking itself. Achieving a state of ecstasy through alcohol consumption may have been a goal of archaic and medieval drinking bouts,[21] but drunkenness for those in the early modern period was more often a side effect than a goal of drinking. Even at the competitive drinking bouts of the privileged classes, which could end with the entire company drunk into a stupor, the goal of the wine hero was not to pass out but to consume more than his fellows and yet remain standing. Drunkenness was tolerated, occasionally utilized, and undoubtedly enjoyed, but to claim drunkenness as the goal of early modern drinking bouts oversimplifies the cultural uses of the process of consumption.

The sixteenth century was not only a high point in the production of literature on insobriety. It was also witness to a flood of books on brewing, distilling, and wine making as well as printed collections of German drinking songs and poems extolling the virtues of wine. The era of drink literature was more than a period of temperance agitation. It was an era of total fascination, both negative and positive, with alcohol.

Historians and Taverns

German historiography of the early modern period has, for the past thirty years, been ruled by three paradigms: Max Weber's theory of rationalization; Norbert Elias's theory of the civilizing process; and, most recently, Gerhard Oestreich's theory of social discipline.[22] According to Oestreich, the groundwork for an unevenly applied but nonetheless Europe-wide tendency toward shaping society into a model of order and discipline was founded in Renaissance notions of order and harmony. With the growth of the early modern city and the expanded need for communal cooperation, the pursuit of harmony manifested itself in social, religious, and political forms of socialization. The social disciplining process involved not only the enforcement of behavior in the interest of social harmony but also the gradual internalization of appropriate norms of social behavior, including the development of a work ethic. The legal instruments and social institutions designed to implement this vision of discipline (police and discipline ordinances, sumptuary laws, laws controlling beggars and vagrants, and so on) increased dramatically during the century following the Reformation. According to some historians, the process of social disciplining was linked not only to a growing repression of the marginal classes but also to an attempt to control, suppress, or reform popular culture generally.[23]

The position of the tavern poses a particular challenge to this explanation. Regarding England, historians have drawn a connection between the condemnation of alehouses in the sixteenth century and this rising concern with public order and discipline. The English authorities during the Puritan reformation, like their German contemporaries, were becoming increasingly obsessed with disciplining the lives of the populace and controlling communal leisure activities. Taverns threatened order by promoting violence and brawling, providing centers for trafficking in stolen merchandise and other criminal activities, and serving to encourage idleness, which inevitably led to discontented speeches fired by intemperate drinking.[24] Laws that controlled drinking and licenses that regulated the manufacture and sale of alcoholic beverages are often seen as part of an overall effort to prevent social disorder, for it was invariably the lower orders, the "disorderly poor" who took their pleasures there.[25] The tavern in this context became a "stronghold" posed in opposition to "established, respectable society,"[26] and the tavern keeper a person who generated "communal disfavor."[27] Some German historians, following the English model, have also tied growing controls on tavern drinking in Germany to a trend toward increased social discipline.[28]

The image of the early modern German tavern that is portrayed by its sixteenth-century critics certainly supports the notion that it lent itself to social instability. Whenever men joined at table, the advocates of moderation charged, the competitive drinking bouts began, and drunkenness was the only possible outcome. Wine thus imbibed, according to Sachs, Franck, and others who wrote in the drink literature genre, robbed men of reason and virtue and inflamed their nature. The result was violent behavior: brawling, sword fighting, even murder. The abuse of wine in the company of fellows also robbed men of humility, provoking them to insult not only one another but God himself, in swearing, cursing, and blasphemous language. According to a sermon delivered in 1610, drunken and disorderly young men wandered the streets at night committing wanton acts of vandalism and screaming "like young devils from Hell."[29] Sexual lusts, too, were inflamed by wine, making whoremongers of the drinkers and prostitutes of the tavern women. The expense of immoderate tavern drinking, temperance advocates charged, wasted inheritances and led to the pawning of clothing and household goods, reducing productive citizens to beggars and thieves.[30]

Also associated with tavern gatherings were the vices of gambling and idleness. German legend attributes the invention of cards and dice to the devil, who used them to gamble for souls. Games of chance were thus imbued with Satan's wiles. Not only did they carry the risk of financial losses, they also encouraged idleness, incited blasphemous language, and involved belief in fate, or the misuse of divine providence. Idleness was often labeled a source of all evils, particularly as the idle hours spent in the tavern company provided opportunities for discussing politics, organizing protests, and plotting revolts.[31]

As Sachs noted, the love of Bacchus led only to "poverty, theft, adultery, and murder";[32] and the tavern, according to one seventeenth-century preacher, was a "school of every earthly and hellish vice."[33] These charges against tavern life are no doubt at the root of the historian Phillip Ariès's conclusion that the tavern in the sixteenth century was "a place of ill repute reserved for criminals, prostitutes, soldiers, down-and-outs, and adventurers of every sort," that would not be visited by any "decent" person.[34]

There are some inherent problems, however, with this interpretation of early modern tavern life. In the first place, the comforts of the tavern were available only at a price, which (at least in the case of urban taverns) beggars, down-and-outs, and the impoverished prostitutes of the early modern period could hardly afford. Second, urban tavern keepers were not desperate persons living on the edge of poverty; they were for the most part economically privileged members of society, whose interests would hardly be served by entertaining criminals, prostitutes, professional gamblers, or guests who could not afford to pay their tab. In addition, taverns served many crucial functions for the community, including serving the authorities as centers of surveillance to ensure that these marginal social elements did not find refuge within the city walls. Taverns also played an important part in keeping the city functioning and defining appropriate gendered roles for all members of society. Finally, tavern going can hardly be defined as deviant behavior, since it was clearly the norm for most early modern townsmen. We must, in short, look beyond traditional associations of taverns with criminals and marginal elements in order to understand the sobriety movement of the sixteenth century. Certainly, drinking often resulted in drunkenness, and drunkenness often resulted in loud, violent, and otherwise "disorderly" behavior. Yet even drunken behavior had its cultural uses.

The portrayal of the early modern period as a progressive process of repression or acculturation of the popular classes has come under fire for its exaggeration of the gap between elite and popular culture. Critics have also found fault with the work of Burke and others for overstating the unity and lack of resilience of the underclasses.[35] More recently, a number of German historians working in criminal records have begun to explore a model that recognizes shared characteristics among all levels of society and lines of communication between elites and commoners. Prescriptive sources, formerly believed to exclusively represent the norms of the ruling sectors of society, are now understood as representing only one of many possible reactions to popular behavior. Legal norms and prescribed punishments were flexible and were not always consistently applied. The decisions of the elites in matters of social discipline often seem to adhere more closely to the unwritten norms of popular society than to the letter of the law.[36] This is certainly true in the case of elite reactions to drunken comportment among Augsburg's populace, which provide more evidence of shared interests than of repressive discipline.

Methods and Sources

What, then, lay at the root of the sixteenth-century attacks on drunkenness? If tavern drinking was an accepted, even necessary part of life for early modern Germans, why did authorities and moralists join together in condemning it? A key to answering these questions may be found in the construct of the "moral panic." This term is used by sociologists and anthropologists to describe "a condition, phenomenon, issue, or behavior" (such as violence or drug use) that emerges as a threat to society and becomes an area of "intense concern,"[37] or to use Stanley Cohen's term, a "folk devil."[38] Anthropologists studying relationships between dominant and nondominant social groups have found that the dominant sector tends to place external attributions on the nondominant group, based on their own value system. The actions of the misunderstood group are seen as meaningless, primitive, or disorderly, having no relationship to the rule-based society. These groups, however, have their own code of communication, a system of symbols that may present an opaque front to other social groups.[39] As Robert Darnton has suggested, it is sometimes the point at which a foreign culture seems the most opaque that provides a point of entry for the historian.[40] It is with this awareness that we must approach the windows of early modern Germany's urban taverns. Perhaps there was an order to the "guzzling, gluttony, [and] wild, lawless behavior" that one Augsburg preacher described as typical tavern comportment;[41] perhaps there was a system of symbols that formed "rules of disorder,"[42] although they remained unwritten.

The boozing devil of the sixteenth century fits the folk devil construct. Folk devils, according to theories of moral panic, often become images of disorder, representing the evils in society. They serve the purpose of providing the rest of society with the comfort of being right, of holding the reins of order.[43] It is thus possible for a society to overtly disapprove of an idea (that is, drunkenness as excess), and yet to tacitly accept the reality (that is, drunkenness as a way of life). The drunkards of Hans Sachs and Johann Fischart were archetypes, lovers of excess and worshipers of Bacchus. It was easy for representatives of church and authority to disapprove of such characters. Early modern German tavern goers, however, were not archetypes but participants in a world of shifting social relations and competition for status in which the use of alcohol was indispensable. Drunkenness the idea meant excess, sin, and worship at the devil's altar, but the drunkenness of reality most often resulted from nothing more than participation in acceptable drinking rituals.

This study, then, locates the role of the boozing devil and his altar in early modern German society by taking a detailed look at cultural drinking practices in the city during the sixteenth and seventeenth centuries. To this end, I set out to answer the following questions: What cultural value did early modern Germans place on the use of alcohol? How did they understand drunkenness as a construct, and how was their understanding gendered?

Introduction

What did people do in taverns, other than drink, and what benefits did they derive or believe they derived from these activities? Did attacks on drinking represent attempts to Christianize or discipline the populace, or was the tavern itself under fire as a potential threat? Were tavern gatherings viewed as suspicious or disorderly? Did they include women as well as men? Were they divided by social standing, income, profession, or confessional ties, or was it true that "gentlemen, Plebeians and very Coachmen [sat] at the same table," as Moryson noted during the 1590s?[44]

The patterns of behavior among tavern goers, and the attitudes of the authorities toward these behaviors, reveal a great deal about more general patterns of social behavior. According to Robert Muchembled, at the basis of the quest for security during the early modern period was a pervasive need for sociability.[45] The importance of the tavern in meeting this need has been explored by sociologists, anthropologists, and historians studying most societies in which alcohol is consumed.[46] By examining the use of tavern space and the pursuit of tavern sociability by members of early modern urban society, we can uncover reflections of the relationships between authority and populace, individual and community, man and woman, and citizen and state.

The importance of drinking customs to the cultural life of early modern Germans was well known to folklorists and cultural historians of the nineteenth and early twentieth centuries, who wrote multivolume cultural histories on wine, beer, and taverns; translated accounts of tavern visits by foreigners; and collected and published a multitude of drinking anecdotes, anti-drinking legislation, and drinking songs. The best of these works provide a wealth of readily available sources as well as many useful insights on the material. Nonetheless, they are anecdotal in their approach and lack the systematic methodology that modern scholarship requires.[47]

The value of studying public drinking as a starting point for broader questions of early modern social and cultural history has recently been recognized by historians of France, England, and the United States. Although by far the bulk of modern scholarship on the history of alcohol concentrates on the temperance movement of the nineteenth and twentieth centuries, there have been some pathbreaking works that examine early modern drinking patterns at least as a starting point. These include works by W. J. Rorabaugh and Marx Lender and James Martin, which examine alcohol consumption in the United States within the context of general social and ideological issues.

The Culture of Drink in the Early Modern German City

William Taylor's work on colonial Mexico, which draws on criminal trials and related records to investigate drinking behavior within its social and cultural context, laid the groundwork for later historians pursuing early modern alcohol history from an interdisciplinary perspective. And Peter Clark illuminated the social importance of the alehouse in early modern England with his seminal work *The English Alehouse: A Social History, 1200–1830*. Particularly innovative is Thomas Brennan's work on the cultural aspects of tavern drinking in eighteenth-century France. Brennan found in the tavern life of Paris at once a public theater for the culture of the Parisian populace and a target of elite critique of popular culture. Public drinking thus served as a metaphor for suspicion of the underclass and a "battlefield of conflicting cultures."[48]

In Germany, as in the United States, the nineteenth-century temperance movement dominates the historiography of alcohol. The early modern period is treated only fleetingly, when at all.[49] The lack of scholarship on drinking in early modern Germany is particularly surprising in view of the degree of attention the subject received in the literature of the period. Remarkable, too, is the near complete dependency on prescriptive sources by historians who do address early modern German drinking. With the exception of a few observations included in recent histories of a more general nature (especially by historians of crime),[50] those pursuing the issue of alcohol use in early modern Germany have scarcely looked beyond the printed sources (pamphlets, broadsheets, poems, and ordinances) that have until recently occupied the efforts of historians of popular culture. Such sources may provide the norms dictated by ruling authorities and other members of the literate sector, but they shed no light on whether these norms were accepted or resisted by popular society — or indeed, whether they were enforced by those who dictated them. For the most part, modern historians have not even systematically examined ordinances governing drinking and drunkenness; they have tended instead to depend on scattered examples from diverse periods and territories cited in early works by antiquarians and folklorists, scarcely improving on the anecdotal character of the original works.

It has only been during the past two decades, and then in fits and starts at best, that German historians have begun to exploit the opportunities provided by the marriage of a methodological framework borrowed from social anthropology with the rich source material to be found in Germany's collections of arrest, interrogation, and punishment records. As the efforts

Introduction

of historians such as Natalie Davis, Carlo Ginzburg, Lyndal Roper, and David Sabean have demonstrated, court documents can be among the most useful sources for illuminating the values and attitudes of the popular classes and their discourse with authority. Taylor and Brennan both made able use of criminal records in their work on early modern drinking in Mexico and Paris, drawing primarily on testimony from judicial records to locate the voices of illiterate drinkers and looking past particular incidents to discover the underlying attitudes and values revealed by their discourse with authority.[51] At times these attitudes and values are so basic to the society under examination, so much a part of their worldview, that they escape written description in printed texts.

The principal sources on which this study is based, then, are the judicial records of the Augsburg city council. These include interrogation records (*Urgichten*), which contain not only interrogations of defendants but also witness statements, supplications from the relatives of defendants and victims, and other supporting documents; records of arrest and punishment (*Strafbücher*); and lists of fines for minor breaches of discipline (*Zucht*) (*Protokolle der Zuchtherren*). To avoid the danger of selecting unrepresentative years for analysis, I have chosen to examine all existing court records for three five-year periods (1540–1544, 1590–1594, and 1640–1644). This allows a deeper look at three important periods in Augsburg's history, starting with the period immediately following the Reformation and ending with the period of economic and political decline during the Thirty Years' War. The years covered in the sample were chosen not only because they correspond to the rise and waning of the sobriety movement but also to take advantage of the largest collection of court records, which are scanty before 1540 and decline in number as the seventeenth century progresses. Out of a total of 2,230 interrogations covered in the sample, nearly 400 included material relevant to taverns and drinking, along with thousands of entries in the punishment and discipline records.[52] Supporting qualitative descriptions and records of changes in legislation are drawn from additional court cases from between 1520 and 1700. Findings based on these court records are then contextualized by information gleaned from craft and guild records, medical records, military records, city chronicles, church documents, real estate and tax records, council minutes, marriage protocols, and miscellaneous other documents.

In the case of interrogations, drinking was rarely the behavior primarily at issue, for no one would be interrogated merely for being drunk. Instead, drinking behaviors normally emerge as background information that defendants and witnesses provided in their attempt to explain, justify, or describe the details of the incident in question. Because interrogation records were typically filtered through a court scribe, no claims may be made as to their representing a verbatim transcript of the defendants' and witnesses' own words. Nonetheless, each statement, regardless of the scribe recording it, has its own discernible voice. Together with the decisions of the court, these statements form a readable dialogue among those accused of infractions, the witnesses and friends who supported or condemned the defendant's behavior, and the authorities responsible for administering punishment.

How much value should be placed on the statements of witnesses and defendants involved in an interrogation process? Certainly the truth of descriptions and explanations made by persons charged with a crime, who may have had reason to be cryptic about their behavior, must be accepted with caution. This is especially true as some of the most detailed descriptions of tavern life occur in the most serious cases, particularly where a death resulted. Such cases cannot be regarded as ordinary either, for no tavern goer kills someone on a typical evening. Nonetheless, witnesses and defendants rarely went out in the evening with a killing in mind, and they definitely had a stake in avoiding giving the impression that they had. Thus their descriptions of the events incidental to and leading up to a killing generally represent their attempt to appear as normal as possible.

Natalie Davis, in her analysis of pardon tales, has shown that stories told in one's own defense, while not necessarily presenting the raw truth of the event, may be used to reconstruct the social and cultural norms that shaped the story and gave it meaning. Although Davis dismissed interrogation records as overly confined and directed and lacking a beginning and an end,[53] my experience reading interrogations has taught me that when a defendant believed he had a story to tell, he found a way to tell it. Witnesses and defendants who felt strongly about their position often took control of the interrogation process, ignoring the questions and presenting their side of the story as a coherent narrative. In telling their stories, all of the participants in the drama were interested in making their own actions seem as innocent and honorable as possible. The resulting picture, if not necessarily the truth of the incident, represents fairly what the participants considered to be a believable and justifiable truth. In defending their own actions and those of their

Introduction

peers, they described their values and norms in a way calculated to appeal to the values of the authorities — values more often shared than at odds.

Even more intriguing than the effect that these stories had on the authorities to whom they were addressed is the effect they have on those of us who are trying to interpret them hundreds of years later. The use of detail by Michel Foucault and Norbert Elias in describing the horrors of judicial torture and the vulgarity of early books of manners is designed to do more than provide historical accuracy. By forcing us to picture early modern life in graphic detail, they re-create our distance from that world on the level of emotion as well as description. And yet there is much in the way of human nature that we share with our early modern predecessors. While Darnton has made use of our distance from earlier sources to find an opening into what we may not understand of their world, I suggest that we can only access that opening if we approach it with empathy. When we read of a soldier chided by other members of his drinking party into killing a man he described as his "good fellow" or a woman with eight children who pleaded in defense of her husband's immoderate drinking habits, we begin to relate to our sources on a very human level. In so doing, we are able to make sense of codes of behavior that might otherwise remain impenetrable.

Although the documents examined here tell the story of only one city, the drinking customs described were, to use the words of an Augsburg tavern keeper justifying a drinking ritual in 1591, "customary in all German lands."[54] Findings at the local level are thus placed in the broader context provided by the many books, pamphlets, sermons, ordinances, broadsheets, and other printed sources that addressed the drinking problem throughout the German-speaking areas of early modern Europe. In terms of the social makeup of its population and the process of communication between authority and populace, Augsburg did not differ significantly from other German towns, and thus it should be seen as representative of urban life more generally. At the same time, however, the tensions created by Augsburg's bi-confessional character may well have led the local authorities there to take a particularly cautious approach to potential disturbances, especially those of a confessional nature. In respect to issues of institutional authority and specific legal decisions, then, this remains a case study.

This study begins with two chapters introducing the city of Augsburg, examining its taverns and drinking rooms as institutions and underlining the importance of taverns and tavern keepers to urban society. Chapters 3, 4, and 5 locate the cultural construct implied by the term "drunkenness" in the early modern German mentality, beginning with an examination of drunkenness as a physical and spiritual state. This requires an excursion into the more theoretical realms explored by doctors, theologians, artists, and poets. The examination of legal practice that follows returns to the documents to evaluate local Augsburg practice as a case study in the treatment of drunken defendants. In Chapters 6 through 8, the doors of the public house are opened to reveal the cultural uses of alcohol in early modern society. The ritual of the contract drink is first explored both in theory and as local practice in order to emphasize the cultural value that early modern Germans placed on a shared drink. This is followed by a discussion of the role of drinking in defining household, family, and gender relations and the importance of drinking bouts and rituals to social and cultural identity. Finally, chapters 9 and 10 examine the role of the tavern in supporting the aims of the authorities, the variations that existed between norms of control and norms of practice, and the process of negotiation that took place between authority and populace in establishing and enforcing norms of drinking behavior.

The tavern in early modern society was a public theater, in which its patrons performed rituals of social and cultural identification. Elites and commoners, men and women, and respectable and less than respectable elements all had a stage there. Upon that stage they acted out their particular part in the social play. When we look through the right windows, we find neither a society of beggars and thieves nor a society of disorder. What we see reflected is an urban community functioning according to its own rules. These rules differ from ours, but they varied surprisingly little among the layers of urban society. Taverns and popular drinking traditions did not stand at the point of division between populace and authority. They stood in support of both.

1

The City and Its Taverns

THE FREE IMPERIAL CITY OF Augsburg was at the height of its wealth and power as it moved into the sixteenth century. Home to the fabulously rich merchant houses of Fugger, Welser, and Baumgartner, Augsburg was renowned for its splendor.[1] Its population of over thirty thousand meant it was one of the largest cities in Germany, and the far-reaching interests of its leading merchants made it one of the wealthiest. The Fugger family, under the leadership of Jacob, "the Rich," as the sixteenth century began, had established a close relationship with Emperor Maximilian I, and the emperor and his entourage were regular visitors to the prosperous merchant city. Augsburg lay at the junction of two rivers, the Lech and the Wertach, directly on the ancient trade route leading to Venice. The proximity of the waterways allowed the construction of a complicated system of canals and fountains that provided the city with water power to turn its mills, carry away its refuse, and furnish private sources of water for individual homes, workshops, and breweries. A major center of printing, weaving, banking, and gold- and silversmithing, Augsburg was also home to an important circle of humanists led by Conrad Peutinger. One historian, noting the extent of the city's financial connections, technological innovations, and cultural achievements, described Augsburg at the beginning of the sixteenth century as the most modern city in Germany; Michel de Montaigne in 1580 called it "the most beautiful."[2]

In spite of its international renown, however, the early modern city within its walls maintained an independent local identity. City leaders were concerned not only with their banking ties to Venice and Antwerp but also with sustaining stability and order among the local citizenry, on whose labor their trade interests depended. Throughout the early modern period, city councils in German towns invested much effort in building, upholding, and protecting an orderly community of responsible, taxpaying citizens. The architectural achievements of the century following the Reformation in

Augsburg provide a visual articulation of this goal. The outer fortifications were raised and accented by impressive gates and towers, a bastion that would prove more effective against the increasing numbers of wandering poor and vagrants than against military attack. The Gothic courthouse and the Lords' Drinking Room, centers of elite power, were torn down and re-built in the massive, mathematically rational style of the late Renaissance, facing each other in an imposing display of secular splendor.[3]

Augsburg's Catholic poor were fortunate enough to be among the world's earliest recipients of social housing, quartered in a settlement financed by Jacob Fugger and named in his honor the Fuggerei. Surrounded by its own walls, the Fuggerei consisted of 106 individual dwellings, neatly arranged in straight rows. The tiny planned community contrasted sharply with the less rational, medieval character of the city surrounding it. Jacob Fugger may have been motivated by the hope of winning salvation in return for his charity, yet the orderly little community served a calculated worldly inter-est as well. Impoverished people with a home were less likely to risk social protest than those with nothing to lose — and as an added precaution, the gates to the Fuggerei were locked, with its residents inside, during the hours of darkness.

Lining the streets just inside the city's gates, clustered in its center, and thinly scattered among its back quarters were Augsburg's taverns and drink-ing rooms. These institutions ranged from the poorly lit rooms of backstreet wine sellers to the elaborate marble halls frequented by society's most privi-leged members. Urban drinking rooms provided more than food, drink, and lodging for their guests. They also conferred on their visitors a sense of so-cial identity commensurate with their status. Like all German cities, Augs-burg's history during the sixteenth and seventeenth centuries was shaped by the political events attending the Reformation, the post-Reformation, and the Thirty Years' War; it's social and political character was also reflected and supported by its public and private drinking rooms.

Augsburg and the Reformation

By the time the Fuggerei was completed in 1523, the Reformation had dawned in Germany. Despite the conservative influence of the Catholic Fuggers and the humanist civic secretary Conrad Peutinger, Augsburg's guild-based government would prove fertile ground for the ideas of the reformers during the years that followed. The guild constitution, established in 1368, provided for the Small Council (*Kleiner Rat*), made up of thirty-four guild masters (raised from twenty-nine in 1478) and fifteen representatives of the patriciate. The larger guilds, including the brewers, each contributed two representatives to the Small Council, and the smaller guilds provided one. The Small Council was the highest governing body in the city. Supporting it in major decisions was the Large Council (*Großer Rat*), which included twelve representatives of each guild. Two mayors (*Bürgermeister*) headed the government, one selected from the patrician class and one from among the commoners.

The balance of power between different religious groups among Augsburg's leading families ensured a late start for the Reformation, but it did not manage to stop the tide from coming. The city's taverns, as meeting places, centers of news and debate, and in some cases doubling as printing houses and bookshops, played an important role in fostering and spreading Reformation ideas. In 1524 tavern meetings served as organization points for the protests that broke out in response to the banishment of the evangelical preacher Johann Schilling. Interrogation records of those arrested in connection with the disturbance reveal that their concerns were primarily economic and religious, rather than political or revolutionary.[4] Nonetheless, the planned coordination of common craftsmen in this incident seemed threatening to the authorities, who issued a special ordinance within a week forbidding further meetings or inflammatory discussions.[5]

The city council, influenced by Peutinger, attempted to steer a middle course that would appease both the emperor and evangelicals. The incidents of 1524, however, had marked the beginning of a process of institutionalization of the Reformation, which gained more ground with every election. In 1529 the council appointed a committee of six Punishment Lords (*Strafherren*), tasked with controlling "blasphemy, swearing, and toasting."[6] The Reformation process culminated in 1537 with the election of Mang Seitz and Hans Welser as mayors, both of whom were strongly influenced by the ideas of Ulrich Zwingli and Martin Bucer. In that year the Large Council took steps to eliminate all vestiges of "papist idolatry."[7] The Zwinglian-style phase that followed was characterized by an assault on sin, riotous living, and excessive drinking. The Punishment Lords became the Discipline Lords (*Zuchtherren*), heading a special office of discipline, and a marriage court was established as well. Lyndal Roper has explained the zeal with which the artisans and the guild government embraced the Zwinglian message by noting its appeal to traditional guild-based moralism.[8] The concerns related by those involved in the Schilling incident, however, also reflect certain economic interests — interests that were not necessarily aligned with Zwinglian ideas of moralism. Among their demands were the reinstatement of the former, larger measure of wine and beer, which had been reduced in 1474, and the elimination of excise taxes on alcoholic beverages.[9]

While the bulk of the population favored the new religion, both the social and financial interests of the patricians and merchants were closely tied to those of pope and emperor. Indeed, it was the financial backing of the Fugger family that had ensured the election of Emperor Charles V in 1519. Many patricians clung to the old religion, and some left the city when Augsburg entered the Schmalkaldic War on the side of the Protestants in 1546. This fact worked to their advantage when the Protestant-dominated phase of Augsburg's Reformation came to a forced end in 1548. Charles, having defeated the forces of the Protestant Schmalkaldic League, took steps to eliminate the political power of local guilds, whose authority had increased under the Zwinglian-style government. Charles blamed Augsburg's guild leaders for accepting the new religion, for the city's participation in the Schmalkaldic League, and for what he considered a "disorderly government."[10] Craftsmen, Charles pointed out, were not suited for government; they should concern themselves with their craft and subsistence. Under Charles V's direction, the guildhalls in Augsburg were closed and their property sold; the large guilds were divided into smaller crafts; and city rule was placed firmly in the hands of the patricians. The two mayors were replaced by patrician caretakers (Stadtpfleger), and elites dominated both the Small Council and the Large Council. Replacing the guild masters, who had formerly been elected by the guild members, were council-appointed principals (Vorgeher), and the city council took over the responsibility for regulating the crafts and settling their disputes — functions that guild leaders had performed in the past.[11]

After a brief period of wrestling for power among the confessions, the Peace of Augsburg in 1555 officially sanctioned both Catholicism and Protestantism within the city. Under Protestantism, however, the settlement allowed only Lutheranism, and it excluded Zwinglians, Calvinists, and Anabaptists. Nonetheless, the guild-based moralism associated with the

Zwinglian movement continued to influence city politics, and the Zwinglian-style institution of the Discipline Lords continued in force. The populace of Augsburg after 1555 remained predominantly Protestant, a bastion against the primarily Catholic countryside outside its walls.

The influence of the emperor ensured that Catholics remained the majority in the Augsburg government after 1548. The late sixteenth century was marked by religious instability, and the city council responded to the tense situation by again attempting to steer a middle course in confessional matters. In 1584 the tension exploded in riots, as Augsburg Protestants stormed the armory and threatened the courthouse in reaction to the introduction of the Gregorian calendar.[12] Questioning more than one hundred of those who participated in the riots, mostly craftsmen, revealed that their complaints this time were social and political rather than confessional in nature, calling not for the return of the old calendar but the reinstatement of the old guild system. Fear of social unrest prompted the Protestant city council members to reach an agreement with the Catholic majority, and Protestant leaders subsequently supported the new calendar. Legislation of the late sixteenth century reflects the interests of the council in controlling social unrest, increasing restrictions on those elements that seemed threatening or unruly, and yet remaining cautiously neutral on confessional issues. The shared social identity and interests of city leaders overpowered their confessional differences.[13]

The dismantling of the guilds and the sale of their meeting halls was a move calculated to decrease their ability to meet privately and form a center of power. Afterward, many of the functions formerly served by guildhalls were taken over by public taverns, where artisans continued to meet for both official and unofficial purposes. These institutions, which had served as breeding places for Reformation ideas and centers of information even before the guildhalls were closed, were a likely target for those wishing to suppress social unrest and control disorderly elements. This pattern is exactly the claim that historians made regarding England, as they placed attacks on taverns and drinking during the late sixteenth century within this context. Such a correlation, however, does not hold true in Augsburg, where taverns, their landlords, and their customers were in many ways more stable than the world outside their windows. In practice, Augsburg's taverns served more to underscore than to threaten the lines of the social hierarchy.

Urban Geography

Historians are accustomed to thinking of the Society of Orders (*Standes-gesellschaft*) as a vertical picture of society. The populace of the early modern city we can see as an onion-shaped diagram, with a small triangle of social and economic elites at the top, a bulbous center of artisans whose economic means varied from nearly wealthy to borderline poverty, and a thin but wide layer of poor at the bottom. In reality, of course, this population was distributed throughout the city on a plane that was more horizontal than vertical. The city spaces occupied by these various segments of society say at least as much about their culture, that which was shared and that which was not, and their relationship to one another as any other cultural artifact.

Fortunately, the citizens of and visitors to early modern Augsburg have left a variety of sources that allow the reconstruction of this horizontal picture of urban society. Precise maps of the city, showing individual streets, houses, and even traffic, provide us with a view of the developments in urban topography. Tax and real estate records allow us to match the houses, streets, and city quarters depicted on these plans with the economic and social status of their residents. The elites in this horizontal view naturally carve out a much larger chunk of the picture than is reflected by their numbers, with just over 4 percent of society paying more than 80 percent of the property taxes and owning 28 percent of the real property.[14]

Let us now imagine a traveler to Augsburg in around 1600, exploring this urban world from the ground. A likely entry point would have been Red Gate (*Rotes Tor*) at the city's south entrance. Nonresident travelers coming into town were restricted to the four primary city gates, and they most often entered via either Red Gate or Wertach Bridge Gate (*Wertachbrucker Tor*) to the north. At the gate, our visitor would be challenged by the guard and allowed to enter the city only after stating his name and the nature of his business in the city.[15]

A traveler entering Augsburg through Red Gate, should he glance to his right, could not miss the imposing water towers that supplied the upper half of the city with water, for three of the city's seven water towers were located at the waterworks just inside this gate. Elaborate pumps driven by water-wheels moved the water up into the towers, and gravity provided enough natural power to supply the city with running water. Augsburg's first running fountains and water pumps were installed in 1416, and by the sixteenth century the city was equipped with a system of running water that supplied private homes as well as public fountains. Over two hundred private and public buildings had a private water supply by 1600; the number topped three hundred by 1625.[16]

Many of Augsburg's taverns were supplied with private water. Beer tavern keepers, who brewed their beer on the premises, were especially dependent on a ready supply of clean water. This partially accounts for their concentration in three major groupings: along Baker Lane (*Bäckergasse*) in Lech Quarter (*Lechviertel*), in the center of town around the courthouse and slaughterhouse (*Metzg*), and in the north quarter of town known as the Frauenviertel after the Cathedral of Our Lady (*Unserer Frauen Kirche*) (see map 1).[17] The impoverished quarter surrounding St. Jakob's church, called Jakob Suburb (*Jakober Vorstadt*), was poorly supplied with private water, and the few breweries scattered through its streets in 1603 accounted for over half of the water licenses in that quarter.[18]

A thirsty traveler entering town after an exhausting journey would look first for refreshment, a place to stay, and (unless he were traveling by foot) a stable for his horse. For this, our wanderer would not have far to go. The rows of taverns that lined the streets leading from Red and Wertach Bridge Gates were strategically placed to offer immediate hospitality to the weary stranger. The greatest concentration of taverns in Augsburg was along Baker Lane, which was located only a couple of blocks from Red Gate. The street is believed to be so named because of the many bakers who resided there (fig. 1). Historians have noted, however, that Baker Lane might have easily been called Brewer Lane, for every third building housed a brewery.[19] This can be explained not only by its proximity to a water supply and to the city gate but also by the fact that it lay along the route taken by merchants and wine carters heading for the Wine Market (*Weinmarkt*). The regular traffic of well-to-do travelers helped support a thriving brewing business. Yet travelers were not the only visitors to the taverns of Baker Lane; tavern keepers here profited from local customers as well. Centered in a thriving artisans' quarter of middling economic status, Baker Lane provided a lively social center for Augsburg's craftsmen.[20]

If our traveler's appearance and the coins he carried were both reputable, a visitor of common status might find a bed in one of Baker Lane's taverns,

The Culture of Drink in the Early Modern German City

Figure 1. Baker Lane. Note the heavy traffic of wagons and horsemen passing to and from the town center (at the upper right). (Detail from Wolfgang Kilian, Vogelschauplan 1626. Courtesy of the Kunstsammlungen der Stadt Augsburg)

which he would be likely to share with another guest. If he arrived very late, however, he might have to make do with sleeping on a bench in the public room (*Stube*). Before retiring, he undoubtedly would enjoy some refreshment, possibly sharing an evening drinking bout with other guests in the public room. Here he would find one or more tables, depending on the size of the tavern, and an oven by which he could warm himself. A regular visitor to the city might know the tavern keeper personally, in which case his stay would raise no questions. If he were a stranger, however, his landlord would be obliged to ask how long he planned to stay. For a visit of more than three days a report to the mayors' office would be necessary.[21]

If our traveler were a member of the merchant class, his social rank would be sufficient to exempt him from this requirement. In that case, he would most likely make his way to the Wine Market, like many of the arriving merchants and other visitors who passed by the taverns of Baker Lane. The Wine Market was located parallel and to the west of Baker Lane on what is today Maximilian Street (*Maximilianstraße*), part of the ancient Roman trade route that formed the north-south axis of the wealthy Uptown Area (*Oberstadt*). The Wine Market was the social center of Augsburg's elites and was lined with the palaces of the city's most affluent families (fig. 2). For wealthy visitors the impressive facades on the Wine Market symbolized Augsburg hospitality, for here were the establishments of the privileged innkeepers (*Gastgeber*). The elite clientele of this group of tavern keepers differed considerably from the common tavern goers of Baker Lane. Innkeepers, because of the wealth, prestige, and volume of their visitors, were granted special tax privileges to help alleviate the burdensome expenses of providing for their guests.[22] One innkeeper, petitioning for this privilege after newly inheriting an inn, claimed that without a special tax consideration he would be forced

Figure 2. The Wine Market. The Wine Market was flanked by the Hallmark House (*Siegel Haus*), where wine was measured and taxed (44), and the elite Dance House (46). (Detail from Hans Rogel d. Ä., Stadtplan, 1563. Courtesy of the Kunstsammlungen der Stadt Augsburg)

to give up lodging the nobility during imperial diets—a calculated argument, for appropriate quarters for persons of rank during these events were often in short supply.[23]

The power of the wealthy innkeepers at the end of the sixteenth century was sufficient to allow them to represent themselves as an institution with exclusive rights to public hospitality on the Wine Market. When the former wine clerk (*Weinschreiber*)[24] Elias Mair requested a license for an inn on the Wine Market in 1587, the six existing innkeepers petitioned against the new establishment. Mair responded by claiming that their facilities were not sufficient to meet the needs of the many wine merchants who traded at the market, and they were especially inadequate for stabling their horses. The "Six Innkeepers" (*Sechs Gastgeber*) then drew on tradition to support their cause, noting that "since times long past there have not been more than six innkeepers [on the Wine Market]" and citing their tax privileges as evidence of their elite status. Ultimately, the powerful innkeepers were successful in forcing out the competition.[25] As the city council had pointed out in response to a petition for increased privileges in 1562, these elite tavern keepers certainly had "more reason to be thankful than to complain."[26]

It was one of these prestigious inns that impressed Montaigne during his travels through Germany in 1580. The inns on the Wine Market were among the few wine taverns provided with an indoor water supply, and the indoor pump that supplied water to the Linden Tree Inn (*Zur Linde*) was a source of wonder to Montaigne. He was also impressed with the cleanliness of the inn, which was no doubt made possible by the availability of water on the premises.[27]

Visitors of an even higher status might expect an invitation to lodge privately with one of Augsburg's privileged families. Otherwise, however, our visitor's search for accommodations would be likely to end in one of the concentrations of taverns already described, for a walk either through the meandering streets of the poorer sections of town or the broad lanes of the wealthy Uptown Area would yield little in the way of lodgings. These sections of the city, populated by the two extremes of Augsburg's social and economic scale, were conspicuously lacking taverns.

The poor, sparsely populated area encompassing the northern section of Jakob Suburb had little to offer a tavern keeper looking for a desirable location to run his business. The houses here were small and the streets unpaved, and the residents in this section of town (among them the deserving Catholic poor who lived in the Fuggerei) paid the lowest per capita rate of property taxes in the city. Few would have had large amounts of excess income to spend on tavern entertainments. One of the few wealthy residents of the northern Jakob Suburb was the city executioner, whose presence was not welcome in tavern society.[28]

The Frauenviertel, too, had very few taverns, with the notable exception of those along the main roads leading into town from Wertach Bridge Gate. Wertach Bridge, known to locals as Beggars' Bridge (*Bettelbrücke*), was a traditional haunt of the beggars, vagrants, and gypsies who gathered outside the city, hoping for a handout from a passing traveler or a chance to slip into the city to beg. The back streets of the Frauenviertel were not often frequented by Augsburg's local artisans, who preferred the more pleasant society of Baker Lane.

Also virtually without taverns was the Uptown Area, the section populated by Augsburg's leading citizens. The patricians, merchants, and scholars of medicine and law who lived in the luxurious homes of the Uptown Area had little need for neighborhood taverns. The residents of this quarter, when not attending one of the many private banquets for which the elites of the sixteenth and seventeenth centuries were renowned, had easy access to the nearby Wine Market with its fine inns and elite Dance House. The inns on the Wine Market, however, for all their elegant appointments and privileged status, remained public taverns. An even more exclusive establishment was necessary to meet the needs of the highest strata of Augsburg society. Many of the residents of the Uptown Area were members of the most privileged drinking establishments of the city — the closed societies of the Lords' and Merchants' Drinking Rooms.

The tradition of the Drinking Room Society (*Trinkstubengesellschaft*) dated back to the establishment of the guild constitution in 1368. The new constitution made membership in a guild mandatory for citizenship. Citizens from noble or patrician families who did not choose to enter a guild formed their own Society of Nobles (*Geschlechtergesellschaft*), which served the same political function as a guild. These urban patricians, who once dominated and now shared city government, initially continued to hold their social and business meetings in the courthouse, as men of their class had done for centuries. The fact that common guild masters served on the city council and had access to the courthouse, however, threatened the exclusive nature of their society. In 1412 Paul Riederer, a member of the Society of Nobles, provided his house on the Perlachberg (the street adjoining the courthouse) for the private entertainments of the society's members. Thus the Lords' Drinking Room, or *Herrentrinkstube,* was born. Later, its members would call themselves the Lords' Drinking Room Society (*Herrentrinkstubengesellschaft*), or simply the Lords' Room (*Herrenstube*). The purpose of the drinking room, according to the patrician chronicler Markus Welser, was to provide patricians' sons (*Geschlechtersöhnlein*) a place for "gaming and drinking, to the avoidance of other drinking rooms, only to those, who have been registered as members, as befits the preservation of their station and reputation."[29] The Lords' Drinking Room originated as an exclusive social club, with no overt political function beyond the maintenance of the lines of the Society of Orders. Ten years later, the Lords' Drinking Room moved into the newly erected Dance House; when it burned down in 1451, the society returned to the building on Perlachberg. This house also burned down, in 1488. After it was rebuilt, the new house became the joint property of the society. In 1557 city officials tore down this building and began construction on an imposing house, built specifically for the purpose of housing the Lords' Drinking Room Society. The new building was completed in 1563.[30]

By the sixteenth century, the Lords' Drinking Room had become the political as well as the social center of Augsburg's most privileged circles. Here elite society met to swear in members of the city council, honor visiting dignitaries, and debate political decisions, as well as to eat, drink, and play at cards or other games. The traveling knight Hans von Schweinichen described an impressive reception held in Augsburg's Lords' Room in honor of his lord (the duke of Liegniz) and another visiting dignitary in 1575. The banquet, which was fit for the emperor, took place in a hall "where one saw more gold than any color. . . . The floor was of marble and as slick as ice."[31] Less formal drinking bouts took place in the drinking room upstairs, where those with the proper status (and sufficient funds) could buy each other rounds of the finest imported wines. There, Schweinichen wrote, one found "fine amusements . . . gamblers, drinkers, and other knightly games."[32] When prestigious visitors to the city arrived unannounced, the members of the Lords' Drinking Room sent representatives to discover the rank of the visitor, so that an appropriate ceremony could be prepared; for, as Montaigne noted, "they [gave] more wines to some than to others."[33]

Visitors to the Lords' Drinking Room blended in their descriptions details about social drinking bouts with political interests and matters of state, for

German convention tended to combine the two. Debate and compromise, according to German cultural tradition, were more fruitful when conducted under the congenial influence of wine, and no contract was binding unless it was sealed with a drink. Drinking together, according to tradition that predates Christianity, implied social intimacy and bound the participants in a form of brotherly trust. Political negotiations and contracts were therefore best conducted at the drinking table, and the cost of wine that the members of government drank while performing their duties appears in financial records as an official bureaucratic expense.[34] It is no surprise, then, that the Lords' Drinking Room served not only as a social center but as a potential hub of political power.

The membership of the Lords' Drinking Room Society was more broadly defined than the membership of the patriciate. The patrician class, with few exceptions, was closed to new members from the end of the 1300s until 1538. In that year, thirty-eight families were admitted in order to increase the power of the patricians, whose numbers had dwindled to eight families.[35] Membership in the Lords' Drinking Room, although still an extremely restricted society, was somewhat more accessible. In addition to Augsburg patricians, membership was open to titled nobility and patricians from the imperial cities of Strasbourg, Nuremberg, and Ulm, and to those who married into the society. The society was completely closed to all commoners except for merchants who came as guests of members. Improper behavior could lead to a temporary ban from the drinking room, and marriage with the wrong party was grounds for exclusion entirely.[36] Membership in this exclusive society, attainable only by birth or marriage to a holder of this legacy, was the epitome of social status and recognition in Augsburg. Neither wealth nor political influence could buy one the right to drink with those born to the Lords' Room.

In 1479 a second elite society—the Merchants' Drinking Room Society—was formed on a basis different from that of the Lords' Drinking Room Society. While one had to be born to the Lords' Society, membership in the Merchants' Drinking Room Society was a question of finances. The requirements for entry into the Merchants' Society were the social standing of a merchant, attained via economic success, and the payment of a membership fee. The members of the Merchants' Drinking Room (*Kaufleutetrinkstube*) met in rented rooms until 1539, when they bought a building in the vicinity of the courthouse for 4,500 gulden, 4,000 of which the city council put up as credit. The purchase of their own building improved the merchants' position as a rival to the Lords' Room; in fact, the members of the Merchants' Room were confident enough of their position to practice their own form of exclusivity, closing their society even to patricians.[37]

The independent status of the Merchants' Society allowed the creation of a power base for the "elite commoners." This opportunity was seized during the 1540s by the master furrier and fur trader Jakob Herbrot, who used the Merchants' Drinking Room as a center of power on his rise to the position of mayor, in 1545. Herbrot's aim was to make the Merchants' Society into a political organization representing the interests of the guilds, merchants, and common intelligentsia, and capable of challenging the monopoly of the patricians. A new set of statutes governing the Merchants' Society, introduced in 1541, would allow members of any guild to join the society. Herbrot's rise to power through his connections in the Merchants' Room was a source of concern for the patricians and an added thorn in the side of Emperor Charles V, for Herbrot used his considerable wealth and power to back the Protestant Schmalkaldic League.[38] When Charles ordered the closure and sale of the guildhalls in 1548, the Merchants' Drinking Room was included in the sale. The merchants' request to allow their society to continue its meetings was granted only on the condition that the society be closely supervised by the Lords' Society and, to that end, that their building be located next to the Lords' Drinking Room. In 1549 the merchants purchased the neighboring building and reopened their society, but political control of the city remained centered next door at the tables of the patricians. From this point on, all members of the Lords' Society had access at will to the Merchants' Drinking Room, and the patricians supervised the merchants' elections and activities. The right of visitation was, of course, one sided—the merchants were not welcome in the Lords' Room.[39]

The space occupied by these two institutions, side by side and directly across from the courthouse, symbolized both their elite social status and their relationship to one another. The Merchants' Drinking Room stood literally as well as figuratively in the shadow of the centers of secular power in Augsburg. While the building allowed its members an exclusive meeting place that set them apart from more common society, it also served to confine and control the merchants' activities and keep them under the watchful eye of the ruling patricians.

The Merchants' and Lords' Drinking Room Societies had developed into much more than simply exclusive social clubs. These institutions defined the social order of their members. Clothing ordinances, wedding ordinances, chronicles, and other documents, in describing the restrictions and privileges that applied to members of society based on their social standing, often indicated the status of the patricians and merchants by referring to them as "those belonging to the drinking rooms," or simply "the society of the rooms."[40] In 1555 the new patrician government officially confirmed what was already a social reality and designated the Merchants' Drinking Room as the formal political agency of the merchant class.[41] The drinking room, which represented the privilege of drinking with others of one's social standing, itself became a metaphor for social class.

The dismantling of the guilds in 1548 did not eliminate the need for artisans to meet in their own craft-associated drinking rooms, but, unlike the merchants and patricians, the individual crafts were hardly in a position to purchase a private building. Only the weavers, Augsburg's largest and most powerful craft, kept their guildhall, now supervised by the city council. The smaller crafts continued their professional activities and drinking rituals in designated public taverns. Most of these craft hostels (*Handwerkerherbergen*) were ordinary taverns in which a room was set aside for the artisan gatherings, and they were otherwise open to other visitors.[42]

Even the public tavern, which was open to all respectable members of society, had a measure of exclusivity. Beggars, persons taking alms, and those who had proven themselves to be irresponsible householders were banned from tavern company. Thus each order of drinking society in the city was open to those of equal or higher social status but closed to those below it. Together, these establishments formed a hierarchy of drinking circles that corresponded both socially and geographically to the distribution of the Society of Orders.

The wealth and power enjoyed by the city of Augsburg during the sixteenth century was not destined to last. Hints of economic decline were already in evidence as the seventeenth century began; if Augsburg's citizens held any hope of recovery, they were dashed by the devastation of the Thirty Years' War. The war decimated the economic power of the city, intensified confessional differences, and left the population reduced by more than half. The prewar population level would not be reached again before the nineteenth century, and, largely due to the financial losses experienced by the city's wealthiest citizens, Augsburg would never regain the position as an important regional political and economic power that it enjoyed during the

The Culture of Drink in the Early Modern German City

sixteenth century.[43] To stabilize confessional tensions after the war ended in 1648, a system of confessional parity (*Parität*) was instituted that ensured equal representation for Catholics and Protestants in government institutions and bureaucratic offices. Eventually, craft hostels would also be confessionally divided.[44]

A look at the distribution of taverns at the end of the war in the mid-seventeenth century reveals certain changes. Most notable is a growth in the number of beer taverns and a corresponding drop in wine taverns. Additionally, taverns appear in areas in which they were formerly lacking, especially in Jakob Suburb. There are two probable explanations for this

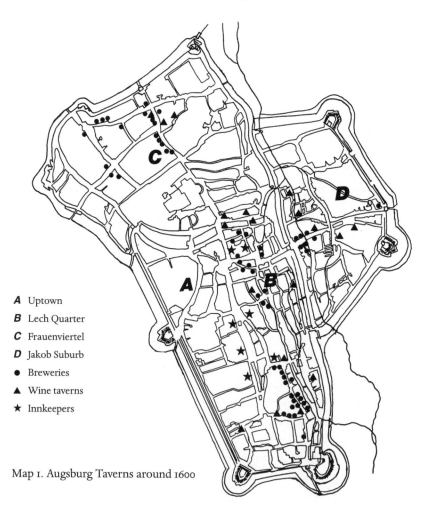

A Uptown
B Lech Quarter
C Frauenviertel
D Jakob Suburb
● Breweries
▲ Wine taverns
★ Innkeepers

Map 1. Augsburg Taverns around 1600

development. First, the city water system had by this time extended into this section of Augsburg, which made tavern keeping and especially brewing more practical. Second, a slight leveling of wealth among specific strata of society is evidenced by the fact that, while the tax payments in the wealthier areas of town decreased after the Thirty Years' War, they increased in exactly those areas of central Jakob Suburb in which the new taverns appeared.[45] Again, the taverns that cropped up in this quarter were concentrated along the major road into town from the east (*Jakoberstraße*). The area in the northern Jakob Suburb, where the executioner had his home, remained free of public taverns (map 2).

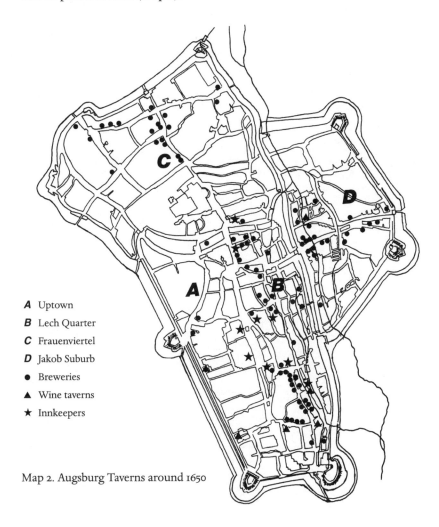

A Uptown
B Lech Quarter
C Frauenviertel
D Jakob Suburb
● Breweries
▲ Wine taverns
★ Innkeepers

Map 2. Augsburg Taverns around 1650

The just over one hundred breweries in operation in 1650 became permanent fixtures with new restrictions on brewing license transfers established in 1657. This law remained in effect until the nineteenth century, and the pattern of taverns identifiable by 1650 changed little over the next 250 years. The elite inns also remained well established, serving as luxury hotels in the eighteenth and nineteenth centuries. Most of the taverns established by 1650 were still in operation, names unchanged, at the beginning of the twentieth century.[46]

2

Augsburg's Tavern Keepers

Sᴇʀᴠɪɴɢ ᴛʜᴇ sᴏᴄɪᴀʟ ɴᴇᴇᴅs of Augsburg's populace during the sixteenth and seventeenth centuries were between 90 and 110 public taverns. The previous chapter outlined their locations and role in defining and supporting social status. But what exactly was a public tavern? What services did it provide and what drinks did it serve? How did tavern keepers identify themselves with their trade? What status within the community did their position confer on them? An examination of the drink trade in Augsburg offers further support for the thesis that taverns buttressed rather than undermined established norms of status and identity.

This point is illustrated first by the gradual rise in the status of wine in relation to beer during the late sixteenth and early seventeenth centuries. Although both beverages were popular with all of Augsburg's inhabitants during the early sixteenth century, wine eventually came to be identified with the wealthier classes and beer with more common folk. Just as drinking rooms were segregated according to social status, the dynamics of supply and demand led to a gradual segregation of the drinks themselves. The process was accompanied by a professionalization process in the licensing of wine taverns. Also of significance is the relatively high economic and social status of Augsburg's tavern keepers in the community. The purveyance of drink reveals itself as an especially stable and lucrative trade even in difficult economic times, and the social status of tavern keepers was boosted by the importance of notions of hospitality to the city's corporate identity as a merchant city of international reputation.

The Drink Trade

Public taverns (*Offene Wirtshäuser*), according to the definition provided by Augsburg's licensing laws, were institutions licensed for seating customers, serving food and drinks, and putting up overnight guests. They were not the only suppliers of drink in the city. In addition to the elite drinking rooms discussed in chapter 1, virtually any citizen could obtain permission to sell beer or wine on a retail basis for customers to take home. These tap landlords (*Zapfenwirte*), however, who were not licensed to seat guests at tables or serve food, could not normally earn an independent living through alcohol sales. Rather, tap landlords were practicing craftsmen who bought and resold drinks only as a sideline to supplement their incomes. Although customers occasionally gathered in front of a tap landlord's shop for a drink or two, these shops did not have the character of a public tavern and will not be considered as such.

In addition to wine and beer, Augsburg's citizens enjoyed mead, brandy, and gin. Mead taverns, however, were few, and by the seventeenth century only one permanent Augsburg mead tavern is identifiable. The sale of brandy and other spirits was illegal in public taverns throughout the sixteenth and most of the seventeenth century. Distilled liquors were available only in apothecaries, grocers' shops, and directly from brandy sellers, who could legally sell their wares only for taking home or in limited amounts for immediate consumption standing up. Although distilled liquors were popular by the end of the sixteenth century, they did not yet belong to tavern life, and brandy sellers could not in this period be defined as tavern keepers.

Early modern people also drank milk, juice (both sweet and fermented), and other beverages at home, but there is no record that they were served in taverns. Tavern visitors never reported asking for milk or juice, nor are such beverages listed in ordinances regulating food service in taverns or in bills for tavern service. In defending their right to keep cows against infringement charges brought up by the butchers, brewers did make the claim in 1604 that they provided an important service in supplying milk for the city's young children; it is unlikely, however, that this milk was served at tavern tables, where the only drinks appearing in the records are those containing alcohol.[1]

In order to seat customers at tables, thus allowing social drinking, gambling, food service, and other entertainments, tavern keepers had to offer facilities for overnight guests and the stabling of horses. This rule was enforced only intermittently until 1563, when the council charged the city steward (*Stadtvogt*) with inspecting all city taverns and closing down those that did not provide at least four beds and stables for eight horses.[2]

Most Augsburg tavern keepers specialized in the sale of either wine or beer. Beer taverns differed from wine taverns in that beer was brewed on the premises, whereas wine had to be purchased at the Wine Market and then resold (there were no local wines, for Augsburg is not situated in a wine-growing region). Although beer was also imported into the city before the sixteenth century, increasing restrictions made at the request of local brewers as the century progressed served to ease the competition. In 1511 the city council restricted public selling of nonlocal (*fremdes*) beer to two days a week, and in 1554 the council closed the communal cellar used for storing and selling nonlocal beer entirely. Afterward, local brewers had a near monopoly on legal beer sales within the city.[3] Brewers made their living primarily with retail sales in their own taverns, the designation "brewer" essentially being equal to "tavern keeper." Throughout the early modern period, brewing in the city remained a private industry. Although large, commercial breweries could be found in territorial towns or attached to monasteries, Augsburg had no large wholesale breweries before the nineteenth century.[4]

Breweries, equipped with special ovens and brewing pans (often housed in a separate, attached building to reduce the danger of fire) and dependent on a ready source of clean water, tended to be larger and more permanent operations than wine taverns. The need for special equipment may have been at the root of the association of the brewing license with a particular house rather than a particular brewer. The practice of selling the brewing right (*Braugerechtigkeit*) with the house was an established tradition by the early sixteenth century, and the license became officially nontransferable, or permanently attached to a specific building designated as a brewing house, in 1657.[5]

Another major difference between wine sellers and brewers was the designation of brewing as a craft and the resulting political organization of the brewers into a guild. The requirements for becoming a brewer were more stringent than those for becoming a wine seller, including a minimum period of apprenticeship and higher licensing fees.[6] Because the brewers were thus organized, their activities are better documented than the wine sellers'. As early as 1156 the Augsburg Civic Code (*Stadtrecht*) provided quality controls for Augsburg brewers, making it the oldest known brewing ordinance in Germany.[7] The brewers became one of Augsburg's original seventeen guilds in 1368 with the establishment of the guild constitution, and as one of the larger guilds was entitled to two representatives on the Small Council.

The number of brewers operating in Augsburg remained fairly constant at around sixty throughout the sixteenth century.[8] After 1600, however, the number of breweries began to increase to meet a growing demand. During the financial crisis of the latter part of the sixteenth century, authorities attempted to alleviate shortages and extend city income by raising the excise tax on wine. Economic difficulties in this period were partially due to a run of poor weather (associated with the *kleine Eiszeit,* or "little ice age"), which also resulted in a shortage of wine that forced up prices.[9] By the onset of the Thirty Years' War in 1618, the cost of wine and the accompanying tax were high enough to put it out of reach of many commoners, and the demand for beer increased proportionately. In addition, the sixteenth century had seen improvements in brewing techniques, notably the switch from oats to barley, rye, and wheat as the basis for beer; the standardized use of hops; and the introduction of the famous Bavarian purity laws (still in effect today) restricting the ingredients from which beer could be made.[10]

As beer became a more attractive alternative to wine, more brewers were needed to meet the demand. During the Thirty Years' War the trend accelerated, as the destruction of many vineyards put wine in increasingly short supply. The improved transportation networks of the seventeenth century ensured a supply of imported Italian and Spanish wine for the elite wine drinkers, and the commoners contented themselves with beer and brandy. By the end of the war, the number of brewers in Augsburg had grown to over ninety, while the city's population had dropped by more than half.

Although lists of wine sellers for the sixteenth century do not exist, real estate records and military musters of the seventeenth century do allow an estimated count of wine taverns for the period. The switch of the general populace from wine to beer as the drink of choice is particularly evident in the drop in numbers of wine taverns between the military muster of 1610, which listed fifty-two wine tavern keepers, and that of 1635, which listed only eight. Real estate records (*Grundbücher*) for the same years show a similar trend, with houses defined as wine taverns dropping from twenty-seven around 1600 to only fifteen in 1650. These figures, however, are almost certainly lower than the actual number of wine taverns operating in the city, for real estate records identify only permanent taverns. Particularly during the years before the war, many struggling craftsmen in need of supplemental income ran wine taverns on a temporary basis in addition to practicing their craft. Anyone who could afford to purchase a stock of wine and provide beds and stables for guests could obtain a license to operate a wine tavern; all that remained was taking the required civic oath to serve only unadulterated, properly taxed wine; paying a fee to the city; and hanging a sign over the door. The ease with which craftsmen could obtain wine tavern licenses was a source of concern to those who operated wine taverns full-time, as they thought themselves disadvantaged by competition from persons with other sources of income. Thus wine sellers petitioned against the practice in the late sixteenth century. Artisans who sold wine on the side, however, were able to defend their position successfully by pointing out that the wine sellers themselves were at fault for their lack of industry and failure to learn a craft.[11]

Brewers, too, like any other craftsmen, apparently could serve wine in addition to their own product up until 1657, although the practice was rare. Wine tavern keepers of course opposed this practice as well, but their petitions remained unsuccessful as long as selling wine was a common man's privilege. As wine drinking became increasingly associated with elites, however, the trade was gradually professionalized and restrictions on opening wine taverns became tighter. In 1656 brewers were officially forbidden to serve wine at weddings, and after 1657 they could not serve wine at all.[12] The city council issued these decrees after wine landlords complained about the unfair competition, noting among their arguments that "while there were formerly only around twenty brewers as opposed to one hundred wine sellers, there are now only around twenty wine sellers against one hundred brewers."[13]

The trend toward social stratification of drinks was further institutionalized in 1683, when sumptuary laws limiting the serving of drinks at wedding breakfasts specified that commoners of the third class (socially, immediately beneath patricians and merchants) could serve two types of wine, those of the fourth class one kind of wine, and those of the fifth class, beer only.[14] By the eighteenth century city ordinance also required two years' experience as a cellar boy or apprentice wine seller as a prerequisite to opening a wine tavern, a requirement that paralleled the apprenticeship requirement for other crafts.[15]

The Social and Economic Status of Augsburg's Tavern Keepers

If we are to believe the picture of tavern keepers that some historians have gleaned from Hans Sachs's Shrovetide plays (*Fastnachtspiele*), they were "generally poor" and occupied a "low social position, not just because of their poverty but because of their association with beggars, rascals, and thieves and their own common trickery in diluting drinks and overcharging."[16] The German historian Johanna Kachel, writing in the 1920s, differentiated among classifications of tavern keepers, concluding that there was a correlation between their socioeconomic status and degree of morality. According to Kachel, a class of urban tavern keepers existed whose houses were frequented by beggars, vagabonds, and common women, and whose establishments were shunned by honorable society. Kachel interpreted the numerous ordinances and decrees forbidding the mixing of wine with water, restricting lodging of vagabonds and dangerous persons, and establishing tavern closing times as evidence of the low morals of the typical sixteenth-century tavern keeper.[17] She was correct to assume that the social and economic status of the tavern keeper was closely tied to that of his clientele — as Sachs expressed it, "The landlord is just like the guest, the birds are just like the nest."[18] But here any similarity with the impoverished and dishonorable class of tavern keepers described by Sachs and Kachel ends, for beggars, vagabonds, and thieves were rare visitors in these urban taverns.

The mean property tax Augsburg tavern keepers paid in the seventeenth century was the highest for any nonelite group, exceeded only by taxes exacted from patricians, merchants, and doctors. Based on other economic indicators such as numbers of journeymen per house and home ownership, the high taxes tavern keepers paid represented a fair estimate of their financial health.[19] Within this overall picture of economic strength, however, there was considerable variation in the wealth of individual tavern keepers. A breakdown of the tax payments by profession reveals, not surprisingly, that the wealthiest group of tavern keepers were the innkeepers, most of whom were located on or near the Wine Market. The second wealthiest group were the brewers, with wine sellers the poorest group before the war, and their numbers diminishing by the end of the war to the point that a comparative evaluation is impossible.[20]

An examination of the average tax payments according to location rather than profession, however, indicates an interesting concentration of wealth before the Thirty Years' War. The highest average tax payment came not from the tavern keepers in the wealthiest section of town but from the brewers of Baker Lane in Lech Quarter. These fortunately located taverns drew business from traders entering town from Red Gate and also served as the social center for the Lech Quarter's artisans, an economically strong group until the war. The brewers on Baker Lane averaged 21.5 percent higher tax payments than the beer and wine sellers in the wealthy Uptown Area and nearly twice the overall average for tavern keepers generally. The two tavern keepers who paid over 50 gulden in 1610 (higher than the average tax paid by doctors) were not innkeepers on the Wine Market but brewers in Lech Quarter.[21]

The fact that tavern keepers were relatively wealthy is hardly surprising, for entry into the tavern keepers' profession required a fair amount of capital at the outset. Brewers especially needed a house outfitted with brewing equipment. During the period under consideration, a building thus equipped generally cost over 1,500 gulden and could cost as much as 7,000 gulden.[22] Several of Augsburg's larger taverns had their roots in the dismantling of the guilds in 1548, which proved devastating to the political power of Augsburg's artisans but provided a fortunate opportunity for investment to wealthier tavern keepers. Of the thirteen guildhalls that the new government sold, tavern keepers purchased four, at an average price of 3,575 gulden.[23] The brewing equipment, if purchased independently of the house, also required a significant investment. A brewer purchasing a brewing license with all the necessary brewing utensils paid 1,800 gulden in 1614, about 600–800 gulden more than the probable cost of the license alone for that year.[24]

The license was the second basic necessity for operating a tavern. This was considerably more expensive for a brewer than it was for a wine tavern keeper, for a beer brewing license or franchise (*Gerechtigkeit*), independent of the tavern, could cost as much as the building. Although the brewing license was normally attached to the house, it could sometimes be inherited or sold separately as an independent asset. The official price for a license purchased from the city government was only 24 gulden. Licenses were limited, however, and began to rise in price as higher beer sales increased competition for breweries. The brewers' ordinance forbade transferring licenses in 1572, but an exception to the rule allowed by the council in 1593 set a precedent for what would become a thriving business in license sales. Thus it was possible, as the brewer Georg Siedeler complained in 1607, to "take the brewing license in a sack or basket and carry it around the city, and set it down at will."[25]

Exactly why Siedeler opposed this practice is not clear, but it is possible that he was concerned about the effect of such transfers on the price of brewing licenses. A list of brewing license sales gathered from various sources shows prices circa 1600 ranging from 350 to 400 gulden, then gradually rising to a peak of 2,400 in 1620. After dropping back to 300–450 gulden around 1640, the value of the franchise began to increase again until it stabilized at approximately 900 gulden in 1646–1647. In some cases, the cost of the license was higher than that of the brewery itself.[26] The value of the license, which was not defined as property, was a form of wealth that would not be reflected in tax tables. By comparison, records of wine and mead sellers do not include a licensing fee for the sixteenth century, but in keeping with the general trend toward professionalization of the trade, the fee for purchasing a wine seller's franchise was established at 10 gulden by the mid-seventeenth century and 15 gulden at some point before 1688, when it was raised to 100 gulden.[27]

The cost of providing beds, linens, and stables for overnight guests and their horses was also a significant expense. As noted above, taverns that failed to provide these facilities were forced to close their doors to guests. A glimpse at the expenses involved in outfitting a well-equipped tavern is provided in the will of the brewer Paul Hegele, who died in 1608 and left to six heirs his brewery at the entrance to Jakob Suburb. The will lists two adjoining buildings and one stable valued at a total of 4,000 gulden; over 95 gulden in silver dishes; 624 gulden worth of beds and linens; and a supply of barley, malt, and hops valued at 355 gulden.[28] There were undoubtedly taverns that offered more modest accommodations, but every tavern keeper had to have at minimum a house, an eight-horse stable, four beds with linens, a tavern license, and a supply of wine or beer.

Another indication of the economic status of Augsburg's tavern keepers can be found in the healthy dowries that their widows and daughters brought to their marriages. Assets of 200 to 300 gulden were typical, with some dowries reaching four figures. These amounts parallel property taxes in that they are generally higher than those of ordinary craftsmen but less than the dowries of merchants, doctors, and patricians.[29]

Although the Thirty Years' War had a devastating effect on all of Augsburg's society, tavern keepers as a group did not suffer as much as did many in other trades. The total number of city taverns remained fairly consistent despite a 50 percent drop in Augsburg's population, so that while there was approximately one tavern for every 460 inhabitants around 1600, by 1646 the ratio was greater than 1:200. This degree of success in the face of adversity contradicts the assumption that the sixteenth-century attacks on drunkenness died out during the seventeenth century because the common classes could no longer afford the luxury of drinking bouts.[30] Even if the overall tax picture shows a reduction in the average wealth of tavern keepers, with the wealthiest brewers no longer in evidence and a rise in the numbers at the bottom of the scale, the relative growth in taverns per capita indicates that social drinking bouts continued despite the pains of war.

Also by 1646 a greater concentration of wealth emerged in the middle ranks, a trend reflected to a lesser degree in society at large. In the relatively poor Jakob Suburb, an increase in the number of tavern keepers was accompanied by a rise in their average tax payment, a rare phenomenon after the devastation of war. Several of the brewing families, far from suffering financially, spent the war years expanding their business into larger breweries, so that by 1646 a number of taverns existed that incorporated two or even three buildings. Overall, the greatest number of tavern keepers in 1646, as in 1610, paid a property tax of between 1 and 50 gulden, placing them in the upper-middle ranks of society. The sale of beer and wine remained a solid and profitable business even in the worst of times.[31]

These indicators, then, all point to a relatively high and particularly stable economic status for Augsburg's tavern keepers, a phenomenon typical for keepers of city taverns throughout Germany.[32] Economic status, however, did not always equal social status. The social stratum known as *Mehrer* (members of the Lords' Drinking Room who did not have patrician status), for example, had a higher mean property tax level in the seventeenth century than did the patricians themselves, and by 1646 the merchants had surpassed the patricians as well. The city executioner, too, although a social pariah, could be quite wealthy.[33] Where, then, did tavern keepers fit into the social picture?

The social position of tavern keepers probably did not quite equal their economic strength. Wedding protocols indicate that tavern keepers and their widows and daughters made more matches with bakers, butchers, and craftsmen than they did with members of the elite trades (goldsmiths, merchants, doctors, and lawyers) with whom they had more in common economically. There is, however, no evidence of a class of disreputable publicans who consorted with beggars and thieves. The doctors, lawyers, goldsmiths, artists, and their families who appear only rarely as brides and bridegrooms nonetheless served as witnesses at many tavern keepers' weddings, evidence of social or professional contact or ties of kinship.[34] Tavern keepers also participated in city government, a further indication of social acceptance. The Small Council in 1549 included two brewers and the Large Council a total of twenty tavern keepers. Their numbers on the Large Council came to over 14 percent of all the commoners on the city council, an amount far exceeding the less than 2 percent of the population at large made up of tavern keepers.[35] For the years 1548–1648, a total of five tavern keepers served on the Small Council, 7 percent of the total number of commoners who served throughout the period.[36] Although tavern keepers who were privileged enough to serve on the city council cannot be considered representative of the trade in general, their presence provides evidence of a high degree of social acceptance for their profession.

Society, then, conferred on tavern keepers a level of economic and social prestige generally higher than that enjoyed by the average craftsman. The high sense of self-esteem that many tavern keepers associated with their profession is evidenced by their commissioning of portraits and family coats of arms and the keeping of family chronicles, hardly earmarks of a disreputable trade.[37] In fact, the view of the tavern keeper as disreputable gleaned from Sachs's works is based on an unbalanced selection of his plays. A systematic examination of Sachs's Shrovetide plays reveals that the tavern keeper appeared at least as often as a spirit of generosity and hospitality, or as the voice of reason in mediating the disputations of his guests, as he did in a more negative light.[38]

Hospitality

"A guest will sometimes judge an inn, by the pretty maid therein; The inn should suit the guest just fine, as long as there's good food and wine," counseled the Augsburg schoolmaster Georg Mayr in his advice for travelers — "although," he added, "the guest will also be well pleased, if the sheets are good and clean."[39] Providing food, drink, and lodging for guests to the city was, of course, the function that defined the tavern keepers' trade. For as we have seen, the right to seat and serve local guests was dependent on the capability to put up strangers.

Augsburg's Tavern Keepers

Hospitality was a matter of honor in any German land and a matter of survival to a city dependent on trade. Augsburg's ruling classes prided themselves on the luxurious receptions and well-appointed accommodations they were able to offer visitors. The arrival of exalted guests was met with sword dances and extravagant displays of fireworks on the Wine Market, followed by banquets, dancing, and toasts in the Merchants' and Lords' Drinking Rooms. Wine on these occasions was served in elaborate vessels made of gold or silver or even Venetian glass in the shape of merchant sailing ships. The skilled handwork of Augsburg's gold- and silversmiths also glittered on the walls, ceilings, and furniture of lavishly decorated reception and banquet halls.[40] The huge banquets and great vessels of wine consumed at such occasions have been described in detail by many chroniclers and cultural historians. These extravagant displays of hospitality were calculated to impress visitors with Augsburg's wealth, power, and ability to provide for its guests. A city of international renown needed a reputation for generous hospitality.

During the peak of Augsburg's period of prosperity, the so-called *Blütezeit* (blossoming) of the sixteenth century, the emperor himself often chose Augsburg to host his official gatherings. A guest as distinguished as the Holy Roman Emperor did not, of course, seek refuge in public taverns. Visitors of high caliber were welcomed in the private palaces of Augsburg's merchant bankers.[41] The great merchant houses of the city, located adjacent to the Wine Market, were famous for their generous private hospitality. This was a function that the merchants had taken over from the nobility in earlier centuries, when travel and personal contact were still crucial to successful commerce.

Private hospitality had been the rule for most travelers during the Middle Ages, when pilgrims and tradesmen found lodging in churches or private homes and knights and other persons of higher birth could expect generous hospitality in the country homes of the nobility. Between the twelfth and fourteenth centuries, as cities grew in size and traveling became more commonplace, this form of early hospitality declined in favor of the commercial tavern. Taking money in exchange for hospitality, unthinkable in the Middle Ages, now became the rule.[42] Extremely exalted guests, however, still honored the private homes of Augsburg's elites, for the status they conferred on the house could not be measured in money.

The development from private hospitality to commercial tavern was more than a utilitarian adjustment accompanying the emergence of a money economy. It was part of the evolution of the separation of spaces defined as public and private. Houses specializing in providing food and rest to outsiders took on a public character and, in the process, became increasingly subject to the control of the authorities. During the age of private hospitality, guests in private homes were entitled to the protection of the house and were in turn bound to respect the peace of the household. Even when enemies took hospitality under the same roof, convention required them to keep peace for the duration of their stay. The sanctity of the private home was not to be violated. The head of the household in this arrangement could be directly accountable for the safety of his guests.[43]

The public tavern, in contrast, offered its guests no protection from their adversaries. While the tavern keeper did remain responsible for maintaining peace in his house, he was not bound to protect the lives of his guests or provide them with asylum. Neither law nor hospitable tradition prevented an adversary from seeking satisfaction against a tavern guest. On the contrary, the public tavern provided the ideal stage for settling disputes, whether through peaceful negotiation or violence. The early modern tavern, then, although it served as home for the tavern keeper and his household, had a different status from the homes of other citizens. Territorial, town, and city officials slowly took over the role of regulating and protecting travelers and, in turn, controlling the houses in which they stayed. Only in a public house could the city government regulate the amounts and types of food and drink that could be served, the hours during which hospitality was available, and the sorts of facilities guests could expect. City ordinances, in the tradition of sumptuary laws, limited the tavern keepers to certain mealtimes between which only bread, cheese, and fruit could be served. Only tavern keepers were subject to fines for serving meat on Fridays, Saturdays, and during periods of fasting, and special restrictions on public food service went into effect during times of shortages.[44]

City ordinances also required tavern keepers to announce the public nature of their house by hanging a sign identifying the building as a tavern. The tavern sign was a fixture throughout Europe by the fifteenth century, identifying the tavern not only to the traveler seeking lodging but also to the authorities trying to control taverns and their guests.[45] Signs generally carried the name of the tavern along with an identifying symbol, often reflecting the reputation of the house for hospitality. Thus many taverns based their names on famous or legendary guests, such as the Three Kings (*Zu den drei Köni-gen*) or the Three Moors (*Zu den drei Mohren*). Also typical were religious sym-bols, reflecting a feeling of hospitality because of the traditional image of the church and tavern as havens for pilgrims. Tavern symbols thus included not only names of saints but also animals connected with Christian symbolism, such as the ox, lion, and eagle, symbolizing evangelists; the deer and lamb, symbols of Christ; and the whale, dragon, and swan, associated with Bible stories and medieval church legend.[46]

The tavern sign guaranteed potential guests that drink as well as lodging were available, for a tavern keeper whose cellar lacked a supply of wine or beer had to remove his sign. Licensed tavern keepers were not allowed to turn away honorable guests unless the tavern was full, and they could be fined for refusing to serve drinks to their customers.[47] In some parts of Ger-many, even good cheer was a matter of public decree. A Heidelberg ordi-nance required that tavern keepers receive all guests with "friendly words and behavior" and provide whatever information, food, drink, and overnight lodging the traveler requested. Elsewhere, tavern keepers were also bound by law not to refuse wine to their guests.[48]

In return for their compliance with the ordinances governing the licensing and operating of taverns, tavern keepers enjoyed a monopoly on lodging and entertaining visitors. With the exception of visiting elites already noted, only licensed taverns could lodge nonresidents, for pay or otherwise, and only tav-ern keepers could serve meals and drinks for a profit. Their capacity to feed and lodge visitors to the city was an important part both of the tavern keep-ers' identity with his trade and Augsburg's civic identity as a merchant city.

Augsburg's publicans, in providing the city with lodging for its guests and tables for its public gatherings, occupied a key position in the community, and their social and economic status reflected the significance of that posi-tion. But with the possible exception of the most prestigious innkeepers, the tavern keepers' income was less dependent on the provision of space than it was on the provision of drinks. The consumption of alcohol, especially in a public space, could serve certain social functions. At the same time, it could be a potential source of disorder at many levels. We will now turn from the institution of the tavern to the effects the alcohol served therein had on its customers and how early modern townsfolk, as social, spiritual, and physi-cal beings, made sense of those effects.

3

The Drunken Body

In 1570 THE Augsburg physician and humanist Achilles Pirminius Gasser gave
a speech to the members of the Lords' and Merchants' Drinking Societies
warning against the dangers of drunkenness. Gasser preceded his list of possible dangers with a general explanation, based on the current state of medical knowledge, of how alcoholic drinks affect the body. His description of
basic temperaments, shifting humors, and multiple types of drunken bodies was grounded in the Galenic tradition that dominated Renaissance medicine.[1] The recipients of Gasser's information were the city council members,
magistrates, and Discipline Lords who issued local legislation against drunkenness and made decisions about its enforcement. Contemporary medical
theories affected notions of physicality on a more general level as well, for
popular cultural images such as woodcuts, broadsheets, Shrovetide plays, and
even drinking songs also drew heavily on Galenic theory.[2] In order to make
sense of any of the topics covered later in this volume, from the attempts
by early modern authorities to control drunkenness to the shared cultural
experiences of early modern drinkers, it is necessary to understand how early
modern people made sense of the physical sensations and behaviors that resulted from alcohol consumption.

The body, intensely personal and yet physically and metaphorically a social
object, was in a process of redefinition during the early modern period. The
Renaissance humanists turned to the body as an object of intense observation, exploring its functions, mapping its parts, and recording their personal
experiences with its inexplicable disorders. This process of discovery of the
physical body also led to a reexamination of the relationship between the corporeal and the ethereal.[3] Anatomical discoveries affecting medical theories,
religious debates centering on saints' relics and transubstantiation, and philosophical concern with the relationship of the body to the soul, the state, and
the cosmos were all part of an intellectual movement that increasingly pri-
vatized and individualized the body, while at the same time subordinating it

to the mind as the center of human identity. Bodies, which could exist and function only in accordance with prevailing social experience, were thus undergoing a transition from their medieval construct as fluid, permeable, and cosmically networked toward the more mechanical, bounded, and private Enlightenment bodies.[4]

The early modern body, then, cannot be understood as a natural object, one subject to universal experiences that can be labeled in accordance with our own terms. People experienced their physicality, including drunkenness, in accordance with culturally available discourse. The physical state of drunkenness might be described, treated, condemned, or celebrated; but without an objective test for blood alcohol levels, it could not be measured. A degree of drunkenness could only be assumed based on outward appearance, behavior, and the drinker's own sensual awareness of his or her condition.

Scholarship on the early modern body is primarily concerned with modes of its suppression. Influenced by the work of Norbert Elias, Michel Foucault, and Gerhard Oestreich, scholars of the early modern period generally accept a paradigm that assumes an increasing emphasis by the dominant elements in early modern culture on establishing boundaries and enforcing order and control.[5] Calvinist ideology in particular intensified the notion that the body was something to be mastered or conquered.[6] The early modern body was still a humoral body, defined internally by shifting and transmutating fluids and permeable via its many orifices; thus it was an inherently unstable vessel, threatening order with its physicality.[7] Much about the human body seemed separate and unknowable, so that early modern writers often ascribed to it a separate identity or animistic life of its own that was at war with their intellectual side. When in a state of disorder such as illness or drunkenness, the body seemed rebellious, even treasonous. Constantly threatening to violate its precarious boundaries and pollute its environment with dangerous and unhealthy fluids, the corporeal was in a constant struggle with the spiritual, undermining reason and not confinable by order.[8]

It was this humorality of the body that was being silenced in the repression of functions identified by Elias. Scholars of literature discuss the conflict between the tradition of disorder, defined as peripheral, popular, and corporeal, and the discourse of discipline and order, defined as central, aristocratic, and spiritual, in terms of oppositional hierarchy. The corporeal aspects were associated with low or popular culture while the controlled and intellectual culture was elevated. Mikhail Bakhtin thus identified in the open, grotesque body of Rabelaisian tradition a direct opposition to the controlled and closed classical body represented by intellectual tradition.[9] And yet the propagators of order themselves seemed to share much of the baser traditions associated with Rabelaisian culture. Attacks on disorderly behavior were often illustrated with provocatively corporeal images, and literature defining the body in humoral terms persisted until the time of Newton.

Drunkenness, both by decreasing the newly imposed inhibitions about bodily functions and intensifying humoral disorder within the body, softened boundaries between the personal and the social, providing a portal for the transition from confinement of bodily fluids to their spillage. Thus it seemed to threaten order. At the same time, however, drunkenness could provide a portal from the physical to the spiritual, the creative, and the procreative. Just as fasting and temperance represented both worldly discipline and concern for cosmic order, feasting and drunkenness could be an expression not only of worldly pleasure but also a celebration of the expansiveness of God's universe. The grotesque body, like a bursting wineskin, could represent both physical and spiritual plenitude; and drinking, even drunkenness, had positive uses both physically and metaphorically. Harmful drunkenness was represented less as a physical state than it was as a cultural archetype, indicating disorder and a descent to the realm of the senses. Moderate drunkenness was in some cases considered healthy by physicians, and even extreme drunkenness could be a positive cultural metaphor. It is precisely because the early modern period was characterized by a process of repression of the body that the image of the drunkard during this time was such an ambiguous figure, inviting ridicule while at the same time glorifying the fluidity of the boundaries between body and environment and reveling in a culture of excess.

Learned Views on Alcohol and the Body

How did early modern physicians understand drunkenness as a physical condition? A brief overview of learned views on the use and abuse of alcohol reveals that physical drunkenness was not a single objective construct but represented a multiplicity of concepts. Although advances in science of the early modern period raised a challenge to the ideas of Aristotle and Galen, the new ideas entered into the practice of science very slowly, and medical and chemical texts of the sixteenth and seventeenth centuries persisted in describing the material world and the physical self in Aristotelian and Galenic terms. More than just an ancient tradition, Galen's theories became the subject of intense scrutiny and reevaluation during the Renaissance, with new editions of his works numbering among the most popular of Renaissance texts.[10] According to Galen, treatments for bodily disorders needed to take into account not only the characteristics of the illness but also characteristics of the patient and his or her environment. This applied to the self-imposed humoral imbalance resulting from alcohol consumption as well as to disorders caused by disease. Whether one was drunk, and whether this drunkenness was a positive or a negative state, could thus depend on a variety of factors, including age, gender, temperament, state of health, and astrological conditions.

Medical authorities by the sixteenth century had clearly recognized that drunkenness, especially habitual drunkenness, was harmful to health. "Drinking a lot of wine is unhealthy," a 1474 health text warned; "it upsets the nature of the body."[11] Sixteenth- and seventeenth-century medical texts described numerous afflictions caused by habitual drunkenness, including lameness, shaking limbs, digestion problems, loss of appetite, inflammations, and damage to the heart, liver, and eyes. These texts especially drew attention to the harmful effects of misusing brandy.[12] Gasser in his speech warned the members of the Lords' and Merchants' Drinking Rooms against stroke, laming, epilepsy, and early death, all of which could result from drunkenness. The problem, then, arises not in asking whether doctors considered immoderate drinking to be harmful but in asking how they defined immoderate.

The science of alcoholism is a recent one, and the label "alcoholic" is in no way synonymous with the early modern application of the term "drunkard." The concept of a physical addiction was not possible from the standpoint of anatomical knowledge of the sixteenth and seventeenth centuries. Physicians of the early modern period could make no distinction between a drunken alcoholic and a drunken nonalcoholic, nor would they have considered an alcoholic who showed no outward signs of intoxication to be a drunkard. "Drunkenness," then, in early modern use, cannot be regarded as a description of either alcoholism as defined in the twentieth century or merely the consumption of large quantities of alcohol. "Drunkenness" implied some degree of evident intoxication, and chronic drunkenness was viewed as a choice of the will, not a disease of the body.

Nonetheless, medical authorities did recognize by the sixteenth century that different people reacted differently to alcoholic drinks. Doctors then, as now, were trying to find explanations for these differences. Why did some men become violent when drunk, while others seemed relaxed or even lethargic? Why did wine make some men happy and others sad? Clearly, these variances could not be explained simply by the amounts or types of beverages consumed. The answer, then, had to lie in the fundamental differences among people: their various temperaments, which early modern scholars understood to be related to the Aristotelian and Galenic view of nature as defined by the four basic elements. According to this tradition, the four elements (earth, water, air, and fire) were defined by the four essential qualities of heat, cold, wetness, and dryness. Each element was associated with two of these qualities. The elemental earth was essentially dry and cold; water was cold and wet; air was wet and hot; and fire was hot and dry. Each of these combinations was in turn related to one of the four cardinal fluids, or humors, of the body, the balance of which established the human temperament (*Complexion*). While an ideal, healthy anatomy would consist of a perfect balance of all four, most people displayed temperaments that suggested a prevalence of one or another of the humors. The resulting individual temperaments were related to the four qualities of wet, cold, dry, and hot. The cold quality made one pale, often heavy, with a weak pulse, thin hair, and problems with digestion; the wet quality meant a person tended to be fleshy in body and face, soft, with an excess of bodily fluids and a need for much sleep; the dry quality made one lean, with a fast pulse, and little need for sleep; and the hot quality was identifiable by a person's red color, hearty pulse, strong voice, and hairiness. These qualities combined in the four primary temperaments, each associated with a predominance of one of the four humors working in the body: blood, with the qualities of air (wet and hot), the sanguine temperament; phlegm, with the qualities of water (cold and wet), the phlegmatic temperament; black bile, associated with earth (dry and cold), the melancholic temperament; and those ruled by yellow bile, with the qualities of fire (hot and dry), were of the choleric temperament.[13]

Like people, beverages were believed to have certain characteristics, or complexions, based on their cool, warm, light, heavy, or other qualities. Older wine was considered warmer than new wine, and white or yellow wine was warmer than red. Likewise, dry or sour wine was thought to be colder and dryer than sweet. Some physicians believed that drinking wine mixed with water would cause drunkenness more quickly than drinking wine alone, because the heavier, colder qualities of the water would cause the wine to move through the system faster. According to the sixteenth-century physician Lorenz Fries, this was the reason that the wine available in public taverns (which he assumed would be watered down) made one drunker and caused greater headaches than wine served in more reputable locations. Physicians also found beer to be generally cold and wet in quality, and they warned that immoderate consumption of beer could lead to a more phlegmatic drunkenness than that resulting from wine, lasting longer and causing a greater hindrance to movement.[14]

Besides wine and beer, distilled liquors were gaining ground both for medicinal and pleasurable purposes. Distillers described the distillation process as the drawing out of a fifth, essential element (*quinta essentia*) from a base material. This transformation could be achieved only through the application of fire, the purifying element, and the resulting spirit also contained the qualities of heat and dryness.[15] An example of how such beliefs affected local legislation is provided in the Augsburg authorities' concern that craftsmen who got themselves too "heated up" (*erhitziget*) on brandy would find it necessary to "cool down" again with beer (*in dem Bier abzukühlen*).[16] The city council thus justified the severe limits placed on the amount of brandy that could be sold for consumption on the premises by noting that brandy often "ignites" further immoderate drinking (*zu weiter füllerey anzündt*).[17] Their fears were apparently not without foundation, as illustrated in the case of Hans Block, a craftsman whose physician recommended brandy to relieve "painful limbs" (*schmertzen seiner glid*) in the winter of 1544. Block testified that the drying effect of the brandy led him to go to a public tavern for some cool wine. The unseemly behavior that resulted led to Block's arrest, after which he was banned from drinking brandy entirely in spite of his doctor's advice.[18]

The qualities associated with various drinks, medical writers believed, acted in turn on the qualities existing in the individual drinker. The extent to which beverages could be useful, harmful, or dangerously intoxicating was enhanced by factors of compatibility between drinker and drink. While health and medical texts agreed that immoderate drinking was generally harmful, the negative effects of intoxication could be exacerbated or reduced based on the balance of humors in the body. Medical texts warned against the use of drinks of a warm complexion by those of a dry and fiery nature, whose resistance to inflammations would be lowered, or the drinking of old wine by people of a cold complexion. Melancholics, however, could benefit from the heavier wines, which calmed and relaxed their mournful spirit.[19]

The least likely to suffer or cause serious harm through immoderate drinking were those of the sanguine temperament. The sanguine was the noblest of the temperaments, making the individual friendly, mild, and cheerful by nature. Persons blessed with this temperament became even more good-natured and happy when drunk. This was particularly true because good wine was believed to have a sanguine nature, which naturally enhanced this noble and especially manly character. The most dangerous drunk was the choleric personality. Possessed by a fiery temperament, the choleric was un-friendly, warlike, and inclined to be lean and restless, the type embodied by Shakespeare's Mercutio. This temperament was exacerbated by drink, es-pecially drinks of a hot character, such as dry wine or brandy. The choleric quality explained the tendency for many people to become boastful, angry, and violent when drunk. Phlegmatics, whose nature inclined them toward heaviness, slowness, and an excess of bodily fluids, became lazy, sleepy, and dull when drunk, and they lost control of their bodily functions. Images and descriptions depict drunkards of this temperament vomiting, complaining, and passing out. Melancholics were believed to be fearful and depressed by nature, thin, sensitive, and given to dark musing. This is the temperament as-sociated with artists and poets; and the comforting effect of drink was con-sidered beneficial to them, although the impact of exaggerating their creative tendencies could cause them to behave irrationally. Drunken melancholics are often accompanied in graphic representations by the symbol of madness, the monkey. Physicians also recognized melancholy as a mood from which anyone might suffer from time to time, and they thought it a circumstance that might be relieved by strong wine or brandy.[20]

Some doctors believed that drink exacerbated the sad temperament of the melancholic, causing them to cry over past sins.[21] This characteristic, how-ever, was attributed by others to the sanguine rather than the melancholic. One moral fable, which told of Noah's planting of the vine after the flood, tied the four properties of wine to the blood of the various beasts Noah used to nourish his four vines — the monkey gave his character to the melancholic, the pig to the phlegmatic, the lamb to the sanguine, and the lion to the choleric. The blood of the lamb, symbol of the baptism of Christ, could only result in a pious drunk. Drunken sanguines, according to this view, are in their most spiritual state, weeping over their sins and wanting to reform the entire world, although their repentance might be forgotten by morning.[22]

The balance of humors, early modern doctors believed, was affected not only by basic temperaments but by illness, pregnancy, moods, and astrological conditions, and it varied according to one's age and sex. Thus how a person was affected by drinking might change over the course of time. Physicians warned against giving wine to children, for example, explaining that the choleric quality was unhealthy for children under the age of fourteen, who tended to have a choleric nature. Physicians compared giving wine to children to "adding fire to fire."[23] Medical texts warned also against drinks of a cool nature (beer, fruit juice, or water) for women in labor or women trying to conceive children; and the immoderate use of beer by German women was sometimes blamed for infertility. Since infertility in women was generally thought to be caused by a too cool temperament, physicians prescribed drinks of a hot nature, especially brandy, to correct the problem.[24] During labor, good, white wine was most often recommended, although in strict moderation.

The elderly were in the enviable position of seeming to benefit from immoderate drinking. The sixteenth-century physician Walter Ryff provided a recommendation for each of life's stages, describing drinking as particularly harmful to the young and acceptable in moderation to adults up to the age of thirty. Once a man reached the age of forty, however, he might be immoderate in his drinking habits. Another text recommended that elderly people drink "as much as they may" (als vil sy mügen), as they tend toward a cold nature, and it recommended strong wine to return them to strength.[25] Medical experts considered brandy, too, to be healthy for older people, who often suffered from a phlegmatic temperament.

Illness could affect one's temperament as well, and the prescription for taking wine when ill could vary according to the infliction. In periods of infection, such as plague, drinks of a fiery nature were thought to weaken one's resistance. Physicians thus recommended the cooler and dryer wines to help ward off plague and cold, wet beverages such as beer to combat fever.[26] During outbreaks of disease, civic authorities sometimes forbade the sale of brandy entirely.[27] Generally speaking, however, wine was believed to be particularly beneficial to the ill and the weak. Civic authorities thus allowed exceptions to rules against buying drinks on credit for persons suffering from illness. As Ryff put it, "God created wine, after all, to warm and comfort the ill, poor, and feeble-minded."[28]

Health manuals recommended occasional immoderate drinking, even to the point of drunkenness, to healthy people as well in order to purge the system of impurities. The thirteenth-century physician and alchemist Arnald of Villanova had already suggested drinking to the point of vomiting once or twice a month to rid oneself of excess phlegmatic humors, and belief in the positive benefits of this medicinal intoxication persisted until the eighteenth century.[29] If excess drink did not suffice to induce vomiting, drinking warm water or inserting a finger in the throat would complete the purge.[30]

How, then, did early modern authorities define harmful drunkenness? Medical descriptions of the harmful effects of drinking are not very helpful on this point. Invariably, the amount considered unhealthy is simply stated as "too much," or it is associated with terms all too general, such as "drunkenness" (*Trunkenheit*), "immoderate drink" (*unmäßiger Trunk*), or "misuse" (*Mißbrauch*). To identify the line between healthy and harmful consumption, we must look also at the positive uses of alcohol, or the effects considered healthy and good. Medical experts agreed that the effect of creating a feeling of joy, high hopes, and wisdom was an absolutely positive one. They celebrated as great virtues the abilities of strong drink to ease pain or bitterness, relieve melancholy, quicken the tongue, and bring cheer to the old and sick. Simple drunkenness, or a feeling of intoxication, could not in itself be understood as harmful; for it was this very feeling of intoxication that the medical authorities lauded as healthy for body and spirit and that they identified as moderate use in contrast to the harmful state of drunkenness defined by the term "*Trunkenheit.*" In fact, Ryff spent more time in his discussion in the chapter "The German Drunkenness" describing ways to lessen the harmful effects of getting drunk than warning against doing it, and he pointed out that for some people wine is better than water for counteracting the effects of a hangover. Gasser also qualified his attack on drunkenness by pointing out that very good wine (the sort available only to the members of the elite drinking societies whom he was addressing) was the healthiest of all drinks.[31]

The Drunken Body

Immoderate drinking was therefore regarded as something more than an occasional feeling of intoxication, or even occasionally drinking to the point of vomiting. Gasser, like many of his contemporaries, identified the habitual drunkard or "sot" (*Trunkenbold*), who "lives to drink, rather than drinking to live" as the person most likely to suffer physical harm from drinking.[32] His description of harmful drunkenness included interference with movement and weakening of the body and the senses, and he concluded with the generalization that "in all of [the four temperament types], both the tongue and the legs become so heavy, that they can neither speak nor walk."[33] According to Gasser's description, then, drunkenness was defined as the point at which the drinker literally lost all control of his physical self.

The question of how much was too much, to the sixteenth-century physician, is one that could only be answered with respect to the age, gender, state of health, and temperament of the individual drinker. Moderate drinking was considered healthy for everyone, and early modern medical opinions suggest that "moderate" meant something quite different from our current use of the word. The medical community agreed that moderate drinking included moderate intoxication, which could be useful and healthy. Harmful drunkenness was chronic drunkenness, or drunkenness to a point somewhere beyond mere intoxication—exactly where that point was, unfortunately, escapes uniform description.

During the course of the seventeenth century, Galenic medicine passed from favor and was replaced by a more mechanistic view of the body. Although descriptions of the four temperaments do not disappear entirely from medical texts, they become less prevalent after mid-century, and seldom is Galen cited as the source. Nonetheless, medical writers throughout the seventeenth century persisted in describing the body and its reaction to drink in terms of warm, cold, wet, and dry qualities. Wine could be warm or cool, depending on age and quality, and physicians continued to recommend the warmer wines to the elderly and others of a cool temperament.[34] Similar language is used in describing the new stimulants introduced during the seventeenth century (tobacco, chocolate, and opium), which might be more or less beneficial depending on the physician's interpretation of their warm, dry, cold, or wet qualities.[35] Brandy in particular received a great deal of attention during the seventeenth century and well into the eighteenth for its fiery nature, leading in the eighteenth century to the notion that excessive brandy drinking, especially by old "dried up" widows, could lead to spontaneous combustion of the body from within.[36]

In spite of the persistence of such beliefs, some changes in medical approaches are apparent by the later seventeenth century. Positive descriptions of drunkenness, even as an occasional habit, are lacking in the later works. Water also appears more often as an alternative to alcoholic beverages, although the texts warn of the dangers of drinking too much of it; water was believed to be unhealthy for the stomach and limbs. Most notable, however, is the decrease in emphasis on the physical effects of drinking in favor of descriptions of its impact on the mind. Texts of the later seventeenth century are less likely to include detailed descriptions of the various temperaments and their reactions to drink and more prone to concentrate on warnings against destroying reason and annihilating the will.[37] It is in this context that theories of addiction begin to develop by the end of the century; once the will is destroyed, the drinker loses control and succumbs to temptation. Addiction thus remained tied to the will rather than physical need.[38]

In a world before the introduction of any means by which to measure blood alcohol levels (or according to Barbara Duden, even before the locus of bodily perception moved from patient to physician),[39] neither drunkenness as a physical state nor the power of addiction could be objectively defined by the external observer; it could only be perceived sensually by the drinker. This perception not only varied from one individual to another but shifted along with changing paradigms about the body. Not until the end of the seventeenth century, with the triumph of the mechanistic view of the body, would the way be paved for theories of physical addiction that would emerge a century later. During the sixteenth and seventeenth centuries, the term "drunkenness" remained an abstract and conditional construct.

Toward an Iconography of Drunkenness

In turning from learned to more popular treatments of the drunken body provided by early modern German literary and artistic sources, it is important to note that the cultural body was also a humoral body. Descriptions of the four temperaments and their reactions to drink can be found in woodcuts, broadsheets, plays, and songs, as well as in medical texts. Typical of the genre is Hans Sachs's 1528 poem "The four amazing characteristics and effects of wine":[40]

The Drunken Body

The first sort [wine] makes kind and hearty,
Benevolent, a merry party.
The second it incites to ire,
To set with rage and brawl on fire.
The third it renders virulent,
Uncouth and childish, insolent.
The fourth takes wine as an indenture
To fantasy and to adventure.

(*Eygenschafft vnd würckung des Weins, 9–16*)

Erhard Schoen's woodcut "The Four Characteristics of Wine," printed in Augsburg in the same year, was probably intended as an illustration to Sachs's poem (fig. 3). The sanguine personality is represented by the drinking party on the upper right of Schoen's print, men who are conversing pleasantly and are accompanied by their wives, indicating affection. In front of the table is

Figure 3. The Four Characteristics of Wine
(Erhard Schoen, Die vier wunderlichen eygenschafft und würckung des weins. Augsburg, ca. 1528).

the iconographic representation of the sanguine drinker, the lamb. On the upper left, the choleric personality is depicted by a group of soldiers with drawn weapons, accompanied by the symbol of discord, the bear. The phlegmatic persons on the lower right are shown as drowsy peasants who are vomiting, defecating, and passing out; and they are represented by the pig. Finally, those in the group on the lower left, the melancholics, are behaving irrationally, playing foolish games and attempting acrobatics. They are accompanied by the symbol of madness, the monkey. Wine is represented in the woodcut by the tending of the vineyard (top center).[41]

Such images, if not necessarily received by the majority of the population as medical knowledge, nonetheless reflect a worldview that was accepted on a broad level. The animals present in Schoen's print are part of a larger genre of drunkenness imagery, showing the ability of alcohol to rob sane adults of reason and reduce them to the level of fools, children, or beasts. Numerous broadsheets and pamphlets criticizing drunkenness show various animals, either as companions to the drunkard or themselves appearing drunk, each standing for one of the baser elements of human character that might be released by drink.[42] The beastly or animal side of the human was often represented in the literature of the early modern period as the bodily side, that which is governed by the senses and without reason, representing the corrupt counterpart to the spiritual or intellectual, godly side. The descent into sin was sometimes described as a fall from the kingdom of angels to the kingdom of the animals.[43] Drunkenness, which resulted from the physical sin of gluttony and also destroyed reason and intellect, was well-suited to aid this descent. According to Sebastian Franck's influential tract "On the horrible vice of drunkenness" (Von dem greüwlichen laster der trunckenheyt), the drunkard "becomes a dumb, unreasonable animal . . . with nothing left of the human in him."[44] Police ordinances (Polizeiordnungen) mirrored these concerns, warning against "distorting noble reason into beastly absurdity" or succumbing to drunkenness as a "brute vice."[45] As soon as the sensory gained primacy over reason, the person would take on the negative characteristics of the animal. Drunkenness in this case, moralists claimed, was anything but manly, leading instead to its opposite—descent into the subhuman realm.

Images that warn of the potential of alcohol to reduce humans to animals illustrate fear of the disorderly nature of the body, especially the danger of a body out of control. Depicted in a sixteenth-century broadsheet from

Figure 4. Pay Close Attention to This Figure, It Shows the Drunkard's Nature
(Betracht mit fleyß dise Figur / Sie zeigt Weynvoller Leuth Natur. Zürich,
sixteenth century. Courtesy of the Zentralbibliothek Zürich)

Zurich (fig. 4) are all the icons of loss of control and deterioration into less than manhood that characterize the "Nature of the wino" (*Weynvoller Leuth Natur*). The horns represent the beast-like behavior of the drunkard, or loss of reason; the fallen crown depicts loss of honor (the piercing of the crown by the pole suggests a sexual connotation); urination portrays loss of bodily control; the book on which the drinker stands exemplifies disrespect for the law; the spilling purse is financial ruin and the inability to control the household; the drawn sword denotes wrath, the inability to control temper; the death bier stands for illness and early death (or the inability to control one's health); and the image itself is that of a child, incapable of controlling its body or its life. Shown spilling coins and urine, the figure metaphorically breaks other bodily boundaries as well, with symbols representing the potential spillage of semen, blood, and its own life. The child drunkard is chained to the devil, who smiles maliciously as he offers his huge cup. The image of the devil here might also be understood to represent the boozing devil (*Saufteufel*), the personification of the vice of drunkenness.[46]

Hans Weiditz's Augsburg print "The Winebag and His Wheelbarrow" ("Der Weinschlauch") also appears in the first analysis to illustrate the archetype of the disorderly drunk (fig. 5). No longer in control of his body, the Winebag must carry his bloated belly on a wheelbarrow. This drunkard is also clearly no longer a man—not only does he wear the shoes and cap of a fool but he has been reduced from a body to a mere vessel, whose only function is to be filled with wine until he bursts to overflowing. The senses-driven vessel of the body has triumphed completely over the reason of the soul.[47] Spillage in this case, in the form of vomiting, represents not just loss of control but also to points out the wastefulness of overindulgence. Vomiting was a typical icon for portraying drunkenness.

The broadsheets depicted in figures 4 and 5, in representing drunkenness as a disorderly body, express concerns that went beyond the physical state of drunken individuals, or even the spiritual state of sinners. A body out of control could be a microcosm for a community out of control. Not only did authorities fear that wasteful expenditure on alcohol could lead to the collapse of the household and ultimately reduction to dependence on alms but civic leaders often issued ordinances in times of particular stress (such as war, pestilence, or famine), blaming the collective sins of drunkenness and blasphemy for arousing the wrath of God and leading him to punish the entire

Ich bin ein rechter weinschlauch
Für auff der Radwerb meinen bauch
Ich hab mir zogen ein faysten bachen
Und mag mir sein yetz wol gelachen

Im alter aber wirds mir schweer
Wen mir mein grosser wamst steet leer
Und ist alls durch den Ars gefaren
Das müß ich waynen in alten Jaren.

Figure 5. The Winebag and His Wheelbarrow
(Hans Weiditz, Der Weinschlauch. Augsburg 1521).

The Culture of Drink in the Early Modern German City

community.[48] More than just an individual case of sin, the drunken body, threatening to burst from its bounds and spill its contents into the environment, became a metaphor for the disorder of the world. Held only by a fragile fence of authority-imposed discipline, disorder threatened to erupt at any time in a stream of potentially polluting evil.[49] Popular illustrations that depict the bloated and vomiting drunkard as a disorderly fool, then, may be seen as an invitation for their audience to join in ridiculing and condemning drunkenness. Thus interpreted, these images became part of an overall attempt by the authorities to encourage orderly behavior.

Yet the icon of the vomiting drunkard cannot be reduced to a mere moral statement. The sixteenth-century fascination with bodily functions and excess went beyond disciplinary concern. It was also a way of laughing at want and celebrating plenty, and as such it could serve as an expression of joy and revelry. An erupting body might, in the context of social discipline and order, seem to be a sign of wastefulness and sin; at the same time, it had something of the Land of Cockaigne about it. This is, after all, the culture that produced Pantagruel. Caspar Scheit's and Fischart's German versions of the Rabelaisian literature emphasize less the negative results of bodily spillage than the pleasure of the eruption and the eroticism of body openings.[50] In fact, Fischart's description of a descent into drunkenness is anything but negative. The wealth of detail provided in his "Drunken litany" (*Die trunkene Litanei*), in which words trip and spill over each other in an endless stream of senseless joy, whets the appetite more than spoils it.[51]

The popularity of the sixteenth-century drink literature, much of which is satirical, was undoubtedly due more to this joyful expression of the carnivalesque than its didactic value.[52] Norbert Schindler has described the transition from the Middle Ages to the early modern period as a high point of the carnivalesque, defined primarily by its fascination with the grotesque body.[53] The grotesque form of the drunken body takes on a new meaning when placed within the context of the larger carnivalesque tradition. The softening of boundaries portrayed by figures such as the Winebag represented not only a criticism of the excess of individual drunkards but also a more general suspension of order and hierarchy. The boundaries of the self are broken down by drink, which both unites the body with its environment in its spillage and unites drinkers with one another by removing social inhibitions. In the drunkard, senses take priority over the intellect and the stomach takes precedence over the head in an inversion of social and political order. The drunk then becomes a metaphor not just for a cosmos out of order but for an inverted cosmos that is ruled by excess rather than want, freedom rather than restraint, and social integration rather than isolation. The rule of senses over reason in this inversion is cause for celebration rather than condemnation.

Another widespread early modern image is that of the drunk and vomiting peasant (fig. 6). This is one of several representations of the Kermis or peasant wedding from Sebald Beham's school, in all of which the tavern looms larger than the church as the central focus of the supposedly religious festival. Although traditionally viewed as a critical portrayal of peasant excess, art historians have also recognized in the work of Beham, Albrecht Dürer, Pieter Brueghel, and others who worked in this genre a positive kind of joie de vivre among the peasants. Such pictures might have been aimed as much at depicting a simple and earthy celebration of life and the bounty of the countryside as at ridiculing excess. The peasant, like the child or the fool, was a symbol of innocence and simple truth, or even witty social criticism,

Figure 6. The Kermis at Mögeldorf
(Der Kirchweih zu Mögeldorf, Teil 1. Sebald Beham und Erhard Schön. 1528).

as well as immaturity or lack of control. Renate Haftlmeier-Seiffert and Michael Schilling have both identified in the explicit sexual images often occurring in such prints a teasing invitation to take part in the play, purposely serving to titillate the audience even while overtly seeming to admonish. Schilling has suggested that it is precisely this two-sided function that partially accounted for the success of satirical broadsheets; one could uphold the norms of civilized behavior by ridiculing the subjects, while at the same time vicariously taking part in their course and unrestrained comportment.[54]

Images of drunkenness, too, could serve this purpose, inviting participation in the disorderly drama as much as criticism of it. As Alison Stewart has noted, the bodily culture attributed to peasants in festival prints was part of a shared culture, for the tastes of urban elites were also "dirty and bawdy," at least by twentieth-century standards; indeed, Lyndal Roper has found evidence of elite fascination with the bodily side even in police ordinances.[55] The text accompanying the Kermis broadsheet does not condemn the drunken peasant for his boorishness but equates his drunkenness with joy.[56] In Sachs's poem describing drunkenness according to the four humors, too, the tone is less moralizing than it is humorous, encouraging the reader to laugh at the antics of the foolish melancholic, brawl with the defiant choleric, and wallow in the filth of the drunken phlegmatic with obvious pleasure.[57] The image is heightened by the fact that the drunken phlegmatics appear in illustrations to the poem dressed as peasants, recalling the genre of the Kermis prints. Likewise, the cholerics are portrayed as dashing, flamboyantly attired soldiers, for whom even violent behavior might be seen as entirely appropriate.[58]

In all of these literary and artistic forms, the sanguine drinker is depicted as a positive image. The sanguine, blessed with the "nature of the lamb," only "grows altogether sweet and kind" when drunk, becoming a "merry . . . entertaining and quite witty" companion not only to his fellows but also to the other members of his household. Drinking does not incite the sanguine's temper, but makes him more mild and friendly than usual, so that he even bears insults with good will.[59]

The decline in status of Galenic medicine had little effect on the vocabulary of popular literature addressing drunkenness, which remained tied to notions of the four humors throughout the seventeenth century. As is the case in medical writing, however, a slight shift in the direction of a more intellect-centered view is discernible. As the notion of reason was elevated, the descent into the animal realm became even more abhorrent to the critics of drunkenness. This change in perception is most notable in depictions of the drunken sanguine. What was once sanguine joy became the foolish antics of a monkey; the warm heart of the lover became the lechery of a goat; and even the gentle lamb was turned into a mindless sheep.[60] The value placed on intellect, however, in no way led to an overall condemnation of drinking. Added to the already impressive list of positive effects to be gained by drinking good wine was its warming influence on the brain, which would sharpen the intellect and promote elevated thoughts.[61]

The drunken body as it appeared in early modern texts, both learned and popular, was an ambiguous image. A body filled to overflowing, spilling its contents into the environment, clearly expressed excess, but this could be understood in a celebratory as well as a critical sense. Indeed, the same image might signify both sentiments. Jonathan Sawday has described the diseased body during the early modern period as an "image of rebellion," a "hostile entity" poised in opposition to its conscious inhabitant.[62] The drunken body in this world of political and cosmic metaphors could play a similar role; but unlike disease, which was uninvited and often inexplicable, drunkenness was self-imposed and normally a voluntary state. Thus it could serve as a means to assert one's rule over the body by choosing disorder rather than succumbing to it.

The attraction of disorder as a choice was not diminished by the seventeenth-century trend toward locating drunkenness less in the body (as a disruption of fluids) and more in the mind (as a disruption of reason), nor did this shift serve to clarify the boundary between positive and negative uses of alcohol. Early modern drunkenness remained a metaphorical rather than a physical state. Therefore its definition was as porous and changeable as the body it inhabited.

The lack of an objective early modern definition of drunkenness and the ambiguous nature of the culture of the drunkard made condemnation of drunkenness, either as a sin or as a crime, particularly problematic. As we shall see in the following chapters, early modern concepts of drunken revelry do not become less equivocal when explored from the standpoint of theology or law. On the contrary, the culture of excess that images of drunken comportment celebrated was not limited to the physical world; it could also serve as a metaphor for spiritual plenty. As Florence Weinberg has noted, the "gross physical world" portrayed by drunken images could also act "as a comic mirror to the power and majesty of the spiritual world."[63] For according to early modern perceptions, the body housed the soul as well as the stomach.

4

The Drunken Spirit

"THEY GUZZLE," Zwingli lamented in a 1525 tract, "as if wine cannot be poured out and lost in any other way than through the human body."[1] Zwingli in his attack on the abuse of wine deplored not only the damage to body and spirit that excessive drinking caused but also the wasteful squandering of the wine itself. Although the abuse of drink could lead man to sin, the sin in drunkenness rested not in the wine but in the excesses of the drinker. What was being lost in the reformers' view, far from being a sinful substance, was a precious gift from God that should be appreciated and venerated rather than guzzled and poured through the body.

Attitudes toward the use of alcohol in virtually all cultures throughout history share this ambiguous nature. In the case of Christian Europe, it is easy to trace this ambiguity to its religious basis, for the Bible is notable for simultaneously condemning the abuse of wine while lauding its virtues. Attacks on drunkenness in the name of Christian morals were therefore consistent in differentiating between abuse and use, as the use of wine was clearly supported by Scripture. God created wine "to gladden the heart of man" (Pss. 104:15), and Christ's personal intervention at the marriage at Cana implies biblical approval for the generous provision of wine at social occasions (John 2:3–11).[2] Elsewhere, the Bible warns against abuse: "Be not drunk with wine, wherein is excess" (Eph. 5:18); and particularly popular with the moralists of the sixteenth century was Paul's admonition that drunkards will not inherit the kingdom of God (1 Cor. 6:10). The appropriate use of wine, according to Scripture, was neither excess nor abstinence.[3] Medieval poems, too, both condemned and praised the use of wine, and even the saints of the pre-Reformation church sometimes took on this two-sided character. Saint Urban (Pope Urban I) is revered not only as the patron saint of wine and vineyards but also as a protector against drunkenness.[4] Alcohol, then, represented both God's grace and his sorrow — a gift offered, according to one sixteenth-century fable, in the form of his tears.[5] For although God's intention was that man use his gift positively, the devil was always waiting in the wings to encourage him to abuse it.

In order to clarify what early modern Germans meant when they attacked the vice of drunkenness, we must first take a brief look at attempts by the pre-Reformation church to classify drunkenness as a sin, for the literature on drink of the sixteenth and seventeenth centuries is firmly grounded in medieval tradition. We will then turn to the period of the Reformation and post-Reformation to examine the development of reformed notions of sinful drunkenness. At the same time, however, the pervasive image of wine as a gift from God and the enjoyment thereof (even to the point of intoxication) as entirely positive persisted in art and literature throughout the early modern period. Reference to wine (*Wein*) in theological and legal texts should not be narrowly understood as meaning only one type of beverage. The word was often used as a generic term for alcoholic beverages generally. Only gradually during the course of the sixteenth century did specific mention of beer, mead, and brandy begin to appear at all, and the use of "wine" to imply all of the above persisted in records of punishment well into the seventeenth century. Thus wine imagery could represent any form of alcoholic or "spiritual" drink.[6]

We have already seen that depictions of drunkards could have an air of celebration about them. As we move from the microcosmos of the human body to the unlimited cosmos of the spiritual these images become even more celebratory. In religious imagery an overflowing vessel of wine was a metaphor less for gluttony than for spiritual abundance. The notion of drunkenness as a sin, then, was easier to attack than it was to define. Ultimately, drunkenness as a sin could not be defined merely as a state of intoxication but only by either its concretely negative results, especially as part of a general notion of wasteful living, or (more abstractly) by the state of mind of the drinker. Although the reformers of the sixteenth century dedicated much effort to attacking this vice, they were no more successful in establishing an objective means to identify it than their medieval predecessors.

Late Medieval Definitions of Drunkenness

Late medieval penitence manuals defined "drunkenness" as a subcategory of the cardinal sin of gluttony.[7] It did not receive separate treatment. The designation of a sin as cardinal is based not on its gravity but on its role as a start-

The Drunken Spirit

ing point for multiple sins and the decision to live a sinful life.[8] By the fifteenth century, penitence manuals went to great lengths to identify, define, categorize, and condemn sins and to establish an appropriate penance to be carried out by the parishioner. Gluttony generally appears in these manuals as the sixth of the seven cardinal sins. The tracts do not define the sin of drunkenness as distinct from that of overeating, however, and definitions primarily concentrate on infractions that are applicable to both (for example, eating or drinking between meals, in violation of fasting rules, or in excess of bodily requirements). Nonetheless, preachers and writers of penitence manuals clearly recognized that immoderate drinking could lead to a very different outcome. Their lists of the possible effects of the sin of gluttony included talkativeness, unseemly joy, loss of reason, gambling, unchaste thoughts, and evil words — vices that would not seem to follow from overeating.[9]

Physical health also played a role in defining the sin of immoderate eating and drinking, for knowingly harming the physical self was a form of suicide (a mortal sin). As one manual put it, "overeating and over drinking kill more men than the sword," and the sin is equally great whether one kills oneself slowly or quickly.[10] The fifteenth-century theologian Johannes Wolf interpreted this notion as spiritual rather than physical; and he accused those who purposely became drunk of breaking the commandment "Thou shalt not kill," not because of the danger to the body but because drunkenness killed the judgment of the soul. Here, the damage was to the health of the spirit rather than the body. What followed was behavior without conscience — swearing, fornication, even murder.[11]

Sins were grouped in some manuals according to the specific action involved as sins of thought, word, action, or inaction. Gluttony and drunkenness belonged here to the sins of action, commitment of the sin being dependent on a specific physical action (immoderate consumption). The degree of sin, however, was not established by the measure of consumption but by the extent to which free will was involved in deciding to commit the sin. Although action by the material body was required to be gluttonous, it was will, or the spiritual self, that defined the sin.[12] This was true in earlier books of penance as well, where divisions were made in the severity of penance for becoming drunk through (in ascending order of severity) ignorance, negligence, or contempt.[13] Purposely getting someone else drunk was also a sin, and several medieval canons distinguished between compelling someone else to get drunk out of fellowship, which required the same penance as becoming drunk oneself, and getting another drunk out of hatred or spite, in which case the offender would be judged as a murderer.[14]

By the fifteenth century, then, the definition of drunkenness as a state of sin depended on this decision to sin, or the goal of the sinner in getting drunk. Books of penance from this period do not contain the physical descriptions present in earlier canons, which often cited vomiting as the point at which penance was required. Vomiting, a physical sign of excess, as the point of determining gluttony was linked to scriptural admonitions against drunkenness.[15] The excess was not in drinking wine but in abusing it to the point of wasteful spillage.[16] By the late Middle Ages, however, the issue had become a less physical and more spiritual one, in which levels of will rather than levels of consumption determined the state of sin.

Reformation

The issue of free will in determining sin was a central area of debate during the reform movement. The fideistic doctrine of Luther and his contemporaries departed from the doctrine of free will as a determinant in defining either sin or salvation. Once they had identified sin as unavoidable in human nature rather than a voluntary act requiring a specific form of penance, Luther and his followers saw no further need to classify, quantify, or otherwise rate levels of sin and criticized the proliferation of detail in the late medieval penitence manuals as undue legalism.[17]

Despite this radical departure in defining sin, the moralist tracts associated with the reform movement continued to depend largely on the medieval tradition in describing the sins and vices they were attacking. The sin of drunkenness remained tied to the Catholic-defined cardinal sin of gluttony well into the seventeenth century. Moralists most often phrased their attacks on the sin of drunkenness in a language of sumptuary control, as part of the general assault on luxurious living. Although drunkenness could lead to other sinful behavior by weakening the will and robbing humans of reason, the sin in drunkenness itself seemed to rest in a notion of a wasteful abuse of one of God's gifts.

Much of the literature on drunkenness was influenced by Sebastian Brant's late-fifteenth-century work *The Ship of Fools* (*Das Narrenschiff*). The sixteenth chapter of Brant's satire is dedicated to the folly "stuffing and feasting" (*Füllen und Prassen*). Although both of these terms can be translated as gluttony, applicable to either food or drink, Brant's attack concentrated specifically on the abuse of wine. The theologian Sebastian Franck, in his "On the horrible vice of drunkenness" (*Von dem greüwlichen laster der trunckenheyt*, ca. 1531), also placed drunkenness within the context of gluttony, as a sin of the flesh. The flesh, Franck wrote, is the enemy of the spirit and the child of the world, and both overeating and drinking feed the flesh at the expense of the soul.[18] Similar connections were made by the moralist writers Matthaeus Friderich, Johannes von Schwarzenberg, Johann Eck, Jörg Wickram, and others who wrote in the drink literature genre.

Although drunkenness itself remained a form of gluttony, early modern writers also addressed its potential as a catalyst to falling into other sins. Drinkers were aided in this transition by the efforts of the boozing devil (*Saufteufel*). Catholics and Protestants during the early modern period shared a belief in devils, spirits, and demons as the creators of disorder and impetus for sin, and literary allegory often personified specific vices or sins in the form of vice demons (*Lasterteufel*). The boozing devil made his first known appearance in 1517 in Hans Schäuffelein's illustration to Hans von Leonrod's theological tract "Heaven's scales" (*Hymelwag*).[19] The allegory reached its peak of popularity in the devil literature (*Teufelsbücher*) of the late sixteenth century, encouraged by Luther's theories on demonology. The first of the Protestant devil-books was Matthaeus Friderich's "Against the boozing devil" (*Wider den Sauffteuffel*), which first appeared in print in 1552.[20]

The boozing devil was a favorite literary device in the drink literature, encouraging drunkenness, chuckling in the corner at the misdeeds of his followers, and turning God's gift into the devil's poison.[21] Typically, he was depicted with great breasts, grinning and offering a huge cup to his followers. Luther, himself a defender of moderate drink, at times saw in the tavern a counter-church, an altar of the devil. Other moralists condemned those who made a god out of the boozing devil, choosing to spend their Sundays worshipping in their cups at the tavern rather than attending the sermon.[22]

It is perhaps fitting that the devil-books, numbering at least thirty-two by 1588,[23] began with the vice of drunkenness, for this was the vice that opens the door to all vices and destroys the soul, leaving one unprotected from the devil's wiles: "When [the devil] has caught us with wine, deprived us of our senses and made fools of us, he uses us for his mockery, amusement, and carnival games, driving us from one vice to the other," Franck wrote.[24] Once the boozing devil had robbed one of reason, the other vice demons (as many as

The Culture of Drink in the Early Modern German City

six thousand, according to Friderich) were free to reign. As noted above, the tendency of certain sins to serve as a source or starting point for additional vices was at the root of their medieval designation as cardinal or capital sins. Despite its association with gluttony, the fruits of drunkenness (blasphemy, unchaste behavior, violence) invariably appeared in the literature of the sixteenth century as following from the abuse of wine, not overeating.

The vices that followed from drunkenness rather than drunkenness itself were the focus of much of the drink literature. Common to all the major works in this genre was the association of drunkenness with damage (*Schaden*) to soul, body, honor, and property.[25] Damage to the soul not only meant sin but also the destruction of reason, that which separated mankind from the level of beasts. Moralists often used animal images to represent the drunkard, ruled by the flesh and behaving like a pig. The metaphor of an "irrational sow" appears repeatedly in Luther's well-known "Sermon of Sobriety and Temperance" delivered in 1539.[26] The definition of drunkenness as a root of otherwise sinful behavior was at the core of Catholic attacks on immoderate drinking during the Reformation as well. For while visitation records reveal that drunkenness among the Catholic clergy was a common concern of Catholic reformers, drunkenness in this case was defined specifically by its interference with the spiritual duties of the clerics or by otherwise undisciplined behavior.[27]

Although Luther attacked drunkenness as a sin, he was known to be fond of beer and wine, and moderate use in his view did not preclude occasional inebriation. Luther drew a distinction between habitual drunkenness (*ebriositas,* or *Trunksucht*), a vice to be avoided, and mere intoxication (*ebrietas,* or *Rausch*), which God would certainly tolerate, especially where it was earned through hard work and trying difficulties and as long as it did not occur daily.[28] Luther in fact recommended drink, even immoderate drink, to strengthen the Christian spirit against the devil. A minor sin, such as drunkenness, was to Luther preferable to the major sin of turning one's back on God during a period of melancholy spirit. He gave his student Jerome Weller this advice: "Whenever the devil pesters you . . . at once seek out the company of men, drink more, joke and jest. . . . Sometimes it is necessary to drink a little more, play, jest, or even commit some sin in defiance and contempt of the devil . . . . Accordingly if the devil should say, 'Do not drink,' you should reply to him, 'On this very account, because you forbid it, I shall drink, and what is more, I shall drink a generous amount.'"[29]

The Drunken Spirit

Intoxication, then, as a minor sin, could be excused as an occasional anti-dote to combat melancholy thoughts, the pressure of hard work and study, insomnia, spiritual weariness, and doubts and insecurities brought on by the devil's influence—maladies, incidentally, from which Luther himself (according to his own account) suffered regularly.[30] Nonetheless, he denounced habitual drunkenness, that which is injurious to body, soul, and property. Luther defined the differentiation in levels of sin neither by the amount consumed nor the role of free will; he determined the level of sin by a combination of frequency, purpose, and (perhaps most important) results. Habitual drunkenness (*ebriositas*) as the sow-like vice that held the entire German nation in its grip, causing damage to body, soul, and property, was a sin that would land them all "wet and drunk in Hell."[31] Intoxication (*ebrietas*), in contrast, while still a sin, was a sin of a minor and excusable nature, "to tolerate and to overlook" (*zu dulden und zu übersehen*).[32]

Luther's theology of sin was primarily concerned with the personal relationship between the individual Christian and God. The strict moral world demanded by Bucer, Zwingli, and Calvin, however, differed considerably from Luther's world of minor and excusable sins. These reformers shared a vision that was more worldly and social, and yet grander, with the aim of creating entire communities on earth that were deserving of God's favor. Calvin and his followers sought, even demanded, a conformity between inward piety and outward behavior. The Protestants did not differ from the Catholics in believing the natural world to be piloted by divine agency, and they depended on God's good will to protect them from catastrophe. The Protestants also understood plagues, famines, and other natural disorders, as well as wars and military losses, as punishment for collective sin. Their answer to disorder in the world was piety expressed through discipline, and the responsibility for controlling and disciplining sin in the community according to these more radical reformers rested with civic authorities. They thus criticized both Luther and the Catholic clergy for their drunkenness.[33]

Initially, it was the orderly vision inspired by Bucer and Zwingli that had the greatest influence on Augsburg's reformed city council as they set about to create their godly community. Like many other cities during the reform movement, Augsburg's authorities translated their vision of reform into public decrees and ordinances, attacking drunkenness as a vice that both angered God and corrupted the soul. While civic ordinances often tied drunkenness to the sin of gluttony, they particularly stressed its results—disorder and damage to soul, body, honor, and property. What exactly constituted the state of sin is not clear. Although much was written about the sin of drunkenness during the sixteenth century, it was never explicitly defined as a spiritual state.

The theologians of the seventeenth century dedicated much less time and creative effort to attacking the vice of drunkenness than had their sixteenth-century predecessors. Sermons and moralist tracts that do address drunkenness depend heavily on the literature of the sixteenth century, especially the works of Luther. Thus drunkenness continues to be tied in many texts to overeating, as part of a general notion of excess. At the same time, the issue of will plays an even greater role in these texts, adding to Luther's distinction between intoxication and drunkenness a definition more dependent on intent.[34] According to a sermon delivered in Gotha in 1644, drunkenness occurring out of "weakness," with only "joy" as a goal, is thus forgivable in the eyes of God, for a delicate lark is not a sow.[35] The sin of drunkenness could not be defined by either the amount consumed or the extent to which control was lost but only by the conscious decision on the part of the drinker to enter into sin. To the external observer, then, it became an even more nebulous construct.

Spiritual Imagery

The goal of the city council in issuing ordinances aimed at disciplining behavior was the creation of a community based on an ideal of order. The sin of drunkenness, and especially the sins that followed from it, represented an archetype of disorder. Considerable tension remained, however, between the vision and the reality, and this tension was heightened by the ambiguous attitudes toward drink that characterized early modern spiritual life. The construct of drunkenness could have layered meanings, as much so in the spiritual as in the physical realm. The absence of a clear definition of the sin of intemperance was complicated by a profusion of positive spiritual images involving wine, and especially an abundance of wine. As Luther's approach to drinking suggested, reveling in its consumption could as easily be identified with the grace of God as with the temptations of the devil.

Perhaps the most pervasive image of alcohol consumption in early modern Europe was the most positive of all, that of the Eucharist. In churches throughout the Western world, images of Christ and Mary are repeatedly represented with grapes, vines, cups, and other symbols of the vine. A popular theme for religious broadsheets of the sixteenth and seventeenth centuries was Christ crucified on the vine, in which the vine was a symbol of rebirth; for just as the grape is born again as wine, the Christian is born again through Christ. In one seventeenth-century print based on this theme, the abundance of the Holy Spirit is depicted as wine overflowing from great barrels onto the joyous Christians below.[36] Such images were most prevalent in Catholic churches, but Protestant artists employed them as well. Although meant in a metaphorical sense and occasionally accompanied by warnings against drunkenness, the simple association of God with wine in these images had to be inescapable to the laypersons who viewed them.

A related positive image can be identified in a news account showing a miraculous giant bunch of grapes reportedly harvested in 1590 (fig. 7), one of several broadsheets depicting marvelous grapes that appeared during the sixteenth and seventeenth centuries.[37] According to the words accompanying the picture, such a wonder could only be seen as a positive sign from God. The author of the text compared the grapes to the giant bunch of grapes described in the fourth book of Moses (Num. 13:23–24), so large that it had to be carried on a pole between two men and signifying the abundance of Canaan. The huge grapes symbolized wine, and wine represented joy, plenty, and the abundance of God's blessings. Giant bunches of grapes also often appeared in pictures of Christ crucified on the vine or in connection with the popular late medieval theme of Christ in the wine press.[38] Similar imagery can be found mirrored in broadsheets depicting giant wine barrels as symbols of success and fruitful wine gardens as metaphors for God's grace, and such imagery even appears in the portrayal of an incredibly obese man whose good fortune (Glück) could be traced partly to living in a region blessed with good vineyards.[39]

These attitudes were shared even by the most temperate of the European religious groups, the Anabaptists. Refusal to participate in heavy drinking in taverns has been cited as a means of identifying members of this heretical sect; but even Anabaptists, although admonished by their leaders to shun the worldly society of the public tavern, did not advocate total abstinence, which they denounced as papist fasting. Anabaptists drank wine, occasionally

Figure 7. Truthful New Tidings of a Wondrous Bunch of Grapes
(Warhafftige newe Zeyttung von einem wunderbarlichen Weintrauben.
Augsburg 1590. Courtesy of Staats- und Stadbibliothek Augsburg)

immoderately, and they conducted some of their meetings and even baptisms in taverns. A voice for true abstinence as the only way to avoid sin would have to wait until the Pietists of the eighteenth century.[40]

Although the proliferation of literature attacking the vice of drunkenness that appeared in the sixteenth century seems to indicate a change in attitudes toward drinking, the inability of the writers of these tracts to differentiate between drunkenness and other forms of gluttony or to objectively define drunkenness as either a spiritual or physical state suggests a high degree of continuity with medieval constructs of sin. The sin of drunkenness that came under attack in the literature attending the Reformation was not simply a state of intoxication brought on by the enjoyment of large amounts of alcohol. Wine remained a symbol of spiritual plenty, so that even liberal enjoyment thereof was difficult to condemn on religious grounds. After all, the intoxicating effect of wine was a creation of God, not the devil. Drunkenness was a sin only when it represented a waste of God's gift. In order to sin, according to both Catholic and Protestant definitions, one had to turn willfully away from God, forfeiting the soul and thus reason. Evidence of this state of mind, in the case of drunkenness, could be seen in one's indulging in a luxurious lifestyle that squandered material goods or in committing some sin that followed from alcohol-induced loss of conscience and discipline. Drunkenness that did not lead to either result, to the early modern German, did not seem sinful.

5

Drunkenness and the Law

THE CIVIC INSTITUTIONS that resulted from the South German Reform movement represented the partnership between city government and urban church envisioned by Zwingli. During the early years of the Reformation, reformed urban governments issued new laws to control marriage, police moral discipline, establish religious doctrine, and control the church and clergy. This civic control of religious life is the process historians have called the "domestication" of reformed religion.[1] Influenced by the ideas of Zwingli and Bucer and their goal of reordering society according to God's will, Augsburg's reformed city council seemed to have no place in their vision for drunken Christians, whatever the circumstances. But drunkenness was an ambiguous cultural expression. How, then, was it treated as a legal construct? If drunkenness as a state could not be clearly defined physically or spiritually, how could it be made a point of law?

Before the late fifteenth century, laws pertaining to alcoholic beverages were generally limited to regulating prices, quality, and good measure.[2] Only during the period of moral fervor preceding the Reformation did civic authorities begin to pass laws specifically aimed at controlling drunkenness. But drunkenness according to law has always had two distinct, in some ways irreconcilable, legal definitions. It is understood both as a criminal offense and as a legal defense for other offenses, when the perpetrator is drunk at the time of the crime. The balance between early modern German legal definitions of drunkenness as an offense on the one hand and as a defense on the other shifted in accordance with prevailing ideologies. The definition of drunkenness as an offense thus reached its height during the Reformation years, when its function as a defense for other crimes was de-emphasized.

In practice, however, drunkenness did not objectively function as either an offense or a defense. The actual treatment of drunken defendants reveals that it could be identified only by certain unruly behaviors. These behaviors were in most cases dealt with without regard to the drunkenness that may have precipitated them. Drunkenness also did not normally excuse delinquents for their actions. The fact that a defendant was drunk when he committed an illegal act functioned as a defense only when it was in the interest of the authorities to overlook the crime. The decision to consider drunkenness in either context ultimately was left to local decision makers on a case-by-case basis. As a rule, it was simply ignored, but the very ambiguity of the construct could also provide the authorities with a convenient measure of subjectivity they could utilize to support their interests.

Drunkenness in Traditional Legal Codes

German townspeople at the beginning of the sixteenth century were subject to both imperial and civic law. Legal practice was not entirely dependent on established laws, however, which tended to be extremely general both in defining crimes and in determining punishment. Much was left to the interpretation of those responsible for the local justice system who were influenced by other legal interpretations and the law books that explained traditional practice. German legal practice of the sixteenth century drew largely on medieval German civil law codes and canon law, but it was also increasingly affected by the introduction of Roman law principles rediscovered during the Renaissance, which began to influence legal practice from about the fifteenth century.[3]

Drunkenness was not an issue in German civil law codes of the Middle Ages.[4] It was also not punishable in Roman law but was recognized as a form of diminished capacity, so that a deed committed while drunk might go unpunished or carry a reduced sentence. Guilt was not entirely eradicated by drunkenness, but it was mitigated. In contrast, medieval canon law placed greater emphasis on the decision to enter into a state of sin in determining the degree of guilt. Thus it was possible under canon law to make drunkenness a crime and yet to allow the deed committed under the influence of alcohol to go unpunished, since the state of drunkenness had affected or annihilated the will.[5]

The primary instrument of the sixteenth century governing imperial law was Emperor Charles V's *Peinliche Halsgerichtsordnung* (commonly known as the Carolina), which included elements from both canon and Roman law.[6] The Carolina, however, deviated from both of these legal traditions in that

The Culture of Drink in the Early Modern German City

it did not address drunkenness at all, either as grounds for a reduced penalty based on diminished capacity or as a punishable offense. The German legalist Franz Lubbers suggested that the authors of the Carolina purposely omitted mention of the drunkenness defense in order to discourage recourse to it. Elsewhere, the lack of a clause against drunkenness in the Carolina has been cited as evidence that the emperor believed such bans to be useless.[7] Charles V did, however, follow the example of his predecessor Maximilian I in including attacks on immoderate drinking practices in the imperial police ordinances issued during his reign.

The drinking practice specifically addressed in most of the ordinances of the early sixteenth century, along with much of the moralist literature of the period, was the tradition of pledging healths (*Zutrinken*, literally to drink to). The purpose of the legal attack on the pledging of healths was certainly to curtail excessive drinking, and the term *"Zutrinken"* often appears in conjunction with "gluttony." Nonetheless, the language of the ordinances consistently targets pledging healths specifically, without respect to the amount consumed. The imperial ordinances, while recognizing drunkenness as the root of other vices (blasphemy, murder and manslaughter, adultery), did not make the state of drunkenness the point of law but the pledging of healths that precipitated it.[8] Drunkenness was not defined as illegal in any of these ordinances.

Imperial ordinances including clauses forbidding the pledging of healths appeared in Augsburg in 1500, 1530, and 1548 and in Cologne and Trier in 1512. The ordinances appealed to the territorial lords and princes to forbid pledging healths in their lands and at their courts and especially to set an example for their subjects. Local authorities at the levels of prince, lord, and town were responsible for implementing the emperor's policies, since any interference by the empire in local law-making would have infringed on the territorial rights of the imperial estates. Local laws against pledging healths were subsequently passed by territorial princes and civic authorities throughout the German lands.[9]

Although the imperial ordinances were primarily concerned with pledging healths and the Carolina did not mention drunkenness, Ulrich Tengler's *Layen Spiegel*, the most influential German law book of the sixteenth century, did state in a section on gambling and toasting that excessive drinking (*Übertrinken*) was illegal under imperial law. The term "immoderacy" (*Un-*

mäßigkeit) also appears, but there is no other term that could be understood as drunkenness.[10] In the 1512 edition of this law book, *Der neu Layenspiegel*, edited by Tengler's theologian son Christoph, the addition of a section dedicated to the court of God promises punishment in hell for feasting and pledging healths.[11] Specific guidelines for earthly courts, however, are lacking in both editions, and no clear guidance is provided for establishing appropriate controls and punishment for immoderate behavior or defining excessive drinking.

Like the Carolina, Tengler's law book also leaves out any mention of drunkenness as possible grounds for diminished capacity. The drunkenness excuse reappears, however, in the law books that followed the Carolina. Jost Damhouder's description of legal practice, widely used throughout the sixteenth century as a guide to interpretation of law, included drunkenness under a list of circumstances that could excuse an offense entirely. By "drunkenness," Damhouder did not mean mild intoxication but a degree of drunkenness that made it impossible for the offender to judge his or her actions. "The drunkenness, that may pardon [a crime is] the great and entirely immoderate drunkenness, which is so extreme, that it takes away a person's faculty and reason, and not the . . . slight drunkenness, which does not pardon from punishment."[12] Moreover, Damhouder was in agreement with the Scholastics on the point that the drunkenness had to be the result of misjudgment by the drunkard rather than an act of free will in order to excuse an action. It would, otherwise, be possible to become drunk on purpose before committing a planned crime to create a legal alibi. Guilt in cases of blasphemy and manslaughter, according to Damhouder, was moderated by drunkenness, but it was not entirely excused. "Thus . . . drunkenness excuses guilt to an extent," Damhouder wrote, "but not altogether."[13] The interpretation was, at best, ambiguous.

The seventeenth-century legalist Benedict Carpzov also saw drunkenness as a form of extenuating circumstance that could mitigate guilt but not entirely eradicate it. Carpzov, an orthodox Lutheran who held that the Bible should serve as the major source of law, was influenced by canon legal tradition, returning to the practice of pardoning the offense committed when drunk while holding the offender responsible for the drunkenness itself. Carpzov also made a legal distinction between slight inebriation (*modica ebrietas*) and immoderate inebriation (*immodica ebrietas*), with only the more extreme inebriation leading to a mitigating effect. Carpzov recognized the inconsistency of allowing immoderate drinking as grounds for moderating punishments for the very crimes that it precipitated. Ultimately, however, he was unable to effectively reconcile the moral condemnation of extreme drunkenness with the legal recognition of diminished capacity. Carpzov's conclusion that extreme drunkenness can serve to mitigate but not eradicate guilt represented an uneasy compromise. Carpzov, like Damhouder, also sought a means to differentiate between malicious and accidental drinkers. Thus he disallowed drunkenness as a mitigating factor in cases in which the drinker knew before becoming drunk that he or she was liable to commit the offense and became drunk anyway, the person failed to repent of the crime afterward, or they became drunk intentionally with the crime in mind. When the extent of drunkenness was in question, Carpzov placed the burden of proof on the defendant, who had to provide witnesses or withstand torture to prove that he had been drunk enough to be unanswerable for his actions.[14]

A legal comparison is possible between this problem of identifying intentional or "malicious drunkenness" with feigned madness, which the seventeenth-century legalist Justus Oldecop of Halberstadt believed to be a prevalent form of avoiding torture and punishment. Drunkenness in the seventeenth century was described as a "voluntary madness" in which drinkers, by their own voluntary action, robbed themselves of their reason.[15] The extent to which a defendant exercised free will or acted maliciously in deciding to get drunk or the depth of repentance after the fact, however, were points that were extremely difficult to prove in court. The ambiguous interpretations of the legal writers of the sixteenth and seventeenth centuries thus provided authorities with no clear guidelines for handling individual cases involving drunken defendants. Ultimately, the decision to prosecute an offender for drunkenness or to accept drunkenness as a viable excuse for committing a crime was left to local magistrates on a case-by-case basis.

Augsburg's Local Policy on Drunkenness

Officially, Augsburg's Civic Code of 1276 (*Stadtbuch*) was still in effect in 1500, for no other general book of law had been conceived to replace it. Local authorities recognized, however, that the medieval text was outdated.[16] In practice, the many decrees, regulations, and ordinances issued by the council made up Augsburg's system of civic law.[17] These local laws were much more specific in their attempts to define drunkenness than were books of legal theory. Augsburg's city council issued at least eight printed regulations against pledging healths and drunkenness during and after the years of the Reformation (between 1524 and 1553). The last of these was reissued with some modifications in 1580 and remained in effect until well into the seventeenth century.[18]

All of the ordinances controlling drunkenness had in common specific clauses against pledging healths and immoderate drinking, expressed as drinking gluttonously or filling (*Füllen*) with wine, beer, or mead or simply as drinking to the point of drunkenness (*Trunkenheit*).[19] In 1537 offenders showing "noticeable signs of drunkenness" were to be punished with two days in the tower on bread and water.[20] Tavern keepers were made responsible in this ordinance for warning their customers against immoderate drinking, and they could be fined for failure to do so. The city's bailiffs were also charged with visiting taverns that sounded rowdy and removing drunkards to the "fools' house" (*Narrenhaus*), a small cage-like cell located on the square next to the council house that both restrained and subjected the delinquent to public humiliation. Drunkards were detained in the fools' house overnight, until the appropriate penalty could be levied. In 1541 the Discipline Lords were charged with punishing "evidence and appearance of drunkenness . . . with even more diligence."[21]

By 1553, however, the penalty for noticeable signs of drunkenness was reduced to a minor fine (½ gulden).[22] In 1580 this penalty was clarified as applicable only to those drunks who "go home peacefully, without doing anything to anybody in the streets";[23] four years later, those who went home peacefully were exempted from the fine, which was now to be applied only in cases of "offensive and shameful" behavior.[24] Repeat offenses of drunkenness carried increasingly stiff penalties and could result in banishment from the city.[25]

A more heinous crime than getting oneself drunk was causing another to fall to the vice. Thus pledging healths or otherwise forcing (*Dringen*) another to drink immoderately could lead to a penalty worse than that imposed for drunkenness itself. This conforms to medieval definitions of sin, which held that getting someone else drunk out of spite or contempt is a greater sin than getting oneself drunk.[26] In the legal definitions of the sixteenth century, how-

The Culture of Drink in the Early Modern German City

ever, responsibility was not diminished if the intent of forcing another to immoderacy was merely fellowship, since the law interpreted engaging in pledging healths or other coercive measures as contempt for Christian duty and imperial and civic law.

The ordinances expressed concern not just with the sin of gluttony as manifested in noticeable signs of drunkenness but also with resulting behaviors and the danger they represented to "soul, body, life, honor, and property."[27] Evident in all of the council's decrees, for instance, is the association of drunkenness with blasphemy, a sin that would incur God's anger and lead to many catastrophes.[28] Later on, the vices resulting from drunkenness came to constitute its definition. By 1621 noticeable signs of drunkenness were expressly defined as problem behavior—rowdiness, yelling, or other aggravating or abusive conduct.[29] Drunkenness, according to the legal language of the seventeenth century, was not so much punishable as a state of body, or (even less so) as a state of will, as it was defined by other punishable behavior. In fact, this development in the language of the ordinances was nothing more than an adjustment of law to conform to practice.

Although Augsburg ordinances throughout the period were consistent in addressing the ruinous fruits of drunkenness, they also reflect changing concerns with the particular type of ruin that immoderate drinking provoked. The legislation passed during the first half of the sixteenth century, under the influence of the Zwinglian-style phase of the reform movement, concentrated on damage to the soul. Sins such as immoderate drinking and eating and blasphemous swearing, warned the council during the early sixteenth century, not only led to damnation of the soul but angered God. The entire community of Christians, guilty and innocent, suffered the unavoidable consequences of God's wrath: famine, plague, inflation, and military losses to the Turks.[30]

By the seventeenth century, however, legislation was clearly less concerned with the eternal damnation of the soul and more concerned with the immediate damnation of the budget. The ½ gulden fine for drunkenness appeared in the Police Ordinance of 1621, but later decrees did not target drunkenness specifically.[31] Instead, ordinances that addressed drinking and tavern going concentrated on tavern closing times, collection of excise taxes, and the control of city provisions, especially grain and meat. Particularly of interest during this period is a shift in emphasis from general control to the control of only certain members of society. The ordinances of the Reformation years were applicable to "all citizens and residents" of the city, "young and old, male and female," and, notably, "rich and poor,"[32] but later legislation concentrated on the "common man." In 1590 a law was introduced forbidding craftsmen and those of "lower status" to drink in taverns during the week.[33] The purpose of the law, according to the council, was to help the craftsman better provide for his wife and family by discouraging excessive spending in taverns. The urban elites were not subject to the rule. The problem in this case could hardly have been the sin of gluttony, for that was certain to have been more a vice of the wealthy than a problem among the craftsmen. Wasting money at the expense of providing for the family, however, could also be understood as immoral or frivolous behavior, and this was especially true for those who could not afford it.[34]

In 1622, during the first phase of the Thirty Years' War, a special decree appeared forbidding immoderate eating and drinking in taverns among the craftsmen. This document, like those of earlier years, warned against inciting God's wrath and bringing even more devastation to the already ravaged German lands, noting that wartime should be a time for penance and piety rather than high living and revelry. Still, the language of the decree differs from earlier documents. The call to penance appears as an admonishment but not as the purpose for issuing the decree. The reason for limiting expenditures in taverns, the city council stated frankly, was because of the current shortage of provisions, especially grain, bread, wine, beer, meat, fish, fat, and wood. Eating between meals, drinking immoderately, and staying in taverns until late at night constituted wasteful consumption of these precious commodities. No particular significance was placed on drunkenness in this ordinance that did not apply equally to snacking or to burning too much firewood. The city elites, whose fires burned latest of all, were again exempt from the rule.[35]

Treatment of Drunken Defendants

These, then, were the laws issued to regulate drunkenness. We now turn to the way in which these laws were put into practice. Was drunkenness in fact treated as a legal offense? The fines collected for drunkenness during the sixteenth century were so inconsistent that they raise more questions than they answer. Between 1540 and 1544, a total of 212 charges of drunkenness were recorded, or an average of 42.4 per year. This represents 12.8 percent of all entries in the books of fines for these years. The normal penalty for drunkenness, according to the Police Ordinance of 1537, was two days in the tower, and this was the punishment levied for 64 percent of the drunken offenders. Nine percent were given only a warning, and 27 percent served longer sentences for gambling, swearing, fighting, or other offenses. Of the 135 cases in which the minimum penalty was served, however, over 50 percent (71) were in fact also accused of other disorderly behavior, also punishable by two days in the tower. According to the Police Ordinance of 1537, the penalty for drunkenness should have been served in addition to any other punishment. Instead, the penalties for drunkenness accompanied by brawling or swearing were served concurrently in most cases, rendering the drunkenness penalty ineffective.

If we compare these findings with fines collected fifty years later, we see a rise in fines to 317 between 1590 and 1594 (63.4 per year). By the 1590s the process of recording and collecting fines had become much more rational and bureaucratic, reflecting increasing efforts to control unstable elements in society. In addition, Augsburg's population may have increased over the course of the sixteenth century by as much as 33 percent.[36] Thus the increase in the number of fines for drunkenness of around 50 percent cannot be taken uncritically as evidence of a rise in concern over drinking specifically. As a percentage of total discipline fines collected for these years, they accounted for less than 4 percent of the total entries (compared to nearly 13 percent for the earlier period). Books of fines for this period identified penalties as either for discipline (*Zucht*) offenses, generally infractions of moral codes, or for offenses involving violence (labeled *Frevel*), usually fights of some kind.[37] Simple drunkenness here fell under the heading *Zucht,* but the majority of drunkenness fines (84.4 percent) were recorded under *Frevel* in conjunction with brawling, for which a separate fine was charged. In other words, in over 80 percent of cases in which drunkenness is evident, those who paid the ½ gulden fine were involved in some sort of fight.

A total of 4,576 fights and brawls are entered altogether between 1590 and 1594, 259 (5.66 percent) of which include a drunkenness fine. Complete books of fines unfortunately do not exist for the period from 1640 to 1644, but those reports of brawls (*Frevelanzeigen*) that do exist do not record any fines for drunkenness.[38] An examination of discipline books for the second half of the seventeenth century reveals that the downward trend continued. The drunkenness fine remained at ½ gulden in spite of inflation, and it was charged only nine times during the ten years from 1677 through 1686, twice in conjunction with brawling.[39]

Exactly what criteria were used in deciding whether to apply the drunkenness fine is not evident in most cases. What is clear, however, is that being drunk in itself was not sufficient grounds for paying the fine. There are many cases (identifiable in the interrogation records) in which defendants described themselves as drunk at the time of the incident, or were described as drunk by witnesses, but for whom no drunkenness fine was levied. As noted above, most of the offenders charged with both drunkenness and brawling during the 1540s served time for only one of the offenses, and in no period are doubled fines for repeat offenders recorded. These facts raise questions about those fines listed simply for drunkenness, which may actually mask other unrecorded behaviors.

The protocols listing fines collected in the later seventeenth century support this suggestion. While the fines occur less often, they appear with more detail. In most of the cases that did not involve a fight, some behavior can be discerned that the authorities found questionable but in itself may not have been punishable. An alms official was thus fined for drunkenness in 1655 after he falsely accused a tavern keeper's widow of inflicting head injuries apparently caused by his own inability to remain upright. In another case, the drunkenness fine a bricklayer paid in 1663 was for appearing before the Discipline Lords themselves (for another infraction) in a state of drunkenness and behaving rudely in their presence. Also in 1663 a craftsman who was unable to explain why he climbed into a patrician's garden and behaved in a loud and unruly fashion was fined only for his drunkenness. In these and other similar cases, the drunkenness fine served as a convenient means of disciplining persons whose behavior implied disrespect for authority without overtly violating any other ordinance.[40]

Penalties for simple drunkenness, then, were sporadic at best, and probably they were dependent on the occurrence of some other form of misconduct. But drunkenness did play a role in many offenses, at least those of a violent nature. Did the fact that a person was drunk when committing an offense affect the punishment? How did the authorities react to crimes committed by drunken defendants?

Beginning in 1541, in accordance with the decree of that year promising "more diligent" control of drunkenness, interrogators did ask all delinquents involved in domestic or other violence at the outset of questioning with whom they had drunk, where they had drunk, and how much. This suggests an interest in the role of alcohol in incidents of violence, and in fact, virtually all of these cases did involve social drinking.[41] However, it is remarkable that once this question had been disposed of, it was not followed up in any way. The city council made no apparent use of the information. Witnesses were not asked if defendants were drunk, although they sometimes volunteered this information; and there is no evidence that the authorities attempted to verify the amount drunk as reported by defendants (always expressed as a monetary amount). When defendants testified that someone else had paid for the drinks, this served as sufficient grounds to claim ignorance of the amount consumed. By 1547 interrogators had ceased to ask specifically if defendants had been drinking before the incident.

Regardless of the interrogation technique, there is no evidence that defendants who admitted to drunkenness were treated any differently from those who, based on their testimony or that of witnesses, were drinking moderately or not at all. Aside from the occasional levying of drunkenness fines discussed above, defendants identified as drunk at the time of the incident were invariably punished for the offense itself, without respect to their condition when they committed it. Even during the morally charged 1540s, no real attempts were made to determine how much a defendant had actually imbibed or whether drink affected the person's behavior.[42] The amount consumed was simply not an issue in the pursuit of truth about the event.

We are left with the inescapable conclusion that the state of drunkenness was not a matter of serious concern to the authorities. In their pursuit of an orderly, functioning society, the city council did not target individual cases of drunkenness either as a sin or a disorderly state. Instead, they targeted violent, destructive, or otherwise disruptive behavior without regard to the state of the offender. As the sixteenth-century theologian Jakob Andreae noted, drunkenness was "considered no disgrace either for those of high or of low order."[43]

Attacks on drunkenness, then, cannot be viewed as part of a larger attempt by urban authorities to discipline or control popular society. Certainly, the ordinances and decrees attacking excessive drinking that appeared during the early phase of Augsburg's Reformation were part of the overall campaign by religious reformers to impose moral discipline and create "godly" cities. These decrees, together with the critical pamphlets in the drink literature genre, are indicators that certain members of society were alarmed by alcohol abuse. This concern, however, was not universally shared by those responsible for enforcing the decrees. Ultimately, Augsburg's authorities did not view drunkenness as a particular problem and did not treat it as such. The sixteenth-century proponents of temperance failed to convince urban authorities that drunkenness should be treated as a criminal offense.

The Campaign against Pledging Healths

Much of the literature and many of the ordinances attacking drinking during the sixteenth century focused on the practice of pledging healths, or *Zutrinken*. Johann Heinrich Zedler in his eighteenth-century *Universal-Lexicon* would define *Zutrinken* at base as "nothing more than drinking together or in company" but then add that the term in its traditional usage meant more specifically, "such a drinking bout . . . in which one tipple- or drinking-partner or fellow forces the other to empty as many tankards as he himself can pour into his full paunch."[44] The definition accurately reflects the behavior described by contemporaries in sixteenth-century Germany. The competitive drinking bouts that were particularly popular at court made accepting repeated pledges of health virtually compulsory, and drunkenness was the unavoidable consequence. Drinking bouts were not only associated with masculinity, the better man being he who could hold the most alcohol, but also with early modern notions of honor among the aristocracy. The provision and acceptance of wine were symbolic acts that elevated the honor of the host. The association of largess with honor and fame is at the root of the conspicuous consumption of the sixteenth century, for which the Germans and the Dutch were especially renowned.[45] It was a comparatively wealthy period in Germany, and the power of aristocratic families and cities remained linked in popular tradition to displays of grandeur. The rising merchant class, too, by this time beginning to rival nobles in wealth and power, began to display and expand their status through generous hospitality.

Zutrinken was a custom particularly associated with the Germans. Montaigne, for instance, reported that the Germans invited him to take part when they were drinking rounds in competition, but only out of courtesy, for he was as a foreigner not obligated to participate.[46] Drinking rounds at the conspicuously grandiose banquets in which the wealthy noble and merchant classes participated took the form of ritual, each member of the party obligated to pledge to the health of his fellows and empty his glass as they pledged in return. One of the best descriptions of the form this ritual took and its competitive character is that provided by Vincentius Opsopaeus (*De Arte Bibendi Libri tres,* first published in 1536), in which he compared the never-ending assault of wine glasses to arrows launched in battle and provided advice on how to save one's honor by out-drinking the opponent.[47] The sixteenth-century Swiss theologian Johann Wilhelm Stucki described the duty of returning a toast as an "utterly holy and religious contract." Failure to live up to this duty could result in ostracism from the company.[48]

The first Augsburg ordinance against pledging healths appeared in 1524. The ordinance forbade both the practice itself and efforts to force or coerce others to participate in it. A 1529 ordinance attempted to close any loopholes that might result from misinterpreting the ban on toasting, specifically warning against "compelling, forcing, admonishing, suggesting, pushing, or in any other way that human reason can devise" moving another to pledge healths through "insulting language or in any other way." The language was similar to that of decrees appearing in other German towns during this period.[49] Tavern keepers were also made responsible for warning customers against the dangers of pledging healths and reporting those who did not heed their warning to the authorities.

The Police Ordinance of 1537 introduced a fresh approach to controlling the vice. While the ordinance threatened to punish drunks with two days in the tower on bread and water, those who became drunk as a result of pledging healths were to suffer double the penalty, or four days. The penalty was to be doubled again for repeated offenses. In 1538 guild masters were stripped of the traditional right to punish their own members for drunkenness and pledging healths, a right newly declared to belong exclusively to the city council.[50] The ordinance governing the Lords' Drinking Room, however, allowed that the drinking room master might continue to take responsibility for punishment for these offenses in cases not of a "serious" nature, although the accounts of travelers to Augsburg suggest that the custom of pledging healths was more likely to become serious in the Lords' Drinking Room than anywhere else.[51]

In 1541 legislation was introduced forbidding not only the pledging of healths but also other traditional drinking practices that could lead to competitive drinking bouts. A decree issued in this year forbade the traditional drink concluding business transactions (the *Leikauf* drink) "over any product or sale."[52] Drinking was the normal conclusion to agreements of all kinds, as much so among leaders of state as among merchants and artisans. The validity of commercial contracts was dependent on the honor of the participating parties, and the drink that traditionally sealed the deal was closely associated with that honor. The 1541 ordinance allowed for a modest monetary gift to be paid in lieu of the drink, which was the standard for major transactions (such as the sale of horses or real estate), but tradition called for a drink even when cash exchanged hands.

Related to the tradition of concluding commercial contracts with drink were the drinking customs associated with weddings. Toasting with wine at these festive occasions signified not only celebration and joy but also had the character of sealing a contract. This was especially true of *Ansing* (literally, sing on) wine, drunk as the wedding guests took the bridal couple to bed, for the couple were not normally considered legally married until they had slept together.[53] Weddings, too, were one of the few occasions at which commoners were able to establish and possibly elevate their social status through the medium of conspicuous consumption and generous hospitality, and trying to outdo one another in the lavishness and expense of the wedding was a normal aspect of social competition. Drinking bouts and hearty toasts to the bridal pair were a part of every wedding celebration. In an attempt to curtail these excesses, wedding ordinances published shortly before the 1541 decree forbade entirely the drinking of *Ansing* wine, along with the entrenched tradition of drinking to the honor of the bride and groom.[54]

As is the case with most other drinking controls, these harsh rules relaxed during the post-Reformation period. Restrictions on the *Leikauf* no longer appeared in the Police Ordinance of 1553; and by 1621 the *Leikauf* was listed as one of the "honorable invitations" for which exceptions to normal tavern closing times might be allowed.[55] By 1550 the drinking of *Ansing* wine was allowed at upper-class weddings, and wedding ordinances issued in 1575, 1581, and 1599 placed no restrictions on either the traditional toast to the bridal pair or the drinking of *Ansing* wine.

Attacks on the custom of pledging healths also changed in character as the sixteenth century progressed, and they virtually disappeared by the seventeenth century. Although the Police Ordinance of 1553 treated *Zutrinken* with the same vigor as had the 1537 decree, imposing extra penalties on the resultant drunkenness, a change is apparent between the ordinance issued in 1553 and that of 1580. The 1580 ordinance in most respects repeats the language of 1553 word for word, but the increased penalties for drunkenness

The Culture of Drink in the Early Modern German City

as a result of *Zutrinken* no longer appear. The conscious decision behind this change is represented clearly in one version of the ordinance, dated 1553 and maintained with revisions until 1624, in which the clause stipulating the double penalty for drunkenness resulting from *Zutrinken* is visibly struck out.[56] *Zutrinken* does not appear in the Police Ordinance of 1621; and where it reemerges later in the seventeenth century, it is noted only as an inducement to blasphemy and swearing and not treated as a punishable offense in itself. The one ordinance after 1553 in which *Zutrinken* appears as a punishable offense is the 1587 *Kaufleutstubenordung,* which governed behavior in the Merchants' Drinking Room. Punishment, however, was left to the discretion of other members of the society.[57]

The relaxing of ordinances against pledging healths does not so much reflect a change in policy as it does an adjustment of norms of control to more closely reflect practice. Only three fines for pledging healths or other coercive drinking practices appear among the more than ten thousand entries in the books of fines for 1540–1544 and 1590–1594, all three of which were issued during the early 1540s (the height of the Zwinglian-style phase of the Reformation).[58] In no case were fines increased as a result of pledging healths. The term *"Zutrinken"* also never appears in the interrogations of commoners, either as an accusation or as part of a description of drinking practice.

Again, this evidence shows a shift in emphasis from abstract notions of sinful behavior to the targeting of specific social groups. The ordinances attacking this tradition were not describing popular drinking customs but the immoderate behavior of the elites. The consistent association of toasting with gluttony in both the police ordinances and the temperance literature provides a hint at this conclusion. The custom of pledging healths as an impetus to gluttony and excess was a habit few commoners could afford. At the spectacular banquets of the elite classes, however, money was not an obstacle to elevating the status of the host through excessive expenditure. The extravagant, almost ridiculous amounts of food and wine purchased for these events are legendary. In 1521, for example, a group of seventy-two nobles were billed for over twelve hundred liters of wine for one evening's entertainment; and the lists of provisions for aristocratic weddings could include several hundred thousand liters of wine and beer, along with enough food for an army. Drinks were consumed from huge, fanciful, and sometimes vulgar vessels.[59] The value of each drink at such gatherings became negligible, so that the consumption rather than the expenditure on the drink conferred status on the participants. Excess was practiced as an end in itself. The imperial ordinances against pledging healths, as well as much of the temperance literature, are addressed to the nobility, criticizing their coarse drinking customs and their mockery of sober men as unfit for aristocratic company or "women-like."[60] Peasants and craftsmen also participated in drinking rounds, and often enough immoderately, but their drinking rituals were constrained by time and expense. A craftsman's casual drinking bout in a public tavern could hardly compare in terms of excess to the banquets of the Lords' Drinking Room Society.

The extent to which the members of the Lords' and Merchants' Societies were subjected to fines or admonishments for pledging healths in their private drinking rooms is not a matter of record, but their generally derisive attitude toward the attempts to regulate the tradition is well recorded. At a royal banquet in 1559, Emperor Ferdinand I reprimanded a group of Augsburg patricians, along with a number of visiting members of the nobility (including representatives of the kings of Spain and France as well as the archbishop of Vienna) for pledging healths. Continued participation in the vice, the emperor commanded, should be punished with banishment from court.[61] According to the Augsburg patrician Markus Welser, Emperor Ferdinand's reprimand was treated as a "joke."[62] Imperial edicts against toasting issued by Charles V at the Imperial Diets of 1530 and 1548 also met with contempt; afterward it became popular among the nobility to follow a pledge of healths with the toast, "Here's to the Imperial Edict!"[63]

Although the massive consumption resulting from pledging healths at banquets was a behavior primarily associated with elite society, commoners did participate in wedding toasts, the *Ansing* wine ceremony, and the drinking of a *Leikauf* to seal contracts. But fines or punishments for these activities, too, are conspicuously absent from the records. No record exists of a fine or punishment for participating in any of these traditional drinking bouts.

The fact that legislation against the traditional drinking practices of wedding toasts, contractual drinks, and pledging healths was short-lived and ineffectual does not negate the possibility that the temperance movement of the sixteenth century had a lasting if moderate effect on the attitudes of the elites toward competitive drinking bouts. The historical sociologist Hasso Spode suggests that while drinking traditions changed but little, convention nonetheless shifted enough to cause the social ideal among elite society to move from drunk to sober. Participants at banquets still got drunk, but they now tried to deny or hide it rather than flaunting their drunkenness as a status symbol.[64] This may well have been true for at least a segment of society, for the temperance movement originated among elite reformers and moralizers. This suggestion, however, applies only to a small minority of the populace. The ordinances addressing pledging healths were conceived in the language of elite society, and they made little impression on the bulk of the population.

The Drunkenness Defense

We have seen that drunkenness and traditional toasting practices, although illegal in many ordinances, were in practice treated with lenience. How, then, did the traditional legal definition of drunkenness as a form of reduced capacity affect punishments? Initially, the problem was not addressed in Augsburg's civic codes directly, so that it was possible in 1524 to declare immoderate drinking to be punishable and yet, in the same decree, to allow a reduced penalty for persons who swore or blasphemed while drunk. In 1537 the city council declared that drunkenness would no longer serve as an excuse for any offense. This declaration, however, hardly represented a permanent change in legal practice; paralleling the treatment of drunkenness in the books of law discussed above, drunkenness again appears as a legitimate excuse for insults in Augsburg's civic ordinances of the seventeenth century.[65]

Interrogation records reveal that it was common for defendants to claim drunkenness either as an explanation or excuse for their behavior or for their inability to remember their actions. Hundreds of defendants did so. Historians examining interrogation records in other cities have taken this fact as evidence that the defendant had something to gain by professing drunkenness, assuming that it functioned as a legal defense.[66] In order to establish the effectiveness of this defense, however, we must examine not only interrogations but also records of punishment.

As records of punishment show, being drunk did not by itself mitigate guilt, regardless of the degree of inebriation. In cases of brawling, personal injury, property damage, or disturbing the peace, all a defendant stood to gain by claiming drunkenness was the possible (although seldom applied) addition of the drunkenness fine. In many cases, the fact that a defendant was drunk simply provided an explanation, rather than an excuse, for otherwise inexplicable behavior. What else could explain, for example, the sixteen-year-old Hieronymus Schwab's behavior on a January night in 1590, when he was arrested for racing his horse through the streets and making a noise like a post horn? Schwab's confession that he was drunk goes further in explaining the incident than his second excuse, provided when pressed and threatened by his interrogators, that his horse had formerly been a post horse and was "used to running." The youth paid a fine for the disturbance as well as paying for damages caused by his recklessness. Other persons who defended violent or injurious behavior by claiming drunkenness are nonetheless recorded in the punishment records as acting "without cause."[67]

When the affront was not against person or property but against honor, the decisions of the council could be somewhat more subjective. In the case of simple insults, an apology and handshake normally sufficed to drop the matter "without injury to honor." The condition of the parties was academic when insults were involved, for anger (*Zorn*) was as legitimate an excuse as drunkenness.[68] Where insults were public, however, aimed at the authorities or the city itself, the council could decide to accept or ignore the drunkenness defense according to their own interests. When Andreas Steiner gravely insulted the city of Augsburg and its residents in 1544, his drunken state did nothing to excuse him in the eyes of the council. Witnesses quoted Steiner, a carpenter and soldier from Klosterneuburg, as publicly calling Augsburg a "Jew city," calling on God to curse its population and threatening to stab the next citizen he met on the street "even if he be garbed in satin or silk." Steiner insisted that he did not remember any such insults and that he was so drunk that he was "not himself." The public insults, however, were too great to be mitigated either by drunkenness or an apology. The incident cost Steiner his honor and his tongue.[69]

In this case, the unfortunate Steiner provided the recently reformed, Zwinglian-style government with an opportune chance for a show of self-righteous power. Even during less volatile periods of Augsburg's history, an insult to public authority was not taken lightly. The Augsburg physician Wilbolt Strumpf was thus banished for life for insulting the city council in 1519; and in 1593 Simon Rayser was also banished for expressing the hope that Augsburg would fall to Bavaria. In neither case did drunkenness serve as an excuse.[70] The council's demand for respect of their power and the power of their city is further illustrated by the leaders' treatment of unruly behavior in those spaces that represented civic authority. Brawling or drunk and disorderly conduct occurring in or in front of the courthouse, or around

The Culture of Drink in the Early Modern German City

the city gates, was fined at more than three times the normal rate.[71] Clearly, respect for the city council's vision of local power was expected even from drunkards.

At the same time, however, when a drunkard's insults to authority were of a controversial nature and drew attention to conflicts that the authorities wished to play down, then drunkenness could serve as a useful context for overlooking the outburst. This course was occasionally chosen during the post-Reformation period in the case of insults of a confessional nature, for civic leaders were constantly struggling to maintain peaceful relations between the confessions. Persons accused of making religious insults to city authorities while drunk could normally get by with an apology. Illustrative is the case of Melchior Nershaimer, a Protestant gunsmith who verbally attacked a Catholic official at a wedding in 1642. The Catholic Lord Sebastian Hueber was sharing a table with a group of Lutherans, and Nershaimer, irritated by Protestant losses in the ongoing Thirty Years' War, banged his hand on the table and challenged Hueber for daring to share drinks with lords of Nershaimer's faith. Although the council described Nershaimer's threats as "rebellious" and "Swedish" (referring to the Swedish occupation of the city between 1632 and 1635), they allowed drunkenness as an excuse for the outburst.[72]

A similar phenomenon is identifiable in the case of sexual crimes. Those found guilty of such offenses as adultery, fornication, or sleeping with prostitutes were equally answerable for their actions regardless of their state of drunkenness. In none of the cases in the sample in which illegal intercourse actually took place did drunkenness excuse the act, nor did the authorities in these cases attempt to determine the degree of drunkenness. The adultery books (*Ehebrecher-Strafbücher*), which list hundreds of adultery fines recorded between 1575 and 1704, also substantiate the fact that adulterers were treated consistently whether or not they were reportedly drunk when they committed the act.[73]

In the event of a thwarted intent to commit intercourse, however, as in the occurrence of verbal outbursts, the degree of guilt could partially depend on the delicacy of the situation. Unlike person or property, damage to honor (or soul) was difficult to establish, and guilt in these cases became a subjective matter. This is best illustrated by a comparison of two separate cases involving sexual crimes. Both involved a drunken defendant who attempted intercourse without success; yet one defendant was severely punished, while the other was excused entirely. The reason for these seemingly arbitrary decisions is revealed by the language of the authorities in their discourse with the witnesses.

The first case took place in 1592, when the married weaver Hans Wagner was walking the streets late at night in the company of Sara Mair, a self-professed prostitute. Wagner was in an advanced state of drunkenness. According to Wagner, Mair attempted to seduce him in the street, opening his pants and fondling him sexually, but "he was unable to achieve anything" (*er hat nichts aussrichten künden*) because he had been drinking and "had no desire" (*er kain lust gehabt*); thus he did not complete the act. He then added in his defense that he was in any event "no man when drunk," to which his wife could witness.[74] Mair herself testified that she attempted to excite him manually but that "nothing helped."[75] After this failed attempt, Wagner accompanied Mair to her home and again attempted intercourse, this time with Mair's daughter, Rosina. Whether he was successful this time was a matter of dispute in the case, for Mair claimed that Wagner completed the act and Wagner maintained not only that he was still too drunk to successfully engage in intercourse but that he was also too drunk to understand what he was doing. In fact, he noted, Rosina had teased him "as if he were no man."[76]

Intercourse with both mother and daughter would have made Wagner guilty not only of adultery but of incest. The authorities decided in this case that, although Wagner was unsuccessful in at least one of his attempts, his intent to commit incest made his crime "greater than an adultery."[77] Neither Wagner's state of drunkenness nor his own awareness of responsibility were of concern to the interrogators, who did not question any of the witnesses or participants in the incident about noticeable signs of drunkenness. Wagner was banished from the city for life. This punishment was considerably more serious than the fine and warning that were the standard penalty during the 1590s for simple adultery.[78] Defendants in other adultery cases who convinced the authorities that they were unable to perform due to drunkenness were sometimes charged as only partially guilty, with a fine at half the normal rate.[79] This does not mean that drunkenness served as an excuse for an illegal act but rather that it prevented the act from actually taking place. Georg Reichlin, a member of the city guard, was given only a partial adultery fine in 1611 when both he and his partner reported that he was "unable to do anything" (*nichts verichten künden*) because he was so drunk. In a similar case involving a bather who lay naked with a married woman in

1643 but did not complete the act, the Discipline Lords recorded the reduced fine with the explanation that, although the act should not go entirely unpunished, still it was "not completely punishable as an adultery."[80]

In another context, then, the unfortunate Wagner might have gotten off with a 12 gulden fine, for although he admitted that he had behaved badly, he denied committing adultery on the grounds that he was too drunk to be a man and therefore unable to complete a sexual act. The incident involving Wagner, however, was only one of a series of trials associated with the mother-daughter prostitution ring, which resulted in a number of public punishments.[81] The city council presumably chose to ignore the mitigating effects of drunkenness because the cases provided them with useful show trials that would serve as a warning for others against consorting with prostitutes.

When the magistrates preferred not to draw attention to a sexual crime, however, the fact that the offense was greater than an adultery did not prevent drunkenness from providing a convenient context for excusing the offender. This was the course the council chose in the case of Balthasar Weiss, a journeyman tailor accused of attempted sodomy in 1644. The accusation was raised by a fellow journeyman, Hans Paget, who was sharing a bed with Weiss in the tailors' hostel after an evening of drinking in their drinking room. Paget testified that the defendant fondled his genitals while he was sleeping and attempted an act of sodomy, which caused him physical pain and made him vomit. According to the tavern keeper's wife, Paget came yelling out of the room and told her to have Weiss arrested. Although she, her husband, and others well acquainted with Weiss all described him as a pious, honorable journeyman, the incident was not an isolated one. Other journeymen reported that Weiss had fondled or tickled them in the night, but they assumed it was only meant as a jest or vexation and never took him for a sodomite. Weiss did not specifically deny the charges, but he claimed he meant it only "in fun" (*aus kurtzweil*), to which his angry sleeping partner responded "fun of that sort is not and has never been permitted anywhere but Sodom and Gomorra." Weiss then further excused his acts on the basis of *Unwissenheit* (ignorance or unconsciousness) resulting from drunkenness.[82]

Unlike many other cases involving drunkenness, in which the authorities refused to allow defendants to excuse themselves with wine, drunkenness in this case became the point of issue in establishing Weiss's guilt or innocence.

Drunkenness and the Law

All those questioned in connection with Paget's accusation were asked to describe the extent of Weiss's drunkenness and to give their opinion as to whether it was possible that Weiss was too drunk to know what he was doing. Paget, in his petition, also concentrated on this point, noting that Weiss's testimony was too precise to allow the conclusion that he was without responsibility for his actions. In fact, Weiss was able to describe his actions to the council and admit that he had acted wrongly, and although he denied any intention to commit sodomy, he concluded his testimony by falling on his knees and begging for mercy. The extent of Weiss's drunkenness was never really established, for most witnesses had not noticed whether he was drunk or not when he went to bed.

According to early modern definitions, attempted sodomy was a sin at least as grave as attempted incest and a crime greater than an adultery. Historians normally see the late sixteenth and early seventeenth centuries as a period in which homosexuals were increasingly targeted, with the normal punishment for sodomy an execution and burning.[83] Yet the city council decided in this case to allow the drunkenness not only as a basis for mitigating the punishment but as grounds for dropping the case entirely. Weiss was released without penalty, and he and Paget were reunited "in friendship" under the auspices of the council.[84]

The basis for this inconsistency in applying the drunkenness defense is not difficult to discern. In the earlier case of Hans Wagner, the authorities chose to make a public example of the prostitution ring with which the defendant became involved, and all of those accused in that incident were dealt with harshly. The council, however, decided against making a public spectacle of Weiss's transgression. We can only speculate about the council's reasons for wishing to keep the case quiet. In a period of economic hardship, when many journeymen were forced by circumstances to remain single, the council members may well have considered it prudent not to draw attention to sexual alternatives to marriage. In any event, the charge against Weiss was dropped, and his plea to avoid a "public scandal" was honored.[85] Contrary to standard procedure, all those questioned in the sodomy case were subsequently sworn to silence. This unusual measure was taken only in cases of extreme delicacy.[86] Drunkenness in this case, then, served not just as an excuse for the transgression but as a convenient rationalization for ignoring the offense in order to keep it out of the public eye. In reality, the issue of legal concern to the city council was neither the degree of drunkenness nor the severity of the offense; it was the positive or negative effects to be gained by drawing public attention to the crime.

The definition of drunkenness as a form of diminished capacity, a temporary madness, or annihilator of the will has been a topic of debate among legalists and theologians throughout history, and one which to this day has not been settled satisfactorily.[87] For the members of Augsburg's council, however, the very ambiguity of the drunkenness defense made it a useful bureaucratic tool. Whether or not a person was temporarily incapacitated when drunk or in fact more likely to speak what was "truly in his heart"[88] could depend on the interest of the authorities in either turning the case into a public theater or sweeping it under the rug. Drunkenness was a valid excuse only when city magistrates deemed mitigation of guilt as the most useful solution.

To the early modern magistrate, drunkenness was defined not as we understand it—that is, as the experience of a noticeable feeling of intoxication or a specific blood alcohol level—but by its negative effects on behavior. Although many ordinances represented drunkenness as part of a general picture of collective sin not pleasing to God, innocuous drunken behavior was not the real target of the controls placed on drinking during the sixteenth and seventeenth centuries. The attack the religious reformers of the sixteenth century launched against the "sin" of drunkenness thus had little effect on legal practice. Attempts to define drunkenness as a crime were further complicated by its traditional definition as a form of diminished capacity.

There were, however, more compelling reasons to place legal controls on the sale of alcohol, which were not tied to either theological or physical concerns with immoderate drinking. Warnings against incurring God's wrath by indulging in gluttony often served as a convenient context for concerns of a more economic nature. As a defense, drunkenness could also serve as a tool for mitigating guilt when it was believed to be in the public interest. The civic authorities of early modern Germany undoubtedly harbored real concerns about collective sin and the archetype of the disorderly drunkard; these rather abstract images, however, rarely affected their dealings with the concrete individuals who appeared to plead their cases in court.

6

The Contract Drink

In any social situation in early modern Germany, a shared drink had many strings attached. This was especially true of the custom of the contract drink, a drink shared by parties in commercial contracts or other forms of agreements. In the case of the merchant city of Augsburg, which took such pride in its reputation as a center of commerce, drinking rituals were crucial to both the economic strength and the commercial image of the city. This view was at work when Augsburg tavern keepers, in protesting a law initiated in 1590 against drinking in taverns during the week, were able to gain concessions from the city council by pointing out that contract drinking was customary in all German lands and that strangers to the city would be offended if local citizens did not conclude their transactions by drinking with them on the spot.[1] Craftsmen placed under a disciplinary tavern ban also excused violations by indicating the necessity of drinking with customers who purchased their goods; and beggars and takers of alms, who were forbidden to enter taverns at all, risked expulsion from the city to take part in these obligatory rituals.[2] One clock-maker, sentenced to a one-year tavern ban for keeping a disorderly household, based his refusal to take the oath to stay out of taverns on his claim that it could ruin his business. The clock-maker, Hainrich Frey, reportedly said in 1593 that he would "rather rot in the tower than allow that the tavern be forbidden to him," and he was subsequently locked in the tower until he agreed to take the oath. Frey spent eight weeks thus incarcerated as a result of his obstinacy.[3]

Frey's tenacity in this case suggests he found that more was at stake than possible loss of business, for eight weeks of incarceration certainly interrupted his profits. The right to participate in drinking rituals was a matter of personal and professional honor, in defense of which this craftsman was willing to make a considerable sacrifice. Faced with this degree of resistance, it is no wonder that the fleeting attempts at curtailing these traditional drinking practices failed. The reformers who formulated the ordinances were not merely attacking excessive alcohol consumption; they were attacking an essential part of the early modern German worldview.

Where did this worldview originate? In a largely illiterate society, where the written contract had limited application, it is understandable that a formal ceremony in front of witnesses was necessary to ensure that both parties would honor the terms of the contract. But a contract drink created a bond between the drinkers that was weightier than a verbal promise, or even a written agreement. What role did alcohol play in this ritual? What force existed in the drink itself that had meaning to the participants? Why could a contract not be sealed by a verbal agreement, a handshake, or a toast with milk or water? Our exploration of these questions begins with a brief examination of the cultural meaning attached to alcohol in the European tradition, followed by a look at the various kinds of contract drinking rituals in which early modern Germans participated, customs defined both as legal practice and as popular ritual. The earnestness with which Augsburg's citizens took these rituals suggests a cultural meaning that went much deeper than a mere legal formality, one that made breaking such a pact virtually unthinkable for the parties involved.

Alcohol and Meaning

The contract drink is a rite rooted in antiquity. The forming of a bond or brotherhood through sharing a drink was a custom as prevalent among the symposiums of ancient Greece as it was to the communal drinking bouts of the Germanic tribes.[4] In these societies, alcoholic beverages were described as containing a spirit or a demon that inhabited the body of the drinker upon consumption of the wine. These mystical properties accounted for the feeling of intoxication caused by the drink; they also had serious connotations for the strength of the bond. The spirit of the drink became a supernatural witness to the pact who could be angered and seek revenge if the pact were broken.[5]

This belief has roots deeper than merely an inability to explain intoxication. The idea that alcohol contains a spirit, sometimes described as a god or a life spirit, is related to the nearly universal association between wine and blood and other essential life fluids. The swearing of blood brotherhoods and the conclusion of contracts in many ancient societies, including Greek, Roman, Scythian, Slavic, and African, involved mixing blood with wine or other alcoholic beverages. There are also many parallels between blood and wine in the myths and legends of antiquity. In Greek mythology, drinking blood could have an intoxicating effect much like that of wine. The association also appears in the use of alcohol to represent blood sacrifice or the spirit of departed ancestors in other premodern cultures.[6] In these cases, alcohol replaces blood, the essential fluid of life. Unlike any other beverage or food, alcohol could become a material sign of a person's spiritual and physical essence.

The association between blood and wine is especially clear in the Christian tradition. Moses sealed his contract of deliverance with sacrificial blood; so, too, did Christ. Noah's first act after the flood was to plant a vine, a symbol of continuity and resurrection after destruction. Just as the grape is reborn in a second life as wine, the world was reborn after the flood. Again, the symbol is reaffirmed in the New Testament imagery of the eucharistic wine, both blood of Christ and symbol of salvation and second birth.[7] In Christ's statement, "This is my blood," he drew a connection between the sacred person of God and the communion wine, making the drinking of that wine into a holy pact that implied a promise ("Ye cannot drink the cup of the Lord, and the cup of devils").[8] The physical association of wine with Christ was popularized graphically in the medieval image of Christ in the wine press, in which by the later Middle Ages Christ was shown literally being crushed like a grape while the blood of salvation flowed into the uplifted cup of the believers. The cup was also a common icon of religious art, representing the community of Christians.[9]

The imagery of the Christian Eucharist is only one example of how a mystical bond could be created and sacralized through sharing wine, which was, in the words of one theologian, "connected by a metaphorical 'leap' with blood."[10] This metaphorical leap from wine to blood (or another concept of a life fluid) was particularly meaningful for the rituals attending the conclusion of legal contracts. Wine represented life, and the exchange of life tokens in contractual arrangements also had a deeply rooted history. Marcel Mauss, in his classic study *The Gift*, identified an animist quality in the exchange of sureties in legal contracts among the Germans of the early medieval period. The pledged item, normally of nominal value, was understood as having a life and virtue of its own. The pledge then became a form of life token, imbued with the personality of the giver. The donor, if he then failed to follow through, left part of himself in the hands of the other party. This life token was also present in meals shared as part of the contract ritual, each party to the contract thus partaking of the other's substance. In this way both parties were caught in a nexus invoking magical or religious power. To renege on the contract would lead to the debasement of the reneging party — loss of honor, loss of prestige, and, even more dangerous, loss of something of the self.[11]

The risk involved in such an exchange, then, represented a temporary sacrifice of the self on the part of the donor. The greatest possible sacrifice is the gift of human life, and wine, as a metaphor for life, represented most clearly the offering of this life spirit. The sacrifice of the gift of alcohol thus symbolized the allegorical pledging of oneself. The risk did not only apply to the donor, however; for as both parties in the contract shared the drink (according to medieval and early modern custom, from the same drinking horn or cup), both also shared in pledging a part of themselves to the contract. The stakes for breaking any pledge or promise therefore became much greater when alcohol was consumed.

By the sixteenth century, the anthropological connection between life fluids and wine as a symbol of a sacrificial pledge or life token was sufficiently blurred to allow beverages other than wine to serve the same purpose. While all of Europe had by the high Middle Ages inherited the wine-drinking rituals associated with their Greek and Roman predecessors, the early Germans were not a wine-drinking people. There is no equivalent to Dionysos and Bacchus in Germanic legend; instead, the Germans honored their gods with beer, mead, cider, and fruit wine (*Obstwein* or *Leit*).[12] Yet beer drinking and mead drinking were not without their sacred parallel. Medieval Germans drank communally and with the overt goal of attaining drunkenness, which they understood as a kind of spiritual ecstasy. This state of euphoria bound them with one another and with the spirit world. A collective state of drunkenness was achieved through ritualized consumption, beginning with a drink in honor of the gods. The resulting ecstasy opened a portal from the profane to the sacred sphere, freeing the consciousness from its earthly constraints.[13] As noted above, these rituals were similar in form to the sympotic rituals of the wine-drinking Greeks.

By the early modern period, Germans were equally at home with wine or beer, mead or brandy, and any of these drinks was equally binding when used to conclude an alliance or contract. The fact that the specific roots of

the spirituality implicit in this ritual vary from culture to culture does not undermine their power; on the contrary, it only underscores the paradigm that
alcoholic beverages in all drinking cultures throughout history have been in-
fused with meaning that goes much deeper than the material substance of
the drink.[14] The contract drink in early modern Germany was not a religious
ritual but a secular one. Nonetheless, it had a spiritual character. The drinker's
cultural awareness of the spiritual aspect of drinking rituals need not have
been any more complex than his knowing that sharing a drink had meaning. The shared drink in the context of sealing a contract represented more
than conviviality and more than the economic sacrifice of its material cost.
It involved a sacrificial ritual that put something at stake. In early modern
German society, at stake, at the least, was the drinker's honor and reputation,
both tangible assets that could be lost. In a more abstract sense, the party in
the contract drink stood to leave a part of himself, a token of his social or
even his sacred identity, in the power of his drinking partner.

Contractual Drinking Traditions

In 1513 the Augsburg chronicler Wilhelm Rem described a fateful toast made
between the Augsburg journeyman Jörg Rigler and a military officer's servant. Although far from a typical incident, Rem's account provides a hint at
the powerful images that the contract drinking ritual could invoke. The two
young men were drinking with other journeymen in Munich. According to
Rem, Rigler and his drinking partner, on a whim, "pledged a toast, that the
next person they met on the street, they would kill."[15] Bound by the drink
that sealed the pact, the pair carried out the grisly dare; and while Rigler managed to escape, his accomplice in the diabolical contract was beheaded.
Whether the binding quality of the drink really had a role in this killing, the
chronicler's entry represents the drink as the point at which culpability for
the act began.

The consumption of wine or another alcoholic drink was the essential ingredient in creating the sort of unbreakable bond described by Rem. The
basic contract drink (*Leikauf* or *Weinkauf*), which was shared by seller, buyer,
and witnesses to the transaction, marked the point at which a contract became binding.[16] When a contract involved a purchase, the buyer paid for
the contract drink as a down payment or surety on the goods or services

for which he contracted, and accepting the drink bound the seller to deliver. Larger purchases, such as a house or a horse, sometimes called for a cash down payment, but this, too, was traditionally spent immediately on drinks for the parties in the contract and their witnesses. A drink alone was equally binding, even though the monetary value of the drink in relation to the transaction may have been negligible. A drink represented a symbolic commitment rather than a financial one.[17] In cases of legitimate business transactions, the contract drink would normally take place in a public tavern in front of witnesses, testifying to the honest and aboveboard nature of the agreement. Following through on the deal then became a matter of personal honor between the parties to the contract.

The tradition of the contract drink was not specific to urban merchants or retail salesmen. Craftsmen, journeymen, day laborers, and even beggars recognized the drink as a symbol of commitment. Peasants contracting field labor bought drinks to share with their workers; communal drinks were shared by landholders and peasants in the countryside; and carpenters and tailors drank to the conclusion of a sale. A *Leikauf* also bound journeymen to a new master. Once a journeyman had accepted a contract drink from the master craftsman, guild tradition prohibited him from seeking work elsewhere. No other honorable master would accept the labor of a journeyman who had already participated in this ceremony.[18] Contract drinking was also much more than a popular custom; both populace and authority took seriously the ritual of the contract drink. The Augsburg city council recognized the importance of these rituals to the working life of its citizens and sometimes allowed exceptions to disciplinary bans on social drinking so that craftsmen could participate in guild drinking rituals or day laborers invited to drink with their employers could conclude their work contract without fear of retribution.[19]

The contract drink was not only necessary to seal sales or work contracts but also for other forms of agreements and settlements. Even on an informal level, a drink accepted on someone else's tab without reciprocation implied to the authorities that an agreement of some kind had been reached. City officials in particular left themselves open to accusations of corruption when they accepted drinks from persons within their jurisdiction. This assumption led to the arrest of two alms officials in 1590, after they shared a table in an Augsburg tavern with an alms recipient and a municipal gate guard. The drinking party aroused suspicions that the beggar, who by his own account paid for drinks, hoped to gain the freedom to beg illegally by binding the guard and alms officials to his favor.[20] Similarly, interrogators charged a beer inspector who was arrested for failure to report accurately the amounts of taxable beer brewed by local brewers with accepting free drinks from the brewers and thus obligating himself to a return courtesy.[21] Officials in Nördlingen accused city bailiffs who turned a blind eye to an illegal dance of paying "more heed to a drink than to oath and duty."[22] In these and other related cases, no evidence existed that explicitly linked a shared drink to return obligations. The authorities simply assumed that such a relationship must exist.

Another contract drinking ritual that occasionally led to sanctions by the authorities accompanied the settlement (*Vergleich* or *Schlichtung*), which bound its participants to an oath of peace following a disagreement or dispute. This tradition concluded the mediation of fights, debts, and charges of personal injury or property damage. The private settlement was a medieval tradition that by the early modern period began increasingly to fall under government jurisdiction. The Augsburg authorities asserted their control over these affairs by requiring that all disagreements be reported to the mayors' office and that the settlement be formally instituted by an appearance before the council and an oath sworn by all participants in the dispute. The authorities preferred public arbitration of disputes because it lessened the possibility of minor insults and injuries escalating into blood feuds. The formal appearance before the court allowed the council to hold a monopoly on violence, as breaking an oath of peace then became a legal offense rather than only a matter of private revenge.[23]

According to popular tradition, the peace was sealed by a drink (*Abtrinken*) shared by parties in the dispute along with witnesses in a public tavern. This spontaneous ritual normally preceded the formal appearance before the authorities, and for the participants the settlement was binding even without the intervention of the city council. Since local ordinances required reporting such disputes to the Discipline Lords, however, who levied a fine when blows were exchanged, any settlement made without an official report constituted avoidance of penalty and could appear to the council to be a kind of secret pact. Craftsmen who admitted having drunk an unofficial settlement after a fight sometimes testified that the communal drink not only bound the participants to peace but also bound the witnesses (often including the tavern keeper) to silence about the affair.[24]

The dramatic case of three butchers who were involved in a bloody fight with a cart puller named Martin Straub in 1643 provides an example of the differences that could arise between tavern goers and authorities over the issue of the unofficial settlement. The incident began with an exchange of insults in a public tavern; and although most of the company claimed to be too drunk to provide details of how the affair began, Straub apparently believed that he had been sufficiently insulted to demand a settlement drink even before exchanging blows. Straub therefore approached the butchers' table and said to one of them, "I don't care for your words, I should think you owe me a quarter of beer."[25] The butchers refused to comply and the insults escalated. The three later waited for Straub outside and gave him a brutal beating.

The following day, Straub and his attackers settled their differences and drank to their reconciliation in the same tavern in which the dispute had occurred. They were joined in the settlement drink by the tavern keeper and several witnesses to the fight. The witnesses testified that the adversaries were satisfied with the settlement, drank to seal it, and offered one another the hand of friendship. Four days later, however, Straub died from injuries apparently resulting from the beating.[26] Those present at the settlement, including witnesses who had no discernible personal interest in the case, all stressed the point that the settlement had been accepted by all parties, that Straub did not complain of any damage, and that he made no further demands or accusations. For these witnesses, the affair seemed settled to everyone's satisfaction, which should have released the butchers from any further obligation to Straub's heirs. The city council, however, could not accept the unofficial settlement as legal and binding, for allowing settlements outside of their jurisdiction would rob them of their monopoly on the control of violence. The council's determination to exert their right of public authority was no doubt heightened by the tavern keeper's admission that as part of the settlement agreement the butchers had agreed to pay his fine should the incident be discovered. In addition, the victim's family was left without provision and might potentially have become a burden to the Office of Poor Relief. The three butchers were ordered to pay damages to Straub's wife in the amount of 150 gulden.[27]

While one drink may have been sufficient to conclude a settlement, witnesses to these rituals more often described not just a ritual drink but a drinking bout. Since the person who initiated the hostility would normally be held responsible for financing the drinking bout, paying for the drinks, always a significant act, represented a public acknowledgment of guilt in the dispute. In the case involving Straub and the butchers, the butchers paid for Straub's drinks at the settlement, which the council took as an admission that they recognized their guilt in the affair. Similarly, the city bailiff Hans Bausch, whose job had already been jeopardized by his chronic drinking and brawling, offered in 1592 to pay for settlement drinks after a dispute if his adversary would officially take the blame for starting the fight. The fact that Bausch subsequently paid over 1½ gulden (enough for nearly six liters of wine) for a drinking bout with his opponent convinced the authorities that he was the instigator in the brawl.[28]

Although the authorities claimed jurisdiction over the settlement of disputes, they did not oppose the drinking ceremony itself. The unofficial settlement was only a problem when it replaced the formal appearance before the council or involved persons not normally allowed in taverns (alms recipients or persons placed under a tavern ban); this issue did not arise when it complemented appropriate legal procedures. As long as the participants in the settlement subsequently reported the incident and paid the required fines, the drinking bout supported the interests of the city council in helping to contain violence, for it was a practical means of bringing a quick and effective end to a dispute and restoring order. According to Fynes Moryson's description of the ritual, brawlers in Germany would cease fighting "when the first drop of blood is drawne," turning immediately afterward to their settlement drinks and requiring no intercession by others present.[29] Even if this account is something of an overstatement, the settlement drinks did function in many cases as an effective peacemaker.

Evidence of official approval of drinking, even hearty drinking, to settle disputes is provided by the Augsburg chronicler Georg Kölderer's description of the adjudication of a confessional dispute in 1584. The problems began with a pair of anonymous letters accusing Endris Zölling, a dyer, of acting as an informant for the authorities during the popular protests against the Gregorian calendar in June of that year. The city mayor (*Stadtpfleger*) Anton Christof Rehlinger presided over the politically charged situation, demanding that the carpenter accused of writing the letters shake hands with Zölling in front of witnesses at the Weavers' Hall (*Weberhaus*). The two were then sent off with their witnesses (*Vertrags leuth*) "to have a good drink to confirm the [settlement], and to tie one on." Thus, noted Kölderer with satisfaction, the two once again became "good fellows" and a potential crisis was avoided.[30] It is perhaps because of its value as a peacekeeper that the settlement was one drinking tradition that was not attacked even during the height of Augsburg's Reformation.

Another occasion that called for contractual drinking in good fellowship was entry into a guild or the start of a journeymanship. Acceptance into a guild or craft implied certain responsibilities, and one of these was participation in communal drinking bouts. Drinking at these rites of passage into young adulthood not only created a bond of fellowship among guild members but it also provided an opportunity for young men to display their drinking ability, for the capacity to consume large amounts of alcohol was a trait associated with adult manhood. Guild membership entitled wandering journeymen to the hospitality of their craft in each town they visited, including hearty drinking bouts both on arrival and departure.[31] Journeymen also met at regular intervals in their guild drinking rooms or craft hostels (*Handwerkerherbergen*) to elect officials, conduct business, and honor visiting journeymen. All of these formal transactions were sealed with drinks. Guild regulations often prescribed elaborate, formalized drinking rituals, which dictated exactly how drinks on such occasions should be consumed. Failure to participate in drinking bouts, arriving late, or leaving early could result in a fine, which would then be spent on drinks for the remaining company. Some guilds set specific minimum amounts of wine or beer that their members were required to consume during the drinking bout, with journeymen being obliged to drink more than the younger apprentices.[32]

Once the journeyman phase had been successfully completed, tradition demanded that entry into masterhood be accompanied by marriage. The wedding ceremony, as another rite of passage into adulthood, also required shared drinks. The consumption of wine by participants and witnesses took special ritualized forms at these events, which symbolized economic as well as physical union and therefore had the character of a commercial contract. In some parts of Germany, the word "*Weinkauf*" appeared in statutes regulating formal marital engagements (*Verlobung*).[33] The engagement was thus represented as a legal contract, requiring witness by sacred authority and verification by a contract drink. Drinks passed around the tables at weddings united the witnesses to the contract in communal consumption, and the special toast of *Ansing* wine to the bride and groom as they were taken to bed symbolized both the legal and the physical consummation of the marriage. The members of the wedding company who witnessed these drinking rituals served to confirm the legitimacy of the match and could be called on later to verify that an engagement or wedding had been celebrated.[34]

The ritual drink used to seal the contract of marriage was often made with wine that had been blessed by a priest, traditionally Saint John's wine (*Saint-Johannes-Wein*). This wine was formally blessed on Saint John's Day (*Johannistag*, 27 December) in memory of Saint John the Evangelist. The wine then took on a sacred power that provided the drinker with the protection of the saint. Saint John's wine was also given to condemned criminals on the way to the gallows and to those on their deathbed, for popular belief held that wine blessed in the name of Saint John protected those whose lives were in danger from the power of Satan. Soldiers or other travelers received Saint John's wine as a way of binding them to a future meeting, either in this world or the next, and guild members drank it in fellowship, invoking the power of Saint John to bind them in true friendship.[35] These religious and semireligious rites involved a sacred communal bond created through wine, paralleling the social, cultural, and legal bonds formed through secular drinking rituals.

These examples show that the traditional practice of the contract drink had meaning that was more personal than a professional fee or down payment and that alcohol was an essential ingredient in the ritual. One function of ritual, especially ritual sacrifice, is to provide the participants with a feeling of control over the "unpredictable element" in human experience.[36] Nothing is less predictable than human behavior. The contract drink in this context served an important function in confirming commercial and personal bonds. The intense cultural meaning attributed to the drink in these rituals provided early modern Germans with the security in agreements and friendships that could not be guaranteed by human nature alone.

My claim is not that early modern tavern goers and businessmen were aware of ancient images of blood offerings or portals to the spirit world when they shared the cup with an associate or fellow. Yet they were aware of the ceremonies involving wine and sacred power that defined their religious life. To Protestants who shared the blood sacrifice of Christ represented in the communion wine, the parallel between the sacred and secular ceremonies was underscored by Luther's setting of church hymns to the tunes of popular drinking songs.[37] In Catholic communities, Saint John's wine and other blessed wines were an important part of the system of sacramentals or semi-sacred materials that provided a bridge between sacred and secular life.[38] The ritual of the contract drink was also part of a culture shared by populace and authority, for it was practiced by men at every level of society. The authorities' recognition of the importance of these drinking practices to the lives of their citizens led to the relaxing of the short-lived controls after the peak years of Reformation. The reformers' attack was aimed at excess, not at ritual, and the strength of tradition ultimately superseded concerns about immoderacy.

In the early modern worldview, the realm of the physical mingled with that of the spiritual. The intense meaning attached to the contract drink made sense within this mental framework. Alcohol was crucial to the ritual because the drink itself, which nourished both the body and the spirit, provided a bridge between these realms. The ritual took its most sacred form in religious ceremony, but even secular agreements retained a metaphysical element. The bond created through these rituals was significant to early modern notions of both spiritual and social identity. At least as far as the chronicler Wilhelm Rem was concerned, it was the power of the contract drink that doomed Rigler and his drinking fellow to committing their act of senseless violence in 1513. If Rem's account was true, then the bond created by the drink must have seemed unbreakable to the murderous pair, at any cost; for once the pact had been sealed with the blood of the vine, there could be no turning back.

7

Drinking and Gender Identity

WHY DID EARLY MODERN PEOPLE DRINK? The seventeenth-century German legalist Matthias von Abele listed forty-five good reasons, among them friendship, honor, virtue, bravery, virility, business and trade, and good taste and fine company; equally compelling were malice and ill humor, roguishness, envy, defiance, boredom and idleness, as well as "prospective thirst."[1] While Abele's language was grammatically non-gendered, his vocabulary was clearly male—besides virility and business, he included knighthood and manliness as reasons to drink. Abele's list makes clear that the drinks men shared in the company of their fellows had cultural uses that went beyond physical thirst. For men, social drinking was inseparable from social identity, which was a key element in early modern notions of honor and status. Although immoderate alcohol consumption often led to quarrels, excess expenditure, and other violations of behavioral norms, there is no evidence of disagreement among different segments of society about how these norms were defined. Drinking bouts, rounds of gambling, and even tavern brawls could be viewed as acceptable behavior by the authorities as well as the participants as long as everyone played by the rules.

Women, too, had a significant, although carefully proscribed role in the tavern company. Within certain bounds, women were a legitimate part of society in the tavern, and women at home, as its natural adversary, actively participated in defining the ground rules for norms of drinking behavior. Drinking was frequently a major issue in the disputes that occurred between men and women over household responsibility. Using the topic of drink as a starting point, we are able to open windows on spaces that normally remain hidden to historians of the early modern period, allowing a rare glimpse not only into the public tavern but also the private household. Through these windows we witness the negotiations for power that defined relationships between men and women, alcohol consumption and work discipline, and political order and family structure. Women do not emerge as passive spectators or victims in this process of negotiation but as active participants, who were able and willing to take action to protect their interests.

Legitimacy for women ended, however, when they crossed the line that defined male drinking behaviors. According to Elisabeth Koch, early modern theorists saw men as the norm in all social relations and at all levels of belief, and women were regarded as the deviation from that norm.[2] In this view, what was the norm for men would become the deviation for women, and what reinforced the honor of a man could taint the honor of a woman, whether it was tavern space, immoderate alcohol consumption, or power. Immoderate drinking by individual women was nearly always associated with either suspicious sexual behavior or a disorderly household. In its more extreme forms, particularly in the case of group drinking bouts by women that community norms did not sanction, drunkenness among women came to be identified with the sexual power of the prostitute or even the magic power of the witch. Both of these characterizations represented inversions of the natural order and the ultimate perversions of early modern notions of female honor—and both inversions were aided, contemporaries believed, by the consumption of alcohol. The fact that the rules for men and women differed to such a degree served to delineate more firmly the boundaries between the sexes.

Drinking and Household Relations

The early modern German city was a patriarchal society, in theory as well as practice. Civic government especially after the Reformation was based on an image of paternal discipline and control, with the city council acting in the role of municipal fathers. The new legal institutions created at the onset of Augsburg's Reformation process—the marriage court (*Ehegericht*) and the Discipline Lords (*Zuchtherren*)—were aimed at perfecting a godly community based on the model of an orderly household.[3] At the head of the household was the house father (*Hausvater*), a label that implied not only husband and father but also master of a functioning economic unit consisting of a hierarchy of subordinates including wife, children, journeymen, apprentices, and servants. The master of this household was charged with certain responsibilities. At base, he was responsible for stable and continuous economic production, in urban society usually the practice of a craft; on a higher plane, however, it was the house father's job to ensure that the members of his household accomplished this production with honor, virtue, and obedience to God. Thus the head of the household was answerable for the honor, souls, and industry of all household members, as the city council was responsible for the moral, religious, and work discipline of its citizens. Providing the material blessings and spiritual grace necessary for this community of households to function was the ultimate house father, God himself.

This orderly household image, however, failed to allow for the unstable nature of the institution of marriage. Many householders were not even able to manage their own lives, let alone that of their entire household. Marriages were often unhappy, and economic resources to support the family industry were frequently lacking. The result was households out of control. One of the paternal duties of the Augsburg city council was the settlement of marital disputes, and their records reveal many households in disorder. Domestic incidents might be brought to the attention of the council by the complaints of neighbors and relatives, or they could be reported by barber-surgeons who treated wounds resulting from domestic violence. More typical, however, the charges were brought by one of the battling spouses, either of whom had the right to petition against the other. The arguments brought into play by both parties in such a case often took the form of a direct confrontation between household and tavern. In a world in which the workshop was synonymous with the home, a tavern could be the only escape from the demands of the household. Where the household structure was cracking, the tavern and its male rituals often stood at the center of discourse in the conflict between the domestic values associated with the Reformation (moderation, thrift, and an orderly household) and the traditional popular values associated with male sociability.

Much of the discourse between men and women over the issue of tavern drinking in early modern Germany was concerned with negotiating the exercise of power in the household. The basis of that power depended on the ability of both partners to live up to the expectations of their gender roles. The ideal of the orderly household provided both men and women with an effective, state-sanctioned tool for negotiating their position within the household hierarchy. When the costs of tavern drinking threatened to upset the household, women did not hesitate to employ this tool to impose limits on their husbands' public drinking behavior.

At the heart of the domestic debate lay a conflict that arose as a result of early modern notions of male honor. In the late medieval sense, honor was more closely related to reputation than to righteousness. The elite members of society turned increasingly to legal and political notions of honor as a means of protecting their privileged status from encroachment by the rising middle classes. Defense of this position required public demonstrations of power and wealth, for honor in feudal society was closely tied to one's ability to provide, especially in public displays of largess. By the early modern period, demonstrations of economic power and generosity served to establish and maintain a man's honor and status at all levels of society.[4] The cases discussed below show that male honor for the early modern householder was defined not only by virtuous behavior but also by the economic health of his household. Both of these could be threatened by the virtually compulsory drinking rituals associated with craft and guild gatherings, business transactions, and male sociability. A man was expected to verify his masculine identity through generous consumption and provision of alcoholic drinks, while maintaining control of his bodily functions, household, and economic viability. It is not surprising that the foundations of many households cracked under the pressure of proving manhood.

Men who let tavern drinking get in the way of effective householding were placed under a tavern ban by the city council. The ban on tavern visits, normally for one year, was applied most often in cases involving domestic violence and failure to provide. Certainly, one effect of banning a habitual pub crawler from visiting taverns would be a curtailment of his spending and drinking habits, and this was at least one motive that moved the council to establish such a penalty. The tavern ban, however, affected more than a man's expenditure on drinks. The exclusion from normal male society was an honor punishment with its roots in medieval Germanic law. The right to honorable society, like the right to bear arms, was exclusive to men of honor; those who were incapable of fulfilling their responsibilities as men were considered unqualified to carry weapons or participate in social rituals.[5] Thus the ban on tavern visits was often accompanied by restrictions on carrying weapons and walking the streets at night, also symbols of masculinity. These constraints, however, could be applied independently and did not necessarily relate to the reason for arrest. Restrictions on social drinking and carrying weapons struck at symbols and rites of masculinity that served to shame more than to control. A husband might therefore be banned from social drinking for suspicion of adultery, although his drinking habits did not seem to be at issue. In other cases, repeated drunkenness or household violence led to weapons restrictions, even when there is no indication that the defendant used a weapon in the incident.[6]

City fathers knew that the men were not always to blame for marital problems, but there was no women's equivalent to the tavern ban. Generally, husband and wife were both admonished and required to take an oath "to house properly" (*wohl zu hausen*), and where the husband's oath might have directed him to stay away from the tavern, his wife also might have had to promise not to give him reason to go there. The men in these cases naturally tended to place the blame for their excessive drinking on their wives, complaining that they were nagging or shrewish and drove their husbands out of the house. A carter in 1592 excused his excessive tavern going by claiming that "his wife . . . leaves him no peace at home or at the table, so that he is forced to go out and seek peace elsewhere."[7] Another craftsman made the argument in 1542 that it was for the sake of his marriage that he drank, for drinking wine in the tavern after a fight with his wife cooled his anger and allowed him to return home in a more peaceful mood.[8]

The most frequent tactic that drinking husbands used was to turn the tables on the notion of household honor and accuse their wives of refusing to fulfill their domestic duties. One unhappy husband's complaint in 1590 was that "there is no one at home who wants to cook for him, so he goes out only out of necessity."[9] Another husband beat his wife in a drunken rage after a fight that broke out because, he claimed, she refused to go out and buy food.[10] The rope-maker Ulrich Hemerle and his wife turned a domestic squabble in 1592 into a virtual battlefield of sexual honor. Hemerle accused his wife not only of contrariness and refusal to cook for him but hinted at the possibility of unchaste behavior by alleging she refused to sleep with him and preferred the company of journeymen. His wife retaliated with accusations that he would rather spend time in the tavern than in church, that he squandered household money on drinking, and that, coming home drunk late at night, he sometimes cooked his own meals without proper attendance to the fire, placing not only their household but the entire neighborhood in jeopardy. Hemerle believed these accusations to be purposeful attempts by his wife to get him dishonored and banished from the city. He testified that she had told neighbors she had gotten him banned from drinking, and she could then turn him in when he did and so be rid of him. The result would be the effective destruction of their household. Unable to identify a guilty party in this case, the city council took no action against the unhappy couple, whose sole recourse was to go home and try harder.[11]

Although the authorities could do little to tame disorderly marriages such as the Hemerles', the veiled threats of fire and economic ruin that they raised presented powerful images of the potential dangers of unstable household relations. Households in ruin not only presented a practical threat to the economic health of the city, they metaphorically threatened the entire notion of a world based on natural and stable hierarchies. City authorities during the sixteenth century thus issued multiple ordinances against immoderate drinking, with the express purpose of limiting expenditures that left wives and children in poverty, hunger, and shame.[12] Many of the claims women made seem calculated to appeal to these concerns. Women most often used an economic argument in complaining against their husbands, presenting a zero-sum relationship between tavern and home in which drinking was only possible at the expense of providing for the household. Accusations of physical abuse often arose merely as an aside to the budget issue. One wife complained that her husband "does nothing but sit in taverns . . . paying not only for his own drinks but buying rounds for everyone, and leaving both his money and his clothes behind." Afterward, she pointed out, she had to go and retrieve his pawned clothing from the tavern keepers at her own expense.[13] Images of men pawning clothes and household goods for drinks or running up debts in taverns to the detriment of their wives and children are also common themes in the satirical literature of the period; even lighthearted drinking songs jocularly described the sacrificing of personal belongings and household relations in the interest of brotherhood.[14] Husbands sometimes submitted detailed lists of expenditures on household goods as a means of defending themselves against such charges.[15]

What does this evidence tell us about the role of alcohol abuse in ruining marriages, squandering household resources, and breaking down family structures? Unfortunately, this is a question that the authorities during the early modern period did not ask. In applying the ban on tavern visits and social drinking, they did not — and in all probability could not — distinguish between problem drinkers, whose marital relations suffered because of their alcohol use, and persons trapped in problem marriages, who sought in tavern sociability only a refuge from the household storm. Furthermore, problem drinking did not always lead to marital problems. Not all wives took the side of the authorities against their husbands' drinking habits. Many women petitioned in favor of their husbands, particularly in cases in which they themselves had not been the victims of drunken violence. These wives urged the authorities to place the blame for unruly behavior on immoderate drink rather than on the drinker, claiming their husbands were otherwise obedient, honorable, and hardworking.[16] The wife of Hans Bausch, a city bailiff whose continuous drunkenness both on and off duty eventually cost him a suspension from his job, presented the remarkable defense that if her husband was at times careless and lazy (*saumbsellig vnd vnfleissig*) it was only because of his habit of getting drunk, therefore he ought to be treated with lenience.[17]

Early modern society provided a number of likely reasons for this apparent tolerance. Many women were undoubtedly more concerned over the economic problems they would face if the family provider was banished or imprisoned than over the expense of his tavern going. Bausch's wife, for instance, had eight children to care for and was pregnant with the ninth when he was suspended in 1592.[18] Some women certainly were content in their marriages, and they viewed occasional or even frequent drinking bouts as an acceptable part of a man's social life. Ultimately, in a society in which women were rarely able to achieve economic independence and the only possible grounds for divorce were adultery or abandonment, a degree of tolerance may have been the wisest option for many women.

Yet women were not helpless in the face of abusive or squandering husbands. When drinking interfered with a man's ability to provide for his family, his wife did have the power to have him banned from the city or locked in the tower, and women who were financially able did exercise this power. Imprisonment in the tower was at the expense of the plaintiff; and where women lacked personal resources, their families often carried the costs. Authorities generally supported wives when marital problems took the form of a struggle over rights of property. This occurred, for example, in the case of Georg Bschorn, whose marital troubles began, Bschorn testified, when his wife refused to give him money to buy a horse. Bschorn had to borrow the money elsewhere and blamed the insult caused by his wife's lack of faith in him for leading him to drink and to threaten her. She ultimately locked him out of the house, and he moved to a tavern. Bschorn's wife took the case to the authorities, complaining that he had not provided for the household since moving out, and her petition resulted in an expulsion from the city for her wayward husband. Only after she relented three months later and interceded on his behalf was he allowed to return.[19] In other cases, men who violated tavern bans excused themselves on the grounds that their wives had allowed them the occasional visit, thus conceding their wives' right to take control when their drinking habits got out of hand.[20] A traveler to Germany noted, too, that while men might make all manner of promises and bargains in their "pots," the consent of the "sober wife at home" had to be obtained before any commitment was binding.[21] The rights of women to secure the economic means necessary for the household could thus extend to the male world behind the tavern doors.

Drinking and Masculine Identity

According to many women, the public tavern was the natural adversary to the domestic demands on the house father. Yet, although the tavern afforded men the opportunity for amusements and pleasant sociability, the pressures of proving manhood did not relax within its walls. Rather, they intensified. The tavern provided a public theater for social exchange, in which men were expected to perform. Here, men reaffirmed the popular values of generosity, reciprocity, and sociability, which included elements not only of friendship and camaraderie but of rivalry and competition as well.

The association of economic health with manhood was not limited to the requirement to provide for a family. The other side of the coin was the pressure for public displays of largess. Sharing and reciprocity, especially in the provision of basic necessities such as food and drink, have been described by social psychologists as the fundamental principles of society. The host in this rite gives something that is his own, and in the society of the public tavern this is represented by a drink.[22] Anthropologists have identified alcohol in many societies as having a symbolic value far beyond either its economic worth or its physical properties, which is related to its status as a sacred liquid. Stanley Brandes called the gift of an alcoholic drink a "principle medium of social exchange," particularly among men.[23] Robert Ashley, in his sixteenth-century discourse *Of Honour,* noted that the honor of the Germans in particular was contingent on the trait of generosity, expressed through the provision of food and drink. It is for this reason that Hans Jakob Fugger, who abhorred wine and insisted on serving his prestigious guests wine that was heavily watered, was derisively called *Wassermann* (water man, or Aquarius) by his peers.[24]

The public display of hospitality as an expression of status took its most luxurious form for all levels of society at weddings. Commoners as well as elites took part in the traditional economic contest of lavish weddings, each trying to top his neighbor in displays of generous hospitality. The greater the amount of money spent at these events, the more status conferred on the families of the bridal pair, and a large part of the expenditure was normally dedicated to drinks. Wedding ordinances consistently attempted to limit expenditures at weddings, placing restrictions on how many guests might be invited, what types of food and drink could be served, and how much might be spent on wedding gifts. Tavern keepers who accepted bribes for serving finer fare than the ordinance permitted were threatened with heavy fines.[25]

Yet the requirement for a public display of wealth — or for the commoner at least of economic health — was not limited to special occasions. Economic competition at the tables of taverns was a daily event. Honor and status were not static commodities that, once established, became a permanent part of one's identity. Rather, they were variables that had to be constantly reaffirmed. Men of honor who participated in tavern society were expected to pay their share of the tab, and being able to pay one's round was a basic requirement of tavern sociability. A craftsman who left his drinking fellows with the tab was subject to insults and could even be accused of dishonoring his craft, and an allusion to outstanding tavern bills could serve to discredit an opponent's testimony at court.[26] The day laborer Lienhart Strobel's proud assertion that "he had always paid his round," which Roper identified as his "metaphor for right living,"[27] thus reflected not only the townsman's sense of his personal honor but also his awareness of the necessity for displaying it publicly.

These economic requirements repudiate the typical representation of taverns as havens for beggars and vagrants. Beggars or takers of alms, who were incapable of running a household through honorable labor, were forbidden by public decree to drink in taverns at all.[28] Yet the value that men, even beggars, placed on their ability to pay their rounds is illustrated in the case of the alms recipient Georg Albrecht, who risked his livelihood to participate in a tavern drinking bout in an Augsburg beer tavern in 1590. According to his testimony, Albrecht paid for a measure of beer in reciprocation for a drink with which he was honored by Samuel Lederer, an alms official. The incident came to the attention of the authorities only after Albrecht bragged about it the next day to Caspar Zoper, another official of the Office of Poor Relief. Zoper had been in the tavern briefly but left early. Albrecht reportedly approached him on the street the following day and asked, "why he [Zoper] didn't stay longer, he would have had enough to drink, for [Albrecht] and Lederer had left two tankards of beer on the table for the gatekeeper and paid out 14 kreuzer, and [they] were so drunk that he no longer knows how they became separated once outside."[29] Not only was Albrecht voluntarily admitting to becoming drunk in a tavern, which was in violation of the alms ordinance, but also to paying for drinks for others, presumably with money gained through begging and receiving alms. Albrecht was accused of buying the drinks for the alms official and gatekeeper in order to gain their favor so that he might beg in the city unimpeded. If true, this could be understood as an investment in his future livelihood, a small bribe in the form of drinks that might allow greater returns later on. Albrecht's behavior the following day, however, is entirely inconsistent with this charge, for describing his illegal activities to an alms official could only have a negative effect on his livelihood. Albrecht was banished from the city as a result of his talkativeness. His need to belong to male society, and to display that belonging to his acquaintances, at least temporarily superseded his basic need for subsistence.

A particularly explicit expression of the ability to pay for drinks as a metaphor for masculine honor is provided in the case of the sixteenth-century baker Hans Hohenberger, who violated a social drinking ban in 1542 by gambling for rounds with a number of drinking companions. The drinking bout had begun at Hohenberger's house and then moved to a tavern. Hans Liepart, a fellow baker in the group, later became drunk and left the tavern, returning to Hohenberger's house in search of former companions. Fuddled by drink, Liepart claimed he then became confused and thought himself at home, so he undressed and got into bed, unfortunately with Hohenberger's wife. In the interrogations that followed this breach of propriety, Hohenberger was accused of squandering money on drink, which he defended by pointing out that he earned as much in one week as Liepart did in two. The statement seems at first glance irrelevant, for Liepart was not on trial for wasting money. Yet to Hohenberger, who had been shamed by the affront to his wife's honor, the issue of economic viability was inseparable from that of sexual honor. Thus Hohenberger attempted to prove his superiority to this male rival in his wife's bed by citing his superior income.[30]

The rules of male sociability required not only reciprocation in buying rounds but also participation in drinking them. Contemporary critics of the immoderate drinking habits of the Germans complained that the god of wine was replacing the god of war as the symbol of German manhood, "knighthood" being bestowed not on the greatest warrior but on the heaviest drinker. "The Germans were once a nation of warriors," lamented the Italian humanist Giovanni Francesco Poggio Bracciolini during the fifteenth century, "these days they seek their manly courage not in weapons but in duels of wine, the greatest hero being he who can hold the most."[31] Elsewhere, the love of drink was described as replacing chivalry, the cup earning more favor at court than the noblewoman, and the consumption of repeated pledging of healths the only remaining goal of German knighthood. Martin Luther and Sebastian Franck saw in this sad development evidence of the decay preceding the end of the world.[32] Another theologian found a sign of God's dismay at the replacement of manhood with drunkenness and unchaste behavior in the birth of a hermaphroditic child on New Year's Day in 1519. A broadsheet describing the child, part of a series of news accounts and broadsheets reporting miracles and wonders that the Swiss theologian Johann Jakob Wick collected as evidence of the imminence of the Second Coming, noted that the child's female genitalia were located above the male genitalia—a sign that drunkenness and lust had "pushed down" all semblance of manhood among the men of the day.[33]

Although the literature deploring these masculine behaviors was most often concerned with courtly behavior, craftsmen, too, participated in ritual rounds of drinks. Even if their economic means did not allow them to enjoy excesses comparable to those of the great banquets of elite society, they were nonetheless subject to pressure to keep pace with their drinking companions. Popular drinking songs chided those who did not keep up with rounds of drinks, threatening to expel slow drinkers from the company and thus to deny them the sociability of their fellows.[34] Artisans did not normally use the term *"Zutrinken,"* favored among the elites, which had the character of an excessive and self-perpetuating drinking bout. For the elite classes, to whom the monetary value of the drink was often insignificant, it was the consumption of alcohol itself that signified brotherhood. Among the craftsmen, however, the economic value of the drink could also be significant, so that refusal to consume a drink purchased by another not only implied a desire to sustain social distance but belittled the sacrifice made by the spender. Commoners thus spoke of offering an honor drink (*Ehrentrunk*) or a drink of brotherhood (*Bruderschaft*). Like their elite counterparts, however, they described the reciprocal aspect of drinking with the phrase "*Bescheid tun*," which can be translated as "pledging a toast" but more literally meant "to give satisfaction."[35]

Failure to give the purchaser of the drink satisfaction by refusing to drink it or leaving it in the glass too long was a social insult. According to the German version of "The law of drinking" (*Jus Potandi oder Zechrecht*, 1616), such an affront to social graces could only be described as a disgrace (*Schande*),[36] for the refusal of a drink represented a symbolic refusal of social contact. This could be taken very seriously in early modern German society, in which sharing a drink with those persons labeled dishonorable could lead to expulsion from a craft and social ostracization.[37] The rejection of a proffered drink might therefore be understood as socially demeaning. The civic employee Lucas Fischer expressed this norm in 1593 when he demanded that Daniel Ostermair, for whom he had brought a glass of wine in brotherhood, do Fischer the satisfaction of emptying it; Ostermair's refusal to do so, Fischer implied, was related to an old affair for which Ostermair maintained a grudge. Fischer responded to the offense with a drawn weapon, seriously wounding Ostermair in the duel that followed.[38] Likewise, Georg Vetter, "the Younger," a son of Augsburg's mayor Georg Vetter, "the Elder," reportedly stabbed another patrician's son in the Lords' Drinking Room in 1518 for refusing to drink rounds with him.[39] Failing to adhere to the rules of tavern society could be a dangerous choice at any level of the social strata.

Taverns and Male Violence

There is no doubt that the combination of pressure to drink and obligation to compete with one's fellows was a volatile mix. Social drinking undoubtedly did play a role in inciting tavern brawls. Although most of the fights that broke out between male antagonists in early modern Augsburg were settled with a fine, so that the details surrounding the incident are not available, the overwhelming majority of participants in public brawls for which interrogation records exist reported drinking socially before the fight started. In a sample of 114 cases of violence between men in which defendants were specifically asked if they had been drinking, 111 of these cases involved social drinking, only 2 cases provide evidence that the defendants had not been drinking at all, and 1 case shows that the defendant became drunk at home with his wife.[40] Such disagreements make up the largest category of arrests for drinking-related offenses (135 out of 375 cases, or 36 percent). Taverns offered two resources that tended to fuel physical violence: alcohol and a public stage. Alcohol not only strengthened ties of sociability but it also relaxed inhibitions and kindled choleric temperaments. Tavern brawls, too, were a form of public display, taking place in the presence of witnesses. While this setting increased pressure to adhere to social rules, it also increased the pressure to perform. As the barriers of propriety were weakened by alcohol consumption, minor disagreements quickly escalated into conflicts of honor.

An illustrative case of the worst possible consequence of defending male honor is provided by a deadly duel fought between two members of the Augsburg city guard, Caspar Aufschlager and Caspar Rauner, on an August evening in 1591. While fights ending in death were far from typical, the detailed statements witnesses gave in this case allow a rare opportunity to join the company of the tavern, to observe the strategies of defense that various parties provided in presenting the case to the authorities, and to evaluate the role alcohol played in the incident. The representative aspects of Aufschlager's case will be contextualized with evidence from 114 additional cases of violent brawls occurring in Augsburg between 1540 and 1650, nearly all of which began in social drinking situations.

The argument began quite typically, with an insult to Aufschlager's male honor. Rauner, having suffered losses at cards, insisted that Aufschlager take a chance gambling for beer because he had not yet paid a round. Rauner was accusing Aufschlager of breaking the rules of tavern sociability. Aufschlager refused, pointing out that his part in the drinking bout had been paid by a companion and that he was not in the habit of gambling—a response that was acceptable to others of the company.[41] Rauner, however, was not satisfied. They came to words; and as Rauner's insults crossed the point of tolerance, other members of the party began to urge Aufschlager to take action.

The insult that triggered the escalation from verbal abuse to physical action was "dog's cunt" (*Hundsfott*), an obscene accusation of extreme cowardice.[42] As many as thirteen witnesses specifically noted that Rauner had used this insult to Aufschlager's honor. A weaver at Aufschlager's side reportedly chided him by saying, "He called you a dog's cunt, are you going to take that from him? I'll hit you in the face myself, if you call yourself a soldier, and put up with that."[43] Another witness reported that Rauner said Aufschlager was "not man enough" (*nit mans genug*) to defend himself, and he challenged that if Aufschlager was an "upright soldier" (*redlicher Landsknecht*) he would meet him in the street. Aufschlager, then, "could not do less" than to meet the challenge.[44]

And meet the challenge he did. Witnesses to the street duel that followed claimed that Aufschlager not only drew his weapon first but also struck several vicious blows, one of which was fatal, after Rauner had been wounded and had dropped his weapon. When he heard that Rauner had died of the wounds, Aufschlager attempted to flee the city. Nonetheless, the majority of witnesses to the event supported Aufschlager's actions as correct and honorable. Petitions from the captain of his guard unit (of which Rauner, too, was a member) also defended Aufschlager's behavior as appropriate, claiming that he was forced to meet Rauner "in defense of his honor" (*zu errettung seiner Ehren*). In fact, the descriptions by most of those present at the scene represent Aufschlager as the true victim in this case: a peaceful, honorable soldier, forced against his will to take the life of a man he himself described as having always been "his good fellow" (*sein gueter gesel*). In recording the relatively mild punishment for manslaughter, the court reporter noted that "Rauner provoked Aufschlager with defamatory words"; Aufschlager did not draw his weapon in defense of his life but in defense of his honor.[45]

The association of taverns with violence appears again and again in the literature, leading one to assume that this sort of drunken brawl—a fight ending in the "murder" of one of the participants—must have been commonplace during the early modern period. According to some historians, sixteenth-century German taverns were veritable dens of iniquity, in which bloodshed and death were daily occurrences. Norbert Elias described a violent nature among early modern commoners that was almost manic.[46] Did the incident involving Aufschlager and Rauner belong to a typical evening in an Augsburg tavern?

No, if one looks only at the outcome. The records of the Augsburg court show a total of nine killings that either took place in taverns or followed from tavern visits during the fifteen years (5,478 evenings) covered in my sample.[47] While tavern brawling rarely resulted in a death, however, fights of a less

Drinking and Gender Identity

serious nature did occur on a daily basis, and the circumstances leading to Rauner's death were quite typical. Drawing on the work of sociologists, cultural historians have recently begun to identify patterns in the behavior of brawlers that indicate conformance to certain social norms, which served in many cases to contain fights somewhere short of serious injury. Thus, forms of "reciprocal social control" existed even among the "coarse tavern company."[48] Violence under these circumstances tended to take ritualized forms, as the presence of peers encouraged the participants to adhere to the unwritten ground rules of popular society.

The public space of the tavern increased pressure to play by these rules, for without witnesses the challenge would go unheard and the defense would have no symbolic value.[49] The public nature of the tavern provided not only witnesses but also a built-in control factor in the person of the tavern keeper. City authorities required that all fights be reported to the city council, and tavern keepers particularly were charged with reporting incidents that occurred on their premises. The tavern keeper, as head of the household, not only had the right to demand adherence to the traditional right of household peace (*Hausfrieden*) but could be held accountable for disorderly behavior in his house.[50]

Few fights that took place in taverns, then, in the presence of many witnesses and under the watchful eye of the tavern keeper, led to serious injury. Only one-third of the fights described in interrogations as following social drinking bouts took place within tavern walls, the majority having occurred in the city streets after leaving. Less than one-third of the fights that did break out in taverns led to personal injury (defined as the shedding of blood).[51] Fights that escalated to something more than mere fisticuffs, such as that between Aufschlager and Rauner, typically moved into the streets, where the presence of drinking companions and the tavern keeper were less restraining. Of the nine fights in the sample that ended in death for one of the participants, two occurred inside taverns, three resulted from fights that began after leaving the tavern, and four followed from arguments that started within the tavern company but escalated to violence after leaving.

The rules governing the resort to violence in defense of male honor were straightforward. Defamatory insults, as illustrated in the case above, required a physical response, for ignoring provocative remarks shamed the slandered party in front of the company and invited further insults. If the defamer could not be made to take back the insults on the spot, then the insulted party was forced to take the case to court to demand a withdrawal (*Aufhebung*) in front of the city council. A public withdrawal of the affront was necessary to restore the honor of the offended party in the eyes of his peers. Among the insults that invited a physical defense were rogue (*Schelm* or *Bösewicht*), coward, thief (*Dieb*), or whore's son (*Hurnbub*), any of which was an open invitation to a fistfight. Persons defending themselves or their companions for having swung the first blow nearly always justified the physical attack as a response to these insults.

Where the slanderer was extremely drunk, the insulted party could avoid a fight by offering to ignore what had been said on the condition that his antagonist cease his verbal attack. Thus Hans Stehele offered to spare the drunken bailiff Hans Bausch for calling him a rogue and a thief in 1592 because Bausch was "especially full [of drink]" (*sonderlich voll*), and the saddlemaker Hans Jakob Eppelin graciously attempted to ignore a barrage of insults from a journeyman in 1594 whom he described as totally drunk (*aller bezecht*). When the insults continued, however, a fight could hardly be avoided, especially where witnesses were present.[52] The pressure from peers to defend one's honor could be considerable. A carpenter who was witness to the growing antagonism between Aufschlager and Rauner ended his testimony by pointing a finger at the young weaver who had chided Aufschlager into striking the first blow. If the boy had tried to calm Aufschlager instead of urging him to fight, the carpenter suggested, the whole thing might never have happened, for Rauner was drunk when he made the challenge. But the status and power men enjoyed in early modern society depended on their ability to play by the rules, and the excuse of drunkenness could only go so far. Drunkenness did not relieve Rauner of the responsibility for his insults, and it did not excuse Aufschlager from the responsibility to defend his own honor.

Starting a fight without the specific provocation of an insult to honor was not acceptable. Where defendants could not claim either insults to honor or self-defense as the catalyst for resorting to violence, they nearly always blamed it on their drunken state or claimed to have been too drunk to remember how the fight started. Although law books include the defense of honor as a legal basis for drawing a sword and even for manslaughter,[53] drawing a weapon for any reason other than physical self-defense was in practice unacceptable to the authorities. Any person who drew a weapon, unless faced by an opponent with a drawn weapon, was subject to a 2 gulden fine.[54]

Aufschlager did not admit to having drawn first. According to his account, the duelers drew their weapons simultaneously. Just as no defendant admitted to hitting an opponent without being either dishonored or hit first, an admission to drawing a weapon for anything other than self-defense was rare. Again, extreme drunkenness was the only reasonable explanation for drawing a weapon otherwise. Although it did not serve as a legal excuse and those accused of drawing weapons paid the same fine whether they were drunk or sober, drunkenness allowed the defendant to avoid providing an explanation for his behavior where no other reasonable justification existed. Hans Khrauer, for example, claimed in 1544 to have no recollection at all of having drawn a weapon against a guard at the city gate, because the wine had "completely robbed him of his senses."[55] Hans Lechmair used a similar argument in 1591 to explain having attacked a city guard with a cooking spit after the guard took away his weapon.[56] The actions of the defendants in these cases were not justifiable by their own code of behavior, and drunkenness allowed them not to justify it.

Of course, this does not rule out the possibility that Khrauer and Lechmair were in fact too drunk to recall their actions. That is almost certainly true in the case of Philipp Zösching, who testified in 1590 that he was drunk on the evening that the unarmed Thomas Gruess was stabbed to death behind a beer tavern; and therefore Zösching did not know himself if he was guilty of the crime. Remarkable in Zösching's case is the fact that he did not attempt to explain his actions even though testimony by others present indicated that he was almost certainly innocent.[57] But Zösching's case is an exception. Where drawing a weapon was justified or witnesses could attest to innocence, the memories of the defendants seemed to be remarkably clear regardless of the amount of alcohol consumed. Aufschlager, for instance, remembered in precise detail the obscene insults with which Rauner had assaulted him. But when faced with witness statements describing his continued and unnecessary attack on an opponent who was disarmed and injured, his memory failed him—he was drunk.

In dramatic cases such as Aufschlager's, the price of male honor could be high. Much more often, however, insults to honor led to a less dramatic end. The fistfights and brawls that broke out over cards and drinks were a normal part of male competition. The aim of the brawlers was not normally to destroy one another but to evaluate one another, to test and prove their respective identities as men in a male society. Men also did not typically brawl just for the sake of brawling, even when drunk. They fought for their reputation. One guardsman involved in a knife fight insisted that he drew his dagger only "because many people were on the street, and he would have been shamed should he not defend himself." The fight took place, he claimed, not because of "animosity" or "ill humor" but out of "necessity," to avoid "dishonor."[58]

Who were these participants in tavern violence, then, to whom honor and reputation represented such a valuable commodity? Do they fit Walter French's description of tavern patrons as "beggars, rascals, and thieves" or that of Phillip Ariès as "criminals, prostitutes . . . and adventurers," including no members of "decent" society?[59] Few tavern incidents involved persons of lower social status. On the contrary, those most likely to fight in defense of their reputation were men who believed they had a stake in protecting it. The brawlers appearing in the records were almost exclusively craftsmen and other citizens who considered themselves men of honor, and they acted on their obligation to defend that honor. Sixty-four percent (92) of the 144 defendants in these cases of tavern violence identified themselves as craftsmen and another 16 percent (23) as soldiers and guards, shopkeepers and tavern keepers, and city bureaucrats. Around 4 percent (6) were peasants and other tradesmen in the city on business. Less than 6 percent of the total (8) belonged to the less respectable ranks of servants, day laborers, and alms recipients; and only 1.5 percent (2) were known criminals or identified as dishonorable. Vagrants or beggars do not appear at all as participants in this sample of urban brawls; it is likely that they confined their squabbles to areas outside the city gates and away from the watchful eyes of the authorities.[60]

Even more interesting is the consistency of the picture when we move up the social ladder. In the matter of violent conflicts in defense of male honor, members of Augsburg's ruling families had a great deal in common with their fellow citizens of lower rank. Only the location of elite brawls set them apart, as they were generally confined to the exclusive drinking rooms of the Lords' and Merchants' Societies rather than occurring in public taverns or on the streets. To be sure, the city council provided for particularly cautious handling of brawls involving visiting nobility, an affront to whom could lead to political consequences.[61] But neither the level of violence among urban elites nor the forms it took varied significantly from that of urban commoners. Fights between patricians and merchants were just as likely to break out during bouts of social drinking and gambling, often as a result of breaking the rules of male sociability. The insults that served as a catalyst to violence among Augsburg's ruling citizens were precisely those noted by craftsmen and soldiers: *Schelm, Bösewicht, Dieb,* and *Hundsfott.*[62]

The fights and brawls that broke out in Augsburg's taverns and drinking rooms were not random acts of violence committed by ruffians or violent alcoholics. While early modern citizens were often quick to resort to a physical response to verbal insults, they were nonetheless constrained by the unwritten ground rules of popular society. The labeling of early modern city dwellers as insensitive or brutish[63] is typical of the tendency, as anthropologists have identified, for observers of a social group to judge actions by the rules of the dominant sectors of society — or in the case of the historian, by the official rules of the group that dominated the historical period. It is tempting to conclude, then, that the actions of those under observation either have no meaning or that their actions are primitive or uncivilized and thus have no relationship to the dominant "rules of order." These groups, however, are simply functioning within their own system of rules.[64] The altercations and violent outbursts that occurred in early modern taverns and streets were constrained by the rules of popular society, and the forms that challenges, insults, and physical responses took had meaning to the participants. Defendants and witnesses, in representing their part in this social play, nearly always described themselves as having adhered to these rules, and they defended friends and neighbors on the same basis. Aufschlager, in the above case, seems to have fulfilled this requirement in the eyes of his peers.

Drinking and Women

Tavern visits, drinking bouts, and even drunkenness and violence were often acceptable and sometimes necessary components of honorable comportment among early modern German townsmen. We have seen that early modern German women were also engaged in the dialogue over tavern behavior that sometimes arose between tavern goers and civic authorities. But did women participate in the tavern company? Did they drink? And if so, how did women's drinking norms and patterns differ from those of men? Archival evidence illuminating drinking behavior by women is much scantier than that available for men, but it is not entirely lacking. It is possible to piece together a fair picture of the place of women in the tavern and the behavior of women drinkers. This picture will be clearer, however, if viewed in the light of prevailing social and cultural norms, which provide a very negative image of drinking women.

Heavy drinking, especially in public, was primarily a male behavior. The drinking rituals and norms that have been discussed in this work so far were all associated with notions of manhood and masculinity. What conferred honor on a man, in the early modern view, could not be honorable for a woman. A material expression of the different cultural expectations for male and female drinking practices is provided by the jointed maiden's cup (*Jungfrauenbecher*) that young men and women used at elite gatherings, a two-part hinged drinking vessel with a generous cup for the man and a tiny cup to hold a measure considered appropriate for a young woman.[65]

The requirement for temperance among women can be partly explained by early modern notions of the physical differences between the sexes. According to the state of anatomical knowledge up to the late sixteenth century, based largely on the theories of Aristotle and Galen, the female temperament was generally colder and moister than that of men. The colder nature of women served as a context for their perceived sensitivity to alcohol, for alcoholic beverages were generally believed to have a fiery quality that was not compatible with the female temperament. Wine especially was believed to enhance the sanguine nature of men, purging the phlegmatic humors associated with female characteristics. Thus men when they drank became more virile, sensual, ribald, and witty — all characteristics considered completely inappropriate in women. Drunken women, by heating their temperaments and becoming more sanguine, were in effect guilty not only of participating in male behavior but of inverting the natural order of the physical world.

What happened when women did cross the line into male behaviors? At the least, they would become the object of public ridicule, as occurred in the case of women whose peers viewed them as overly domineering. Such women could be subject to charivaris or singled out for derision in Carnival rituals.[66] In extreme cases, however, in keeping with late medieval anatomical theories, women who exhibited overtly male behaviors could actually become men. According to Galenic medicine, the woman's internal sexual organs were essentially the same as the male's organs, only inverted. This was also explained by the woman's colder nature; just as a flower does not bloom without the sun, the sexual organs remained inside the woman's cooler, moister body.[67] Aristotle's biology was based on the premise that heat was the basis for the perfection of matter, fire being the highest and most perfect of the elements. The woman was thus an inferior creature. Since nature would always strive for perfection, Galen believed that it was possible for women to spontaneously be transformed into men. A number of medieval writers documented cases of women whose inverted sex organs turned back out, suddenly providing the woman with a virile member and thus changing her sex. Belief in such transmutations persisted until the seventeenth century.[68]

Although seventeenth- and eighteenth-century physicians continued to be concerned that women could develop mannish physical characteristics as a result of overly masculine behaviors, stories of women spontaneously sprouting penises were by then relegated to folklore. Nonetheless, the provocative image of a woman turning into a man persisted, not as a medical reality but as a symbolic or satirical representation. In his popular sixteenth-century satirical tract "Law, ordinance, and instruction for toasters and gluttons" (*Der Zutrincker vnd Prasser Gesatze, Ordenung, vnd Instruction*), Johannes von Schwarzenberg listed a series of diabolical wonders worked by wine. Under the influence of wine, he warned, shame becomes honor and honor becomes shame; day is spent as night and night as day; sheep become wolves; angels become devils; and women become men. It is worth noting that Schwarzenberg did not suggest the opposite possibility — that drinking could turn men into women — any more than he suggested that it could turn devils into angels.[69]

A well-publicized incident involving such a transmutation is depicted on a popular seventeenth-century broadsheet (fig. 8).[70] In it, a woman who stepped over the line into male drinking territory is shown as being punished for her infraction by having to appear before her husband in a peculiarly male guise. The woman in this case was denounced for encroaching on her husband's territory in two ways — not only was she getting ready to go drinking with female companions but she tried to steal money from her husband's purse to finance the illicit drinking bout. As she pressed the purse against her abdomen to open it, the latch became caught on her skin, and she was forced to wake her sleeping husband to free her from what appears as ridiculously male genitals. Her husband, who in one version of the story was drunk himself when she woke him, agreed to help her only after eliciting a promise that she would remain sober in the future.

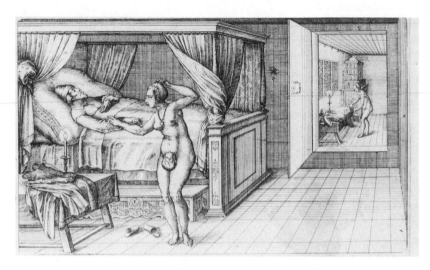

Figure 8. The Lewd Woman's Sack, Snack, Quack, and Tope Leather
(Fürwitziger Weiber Tasch / Nasch / Wasch / vnnd Flaschen Leder. Elsaß, 1620.
Courtesy of the Zentralbibliothek Zürich)

The purse often appeared in early modern German woodcuts as a point
of contention between battling spouses. For like pants and the sword, the
purse was a symbol of male power in the household. This particular broadsheet, although somewhat absurd, thus illustrates both the inappropriateness
of immoderate drinking among women and the assumption of male pre-
rogative in paying for drinks. Although the temperance literature of the sixteenth century most often describes drunkenness as a male vice, drunkenness
among women was also attacked, and the moral reformers of the period expressed concern over both of these issues. Not only was alcohol inappropriate for women for physical reasons, because it could heat up their normally
cool temperaments and release their disorderly sexual desires, but their expenditure on drinks would undermine the financial authority of the household patriarch and waste household resources.[71]

Drinking women, then, threatened to invert the natural order of both their
anatomy and household power. Yet this was not the most heinous inversion
associated with alcohol consumption by women. The effect of alcohol of
heightening sexual desire, expressed positively by men as virility or manliness, would naturally lead to the downfall of women, making them into

prostitutes. "How many whores are made by wine?" warned Sebastian Franck.[72] The ritual of the contract drink, too, became a perversion in the hands of women. Woodcuts depicting procuresses often showed them drinking to conclude the dishonorable sexual contract.[73]

Even more wanton in the early modern mentality, however, and those most guilty of inverting the natural order were the witches. Some representations of the witches' sabbath show women not only participating in unchaste behavior but also decidedly drunk (fig. 9). Witches were routinely questioned about drinking bouts during their trials; a standard accusation was a flight into wine cellars to drink stolen wine.[74] The association of alcohol use with the lewd sexuality that supposedly characterized the sabbath is not surprising, not only because alcohol was believed to incite female sexual desires but also because contemporary theorists ascribed to

Figure 9. The Witches' Sabbath (detail)
(Eigentlicher Entwurf und Abbildung deß gottlosen und verfluchten Zauber-Festes. Matthäus Merian d. Ä., after a sketch by Michael Herr, 1626. Courtesy of Germanisches Nationalmuseum)

women an irrational nature that was enhanced by drink. The devil would have been clever enough to use this tool to aid in his seduction of women, and such scenes served as a warning for women against weakening their ability to resist the devil's temptations by drinking immoderately.

Yet the physical association of women with witchcraft was not limited to notions of a natural tendency toward disorder or weakness in the face of the devil's temptations. The bodies of women were themselves mysterious; and those attributes that differentiated women from men were often credited with magic powers—human milk, menstrual blood, afterbirth, even a dead fetus could be used for magical purposes. Spells that women used to improve crops or quiet storms often involved exposing the vagina, which symbolized the female reproductive role.[75] When perverted, the very traits of womanhood that defined their natural role as mother and nourisher could become instruments of destruction and sin. For many women, especially in Germany, the point of issue in identifying a witch was not the legal question of the pact or the sexual issue of intercourse with the devil but the interference of the witch with cycles of reproduction and nourishment: killing children, drying up milk in the breast, contaminating food, and causing women to become barren and men impotent. As they perverted the female role of bearer and nourisher of children and became murderers and consumers of them instead, witches also stepped across the gender boundary into male territory by engaging in disorderly drinking bouts. The sexual inversion occurred in cases of demonic possession as well, when some women reportedly used a deep, masculine voice to sing ribald drinking songs.[76]

These cultural images provide evidence of an extremely hostile attitude toward the female drunkard. Drinking for women threatened to pervert female honor on every level, making them into men, whores, or witches. The negative images are mirrored in Augsburg's archival documents. The figure of the drunken witch was an archetype rather than a reality; Augsburg's witches did not report being drunk at the sabbath.[77] But the reactions of spouses, neighbors, and other tavern visitors to drinking and tavern-going women show that the fears that alcohol could release disorderly sexual desires and make women into whores, or otherwise disrupt household order, were very real.

The fact that women were not supposed to drink heavily did not mean that they were not allowed in taverns at all. In sixteenth- and seventeenth-century woodcuts and paintings of tavern scenes, women frequently appear among

Drinking and Gender Identity

the tavern company, serving, attending, and occasionally sharing tables or even drinking with the men. However, women virtually never display the attributes associated with drunkenness so clearly exhibited by the men, who often appear vomiting, passing out, fighting, or behaving like fools. The one vice in which women take part in these scenes is that of sexual lust; and even here, it is hard to tell if they represent a female vice or appear simply as passive vessels for the representation of male drunken behavior. A series of etchings of tavern scenes by the seventeenth-century Augsburg artist Hans Ulrich Franck illustrates graphically the different roles of the sexes in the world of tavern sociability. In each scene, men appear in the foreground, etched in bold lines and exacting detail. But the tavern women who serve their drinks and share their tables remain in the background, lightly etched and with details frustratingly obscure (fig. 10). Who were these tavern women? What role did they play in tavern society?

Figure 10. The Recruiting Station during the Thirty Years' War. At right, a recruit receives an enlistment bonus (*Laufgeld*); after his name is recorded in the book of recruitments, he is offered a drink to seal the contract. (Hans Ulrich Franck, Folge über den 30-jährigen Krieg 1656, Die Werbestelle. Courtesy of the Kunstsammlungen der Stadt Augsburg)

Although the space inside the tavern was predominantly a male space, women did have a place there. Three categories of women regularly frequented early modern Augsburg taverns. The first of these included the tavern keeper's wife and her female servants, who played an important role in both serving and controlling the male customers. The wives of brewers especially were routinely left alone with the responsibility for the guests while their husbands busied themselves in the cellar tending to the beer. Brewers' wives thus appear more often than their husbands as witnesses to tavern violence, not infrequently as participants or victims. The brewer Leonhart Schiessler, for example, was in the beer cellar when his wife tried to evict a gambling party from their public room. When the gamblers refused to leave, she took away their cards and tossed them out the window, insulting their honor as she did so by calling them "scoundrels."[78] The gamblers reacted by attacking her physically, without regard for her advanced stage of pregnancy, and she fought back by swinging a beer stein until other guests were able to fetch her husband from the cellar. This incident was not exceptional. Tavern keepers' wives, daughters, and female servants were all subject from time to time to the angry outbursts of their customers, who did not refrain from disciplining the women in this public household as if it were their own.[79]

Women also engaged in fights with one another; but based on fines collected for public brawling, only about one-sixth as often as men and rarely in taverns.[80] The one tavern brawl between women that appears in the records involved a tavern keeper's wife and her servant. A tavern guest who attempted to stop the fight testified afterward that "he assumed that since it was a matter between women, it was of no importance"; thus he did not hesitate to step in.[81] His opinion that fights between women were of less significance than those of men, or at least less liable to cause serious damage, was shared by the authorities, for the fine for brawling between women was only one-half to one-fourth that of the fine for men.[82]

A second important group of women who appear in public taverns were artisans' wives, who visited taverns regularly with their husbands but rarely took part in drinking bouts or tavern incidents. These "silent" customers are mentioned in the documents for the most part only indirectly in the testimony of men. Craftsmen might report coming home after drinking in a tavern with their wives or name the wives of artisans as witnesses present when a tavern incident occurred.[83] One husband charged with running up debts to tavern keepers testified that his wife and daughter shared the blame for the expensive tab, which did not seem to be out of the ordinary.[84] As we shall see, however, female tavern visitors were dependent on the presence of their husbands to legitimate their use of tavern space for socializing.

A less significant part of this group consisted of peddlers, servants, and wives who came to the tavern to sell their wares, make deliveries, purchase wine and beer to take home, or make other minor business transactions. Not unlike men, women were often dependent on tavern space for the conclusion of public business; however, women did not generally conclude the transaction with a drink, and they did not stay to participate in drinking bouts. These women, although often important as witnesses to tavern incidents, were only passersby in the world of tavern sociability.[85]

Occasionally, women came into taverns looking for their husbands or sons in the hope of taking them home, but such behavior appears in the records very rarely. This may be because the brief nature of such a visit makes it statistically unlikely that it would coincide with a tavern incident. It is equally likely that men discouraged their wives and mothers from dragging them home from taverns, for where women seeking to take their men out of taverns do appear in the records of the court, they certainly tended to meet with resistance. One son whose mother tried to force him to stop drinking reacted by throwing her violently to the ground and threatening her with worse if she came looking for him in a tavern again.[86] A woman who went in search of her husband in the morning after he had spent the night in a tavern because, according to the tavern keeper, he was so drunk "he could neither stand nor walk" was chased from the premises at knife point[87]; in another case, a drunken tavern visitor turned his knife on his drinking companions for suggesting that he obey his wife and go home.[88]

The women described above belonged to legitimate tavern society. The last group, however, did not. These were women accused of prostitution or other sexual crimes. Single women and married women who visited taverns without their husbands fell into this group automatically, for they ran the risk of being accused of sexual crimes simply by associating with men in taverns. By far the majority of cases involving women in taverns are of this type.

Prior to the Reformation, prostitution in most German towns was legal in a city-run brothel. The brothel, which offered drinks, games, and sociability as well as sex, shared many of the functions of the public tavern. The strict moral world demanded by the reformers, however, left no room for such an institution; in Augsburg, the city council closed the brothel doors in 1532.[89] After its closure some prostitutes continued to operate out of taverns, and tavern keepers' wives gained a reputation as procuresses. In reality, however, procuresses depended on privacy for their business and were more likely to operate out of private homes.[90] Prostitutes who worked independently were for the most part an impoverished group who could hardly afford the comforts of the tavern, more often conducting their business in the streets. The tavern keepers for their part had little to gain by tolerating prostitutes on their premises and thereby risking the loss of their license and livelihood. Nonetheless, the association of taverns with prostitution was not forgotten by city authorities. Tavern keepers had to be careful about offering lodging to unaccompanied women or they could face charges of involvement in prostitution.[91]

In the majority of tavern cases involving sexual crimes, however, the women accused cannot be identified as professional prostitutes. More often, they were women of either single or married status who made the mistake of appearing in public with a man to whom they were not married. Men and women could be arrested and interrogated for nothing more than sharing a drink, especially if they had fallen under suspicion for sexual crimes in the past.[92] No other questionable behavior was necessary to raise suspicion, for the shared drink implied social intimacy. An expression of this attitude is provided in the case of Rosina Leinauer, the wife of a clock-maker, who was arrested in 1591 after sharing two measures of wine in a public tavern with a journeyman formerly employed by her husband. Although Leinauer linked the drink to business she and the journeyman had conducted together and pointed out that they drank only in the large common room in the presence of many witnesses, returning home "in full light of day," the city council characterized the behavior as not "proper or fitting for an honorable woman."[93]

Even in cases that did not directly involve accusations of sexual crimes, the language of tavern patrons suggests that honorable women did not, or should not, visit taverns alone. Witnesses and defendants in tavern cases tended to describe women alone or in pairs as common (*gemein*) or dishonorable (*unzüchtig*). Although a tavern keeper's wife, daughter, and female servants were accepted members of tavern society, they also seem to have abstained from drinking with the customers. The one case in the records in which a tavern keeper's wife admitted to drinking with her customers falls easily into the category of illegitimate behavior, for she, too, was accused of an affair with her drinking partner.[94] Women were obviously aware of this typecast, and those who wished to avoid suspicion did their drinking at home. Although the risk of being seen was naturally reduced, however, drinking with a man in a private home was no more acceptable than drinking in a public house. The intimacy implied by the shared drink was sufficient to raise suspicions even within the private domain.[95]

If they were not supposed to drink with men, then, did women drink together in exclusively female drinking groups? Folklorists and historians have identified a number of types of women's drinking parties that were formally tolerated, especially in rural areas. These include rituals associated with childbirth (*Kindsbettzeche*, or lying-in party), including exclusively female post-churching ales; and Carnival rituals (*Weiberfastnacht*). Such village drinking traditions were all either tied to formal rites of fertility and reproduction or to Carnival, when cultural inversion was the norm. Most of these events followed carefully prescribed rules of custom and were both financed and controlled by the invariably male village councils.[96] Like other forms of popular ritual, women's drinking parties came under attack during the later sixteenth century as representing unchristian excess.[97]

Sporadic evidence suggests the possibility that women in Augsburg occasionally gathered in public taverns in exclusively female social groups, which may have been acceptable behavior on certain occasions; but sources are too scarce to shed any light on such gatherings.[98] Women were also important participants in the drinking rituals that took place at weddings. Yet while incidents involving men who became drunk at weddings were fairly widespread, I have not yet found any descriptions of women returning home drunk from weddings or other social gatherings. Whether the lack of evidence of women's drinking groups is because of the rarity of such gatherings, or only because they rarely resulted in the kind of disorderly behavior that would bring them to the attention of the authorities, must remain an open question. Either way, it is clear that public drunk and disorderly behavior resulting from social drinking bouts was the exception for women.

In spite of the restrictions that early modern social norms placed on female behavior, virtually everybody drank alcohol regularly, and women were not immune to its negative effects. There were female drunkards; but in view of what we know about the general level of alcohol consumption in early modern Germany, drunken women seem to have been surprisingly rare. This observation is supported by the reports of visitors to Germany, who also tended to describe German women as remarkably sober, even as they invariably described German men as remarkably drunk.[99] In the Augsburg case, less than 1 percent of the fines collected for drunkenness during the sixteenth and seventeenth centuries came from women.[100]

Where women did drink in a disorderly fashion, they did so in forms that differed from those of men. The scant number of women who emerge as problem drinkers apparently drank at home, and, according to the accounts of their husbands and neighbors, they did so alone or only in the company of other members of the household.[101] Thus their behavior came to the attention of the authorities only when they stepped out of the bounds of their prescribed role as honorable women—when they neglected the household, engaged in illicit sex, fought with neighbors, or were labeled drunkards by their husbands as part of more general marital disputes. The consistent exception to this rule were prostitutes who, as public women, were more likely to engage in public drinking and be found drunk in taverns or on the streets.

In all cases of women arrested for drunkenness, the drunken behavior was condemned by relatives, neighbors, and other witnesses, including other women. While drunken men could often count on the support of their fellows, and even their wives, who might testify in their favor in spite of their drunken state, drinking women could not expect support from any quarter. Accusations by husbands and witnesses concentrated on the failure of the female drunkard to live up to their expectations of household honor. Drinking women were charged with shortchanging the household as a result of expenditures on drinks, failing to care for children, abusing servants, or threatening to burn down the house. Witnesses to Anna Krug's drunkenness in 1541, for instance, although admitting that her husband did "beat her viciously," nonetheless characterized him as a "poor martyr of a man" and Anna as a "drunken pot."[102] In many cases, these charges would be accompanied by hints at unchaste behavior, even where little evidence of an affair existed.[103] Drunkenness, widely tolerated among men as an unavoidable side effect of normal sociability, was universally censured as unfitting for an honorable woman.

Also of interest is the attempt of the authorities to control these drunken women. Normally, women who drank were handled simply as unruly wives, and they were sent home with a warning "to house properly" (*wohl zu hausen*) under their husbands' authority. But when all else failed, a truncated version of the tavern ban might be applied, in which women had to take an oath not to drink outside the home and possibly to limit their drinking to a given quantity of wine per day.[104] The limiting of drinking to within the household was essentially a male punishment, intended to address a male behavior, and was part of the wording of the traditional tavern ban. In the case of women, however, it was not possible to underscore their dishonorable behavior by banning them from taverns, because tavern visits were not a right of honorable women. Thus the restrictions placed on women did not specifically include a ban on tavern visits, which would have been as inappropriate as a ban on carrying weapons. Here, the purpose of the restraint seems a somewhat frustrated attempt to control the offender directly rather than an honor punishment. At the same time, such a restriction may well have been intended as a criticism of the ineffective husband, who was apparently unable to control the behavior of his unruly wife.

"Although drunkenness brings honor to none," wrote Johannes von Schwarzenberg in 1535, "it shames a woman more than a man."[105] The silence of archival documents on the subject of drunken women, when viewed in light of the extremely negative reaction of both authority and populace to the few drunken women who do appear, suggests that the cultural norms reflected in literary sources discussed above were generally shared by the populace. The assignment of such a negative image to female drunkards served to more sharply define gender boundaries in early modern German society, for it underscored the importance of alcohol use to notions of manhood and thus enhanced the value of male drinking rituals.

The use of drink and tavern space in early modern German society was subject to social norms that both confirmed notions of male identity and underscored boundaries between the sexes. These norms in most cases formed a common basis for negotiation between men and women, between men and their peers in the public arena of the tavern, and between populace and authority in the adjudication of disputes. Sharing drinks in the tavern allowed for social play that could establish and confirm male honor. Even drunkenness had a role in protecting male honor. For just as it could provide a flexible tool for magistrates to either excuse or condemn an offender at court, drunkenness could also relieve men from explaining their own behavior or, to a point, allow them to forgive that of their companions when norms were broken. For women, accusing a wayward spouse of drunkenness could furnish a tool for exercising power in the home.

At the same time, drinking rituals created boundaries between appropriate and inappropriate male behavior and especially between male and female identity. Truly disorderly behavior was not tolerated even by the tavern company, for as will be shown in the following chapter, social identity depended on one's drinking companions. Men thus ejected from their drinking groups those they considered to be disorderly, and female drunkards were not tolerated by anyone. These clearly established gendered boundaries accentuate the important role that drinking rituals played in defining male identity. Tavern drinking served both to cement social and gender bonds among men and to separate them from women.

Finally, it is remarkable how closely allied the norms of the authorities were with popular practice. City fathers, certainly, were concerned with disorder, and their decisions often seemed to be aimed at restraining unruly brawls and controlling disorderly marriage among commoners as part of a top-down policy of suppression of civic disorder. Yet in regulating against using inflammatory insults, drawing a weapon without provocation, or squandering household resources, the authorities only underscored norms already present in popular society. The negative view of immoderate drinking among women was also shared by all levels of society. Whether or not they actually read civic ordinances, defendants and witnesses in cases of domestic disorder or tavern violence knew what the rules were and where they were broken. Members of the city council were likely to be tolerant of behavior that adhered to norms not significantly different from their own. In defending their actions to the authorities, Augsburg's citizens thus used strategies designed to appeal not just to magistrates but also to men who shared their cultural world.

8

Drinking and Social Identity

The Boundaries of Sociability

THE EARLY MODERN urban tavern provided a routine meeting place in which city dwellers established and maintained group identity with their social network. Augsburg's artisans used tavern space, participation (or nonparticipation) in a drinking bout (*Zech*), and the disputes fueled by alcohol to establish and reconfirm their social identity. Just as was the case with the fights and rituals already discussed, the decision to drink together was governed by certain ground rules. Sociologists and anthropologists have identified similar ground rules in many other cultures in which alcohol is used. As Dwight Heath has observed, "the drinking of alcoholic beverages tends to be hedged about with rules concerning who may and may not drink how much of what, in what contexts, in the company of whom, and so forth."[1] The way in which these rules work in any society can serve as a mirror reflecting the values of society at large; or, more eloquently stated, "Alcohol can indeed serve as a revealing stain on the slide in the historian's microscope, highlighting the structures and relations of a society."[2]

Drinking together implied more than casual acquaintance, and the documents reveal that Augsburg's citizens were cautious about in whose company they drank. When fights or other incidents occurred in taverns, the participants were often careful to point out whether they were participating in the same drinking bout or drinking separately. Caspar Morhart, a guardsman who was involved in a duel with fellow guardsman Ernst Kratzer in 1642, thus replied when asked with whom he had been drinking before the fight started that he had shared drinks "not with Ernst Kratzer but with others";[3] Morhart apparently considered the question of with whom he had not been drinking more relevant. Similarly, Hans Goff, a member of the city elite who was present in a public tavern in which another tavern guest read aloud an inflammatory letter of insult, was mindful to make clear in his testimony that, although the defendant had invited him for a drink, he had declined the invitation. Goff decided instead to seek company somewhere where "better wine" was served, presumably in one of the elite drinking rooms.[4] Goff's statement suggested social distance from the commoners present and thus nonparticipation in their inappropriate behavior.

Craftsmen were also hesitant to drink with persons whose behavior did not conform to the unwritten rules of tavern society. Overly loud or aggressive behavior or failure to pay one's tab were grounds for refusing to accept someone as a drinking companion. Members of one drinking party warned a journeyman who asked to join their party that he might join them only if he would do so as "a good fellow" (ein guter Gesell); the group subsequently came to blows because the newcomer irritated the company by his loud bragging.[5] A drunken soldier who became loud and insolent was refused "brotherhood" (Bruderschaft) by all tables in the tavern, and a journeyman who asked to join an acquaintance was told that if he had money enough to share the tab, he would be a good fellow, but if not, he should seek company elsewhere.[6] Witnesses to a tavern brawl that took place in 1548 created a boundary between themselves and an unwelcome drinking companion by describing themselves as having been "merry and in a good mood" (fröhlich und guter Dinge) until Georg Enißhofer insisted on joining their drinking bout uninvited. Enißhofer, already drunk when he came into the tavern, offended the company by singing "shameful frivolous songs" (schändliche üppige Lieder). When his wife then tried to get him to leave the tavern, his drinking companions suggested that he take her advice and go home. The suggestion enraged Enißhofer, for it implied that they did not consider him fit company. He responded by demanding that "if someone finds fault with him, they should tell him, they could find none with him," for "he didn't want to mooch his wine."[7] Enißhofer then drew his weapon in defense of his honor, a move that would ultimately cost him his life.

For some persons, social boundaries were drawn irrespective of behavior. Consistently excluded from drinking bouts in public taverns were persons belonging to professional groups designated as dishonorable. The taint of dishonor as defined by profession varied in different parts of Germany, but always at the core of dishonor were the executioner, responsible for both torturing and executing serious criminals, and the skinner (or knacker), whose primary duty was skinning and removing carcasses of animals that had died by natural causes.[8] A literary reference to the exclusion of such persons from honorable drinking bouts appears in Johann Fischart's *Geschichtsklitterung:* "What? Have I skinned a dead sow, that no one will bring me any [wine]?"[9] Although certain kinds of professional contact with dishonorable people were acceptable, social contact was taboo, and the social intimacy implied by sharing drinks with them could have detrimental consequences for members of honorable professions. This problem is illustrated by the case of the loden weaver Hans Seidler, who had a drink with a skinner from whom he had purchased some lard; he was subsequently threatened with exclusion from his craft. Seidler defended himself by pointing out that although he and the skinner had drunk together, he was not really drinking "with" the dishonorable party but "separately." According to Seidler, the skinner had asked him repeatedly to drink a measure of wine over the transaction and Seidler finally agreed to do so. "Then I drank with him," he explained, "and assumed that since we each drank separately, it would not bring any prejudice" (presumably each had purchased a separate measure of wine). Seidler's workshop was closed by craft leaders after a journeyman formerly in his employ brought the matter to their attention. Doing business with a skinner was not a problem, but drinking together, a social act implying social identification, dishonored Seidler and threatened the honor of his craft.[10]

In another episode involving a person designated dishonorable, a shopkeeper was exposed on the pillory and then temporarily banished from the city for inviting a military chaplain quartered in his home to drink at his table. The drinking bout occurred in 1634, during the Swedish occupation of Augsburg. The shopkeeper, a Catholic, had failed to mention that one of the women sharing drinks with the Protestant chaplain was the wife of the executioner. After the chaplain suffered ridicule and exclusion for sharing drinks with the executioner's wife, the city council concluded that the shopkeeper's behavior had been a willful attempt to dishonor the chaplain and his regiment.[11] In many cities, the executioner was forbidden by law to drink publicly with persons considered honorable.[12]

Drinking Groups in Public Taverns

Among social peers, participation in drinking bouts signified social identification and acceptance. As already noted, refusal to accept an offer of a drink was a serious insult, one that often led to blows. Conversely, sharing in a round of drinks was a means of establishing structural ties, whether of business, friendship, kinship, or simple camaraderie. Social identification, however, did not automatically mean social equality, for master craftsmen drank with their journeymen and apprentices, householders drank with their servants, and patricians occasionally shared tables with artisans and others of common status.

A statistical breakdown of drinking groups identified in the court records will allow a closer look at the social makeup of Augsburg's tavern clientele and their structural ties.[13] In this context, the division of the tavern company into individual drinking parties was not based on physical proximity but on patterns of spending and consumption. The identity of the group was determined by sharing measures of wine and buying reciprocal rounds. Different drinking parties could and did share a table without participating in the same drinking bout. Thus drinkers might note that others were present at their table but that they participated in a different drinking bout.[14] At times, a loner at the table might be invited to join in the drinking bout or ask to be admitted. Bringing a drink to someone at another table was an open request to be asked to join in a shared drinking bout.

Not surprisingly, the majority of drinkers in Augsburg's taverns between 1540 and 1644 were members of the artisan class. Groups of artisans, or mixed groups of artisans and other social or professional classes, made up nearly 78 percent of the total number of drinking groups.[15] Looking solely at groups in which artisans were present, we find that 71 percent were made up of artisans only, just under 14 percent included soldiers or guards, and another 15 percent were of mixed social status (that is, craftsmen drinking with elites, city bureaucrats, day laborers, servants, peasants, or others of nonartisan status). Within groups of artisans, variety in status and profession was the rule. Most artisans identified themselves only by profession, without noting whether they were masters or journeymen; but based on cases in which these distinctions can be made, there was no particular tendency for masters to avoid the company of journeymen. Those identified as master were actually more than twice as likely to be drinking with journeymen than with other masters. This fact, however, in all likelihood derives from the inclination of journeymen to note that they were drinking with their master, thus identifying the status of both parties, whereas master craftsmen rarely identified themselves as such.

Over 60 percent of the drinking groups that included only artisans were made up of craftsmen from different professions. Among the professionally homogenous groups (which made up about 25 percent of all groups in which craftsmen were present), the majority were either drinking in their craft hostel or noted some professional reason for the gathering. A group of weavers, for instance, explained that they were drinking together to conclude a sale of cloth; in other cases, an employer rewarded journeymen bricklayers with a drink after completing a long day's labor, or craftsmen were seeking a position among others of their profession or drinking together in celebration of a guild holiday.[16]

If we break down these drinking groups by period, it is possible to observe a slight trend toward increased social homogeneity in drinking company over the course of the years from 1540 to the 1640s. In the earliest period of 1540–1544, two cases appear in which elites (nobles) participated in drinking bouts with soldiers, artisans, and even servants. No evidence of drinkers of this status appears during the 1590s, but there are cases involving members of the elevated crafts (for instance, goldsmiths and clock-makers) and city officials who drank (and brawled) with craftsmen, servants, peasants, and musicians. By the 1640s, however, the only drinker identified as an elite was drinking with others of his status, and elite craftsmen and officials did not appear as participants in tavern incidents.[17] The tendency for artisans to drink with others of their craft, too, increased by 1640. Groups of mixed professions made up around 64 percent of exclusively artisan drinking groups in both the 1540s and 1590s; this figure dropped to 42 percent during the 1640s. The mixed groups of craftsmen and soldiers, which made up 5 percent of the groups including artisans in the 1540s and 18 percent in the 1590s, disappeared entirely during the 1640s. These statistics support the widely accepted paradigm that the lines of the Society of Orders (*Standesgesellschaft*) were indeed hardening during the early seventeenth century; however, the small size of the sample for the later period makes a definite conclusion in this regard somewhat arbitrary.

Also missing entirely from the drinking groups of the 1640s were women. Groups that included women made up 20 percent of the drinking bouts during the 1540s and 16 percent of those of the 1590s (although female customers made up less than 7 percent of the customer total). One of these (in 1541) was an exclusively female drinking group, and all others were either women drinking with their husbands (who made up 27 percent of groups that included women) or women accused of sexual crimes (69 percent). Women who drank with their husbands appeared in the documents only as witnesses and not as participants in tavern incidents. It is unlikely that wives kept pace with their husbands in drinking pledges, the fashion for women being only to take a sip of their drink when pledges were made, while the men emptied their glasses. Alternately, women might only kiss their husband's cup or take a tiny sip of his drink, helping him in dutiful fashion to do honor to his fellows.[18] In any case, none of the women present in tavern drinking groups were described as drunk.

Drinking groups that included family members were not unusual, but they were not necessarily the rule. In addition to the wives who occasionally joined their husbands for a drink, about 12 percent of the groups included persons identified as relatives. Nearly as common, occurring in 10 percent of the cases, was the participation of persons in a common drinking bout who did not know one another's names. Occasionally, a drinker would report sharing a round with someone "whom they call [by some nickname]";[19] more often, they simply noted that "there were others there whom [they] didn't know."[20] Augsburg's citizens refused to drink with people who were dishonorable, people against whom they had a personal vendetta, and people whose behavior violated the norms of popular society. Personal acquaintance, however, was not a prerequisite for shared sociability. The gunsmith Otmar Peter expressed this fact candidly in 1591, when he responded to the court's demand to know who his drinking fellows were by asserting that he needed "no particular fellows — when he goes into a tavern, then he finds a fellow soon enough."[21]

Gambling as Structural Identity

A popular way to share an evening with one's drinking fellows was to pass the time with tavern games. A game of cards or dice added more than entertainment value to tavern sociability. Gambling could serve both as a means of establishing group identity and an opportunity to display positive masculine values such as courage, honesty, risk taking, and good character. The friendly competition of a gambling match provided men not only the chance to experience joy at winning but also to demonstrate strength of character in bearing losses. This characteristic is lauded in early modern books of manners such as Baldesar Castiglione's *The Book of the Courtier,* which represents gambling as an opportunity for members of the elite classes to display their distance from material concerns.[22] Even social groups for whom material concerns were more paramount were expected to be willing to make a financial sacrifice for the entertainment of their fellows, and gambling served this function in a way similar to that of reciprocation in buying rounds.

Gambling as a vice received almost as much attention in the moralist literature of the sixteenth century as drunkenness. It was condemned as an inducement to swearing, blasphemy, and brawling; a means to economic ruin; a violation of the commandment against coveting the property of one's neighbor; and a devilish temptation to believe in fate rather than in God's divine plan.[23] Like drinking, gambling has been traditionally viewed by historians as a means of escape from the miseries of early modern life, an indicator of social distress, or a symbol of "the moral lapses of the laboring classes."[24]

Yet police ordinances were as ambiguous about gambling as they were about drunkenness. Gambling in public taverns was restricted up to the 1530s to bets of 1 pfennig,[25] and it was forbidden entirely on work days and during the sermon in 1539; but subsequent ordinances specifically forbade only "ruinous," "habitual," or "excessive" gambling.[26] Definitions of what was meant by "ruinous" were provided only for those of the elite orders; in the Lords' Drinking Room, gaming was restricted to losses of 50 gulden per sitting, and in the Merchants' Drinking Room, gambling on credit was restricted to 1 gulden.[27] Gambling regulations did not appear in ordinances of the seventeenth century.

Most gambling in taverns took the form of playing for the price of the drinks, so that total losses would not exceed the price of an evening's entertainment. Tavern games did not hold out the "prospect of winning a fortune," as Keith Thomas put it, or function as an escape from the realities of social inequality.[28] They offered only the prospect of getting the best of a friend in sociable competition, getting in on a free round of drinks, and participating in the "symbolic exchange of shared consumption."[29] Those who played at games of luck and skill simply for the price of drinks would, in the long run, be likely to end up paying fairly equitable amounts for their entertainment. The goal of such games was not monetary profit but entertainment and nonviolent male competition. Inclusion in and exclusion from such games also served as a means of solidifying group identity.

The authorities accepted gambling for rounds as a normal part of tavern sociability. Although losses at cards occasionally served as a catalyst for tavern brawls and duels, there is no evidence that the authorities made any attempt to curtail gambling for rounds.[30] A few tavern keepers were fined for allowing gambling on their premises, but in cases for which details of the arrest are available, the reasons for the charges were allowing gambling for very large stakes, seating players in a secret room, or gambling after closing time or in violation of rules against visiting taverns during the week.[31] One tavern keeper accused of seating craftsmen in his cellar to gamble after hours explained that "he didn't think that playing for a haller or a pfennig could cause a problem," noting that he "didn't have the sort of guests who have much to gamble away, [but he is] happy when they can pay their tab."[32] The tavern keeper was not fined for the gambling incident.

The gamblers that concerned the authorities most were of the professional sort, many of whom used trickery or marked cards to win large amounts of money.[33] Heavy gambling normally did not take place in taverns, however, where the watchful eye of the tavern keeper and the regular patrol by city guards made illegal activity difficult. Instead, those interested in serious gambling gathered in the streets or outside the city walls, most often at Schießgraben, shooting grounds located in the moat just west of Augsburg's walls. Gambling at the shooting grounds was specifically forbidden by ordinance in 1539, and repeat offenders caught gambling at Schießgraben were normally banished. It is in the interrogations of these defendants, nearly all of whom were from outside of Augsburg, that the major concerns of the authorities become evident. The questions raised by the interrogators, if not the responses of the defendants, paint a picture of a dangerous archetype: the professional swindler. This menacing character and his band of accomplices made his living by cheating his victims with loaded dice, marked cards, and persuasive language. Questions about cheating were standard in such cases, as were demands for information about conspirators, informants, and related crimes such as theft and counterfeit coinage. In the case of tavern gambling as well, gamblers from outside the city who won large amounts were automatically assumed to have used persuasion and trickery to win their purse.[34] The victim of one such accused gambler, a peasant who lost 50 gulden in an Augsburg tavern, complained that he was "enticed and lured to it with slick and high-handed words." Gamblers found guilty of using false cards or dice could face torture, permanent banishment, or the death penalty.[35]

These dangerous professionals, then, were the real target of ordinances restricting gambling. Artisans who tossed dice for drinks or change to pass the time in taverns were not a cause of official concern. As long as the stakes were affordable and the gambling peaceful, it was not viewed as disorderly by the populace or the authorities. In a petition to the city council written in 1590, the Discipline Lords themselves described one fight that broke out during a tavern gambling bout as having occurred while friends and relatives were enjoying a "friendly drink," a phrase laden with notions of sociability and brotherhood, clearly implying approval.[36] The approval of the authorities for friendly gambling bouts is also evidenced by their revoking of the privilege when it was abused. The tavern and weapons ban for troublesome householders sometimes included a ban on gambling, normally for a period of one year. The right to gamble was revoked in cases of violating tavern bans, domestic violence, and losses at cards significant enough to endanger the household budget. Alms recipients, too, were forbidden to gamble at all.[37] The application of this ban implies that moderate gambling, like drinking and carrying a weapon, was a right of honorable men.

Drinking between the Confessions

Those accustomed to examining the sixteenth and seventeenth centuries in Germany primarily in the light of the process of confessionalization must, by now, be wondering when the important question of confessional ties and religious differences will be addressed. Augsburg was, after all, a bi-confessional city and one that suffered its share of confessional differences, particularly during the period of controversy attending the introduction of the Gregorian calendar and the Thirty Years' War. Would these differences not have been at issue in Augsburg's taverns, affecting group identity, ties of sociability, and violent outbursts?

Surprisingly, the question of confession appears only rarely in tavern discourse. Relations between the confessions were less strained during the sixteenth century than they would become in the seventeenth century, after the bitter struggles of the Thirty Years' War led to a tighter drawing of confessional boundaries. Social contact between Catholics and Lutherans, even mixed marriages, was fairly common before the 1630s.[38] Michel de Montaigne expressed surprise in 1580 that marriages between Catholics and Protestants in Augsburg were a daily occurrence, the party more eager for the match often accepting the confession of their marriage partner.[39] Social contact between the confessions as expressed through shared drinking bouts was also commonplace. There is no evidence that either taverns or drinking parties were confessionally divided during the sixteenth century; and there is not a case either between 1540–1544 or 1590–1594 when a fight broke out as the result of confessional differences. Not until after the Thirty Years' War and the establishment of political parity for Catholics and Protestants were craft hostels confessionally divided.[40]

As religious tensions grew during the course of the seventeenth century, the council took steps to enforce peaceful relations between the confessions. Public taverns, in which social conflicts of many kinds found their stage, appeared to city leaders a likely breeding ground for religious quarreling. Following the establishment of parity in 1649, the bi-confessional council issued a decree warning Augsburg citizens of both confessions against insulting or slandering one another for reasons of faith, "not only in beer and public houses but in the public lanes and streets."[41] The only two cases of confessional disputes taking place in taverns recorded between 1640 and 1660, however, both occurred between persons of different faiths who were participating in a common drinking bout, which does more to suggest the existence of cross-confessional friendships than enmities.[42] Certainly, confessional differences were a reality in Augsburg during the post-Reformation century, but they were not the dominant theme at the tables of Augsburg's taverns, where issues of a less philosophical nature took precedence.

Alcohol has a long history as a cultural artifact. Anthropologists have identified many societies in which "drinking behavior is considered important for the whole social order, and so drinking is defined and limited in accordance with fundamental motifs of the culture."[43] Some patterns in drinking behavior are virtually universal throughout those parts of the world in which alcohol is consumed. Drinking behaviors in early modern Germany generally conform to these basic patterns. It is usually the case, for instance, that heavy drinking is considered more acceptable for men than for women and that sharing a drink symbolizes "durable social solidarity" or identification with the drinking partner.[44]

It is the variations in behaviors rather than the commonalities, however, that provide the historian with insight into a particular society and period. Significant variations occur in the way in which different cultures consume, think about, and react to alcoholic beverages. In this and the preceding two chapters, examining specific drinking behaviors in the light of known commonalities affords a better understanding as to how early modern city dwellers established and played by their own rules. Discerning the legal significance of contractual drinking, for instance, indicates the importance of a shared drink in forming professional and personal bonds. While the reputation of preindustrial society as a community of drunkards is often cited as evidence of their disorderly or "irrational" nature,[45] the idea of conducting daily business without consuming alcohol would certainly have seemed irrational to early modern German craftsmen and merchants. Household discourse over drinks illuminates the dynamics of gender relations, gendered domains, and sexual power. The banning of unsuccessful householders and beggars from tavern company, and the direct link of paying one's round to acceptance in this company, shows the degree of social emphasis placed on economic health, even among craftsmen. The flexibility of drunkenness in functioning as a social excuse reveals where insults went too far, highlighting the key role that personal honor played in the lives of Augsburg's citizens. Finally, the willingness or refusal of tavern goers to drink with certain members of society demonstrates where unofficial culture placed social boundaries.

The carefully constructed ground rules that defined drinking rituals in early modern German society are not consistent with the characterization of the popular classes as irrational or tolerant of disorder. The city taverns in which these rituals took place did not represent a threat to social order, nor did they house criminals, prostitutes, vagrants, or other dangerous or dishonorable groups. Naturally, taverns could not remain entirely free of these elements, but at least within the city walls, they were the exception rather than the rule among the tavern company. By revoking the right to participate in this company from those persons whose behavior did not meet social norms, society defined the tavern as a haunt exclusive to honorable men, not to beggars and thieves. Social drinking had meaning to the citizens of early modern Germany that went far beyond alcohol-induced exhilaration. Drinking rituals served to establish and confirm the social identity of the participants — as men or women, as members of a certain social order or economic class, and as honorable citizens of the "prestigious and renowned city" of Augsburg.[46]

9

The Social Functions of the Tavern

The Functions of Public Space

WE HAVE SEEN that the provision of food, drink, and lodging in return for money was the basic form of economic exchange that defined the tavern keepers' trade. The tavern offered another important commodity, however, for which no direct charge was made: public space. Tavern space, warmed and lit by oven and lamplight and providing protection from the cold, the dark, and other unwelcome intruders, was the natural point of contact for many social and professional activities. The public nature of the tavern also allowed a measure of surveillance over these meetings by city authorities, who at times utilized taverns for purposes of their own. An exploration of the social functions of tavern space, the ways in which this space served the community, and the interests of the authorities in keeping this space available to the populace contributes further insights into the role of the tavern in the early modern German city.

In return for offering space and hospitality to residents and visitors in the city, the tavern keeper received a monopoly on the profitable business of seating guests, serving drinks and meals at a price, and lodging travelers. The public nature of his house, however, did not relieve the tavern keeper of the responsibility for order within it. The profitable nature of his business made it worth his while to try to live up to that responsibility. City leaders also had every reason to support the publican's authority and keep him in business. Not only could the tavern keeper function as a representative of the city council's interests in controlling his guests but the city's network of public taverns was a major part of the framework on which the social structure rested.

The tavern, in serving these social functions, rarely provided a haven for disorder or popular resistance. More often, it supported and enhanced the orderly functioning of society. Tavern space could even be enlisted by the authorities as an aid to social control, which was aimed not at the popular

158

classes generally but at certain elements that were perceived as threatening to order. The use of taverns by respectable craftsmen was accepted and even encouraged. In the case of vagrants, beggars, and other social groups that threatened to become a burden to the community, however, tavern visits were carefully controlled. Tavern space and tavern keepers supported the authorities in regulating the movements of these potentially burdensome groups.

Augsburg's council, as public authority (*öffentliche Gewalt*), understood the public domain as belonging to their exclusive realm of authority.[1] This domain at times extended into areas we would today consider private, such as the financial, sexual, and confessional lives of the populace; for misbehavior in these areas was viewed as a threat to public order and stability. Mismanaging the household, committing adultery, or failing to appear in church were acts that could lead to the disintegration of the family unit and disruption of economic production, or even incur the wrath of God. Either result was harmful to the public (common) good.

In direct opposition to that which was understood as public, or belonging to the domain of public authority, was that which was secret, or hidden from the public view. It was in secret rooms or hidden corners that activities threatening to public stability took place. That which was virtuous took place in the public light of day, and what went on in the dark or hidden from the public eye could only be malevolent. Private meetings and gatherings, simply by virtue of being private and thus secret, often seemed suspicious to the authorities. Any gathering, discussion, or other activity that could potentially take on a political character, in order to be legal, had to be open to the watchful eye of public authority. During periods of confessional struggle, even private gatherings to read the Bible gave cause for alarm.[2]

The designation of the tavern as a public house (*öffentliches Wirtshaus*), and thus a place in which meetings and gatherings were sanctioned by the authorities, was crucial to the city council's perception of a functioning society. Craftsmen, merchants, farmers, and laborers had to meet to conduct their business. Public weddings and other forms of sociability were necessary for the establishment of family, professional, and neighborhood networks. If these gatherings were to take place, then, the authorities preferred that they occur in public taverns rather than in private homes or secret corners. This aim lay at the root of the closure of the private guild drinking rooms in 1548 and the subjection of the Merchants' Drinking Room to visitation by patricians a year later. Thereafter, all Augsburg's drinking rooms remained open to the inspection of the city council and their appointed representatives, the bailiffs and guards who incorporated public authority.

Within the tavern, space was also divided between the public and the private spheres. Only the large public room (*Stube*) was considered by the authorities as belonging to the public domain.³ The cellars, the smaller upstairs rooms used for overnight guests, and other tavern spaces did not belong to that space sanctioned by the authorities for public gatherings. Guests who were seated in separate rooms raised suspicions of illegal gambling, plotting against the government, engaging in sexual crimes, or other illegal activities; and the tavern keeper who allowed them access to such private spaces risked charges of complicity. Interrogators charged tavern keepers in such cases with maintaining a "special, secret, small room" (*sonders haimlich stüblin*) for illegal activities or of hiding guests who were seated in the cellar, the brewing house, or in other private areas.⁴

Conversely, persons accused of illegal activities might cite the fact that they remained in the public *Stube* as evidence of their innocence. Rosina Leinauer, accused in 1591 of an affair with one of her husband's former journeymen, defended herself by noting that she had only had a drink with the journeyman "in the large [public] room, in which many people were sitting."⁵ In another case, a tavern keeper's wife was accused of committing adultery in her public house while her husband was away at war. Her brother, when interrogated about visitors to his sister's house, defended his ignorance of her activities on the grounds that "it was a public tavern" in which she had a right to entertain guests.⁶ Defendants accused of frequenting secret corners, or "evil haunts" (*böse Schlupfwinkel*), denied the charges by naming the respectable taverns in which they were known. One young clock-maker flatly denied any secretive behavior by stating that he "never visited secret corners, but public taverns."⁷

The fact that customers as well as the authorities understood the tavern as public space could at times come into conflict with a tavern keeper's notions of private ownership and the sanctity of his household. Despite the publicity of his profession, however, the tavern landlord remained master of his house. The sanctity of the home in the early modern period was protected by the traditional right of household peace (*Hausfrieden*). Control of the household and responsibility for its peaceful and productive functioning lay in the hands of the family head. A tavern keeper, as master of his household, was also responsible for what went on within his house, and he could be held partially responsible for fights and injuries, illegal gambling, blasphemies, or even the conversations that took place on his premises.[8] When one guest shocked others in his drinking party in 1541 by insisting that there was no life after death, the tavern keeper responded by warning him not to express such opinions in his house.[9] Some customers even tried to blame their own behavior on the failure of the publican to control them, as did one group of singers who violated a wedding ordinance by singing after the dance had ended. The singers defended themselves by claiming that "they assumed that if it was forbidden, the landlord should have warned them."[10]

Tavern keepers were not always successful in enforcing their household authority. Evicting an unruly guest could occasionally be problematic, particularly before closing time. One tavern keeper who made several attempts to evict a drunken soldier who was harassing his other guests was forced by others present to let the offender back in, because it was not yet nine o'clock (closing time). In other cases, guests came to one another's defense in physically resisting the tavern keeper, or they tried to force their way into the house. To these guests, the right to visit the tavern keeper's home was a matter of public ordinance and not private hospitality.[11]

In spite of these occasional challenges, however, a tavern keeper's rights of property took official precedence over a customer's demands on his publicity, and resistance to his authority was the exception rather than the rule. Only 12 percent of the 115 cases of violence occurring in taverns identified in the sample on which this study is based involved the tavern keeper, and in most of these cases, the authorities sided with the publican against the customer. When the furrier Matthäus Nate, for instance, was arrested along with the brewer in whose house he was drinking for exchanging blows, Nate spent time in irons and in the tower and was forbidden to visit taverns for a year. The brewer, because he was acting "in the interest of [household] peace," was released without punishment.[12] Another tavern customer who refused to comply with the landlord's insistence that he quit swearing and leave the other guests in peace was banished from the city.[13] As one tavern keeper expressed it, a customer had no business imposing "either bounds or order in [the publican's] house," for that right belonged to the head of the household alone.[14]

News, Contacts, and Messages

An important tavern function was its role as a center for information. Taverns in the early modern period could serve as bookshops, post offices, lost and found depots, employment offices, advertising agencies, and even museums, where traveling showmen displayed collections of wonders.[15] All of these functions supported communication not only among the network of tavern visitors but also between the populace and city authorities.

Tavern keepers could be called on to hold and pass along messages, letters, and lost or unclaimed goods, which became the responsibility of the tavern keeper until ownership could be determined. Tavern keepers also sometimes held securities for loans. Thus in the winter of 1544, when three journeymen from the neighboring village of Oberhausen stumbled across the body of an unidentified man who had apparently frozen to death, they removed the money from his pockets and took it to the nearest tavern keeper for safekeeping. The money was counted in front of witnesses before being handed over.[16] Similarly, tavern keepers retained temporary responsibility for goods belonging to guests who died while staying at their taverns — and if the stay had been a lengthy one, the tavern keeper might expect to share in the inheritance.[17] One desperate young mother even chose a tavern as the appropriate place to abandon her illegitimate child, which she slipped inside, she testified, so it would not freeze to death.[18]

Public taverns were also the natural choice for the open reading of ordinances, broadsheets, and other news items, as well as for reading and discussing the latest books. Augsburg's publicans were a literate group, for even a cellar boy was expected to be able to read.[19] This fact supported the role of the public house as a circulation center for printed information. Ordinances were both read aloud and posted in taverns, and some Augsburg taverns doubled as book shops. Printers not only sold their books in public taverns on a door-to-door basis but sometimes obtained tavern licenses or operated together with established tavern keepers, taking advantage of the public atmosphere to read, discuss, and sell their wares.[20] By the seventeenth century, early forms of advertising appeared on tavern walls, where printed posters described wonder cures and other products for sale in the city.[21]

Another important function of Augsburg's taverns was that of a point of contact for employment and other business contracts. A tavern was the first stop for any wandering journeyman, servant, or day laborer looking for work. Tavern keepers directed craftsmen to the appropriate guildhall or craft hostel, and they sometimes aided servants and day laborers in making the contacts necessary to find a position. Peasants from the surrounding villages came to taverns looking for field labor and also to contract sales of their produce and livestock. Women contracted sewing, mending, and washing jobs in taverns, even picking up and delivering the clothing there. Tavern keepers at times served as cashiers for the services contracted in their houses, collecting and distributing the payments for various services. Both traveling and local peddlers came into taverns to sell their wares; this was legal as long as their products did not compete with the production of local craftsmen.[22]

While the tavern keeper did not charge directly for the use of his house for such activities, he certainly profited from them. Holding messages, letters, and moneys usually resulted in a tip for the tavern keeper. Since business contracts, at least between men, were invariably sealed with a drink and often accompanied by a meal, this resulted in profits for the landlord. Peasants, traders, and other persons with legitimate business in the city might provide the tavern keeper with overnight guests. In short, any activity that encouraged people to gather at tavern tables to eat and drink was a potential source of profit.

All of these tavern activities were obviously valuable for both a tavern keeper's business and the lives of the tavern goers. But the city authorities, too, reaped benefits from these activities. Taverns aided the dissemination of decrees and ordinances, as well as the popular broadsheets and cautionary tales that were often circulated for purposes of official propaganda. Certainly, the ready availability of employment contacts was in the public interest, and the conclusion of business contracts and sales agreements not only supported local commerce but were linked to the merchant city's corporate identity. By serving to strengthen community and commercial ties through the distribution of information, the tavern helped bolster the social and material foundations of the city.

The Tavern as a Point of Control

The tavern's function as a center for news and information did not always work in the interest of stability or in support of authority. Taverns could and did provide a public theater for social protests and unrest. The printed pamphlets that circulated in the city did not always reflect the interests of the

Augsburg authorities. Social and confessional criticism, satire, and even pornography made the rounds of Augsburg's taverns. Such publications were forbidden by the city council, along with the singing of songs or reading of poems of an insulting or inflammatory nature.[23] Equally disquieting to the authorities was the attraction of city taverns to beggars, thieves, prostitutes, professional gamblers, and vagrants, who came to the city seeking jobs, hoping for alms, or looking for contacts of a less public nature. Yet at the same time, the ready accessibility of the tavern to representatives of authority could make it a useful point of control through which these potentially threatening elements could be observed and suppressed, and tavern keepers could be engaged as civic watchdogs. The early modern tavern keeper thus functioned as the "authorities' ear" in following the movements of strangers to the city.[24]

The public house was more easily accessed and controlled by the authorities than was a private home.[25] In fact, city guards were charged by the council with making regular evening rounds of the taverns and inspecting those from which loud or unseemly noise issued. Therefore, when the council passed laws aimed at limiting the potential for social disruption, they did not shut down or restrict taverns. Instead they restricted certain activities to taverns only. As noted above, games and meetings were allowed only in the public *Stube,* where city bailiffs and guards could easily look in on the activities.[26] Weddings, too, at least those of commoners, were restricted to the public space of the tavern.

Even more stringent, however, were the laws governing the lodging of nonresidents. As the economic problems of the late sixteenth century and into the seventeenth led to growing numbers of vagrants and wandering beggars, urban authorities responded by tightening the control of persons entering the city. City taverns proved very useful for this purpose. The tavern keepers' monopoly on lodging visitors to the city was not established in the interest of the publicans. By restricting the housing of travelers whose presence might prove disruptive or burdensome to public taverns, the council hoped to turn the city's taverns into an internal network of control centers.

The civic law against indiscriminate lodging of visitors dated at least from 1530, when the council decreed that no one in Augsburg was to lodge nonresidents without first obtaining the permission of the council or the mayors' office. The penalty for breaking this rule was loss of citizenship.[27] Tavern keepers, whose tavern license constituted standing permission from the city council to lodge guests, were ordered in 1541 to report to the mayors' office any guest staying longer than three days. In addition, tavern keepers were to observe their guests and report any who seemed "suspicious."[28] Three years later, they were specifically forbidden by the council to offer shelter to beggars without the express permission of the Office of Poor Relief (*Almosenherren*). Even wandering monks and preachers belonging to mendicant orders, whose poverty was a matter of faith, had to be reported to the authorities.[29]

Decrees and ordinances repeating these basic points appeared repeatedly throughout the sixteenth and seventeenth centuries, increasing in frequency, severity, and detail as the city's economic problems escalated. A decree issued in 1594, blaming many harmful occurrences on "nonresident idlers and frivolous persons" staying in taverns, reduced the length of stay permitted without registration from three nights to one, and it specified that the registration should include not only the guest's name and date of arrival but also the intended length and purpose of the visit. These instructions were reissued repeatedly thereafter.[30]

However insistent the tone of these ordinances, they were not specific on exactly who qualified as suspicious or frivolous (*leichtfertig*). The earlier ordinances theoretically required that all guests be registered, but the council's intention was clearly not to hinder those persons who had legitimate business in the city or to prevent journeymen or laborers from seeking employment. Thus the authorities were somewhat subjective in enforcing the rule. Tavern keepers interrogated on charges of lodging disreputable guests defended themselves by claiming that they took their guests to be honorable or noting that their guests behaved modestly and peacefully, giving no cause for suspicion. Only when an unregistered guest attracted the attention of the authorities was the tavern keeper arrested or fined. One brewer testified in his own defense in 1593 that the mayor himself had released him from the responsibility to register guests he took to be honorable. Otherwise, the mayor had told him, "he would need his own mayor to handle all the registrations."[31] Where the lodging of suspicious guests without registration was the only charge against a tavern keeper, he was normally released with a warning.[32]

The decision as to whether or not a guest was suspicious, then, seemed to rest with the tavern keeper, and it was the tavern keeper who had the most to lose should his judgment prove faulty. Far worse than an interrogation and a warning from the city council was the economic damage tavern keepers could suffer at the hands of disreputable guests. Publicans appear much more often as victims of crime than they do as collaborators, with their guests not only slipping out without paying the bill but taking everything from silver dishes to sheets along with them. Few tavern keepers were willing to risk giving shelter to guests who were known to consort with thieves, or destitute persons obviously unable to pay for their visit.[33]

The most costly of dishonorable guests for the tavern keepers, however, were not the poor or the destitute but those who either belonged to the titled nobility or managed to pass themselves off as such. A tavern keeper might lodge for months on credit guests he believed were wealthy. The result, should the lodger prove unable to pay the bill, could be devastating. In 1641 a Dutch aristocrat ended up in the tower (at his creditor's expense, in accordance with debt laws) after attempting to leave the city secretly without paying his tavern bill of over 200 gulden. A year and a half later, the tavern keeper's widow had to give up on collecting the debt, which she had hoped eventually to obtain from her debtor's relatives, because she could no longer afford the expense of keeping the aristocrat locked up.[34] According to the account of the traveling knight Hans von Schweinichen, his lord (the duke of Liegniz) managed during his stay in an Augsburg inn to run up a debt of over 1,400 gulden, which he was subsequently unable to pay. A wine seller whose elite guest ran up a bill of 800 gulden before secretly leaving the city in 1624 was unable to absorb the loss and ultimately had to give up his tavern entirely.[35]

Although broke or disreputable members of the nobility could threaten the livelihood of a tavern keeper, they were not the target of city legislation, for they rarely became a burden to the community at large. The guests that worried the authorities were those of lesser status whose means of subsistence was not clear and who seemed likely to burden the city's system of poor relief or engage in crime to survive. All ordinances addressing the registration of visitors targeted persons described as idler (*Müßiggänger*), frivolous (*leichtfertig*), and suspicious (*verdächtig*), but not until after the Thirty Years' War did the city council provide tavern keepers with a clear definition of the line between respectable and suspicious guests.

Beginning in 1655 city leaders introduced a more bureaucratic system of control, which specifically targeted visitors they perceived as threatening to stability. The new ordinance provided publicans with a list of those visitors who were required to obtain a pass or billet (*Billette*)[36] at the city gate, on which was noted their first and last names, place of origin, destination, where they intended to lodge, how long they intended to stay, and with whom they had business in the city. Persons requiring such a pass included: victims of fire or other catastrophes who might be seeking alms; impoverished soldiers; poor servants seeking positions and others who may be entitled to poor relief; commoners seeking work or service; journeymen seeking a master; and nonresident beggars and poor old people deserving of alms. The aim of the authorities, then, was not just to keep suspicious or criminal elements out of the city but also to keep track of all those who might become a social burden. Legitimate seekers of poor relief could obtain permission from the mayors' office to collect alms for one to three days, and incoming journeymen had three days to find work. Specifically excepted from the requirement to obtain a pass were local residents, persons bringing goods into the city to sell, and familiar neighboring peasants and craftsmen. The gatekeepers at those gates through which nonresidents were allowed to enter were charged with filling out the forms, informing arriving visitors of the rules, and directing journeymen to their craft hostel. Only tavern keepers who ran houses designated as craft hostels could lodge wandering journeymen; other tavern keepers were expected to send them to the appropriate hostel. Finally, city bailiffs and night watchmen, already charged with making regular rounds of the taverns after nightfall and reporting any unruly behavior, received the added duty of reporting all tavern guests in the noted categories to the mayors' office.[37] Through the guards at the gates, the watchmen in the streets, and the publicans in their taverns, the city council hoped to create a tight network of information and control centers that would allow them to keep tabs on all visitors to the city.

Craft Hostels

After the fall of the guild-based government in 1548, Augsburg's artisans no longer had access to the guildhalls that had formerly served as employment office, conference hall, social center, and political base for the various guilds. It was only the last of these that had proved unsettling to the emperor. All the other functions, which were necessary for the social and economic organization of the different crafts, were taken over by taverns designated as craft hostels. The space that public taverns provided for craft meetings allowed craft traditions to continue with an increased measure of control by the authorities.

The designation of a particular tavern as a craft hostel was more than an organizational definition. It bestowed a special honor on the tavern keeper, his house, and his entire household. The tavern keeper who hosted a craft hostel received the title hostel father (*Herbergsvater*) or craft father (*Hand- werksvater*). His wife, accordingly, was often called Mother, and the other members of his household (children and servants) were addressed as Brother and Sister by the members of the craft. These terms convey the artisans' vi- sion of the craft organization as a family-like structure, with all members united in a brotherhood. The father figure of this brotherhood was respon- sible for providing for the welfare of its members in the form of food, drink, and space for craft meetings and hospitality for incoming journeymen. In re- turn, he received not only payment for the drinks consumed at the crafts- men's meetings and rituals but the esteem and respect that the symbolic head of a household deserved.[38]

As noted above, the designated craft hostel was the first point of contact for wandering journeymen arriving in the city. A period of travel, or wan- dering, was a traditional part of the journeyman's education, and it was one of the requirements in many trades for becoming a master. During the Mid- dle Ages, wandering journeymen were normally offered hospitality by local guild masters, but the forced sharing of living quarters by journeymen and masters who had not yet agreed to enter into a professional relationship was an unsatisfactory arrangement. Like other forms of hospitality, the lodging of wandering journeymen was commercialized and taken over by public houses in the early modern period.[39]

On arrival at the hostel, journeymen were welcomed by the hostel father, who provided the newcomer with food and drink (normally without com- pensation) and sent for representatives of the craft. If the journeyman was seeking work in the city, the designated craft representatives helped him to find a position with a master.[40] Nonresident journeymen had three days ei- ther to find a position or to move on. The rule that journeymen seek lodg- ing only in their designated hostel served to control irresponsible or idle craftsmen as well as to streamline the job-hunting process for those serious about finding work.

Besides providing a point of contact for wandering journeymen, the hos- tel maintained a private drinking room for members of the craft (although in the case of the poorer trades, the drinking room might be open to the public when craft meetings were not in progress). The right to a private drinking room was also a matter of prestige to craftsmen, and not every craft could afford the privilege. Those who could, normally crafts of somewhat higher social and economic status, received the prestigious designation *geschenktes Handwerk*. The term *"geschenkt,"* which in modern German translates to the word "given" (as a gift), is often erroneously thought to originate in the gift of food, lodging, and money that was offered to wandering journeymen on their arrival at the hostel. The term more likely, however, derives from the same root as *"Schenke,"* or drinking room, and it refers to the welcoming toast that symbolized the journeyman's acceptance into the local guild or craft (*Geschenk*). The social reputation of these *geschenkte* crafts was represented by the welcome cup (*Willkommen*), an often elaborately decorated vessel of pewter or silver from which the ritual welcoming toast was drunk.[41] The welcome drink, the drinking vessel, and the drinking room were symbols of the honor and prestige accorded the trade.

Members of the craft met in the craft hostel at regular intervals, normally monthly, to conduct the administrative affairs their craft required, to elect representatives, and to honor arriving journeymen and visiting masters with drinks. The focus of these monthly meetings was the *Büchse*, a box or cabinet that contained the property of the craft organization, including money collected from members as monthly fees and fines, governing ordinances, and sometimes the *Willkommen* cup and other drinking vessels. The ceremonial opening of the *Büchse* signified the official start of the craft meeting. As long as the box was open, strict rules of conduct and protocol had to be observed.[42] Although a separate public room in the tavern might remain available to other guests while the craftsmen conducted their business, the meetings themselves were conducted in a private room. The only persons who participated in the rituals other than members of the organized craft were the hostel father and his children or servants (and possibly the hostel mother as well).[43] The authorities tolerated secret craft meetings because they recognized the importance of the ceremonies. Trade secrets needed to be protected, and secret rituals allowed local masters to tell if arriving journeymen had been properly initiated into the craft. The presence of guild masters and the hostel father at the meetings also ensured control by persons of authority. The normally public space of the tavern in this case served to protect the privacy of the craft.

Aside from these regular meetings, craftsmen also gathered in their hostel to celebrate more informal occasions such as important sales contracts or the acceptance of a new journeyman. The copious amounts of alcohol consumed at the various guild activities would have more than offset the small loss of profit that the tavern keeper sacrificed in providing free room and board for arriving journeymen.

With the worsening economic conditions of the later sixteenth century, the status of the journeyman became a long-term position for many, rather than a step on the way to becoming a master and setting up an independent workshop. For these journeymen, the hostel could become a permanent home, for it was often a more attractive alternative than sharing quarters indefinitely with a master and his family. The hostel father and hostel mother in this case played an even greater role as symbolic parents.[44] At the same time, rising prices (which particularly affected alcoholic drinks) meant that the obligatory drinking bouts associated with guild life began to strain the limits of the younger journeymen's purses. Augsburg's journeymen loden weavers, who were low on the economic scale, were particularly hard hit by this demand. In 1591 some tried to refuse to attend the monthly drinking bout. The leaders of their journeymen's association, however, had no choice but to increase the pressure to attend by raising fines. Otherwise, they risked losing their drinking room altogether, for their hostel father threatened to open the room to the public if they did not consume a reasonable amount each month.[45] The result would not only be loss of access to a private room for their ceremony but a loss of status for the craft.

The closing of the guildhalls in 1548 was a political move aimed at breaking and diffusing the political power of the larger guilds. The intent was not to suppress guild traditions or to interfere with the networking and support systems on which artisans depended for their security. The authorities knew that the city's economic strength was tied to the productivity of the artisans, who made up its largest socioeconomic group. Taverns operating as craft hostels provided a stable base of operations for this important class of citizens. At the same time, the public tavern allowed the authorities a larger measure of control over the activities of organized crafts than had the private guildhalls. The tavern thus supported the city council's interests in preventing the organization of politically powerful guilds and controlling itinerant craftsmen.

The Social Functions of the Tavern

Military Recruitment and Quartering

Positions with masters and as day laborers were not the only jobs that one could contract in public taverns. The nature of the tavern as a public meeting place lent itself to another sort of employment operation—military recruitment. The primary concern of the city council in military matters was local defense, and thus it did not tolerate recruitment of local citizens by foreign powers in Augsburg taverns. The penalty for enlisting to a foreign power was loss of citizenship.[46] Foreign recruiters, however, did operate in Augsburg taverns along with local and imperial military representatives, for local citizens were not the only source of new recruits. Persons from outside Augsburg sometimes reported the intention to enlist as their reason for entering the city.[47]

The combination of public space and drink that the tavern offered was particularly convenient for military recruiters. As in the case of other contracts, the fact that the recruitment took place in a public space made witnesses easy to find. The tavern keeper sometimes signed recruiting contracts as an official witness.[48] Persons wishing to enlist not only received an immediate cash payment (*Laufgeld*) from the recruiter but also a drink afterward to seal the contract (fig. 10). The offer of cash and drink was naturally irresistible to some tavern patrons, particularly those who were broke, unemployed, and already under the influence of alcohol. Tavern customers who contracted to enlist while in a drunken state could get out of the contract by returning the *Laufgeld,* for the actual enlistment (swearing in) did not take place until the recruit appeared at the muster, at a time and place designated by the recruiter.[49] However, if the recruit had spent the money in the meantime and was unable to return it, then failure to appear for the muster could lead to arrest and possible punishment. Even more serious was signing up twice and accepting two payments from different recruiters, which constituted fraud (*Betrug*) and was punishable by banishment even after the money had been returned.[50]

Besides functioning as recruitment centers, taverns also served the military as quarters for soldiers. As was the case with other forms of hospitality, soldiers were originally quartered in private homes, but commercial taverns assumed this function during the sixteenth century.[51] Unlike other forms of hospitality, however, the quartering of soldiers was often forced on tavern keepers against their will, and it could be contrary to their interests. Tavern keepers were not expected to provide this service without charge, and some publicans no doubt profited from taking in soldiers; but the many complaints that tavern keepers registered about these unruly boarders leaves the impression that the housing of soldiers was often more costly than profitable.

Soldiers seem to have been most unpleasant guests. Tavern keepers complained that they kept other guests out of the taverns, either refusing to allow them in or frightening them off with their disorderly behavior, and that they threatened the wives and families of their hosts as well. One tavern keeper asserted that he could not be sure of life and limb as long as the soldiers were in his house; another publican reported that a soldier had beaten his crippled daughter.[52] When a group of brewers was arrested for failure to pay excise taxes in 1635, their wives petitioned to the city council for the release of their husbands on the grounds that soldiers were quartered in their houses, which exposed them and their children to "great danger."[53] Tavern keepers in Oberhausen, which was under the jurisdiction of Augsburg's council, who were forced to take on a company of new recruits in 1632 told stories of soldiers wrecking tavern property, injuring other customers, cursing, gambling, and committing all manner of "sins" and "blasphemies." The introduction of tobacco in the seventeenth century led to an even greater threat—soldiers, the tavern keepers complained, were smoking in the stables in a state of drunkenness, and they were certain eventually to burn down their stables, taverns, and yards.[54]

To make matters worse, collecting payment for the expenses incurred by quartered soldiers proved extremely problematic for the tavern keepers. Many complained that soldiers refused to pay or that they paid only "as much as suits their pleasure."[55] One tavern keeper petitioned to the War Commission in 1619 for reimbursement after soldiers left secretly during the night without paying their bill of 500 gulden, leaving an additional 400 gulden in damages and stealing much of his silver, linens, and other property as well.[56] Many tavern keepers submitted itemized bills to the War Commission or to the city council, showing the exact amounts of food and drinks consumed by their military guests who left with unpaid bills of as much as 1,500 gulden. Based on the bills, the soldiers spared no expenses while staying in Augsburg's taverns. Where bills are itemized, they show most guests drinking one or more measures of beer or wine per meal plus larger amounts in the evening.

Officers ate and drank more than foot soldiers, often choosing expensive imported wine, as well as drinking (with their wives) vermouth or brandy in the morning. On many days they invited guests and held banquets, consuming at one meal amounts equal to five or six days' ordinary board.[57]

Tavern keepers rarely seemed to receive satisfaction for unpaid bills. The city council refused one bill because, they claimed, the landlord had overcharged anyway, and others were turned down because the claims were submitted too late. When the quartered soldiers were imperial troops, their hosts frequently reported that they did not know to whom they could turn with their claims; and even when they applied to the appropriate authorities, the processing of the claim could take years.[58] Some tavern keepers complained that the debts and damages caused by quartering soldiers had forced them to go into debt themselves in order to keep the tavern running and that they would be forced to close their doors permanently if their losses were not recovered. One such frustrated publican lamented in 1561 that no matter how long the destructive members of the imperial regiment stayed in his house or how much damage they caused, they refused to pay him "a single Heller," noting only that "his imperial majesty is rich enough."[59]

Despite the burden it placed on tavern keepers, the quartering of soldiers was a function that served the needs of city authorities. Augsburg did have permanent military quarters after 1582 when the first wing of the barbican barracks (*Zwinger*), housing for soldiers and guards, was erected on the city wall. The Zwinger was expanded between 1585 and 1597 to a total of 274 apartments, a development that can only have been welcomed by Augsburg's tavern keepers.[60] The permanent quarters were hardly sufficient for the troops housed in the city during the Thirty Years' War, however, when even private citizens were again forced to take in soldiers. But the burden fell hardest on the tavern keepers. When the beleaguered brewers petitioned in 1634 with the request that more of the share of quartering be taken over by other Augsburg residents, many of whom also had large houses and sufficient stables, the quartermaster reminded them that, unlike other citizens, tavern keepers were bound by "duty and oath" to maintain public space and stables.[61] Thus the beds, stables, cellars, and kitchens of the local taverns, with or without the consent of their landlords, continued to stand ready to meet the needs of civic and imperial defense.

Weddings

The point of marriage was a crucial stage in the life of early modern citizens. For most crafts, marriage was a required prerequisite to achieving the status of master craftsman and thus marked the beginning of an independent career as well as an autonomous family life. The public celebrations attending this step reinforced its meaning to the couple and the community and mirrored the social and sexual differences of the participants.[62] For most of Augsburg's citizens, the tavern provided the center stage on which this public ceremony was enacted. Here again, the public access the tavern provided also allowed the authorities an added measure of control over these important communal events.

The process began with a public announcement of the engagement, which might itself take place in a tavern. A priest sometimes witnessed this exchange of promises. An official engagement was dependent on prior conclusion of property arrangements, and like any other contract, it was sealed with a ceremonial drink. From the point of engagement, the couple was referred to as bride and groom. The engagement was afterward confirmed by an all-male drinking party (*Untertrunk*), which was attended by a combination of journeymen and masters who represented the groom's passage from one peer group to the other. All of these ceremonies served publicly to verify the validity of the marriage promise.[63]

The wedding itself was a very public affair. Most socially significant was the procession through the streets to and from the church, for testimony from witnesses who had seen this public procession more often served to confirm the legitimacy of the marriage than did church records.[64] The public nature of this event was prescribed by ordinance. Weddings were not to be confirmed in "houses or secret corners"; rather, wedding ordinances required the couple to go "publicly to church and street," thus ensuring that the union was witnessed by the community.[65] The processions, parties, and dances accompanying weddings also provided an opportunity for the couple and their families to display their wealth as a symbol of social prestige. Wealthier citizens punctuated their wedding ceremonies with fireworks, tournaments, and other impressive public displays, making the entire city witness to the match.

Augsburg's wedding ordinances distinguished between two categories of wedding celebrations. Although all were meant to have a public character, those parts of the festivities not held openly in the church and the streets—the wedding feasts and dances—were defined and regulated differently according to whether they took place in private or public houses. Citizens who could afford it (normally the elite members of the Lords' and Merchants' Drinking Rooms) held private weddings, for which the bride and groom and their families paid the bill. Most of the festivities for these elaborate affairs took place in the home of the couple, although the Lords' and Merchants' Drinking Rooms could also serve as wedding halls. Wedding dances for private weddings were held in the Dance House on the Wine Market.[66]

Commoners, however, normally held their weddings in public taverns. In Augsburg such weddings were at the expense of the guests—that is, each guest paid for his or her food and drinks. The purpose of this system was to prevent couples from ruining their financial future on their wedding day, for craftsmen, too, were compelled by tradition to provide evidence of their economic viability through public displays of wealth. Wedding ordinances carefully regulated not only the number of guests one might invite but also placed limits on types and amounts of food that might be served, including a clause forbidding people to bribe the tavern keeper to offer richer fare than that which the ordinances prescribed.[67] Even at weddings, then, the tavern in Augsburg represented public rather than private hospitality, for while the bridal pair officiated as hosts of these affairs, their hospitality was obtainable only at a price.

Permitting commoners to hold weddings at the expense of their guests also allowed the authorities to establish two sets of rules. Those able to give weddings at their own expense could invite more guests, dance later, and hold special celebrations in their homes that were forbidden to those holding their weddings in public taverns. Fines for violating the ordinances, too, varied according to the financial position of the bridal pair. Overstepping the more generous rules allowed the financially advantaged resulted in a higher fine, two to four times greater than that charged "the commons."[68] The ability to pay whatever fines were necessary to increase the size and extravagance of the wedding, however, could only have augmented the prestige of the hosts, regardless of their social status. As Lyndal Roper put it, "rule-breaking was itself a sign of social standing."[69]

In addition to the separate rules for private and public wedding celebrations serving to protect the financial resources of the bridal pair, the rules also provided the increased measure of publicity the city council considered necessary for the weddings of common craftsmen. Only those believed by the authorities to be financially stable, thus not likely to become a liability to the community, were allowed to marry. Proof of acceptance into a craft or guild was a prerequisite for the marriage of local citizens; and those applying for citizenship not only had to provide proof of sufficient economic assets but also had to take an oath not to apply for alms or any other form of poor relief for a period of ten years after the wedding. In 1604 the authorities gave tavern keepers a share in the responsibility for controlling the weddings of commoners by warning them not to allow weddings on their premises, or to participate in the invitation of wedding guests, before they had been supplied with a written statement of approval or wedding pass (*Hochzeitzettel*) from the authorities.[70]

Those present in the tavern company at the public weddings of commoners served further to confirm the legitimacy of the match, and they might be called on later to verify that an engagement or a wedding had been celebrated. Birth certificates sometimes named the tavern in which the parents had held their wedding party as supporting evidence of a legitimate birth. The tavern keeper, too, was a convenient public witness to the marriage, often appearing as official witness to weddings that were celebrated in his house.[71]

The marriage union in early modern society represented more than a sexual union. It was proof of acceptance into adult society, indicating stability, citizenship, masterhood, and economic health. The public tavern allowed common craftsmen to celebrate this important event publicly and communally, yet without straining their financial means. At the same time, the professional publicity of the tavern keeper and the tavern premises allowed the authorities an additional measure of control over the weddings of commoners.

The Tavern and the City Budget

We have briefly outlined a number of social functions served by Augsburg's taverns. These functions promoted the interests of the authorities more often than running counter to official aims, and they frequently provided the council with a means of exerting control over the populace as well. In the eyes of the city government, however, the most important contribution made by Augsburg's taverns was to the city budget. In addition to the property taxes paid by tavern keepers, taverns supplied a major source of income to the city in the form of indirect tax payments on alcohol sales.

Taxes on alcohol in Augsburg dated from 1360, when Emperor Charles IV granted the city the privilege of collecting excise taxes on "mead, wine, and beer and . . . all sorts of like drinks that are served," and to use the revenues of the tax for "city debts, use, and necessities."[72] City leaders first exercised the privilege in 1363, establishing a tax on alcoholic beverages for the purpose of financing the completion of city fortifications. The tax was supposedly a temporary measure, initially established for ten years.[73] At the end of the ten-year period, however, instead of lifting the tax as promised, the council imposed additional taxes on other goods (grain, cloth, spices, and iron).

Continued failure to lift the tax resulted in an organized protest in the autumn of 1397, when guild members gathered to demand an end to taxes on wine and beer. The city council met with guild representatives and provided financial evidence to show that the city could not function without taxing beverages, but their efforts did not succeed in quieting the protest. To prevent a full-scale riot, the council agreed to relax the tax temporarily. The chronicles are in disagreement on the details of this event, and it is unclear whether the tax was ever actually lifted. What we can determine from these confused accounts, however, is that many guild members were unhappy with the excise tax but that city leaders, including the majority of the guild leaders on the Large Council, did not believe the city could survive without it. In any case, the tax was back in force less than a year later.[74]

The council was probably not exaggerating when they made the claim that the excise tax on alcohol was crucial to the survival of the city. By the mid-sixteenth century, this revenue had surpassed the property tax to become the city's single most important source of real income (that is, other than loans). The importance of the excise taxes continued to increase in relation to other forms of income throughout the sixteenth and seventeenth centuries, averaging over 50 percent of Augsburg's revenue between 1550 and 1650; in some years, the figure topped 70 percent (see graph 1).[75]

The city account "wine tax" (*Wein-Ungeld*) included revenues from sales on all alcoholic beverages (wine, beer, mead, and brandy).[76] Brandy first appeared as a separate entry in 1472, but after 1543 brandy taxes were included under the *Wein-Ungeld* account. Excise taxes on wine and brandy were paid at the point of purchase at the Wine Market; and beer taxes were charged based on inspections by a beer inspector (*Visierer*), who visited the brewers'

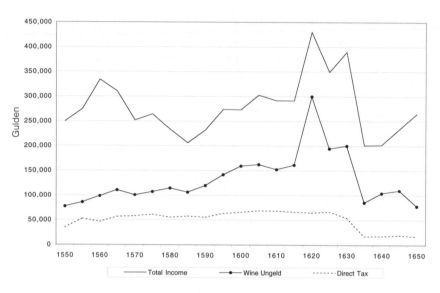

Graph 1. City Income, 1550–1650, in Five-Year Averages

cellars and noted the types and amounts brewed. Kegs of wine and beer that had been properly taxed were marked with a seal. The tax was then passed on to the customer in the price of the drinks. Beer brewed for household use was not subject to the retail tax, and private citizens able to brew beer could therefore avoid paying excise taxes. Civic income from beer brewing came only from public taverns.[77]

   Always an important source of income, the tax on alcohol became particularly crucial during the difficult years of the Thirty Years' War. Temporarily raising this tax had served the city well in the past—a hike in wine tax had helped to finance the cost of peace with the emperor in 1547, and the same measure in 1596 raised money to support the war with the Turks.[78] When the costs of the Thirty Years' War became too burdensome, the city council again found that there was "no more comfortable means" by which to offset them than to raise the tax again.[79] The first major tax raise came in 1623, and the income that resulted made up over 80 percent of the sharp rise in total city revenue that occurred in that year. The tavern keepers found this solution more burdensome than the war, however, and many filed complaints. The following year, the tax was returned to the former rate, although a higher tax on brandy remained in effect.[80]

The Social Functions of the Tavern

The city was forced to raise the tax on alcoholic beverages again between 1633 and 1635, but this time the results were less spectacular. Part of the increase was in the form of an additional duty originating not from the Office of Excise Tax (*Ungeldamt*) but from the Income Office (*Einnehmeramt*), which was responsible for managing the overall city budget.[81] Graph 2, which represents the income from alcohol taxes during the war years, shows that income did increase as a result of the added tax, but the drastic drop afterward resulting from the overall desperate economic situation the city faced during the siege of 1634–1635 effectively eliminated any long-term advantage.[82] In graph 1, which depicts income as a series of five-year averages, the raise in taxes in 1634 is scarcely discernible. Nonetheless, as graph 1 also indicates, the income from alcohol taxes made a quicker and more solid recovery after the siege than did the income from direct (property) taxes. Also apparent is the fact that the relative importance of wine tax to city income, as compared to that of the direct tax, increased steadily throughout the war years.[83]

Clearly, the city was dependent on this source of income, and the authorities dealt harshly with tavern keepers and illegal purveyors of drink who

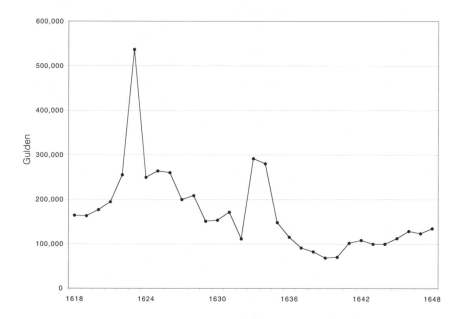

Graph 2. Wine Tax Income during the Thirty Years' War

attempted to avoid the tax. One wine seller caught placing old tax seals on new barrels in 1550 was whipped, exposed on the pillory, and banished for life for his offense against civic duty.[84] Illegal wine sellers and distillers were also dealt with swiftly, and thus they hardly appear in the records, either as a source of concern for the authorities or in the testimony of persons charged with other crimes.

Most often the target of complaints by the Office of Excise Tax were brewers, who brewed their own beverages rather than buying them at the open market and therefore could more easily avoid taxes by understating production. Periodically, groups of brewers were discovered engaging in tax evasion and arrested. Although the large numbers of brewers involved in such cases made banishing or permanently dishonoring them counterproductive, they did face imprisonment in the tower or in irons as well as heavy fines.[85] During one such roundup of delinquent brewers in 1591, the beer inspector was found guilty of collaborating with the tavern keepers. Sixty-seven brewers were interrogated in the case, and a total of sixty ultimately paid fines ranging from 6 to 450 gulden (the average was 136 gulden). Some also spent time in irons. The beer inspector was banished from Augsburg for life, and the city collected a total of 8,170.5 gulden in fines.[86]

Another major arrest occurred during the difficult years of the Swedish occupation in 1632–1635, when a group of twelve brewers faced charges of selling untaxed beer. The brewers defended themselves on the grounds that they were only trying to survive. If they paid the high war taxes on all of their beer, nearly all defendants claimed, they would lose money rather than making a profit and be forced out of business. Similar complaints were filed by other brewers, who noted that the 500 percent rise in beer taxes in conjunction with the burden of quartering soldiers in their houses was more than they could manage. The Income Office responded with the hope that God would see fit to improve the situation soon, but meanwhile, the taxes were unavoidable. The guilty brewers, unable to pay hefty fines like those collected in 1591, nonetheless had to pay an additional surcharge on all beer brewed during the following four years.[87]

Excise tax evasion was more than an infraction of the brewers' ordinance, or even a violation of the brewer's oath. It was a breach of the duty of citizenship. Persons arrested in such cases faced accusations of "injury" to the city, committing tax fraud, and "breach of civic duty."[88] By brewing, buying, and serving taxed drinks, tavern keepers provided the city with its most valuable source of revenue. The welfare of the community depended on the tavern keepers' business and their compliance with the demands of the Office of Excise Tax. As long as they did comply, as the Augsburg patrician Markus Welser noted, "The daily excesses in boozing [brought] to the city coffers a great and notable profit."[89]

The fact that taverns were centers of social interaction and professional contact made them the ideal location for activities threatening to the social order, such as planning social protests, spreading subversive information, and other secret plots. In both of the cases discussed above in which groups of brewers were arrested for tax evasion, for instance, the interrogators spent much of their time trying to uncover a planned collusion or plot among the accused parties, even threatening the brewers with torture. The interrogators charged the brewers with holding secret tavern meetings, having drinking parties with the beer inspector, or providing him with bribes in their cellars. Participants in the uprising of 1524 were also interrogated about tavern meetings, as were convicted thieves and gamblers suspected of having accomplices.[90]

The authorities, however, were rarely successful in proving that taverns provided cover for illegal plots or schemes, and there is no evidence that they considered taverns on the whole to be suspicious. Tavern keepers had little to gain and everything to lose by allowing illegal activities on their premises or lodging disreputable guests. The fact that thieves or other criminals chose certain taverns as haunts seems to be more a reflection of the tavern's popularity than any disreputable associations. The most notorious of Augsburg's taverns was the aptly named *Finstere Stube* (gloomy room), which served as home base for a sinister band of thieves during the 1590s.[91] Yet this tavern was also a regular haunt of Augsburg's elites.[92] The brewer Hans Schnegg's tavern in the Frauenviertel is another one of the spots most often appearing as the site of disturbances during this period; but Schnegg maintained a "Lords' table" (*Herrentisch*) for elite visitors and counted aristocrats and members of the House of Welser among his guests.[93] Clearly, city leaders did not consider these taverns — or, as far as I have been able to determine, any other tavern within Augsburg's city walls — to be disreputable. Thieves, fences, professional gamblers, prostitutes, and other marginal groups appear many times in the thousands of interrogation records on which this work is based, but in describing the details of their activities, they rarely if ever name as collaborators purveyors of drink of any kind.

Sociologists have long recognized that taverns serve certain social functions, including providing a meeting place for establishing and pursuing social relationships, a center for games and recreations, and a community of listeners with whom to work out personal problems.[94] Certainly, all of these functions were served by early modern taverns as well. In preindustrial society, however, the tavern was necessary to more than just the personal and social life of its customers. Taverns served legitimate needs that went far beyond the purveyance of drink and the provision of social space. Their contribution to society also far outweighed the concerns of authorities about suspicious gatherings, tavern brawls and disturbances, or other threats to social order. Taverns aided the authorities in exerting control over the populace. Through the public access that taverns supplied, the authorities were able to observe and at least partially control the movements of vagrants and wandering journeymen, the dissemination of information, the activities of crafts and guilds, and the weddings of commoners. In addition, taverns provided for civic income, defense, and the circulation of news and propaganda.

The public space that urban taverns and drinking rooms offered the community, then, served to support rather than threaten the orderly functioning of society. For how could society function without information networks, employment and sales contracts, meetings, weddings, defense, and income? City leaders therefore had an interest in keeping taverns running and in keeping alcohol sales profitable. This concern was bound to come into conflict with reformers' attempts to curtail excess drinking, for all of the above named activities were linked by tradition to drinking rituals and drinking bouts.

10

Drinking and Public Order

Carnival versus Lent

THE PERIOD OF religious reform in Germany was accompanied by a comprehensive attack on drunkenness that faded out during the late sixteenth and early seventeenth centuries, the era associated with increased social control, enforced discipline, and, according to some historians, reform of popular culture. Drinking controls in Augsburg were being relaxed just as other institutions of social control, such as sumptuary laws and restrictions on vagrants, were being introduced. What, then, were the city leaders actually trying to control, and why? And how were these control mechanisms put into practice? The answers to these questions provide us with a new perspective on the issue of social discipline.

The social discipline model, particularly as applied by historians who see a process of acculturation or suppression of popular culture, not only overestimates the extent to which the ideals of the reformers were successfully received or systematically applied but underestimates the negotiating power of the popular classes as well. The development of tavern controls in Augsburg reveals neither a process of suppression or oppression nor an attempt to enforce religious discipline. What emerges instead is a process of bargaining and concession between government and community along common lines of communication and in observance of shared norms.

This chapter begins with an examination of the controls placed on tavern drinking during the sixteenth and seventeenth centuries, tracing changes in legislation and comparing the strict letter of the law to the variations in treating offenders. This is followed by an analysis of one piece of legislation that reveals some of the motives of the authorities in establishing controls on drinking. The results will provide a basis for drawing conclusions about the relationship between norms of control (written) and norms of practice (unwritten). These unwritten norms often diverge from, or even conflict with, official norms of control. In the case of controlling drinking spaces and practices, the ordinances issued by city authorities seem to represent an attack on popular behavior, but the unwritten norms to which they adhered rarely came into conflict with popular norms.

In his discussion of the conflict between Carnival and Lent depicted in Pieter Brueghel's painting, Peter Burke defines traditional culture as that belonging to the laboring classes, primarily craftsmen and peasants.[1] Poised in opposition to this traditional ethic (Carnival) is that of the educated reformers, the clergy (Lent). Lacking in the analysis, however, is an explanation of the relationship between the clergy and secular authority. The ruling classes of the early modern city belonged neither to the clergy nor usually to the ranks of the learned (university educated).[2] The relationship between populace and authority in Augsburg suggests that Carnival in this model, and by extension the tavern, might have easily been described as representing not just the laboring classes but all of secular society.

The Control of Tavern Drinking

Controls on tavern drinking published in Augsburg during the sixteenth and seventeenth centuries fell into five categories: restrictions of times during which drinking in taverns was allowed (when); restrictions on places in which Augsburg's citizens were allowed to drink (where); restrictions on certain persons (who); restrictions on drinking on credit (by what means); and restrictions on types of drinks (what). The discussion that follows is limited to controls specifically aimed at tavern drinking. Other regulations placed on tavern keepers—such as those controlling the quality of the drinks, tavern licensing, and visitors staying overnight in taverns—do not fall under the definition of controls on drinking, and thus they will not be examined in this chapter. Controls on drinking, however, should not be misunderstood as synonymous with laws against drunkenness, as the purpose of levying such controls could be, and generally was, entirely unrelated to concerns about citizens getting drunk.

Tavern drinking, like drunkenness, was primarily regulated by police ordinances, which provided not only for the policing of morals but also for public security, controlling such areas as public health (especially during outbreaks of disease), market and food regulations, fire and storm safety, and the control of credit.[3] Specific regulations governing tavern hours, drinks, tax control, and licenses also appeared as separate ordinances or entries in city council books or guild and craft records. Wedding ordinances restricted drinking practices at weddings, sometimes with great attention to detail. When all of these types of legislation are examined in relation to one another, it is possible to trace the changing concerns of city authorities over time and to tie shifting attitudes toward drinking not only to questions of a religious and moral nature but also to political, social, and economic conditions.

Generally, ordinances concerned with controlling taverns issued during the Reformation show a trend toward more specific and precise control, which peaks in terms of detailed legalism during the Zwinglian-style Reformation of 1537. The Zwinglian phase of Augsburg's Reformation came to an end in 1548, and after the Peace of Augsburg in 1555, Catholics and Lutherans shared government institutions in an uneasy peace. If the Zwinglian phase of Augsburg's Reformation was supported by the traditional guild values of work, marriage, and order, as Lyndal Roper has suggested,[4] then the traditional values associated with guild drinking customs might well have made possible a compromise with Lutheranism and Catholicism, both more tolerant of traditional culture. Indeed, while efforts to control disorderly elements in society increased during the difficult years of the late sixteenth century, attempts to control drinking did not. The second half of the century was marked by a gradual relaxation in most areas of tavern control; and by the seventeenth century, attacks on traditional drinking practices were no longer evident. Controls placed on tavern drinking over the course of the seventeenth century were increasingly related to fiscal rather than moral concerns. This is hardly surprising given the unstable economic situation; more interesting, however, is the consistency of the authorities in conceding to, and even actively supporting, the cultural drinking practices of the citizenry.

Wine Bells

In his "Drunken litany" (*Die trunkene Litanei*), Fischart sang praises to the all-night drinking bout:[5]

> We want to drink the whole night through,
> until the light of day,
> Bring wine, drink up, there's joy in the cup,

And he who doesn't share our joy,
Should not suffer to stay.

(*Geschichtsklitterung*, 121)

In reality, of course, a full night of carousing was a luxury few early modern Germans could afford. The practice was certainly discouraged by Augsburg's authorities, who placed limits on the time local citizens could spend
in the city taverns. Our examination of tavern controls begins, then, with the
regulation of operating hours.

Temperance historians who have analyzed tavern regulations during the
nineteenth-century temperance movement have linked the establishment
of restricted operating hours for taverns to the introduction of regulated
working hours during the period of industrialization. Closing times in this
explanation become another means of attacking disorder, reducing the opportunity for excessive drinking and enforcing time-regulated discipline.[6]
German historians have made a similar claim for the sixteenth century, placing the imposition of specific closing times within the general framework
of the attack on drunkenness.[7] The tavern closing time, however, was already
an institution throughout Germany by 1500. The traditional closing time for
taverns before that date was 9 P.M. Police ordinances issued in Augsburg between 1472 and 1537 all required tavern keepers to stop serving drinks at the
nine o'clock bell, although guests were allowed to remain to finish drinks ordered before 9 P.M.[8] In some cities, the evening bell that signaled closing time
was called the "wine bell," "beer bell," "drink bell," or "scoundrel bell."[9]

The establishment of a tavern closing time was less a means of reducing
excess drinking than it was a way of controlling public order during the hours
of darkness, which provided cover for possible criminal acts. The wine bell
also signaled the time at which lanterns were required to walk the streets,
and persons found in the streets after 9 P.M. (in some ordinances, 9 P.M. in summer and 7 P.M. in winter) without a lantern were subject to questioning on
suspicion of purposely wishing to remain unseen.[10] Numerous other ordinances also forbade singing, yelling, sleigh riding, and other frivolous activities in the streets at night; and they prohibited the winter carnival custom of
wearing masks to conceal the identity (*Mummerey*).[11] Overnight guests staying at taverns, who did not need to walk home through the streets in the
evening and were therefore not likely to create disturbances, were exempted

from the tavern closing time. Ordinances prescribed no specific time for closing the cellar to these visitors, leaving the decision to stop serving to the discretion of the tavern keeper.

In 1541 an attempt was made to reduce tavern hours drastically. The decree, issued in September of that year, limited serving hours in public taverns and guildhalls to two hours a day, between 1 and 3 P.M., on holidays as well as workdays. Exceptions were allowed only for toasts accompanying guild rituals, "in accordance with tradition."[12] The goal of the city council in issuing this ordinance, which also placed unprecedented restrictions on other drinking activities, was clearly to attack the drinking rather than to control persons wandering the streets at night. The concession to guild tradition was an exception in this unusually harsh decree, although, as we shall see, such concessions were to become the norm in later instruments of control.

A few tavern keepers and their guests did pay fines when guests were found drinking after 3 P.M., but enforcement was neither consistent nor effective.[13] A look at the interrogation records for 1541–1544 shows that in most cases in which any time frame was mentioned, tavern customers reported drinking in the evening or at night, or they said they were coming home shortly after 9 P.M., the traditional tavern closing time. Correlating records of punishments do not indicate that either drunken defendants or tavern keepers in these cases were charged additional fines for drinking or serving after 3 P.M. The last fine for drinking after 3 P.M. was recorded in March 1542.[14] The Police Ordinance of 1553 again established tavern closing time as 9 P.M., where it remained until 1643, when it was extended to 10 P.M. Ordinances throughout the later seventeenth century reflect this change.[15] The short, failed attempt at limiting Augsburg tavern visits was not exceptional, for it mirrored similar efforts in cities in which Protestantism gained a more powerful hold. Calvin's efforts to close down city taverns in Geneva in 1546 lasted no more than two months, and Zwingli was equally unsuccessful in his attempts to severely limit tavern going in Zurich.[16]

Once closing time had returned to the traditional hour, it became even less of an issue.[17] Records of fines indicate that enforcement of the closing time was either very loosely applied or unnecessary. In the periods 1540–1544 and 1590–1594, an average of less than five tavern keepers and their guests per year were fined for drinking after hours, and there are no registers of fines for drinking after closing in the records of the seventeenth century.[18]

Tavern closing times would not have been particularly difficult to enforce, since city bailiffs and night watchmen patrolled the city regularly during the hours of darkness. Most likely, the closing time, as a traditional law concerned more with public safety than drinking, was either not disputed by the majority of the populace or enforced only when it resulted in disorderly behavior. If late-night pub crawling occasionally appeared as a point of dispute between embattled spouses, it was not otherwise a major issue to the authorities.

Tax Fortifications

There were no restrictions on social drinking in private homes other than the individual social drinking ban discussed in chapter 7. The seating of guests at public tables, however, was limited to establishments that met the requirements for a tavern license — that is, to taverns that could provide beds and stables for overnight guests as well as food, drinks, and tables. In 1563 city leaders put a cleanup effort into action to reduce the number of taverns, because, according to the Augsburg physician and humanist Achilles Pirminius Gasser, the streets were overburdened. Thereafter, city bailiffs strictly controlled the taverns to ensure that adequate numbers of beds and stables were maintained.[19] Designation as a public house obligated the publican to take a yearly oath that bound the tavern keeper to provide only unadulterated and properly taxed drinks.[20] In the case of brandy, which was sold not in taverns but by retail grocers (*Krämer*), distillers, or craftsmen in their shops, public consumption was legal until 1614 only while standing on the open street. After that date, guests could drink their allowed measure of brandy sitting down, but regulations severely limiting the amount one could drink at one sitting and forbidding the serving of food with brandy prevented the brandy sellers from coming into direct competition with the tavern keepers.[21]

The Augsburg government's greatest problem in controlling where its citizens drank, however, did not occur within the city walls but immediately without. The lure of the countryside and its bucolic pleasures, especially during peasant festivals such as the Kermis, was often noted in early modern literature.[22] The records suggest that Augsburg's citizens were regular visitors to village taverns not only during festivals but throughout the year. While country taverns might have been appealing to townspeople for various reasons, one of their greatest attractions was freedom from city taxes. The surrounding villages were not subject to excise taxes on alcohol, which could raise the price of wine by as much as 100 percent.[23] Obviously, Augsburg's ruling oligarchy was conscious of the importance to the city budget of excise taxes on alcohol. Many of the controls the city council placed on where drinking could legally occur, both within the city walls and beyond them, reflect the primacy of this concern.

Regulations forbidding Augsburg residents to drink in the outlying villages and monasteries, and also restricting them from purchasing drinks and bringing them into the city secretly, began to appear as a clause in the police ordinances in 1541. During the sixteenth century, the rule against village drinking continued to appear only in the more general police ordinances. By the economically troubled seventeenth century, however, Augsburg authorities started to issue regulations against drinking in the villages as separate decrees and with increasing frequency. Between 1600 and 1699 no less than twenty-one such decrees were printed in addition to the normal police ordinances.[24] The multiple regulations against drinking in the villages were difficult to enforce, since city watchmen and bailiffs could not patrol village taverns; only those caught carrying drinks or in a noticeably drunken state when returning through the city gates could be fined. The fine for craftsmen who drank outside the city was set at 2 gulden at least by the 1590s and gradually raised to 5 by the later seventeenth century. The fine for drunkenness, by comparison, remained at only ½ gulden throughout this period. Although patricians and members of the Merchants' Society, along with upper-level city bureaucrats (and eventually military officers), were exempted from the rule against drinking outside the city, they paid even higher fines than craftsmen for bringing untaxed wine through the gates.[25]

In spite of their obvious concern with the cash drain created by village drinking, Augsburg's authorities included concessions to cultural practice in their legislation against it. In addition to the exemption for city elites, they allowed exceptions to the rule not only for persons who were invited to village weddings but also for those who expected to be involved in legitimate business transactions outside the city that would require a contract drink. These cases were managed by the use of a drinking pass (*Zechzettel*), which was to be obtained through the mayors' office before leaving the city and could then be shown to prevent penalties for village drinking should any questions arise later. In 1607 a clarification expressing this concession was included in the village drinking decree, which noted that the rule against village drinking was to be understood to apply exclusively to those who "go out [of the city] only to drink."[26]

Sixteenth-century versions of the village drinking rule placed it in the general context of alcohol abuse. The 1541 ordinances located the ban on village drinking between statements concerning sots (*Trunkenbolde*) wasting money in taverns and blasphemers avoiding the sermon. In 1577 a revision to the Police Ordinance of 1553 blamed visits to village taverns for forcing families into poverty, because the men were leaving their wives and children at home to go on all-day drinking bouts.[27] The later ordinances, however, were more direct about the reason for the rule. Drinking in the villages, according to a 1630 decree, was affecting Augsburg's revenues from excise tax and negatively affecting the city budget.[28]

Augsburg's council was increasing its controls on village drinking just as it was loosening controls on closing times, distilled liquors, and drunkenness. The interests of the city leaders in controlling each of these areas were not identical. In the later ordinances that address village drinking as a tax issue, there is an indication of the real motivation behind the council's campaign to enforce order. An orderly society was a functioning society; and while drinking within the city walls helped to keep the cogs of government oiled, drinking tax-free in the villages slowed them down. The council's campaign against village drinking was not primarily aimed at controlling immoderate consumption. It was aimed at keeping the consumers in the city.

The Drinking Society of Orders

There was no one in early modern Germany who was not supposed to drink at all. Although physicians warned against giving wine to children, they allowed that a little wine mixed in a child's water was acceptable.[29] Residents in the poorhouse received daily allotments of wine or beer,[30] as did at least some prisoners being maintained in the tower.[31] Even the moralist literature of the period acknowledged that the first glass drunk was for thirst.[32] There were, however, people who were not allowed to drink in public taverns.

The group most consistently prohibited from tavern going were beggars and takers of alms. Organized poor relief was introduced in Augsburg during the sixteenth century, as the growing numbers of poor made institutions of control increasingly necessary. Throughout the sixteenth and seventeenth centuries, those receiving public alms were forbidden to visit taverns. Regulations threatened banishment for alms recipients found wasting their alms in taverns and promised the loss of all future poor relief. Alms recipients were also required by law to wear a white symbol indicating their status. Both the symbol and the ban on tavern visits served to exclude alms takers from the rest of society, placing them in a humiliating social position. These measures were intended not only to bring the rising numbers of poor under control but to discourage those not truly desperate from applying for poor relief.[33]

Although bans on public begging did not remain in force permanently, the rules against spending alms in taverns were strictly enforced when infractions occurred. Those alms recipients caught drinking in taverns were in every case banished from the city. Engaging in a drinking bout for these members of society, then, could mean a complete loss of subsistence and shelter, as well as separation from family. However, the offense was rare. Persons so poor as to be dependent on alms could scarcely afford the comforts of a tavern.[34]

Of even greater concern to the city council were those members of society who were not yet dependent on alms but whose drinking habits threatened to reduce them to begging. Persons in this category, generally married men accused of domestic violence and failure to provide, were placed by the council under the individual tavern ban discussed in chapter 7. Although ordinances threatened banishment for repeated infractions, in most cases in which the tavern ban was violated it was simply extended for an additional year. Only extreme cases of habitual drunkenness accompanied by violence, domestic or otherwise, resulted in banishment.[35] Breaking the oath to stay out of taverns was in any case prosecuted only when a disturbance or complaint, normally a dispute of some kind, brought it to the attention of the authorities. In most of these cases, where no serious crime had been committed, the ban could be extended for years without any noticeable effect.[36]

A final interesting aspect in the regulation of who could drink in public taverns was the problem in controlling the mayors' bailiffs, persons who themselves served as arms of civic control. There were six bailiffs who patrolled the Augsburg streets, representing civic authority.[37] One of the duties of the bailiffs was making regular visits to Augsburg's taverns and removing rowdy or troublesome customers. Other duties included arresting delinquents and escorting those found guilty to the pillory or out of the city. Because of their association with criminals, punishment, and the executioner, the mayors' bailiffs were a group who lived on the margins of dishonor.[38] Their status in Augsburg was not so dishonorable, however, as to make social drinking with craftsmen taboo; and this sometimes led to problems as the bailiffs made their evening rounds through the taverns. It was traditional practice to honor the bailiff with a drink as he made his rounds; and with around 120 taverns operating in the city, the temptation to take advantage of this tradition must have been great.[39] In 1540 bailiffs were forbidden to drink in public taverns, and in 1553 the city council recorded an end to the practice of providing the bailiffs with honorary "drink money," since they were getting drunk "on a daily basis."[40] The regulations were probably temporary, as cases involving bailiffs in taverns in the 1590s do not reflect that the restrictions were still in force. This apparently brief restriction on bailiffs is the only example appearing in the records of any group other than alms recipients and those under an individual tavern ban being officially ostracized from tavern sociability. While the executioner, as previously noted, was officially forbidden in some areas of Germany from drinking publicly with honorable persons, his exclusion from public drinking bouts in Augsburg seems to have been regulated by tradition rather than law.

The fact that poor and irresponsible persons were officially forbidden to visit taverns is not evidence that civic authorities in early modern Germany viewed the taverns as havens for these elements. On the contrary—by illuminating the boundary between acceptable and unacceptable spending and drinking habits, these exclusions show that the norm for tavern goers was responsible behavior. Persons incapable of meeting the requirements of respectability were excluded from the tavern company. If friction existed between respectability and the "poorer sort" during this period,[41] then Augsburg's taverns stood squarely on the respectable side of the conflict.

Drinking on Credit

A certain road to economic ruin for problem drinkers was drinking on credit. Drinking more than a single drink or measure of wine on credit or with a security marker (*Pfand*) was therefore made illegal. To ensure that tavern keepers did not allow credit to their customers, the city council recognized no legal recourse for bringing civil charges against debtors. Customers were not legally obligated to pay for any food, drink, or cash received on credit or with a marker from a tavern keeper.[42] Exceptions were allowed only for ill persons and pregnant women (for medicinal reasons). These regulations, however, were concerned solely with commoners, and they did not apply in the Lords' and Merchants' Drinking Rooms. In the Merchants' Drinking Room, up to 1 gulden credit was allowed, which could be used for food, drink, or gaming; and there was no regulation to control the use of credit by patricians.[43]

Since tavern keepers had no recourse to law should their customers fail to pay their bills, no official record of enforcement exists. Tavern keepers who offered credit did so at their own risk. Nonetheless, leaving a security marker of some sort, normally a knife, was a fairly common practice. If a customer attempted to leave the tavern without paying or was too drunk to understand the amount, publicans would resort to taking the customer's coat or knife by force.[44] Payment of such debts then became a matter of honor and reputation rather than a legal issue. Drinking songs praised tavern keepers who were willing to provide credit without a marker. If a publican was not so generous, the songs lamented, then drinkers would have no choice but to hand over their clothes, horses, and household goods, for that was the price of fellowship.[45]

Although the degree to which credit was actually extended by tavern keepers cannot be determined, the records do show that the extension of credit was not a major source of concern to the authorities. Descriptions of customers leaving security markers for tavern bills occur regularly in cases of tavern disputes, but only as incidental testimony. In no case did the authorities take any action against either the indebted customer or the tavern keeper who extended credit. Additional evidence to support the fact that the city council tacitly tolerated drinking on credit appears in the case of Daniel Schmied, a diamond-cutter who was charged by creditors in 1591 for failure to pay debts totaling over 100 gulden. Among those creditors listed were ten tavern keepers, to whom Schmied owed amounts ranging from ¾ gulden to over 4 gulden. Included in the case were promissory notes Schmied had signed for his creditors, among them a tavern bill witnessed by the mayor himself.[46]

There were exceptional situations in which drinking on credit could lead to serious problems, and in such cases the authorities would take action to curtail the debtor's spending habits. Drinking on credit caused problems for some soldiers, for instance; for unlike other tavern keepers, the beer seller in the private drinking room located in the military quarters (*Zwinger*) had the right to withhold his customer's pay in order to collect the debt. Thus he was more than willing to extend large amounts of credit. This led to a brief closure of the military drinking room in 1603 in the interest of the soldiers' other creditors, who complained about the unfair advantage of this privileged publican. Nonetheless, beer sales in the Zwinger were soon reinstated at the request of the Excise Tax Lords, "for the sake of the taxes" because the soldiers were leaving the city to drink.[47]

Also at issue were domestic cases involving failure to provide, in which drinking debts were occasionally cited as part of a general picture of irresponsible drinking and spending habits presented in the complaints of the drinkers' wives. Although such cases often resulted in a tavern ban, it was not specifically drinking on credit that led to punishment but disorderly householding. The line between responsible and irresponsible drinking was not drawn at the point at which a drinker resorted to credit but only at the point at which debts interfered with his ability to support himself and his household. Otherwise, leaving a marker as a promise to pay the bill was an acceptable and customary part of tavern tradition.

The Intemperate Use of Wheat

The beverages affected by controls on Augsburg's taverns during the sixteenth century and most of the seventeenth were wine, beer, and mead. A challenge was raised to the primacy of these traditional drinks, however, with the introduction of distilled liquors, first brandy and then gin. These new social substances, originally used only for medicinal purposes but gradually gaining ground as recreational drinks, were initially resisted both by the authorities and sellers of the more traditional drinks. City leaders' resistance was especially stubborn in the case of gin, which was nonetheless quickly assimilated by the populace, largely due to its inexpensive production price. By the end of the seventeenth century, distilled liquors were culturally integrated into Augsburg tavern life.[48]

Normally, taverns served only one kind of beverage. Brewers during the sixteenth century were apparently also allowed to sell wine; but as already noted, the practice was rare and was made illegal during the seventeenth century.[49] The city authorities limited beer brewing during periods of grain shortages by placing weekly limits on the amounts of barley and malt individual brewers were allowed to purchase.[50] The only official restrictions placed on wine sales were the requirements that the wines be properly taxed and sold pure and unmixed "as the Lord God gave them" (*wie ihn Gott der Herr gegeben*); although in practice, the better wines were normally reserved for the Lords' and Merchants' Drinking Rooms. The employees of the Lords' and Merchants' Societies had first rights to the purchase of these sweet wines as the wine merchants entered the city. Other residents had to wait until the wines were offered at the open market. Wedding ordinances also limited the use of better or sweet wines (mostly imported from Italy and Spain) at weddings for commoners, in the interest of avoiding excess expenditure.[51] What one might drink in this case was clearly defined by who was doing the drinking.

Police ordinances governing drunkenness and the seating of tavern guests generally included reference to mead along with wine and beer, but there were few mead taverns. The numbers of mead sellers appearing in military muster lists of the seventeenth century are insignificant, and real estate records verify the existence of only one permanent mead tavern between 1600 and 1650.[52] Unlike brandy sellers, mead sellers did seat guests in their taverns, but they differed from beer and wine tavern keepers in that they did not serve meals or provide facilities for overnight guests.[53] Otherwise, regulations on drinking mead did not differ from those on beer and wine. In any case, the drinking of brandy eclipsed that of mead by 1637, when economic necessity forced mead sellers, "because [their] business [had] completely collapsed," to take up selling brandy.[54]

Brandy was legal and taxable at least by 1472.[55] As already noted, brandy was not legally available in public taverns before the late seventeenth century but sold separately by grocers, apothecaries, and distillers. While taverns provided primarily evening entertainments, sixteenth-century Germans drank their brandy in the morning, much as we drink coffee today, for warmth and "strength."[56] The morning nip was supposed to serve as a quick pick-me-up on the way to work, but it was not to take the form of an early morning drinking bout. Regulations by 1536 limited the amount of brandy that could be sold for immediate consumption to 1 pfennig per customer per day, although this was gradually raised to accommodate rising prices.[57] The 1 gulden fine for serving more than the allowed measure of brandy does not seem to have been a very effective deterrent, however, as some brandy sellers paid the fine several times per year.[58] The fine was not raised for repeat offenses, and no restrictions were placed on brandy sales for home consumption.

The most tightly controlled drinks were those made of grain, especially wheat. Wheat beer and grain spirits were both gaining in popularity by the late sixteenth century, but their production came into competition with the provision of bread. Alcohol made with grains was the subject of considerable controversy during the sixteenth and seventeenth centuries. Doctors claimed that wheat beer was harmful to the health, and they occasionally blamed immoderate consumption of wheat beer for disease epidemics. The wheat-based beer was popular, however, and became the drink of choice for home brewing.[59] In 1568 a group of brewers, fearing competition from home-brewing industries, began to lobby against the production of wheat beer. Their protectionist efforts resulted in a temporary ban on commercial production and sales, which were forbidden entirely from 1568 to 1597. Private production and use of wheat beer in the home continued unregulated, and commercial production was resumed in 1597.[60] During the seventeenth century, temporary bans on wheat beer were established only during periods of grain shortage and outbreaks of plague.[61]

Even more controversial was the recreational drinking of distilled grain spirits. Imbibing these products, along with their production and sale outside the city apothecaries, remained illegal throughout the sixteenth and most of the seventeenth centuries. Eventually, though, distilled grain spirits were also institutionalized as legitimate substances. The first legislation specifically forbidding the production of wheat spirits for anything other than medicinal purposes appeared in 1570. It is probably no coincidence that legislation against wheat spirits was initiated in this year, which marked the beginning of the great famine that would peak during 1571–1572.[62] The legislation was introduced by the Office of Excise Tax, which condemned the spirits as "harmful to health, and a useless waste of wheat."[63] The Excise Tax Lords cited regulations against grain spirits already in force in Nuremberg and Frankfurt as precedence for passing an ordinance prohibiting its production in Augsburg. Licensed brandy sellers, they claimed, were not only selling the wheat spirits but they were mixing it with legitimate ("good") brandy, which was made from wine and not wheat.[64] Bringing grain spirits

Drinking and Public Order

into Augsburg was also illegal under the new law; and an official taster (*Kieser*) was appointed, charged with going to the homes of all brandy sellers in the city and tasting the brandy to ensure that it was good brandy.[65] The overt purpose of this measure was to protect customers from being cheated by sellers of "bad" brandy.

By the early seventeenth century, grain spirits, especially juniper water (*Cramatbeerwasser,* what we now know as gin), were gaining in popularity despite the resistance of city authorities; and sellers of legitimate brandy began to take a stand against the competition. They first petitioned in 1613 against the sale of juniper water, which persons coming into the city were selling inexpensively door-to-door. Recipes for a drink made from true brandy flavored with juniper appeared in print as early as 1505,[66] but the "false" (*falsch*) juniper water under attack by the brandy sellers was distilled from grain. The strong juniper taste masked the harsh flavor of the grain spirits, and the brandy sellers complained that the common man, whose judgment was limited (*der wenig Verstand hat*), was fooled as a result.[67] In addition, their brandy business was suffering. The city council responded with a special ordinance governing the sale of juniper water, which was legal only when made from taxed wine brandy and when sold at the apothecaries. The primary concern expressed by the Excise Tax Lords by this time was that the illegal spirits were causing the common man to be cheated out of his money, presumably because grain alcohol was cheaper to produce than wine brandy.[68] Lowering the price of grain spirits was no solution, as it would put the brandy sellers out of business, and it could lead to even greater abuse of distilled liquors.

Despite their continued efforts, the brandy sellers could do little to stem the growing popularity of these rival and inexpensive alternatives to legal brandy, and in 1623 the city council found it necessary to legislate against immoderate drinking of anise and juniper waters. This time the regulation was in response to complaints by Augsburg's apothecaries, who claimed that people were using the burnt, or strong, waters for drinking bouts and getting drunk on them. The apothecaries, who expected exclusive rights to the sale of spirits designated as medicinal, enlisted the help of local medical authorities (organized as the *Collegium Medicum*) to support the opinion that immoderate use of the burnt waters was harmful.[69] In 1631 brandy sellers again petitioned against the retail grocers and distillers, claiming that the grain spirits industry was going on in every corner of the city (*an allen Orthen vnd gassen der Statt*). Furthermore, they complained, the drinks were being sold openly in taverns and were not properly taxed, all of which was harmful to the common good (and to the welfare of the brandy sellers as well).[70]

By the seventeenth century, recreational drinking of distilled spirits was on the rise throughout Europe. The inexpensive spirits made from wheat became particularly popular among soldiers during the Thirty Years' War. New centers of grain spirits production appeared in other German cities as well; and by the end of the war, spirits from grain, including gin, were legal in Nuremberg.[71] Although prices during the seventeenth century increased across the board, wine remained more expensive as a basis for spirits than beer or wheat, and brandy was fast becoming a luxury item. Distillers, powerful enough by the 1630s to organize an effective lobby, were also able to make their arguments to the Augsburg council in the interest of the common man, who could no longer afford the costlier brandy.[72]

The last arrest for illegal production of wheat spirits in Augsburg was in 1643.[73] By 1674 grain spirits were being sold "openly as well as secretly" all over town, even at the Wine Market.[74] Gin was selling at six times the former rate, the brandy sellers complained, while brandy sales had dropped to a fraction of what they had been in past years. The excise tax on the sale of distilled liquors was by this time becoming an attractive source of city revenue. In view of the financial problems the city faced during the seventeenth century, the effect of the constant complaints by brandy sellers that grain spirits were being sold in every corner of the city served to strengthen the case for legalizing and taxing the spirits rather than for enforcing tighter restrictions. Records of the 1643 arrest do not mention the sale of a harmful substance, but they register punishment for "damaging the city" through the loss of excise tax.[75] The practical step, then, was to tax grain spirits and thus gain a financial advantage for the city. By the end of the seventeenth century, gin was fully integrated into tavern life and the stage was set for the "gin epidemic" of the early eighteenth century.[76]

The examination of public ordinances alone would indicate a black-and-white condemnation of grain spirits by civic authorities until the mid-seventeenth century. Afterward, there is no further reference to grain spirits until they reappear as acceptable products around 1700. A closer look at the documents, however, reveals that popular demand pressured the authorities into taking an increasingly moderate view in their treatment of offenders. Despite protectionist efforts by established purveyors of drink, the production and sale of gin became a gray area by the seventeenth century, with a decrease in fines and a shift in emphasis from protecting the people from harmful substances to the more practical concern with the difficulty in controlling and taxing the spirits.

In negotiating the proper role for these controversial beverages, the various members of the alcohol trade attempted to formulate their arguments to appeal to communal values, in the interest of the common man (*der gemeine Mann*) and the city at large (*die gemeine Stadt*). Their personal economic interests, although easily inferred, were rarely directly stated. The city council, likewise, used a moral and communal rhetoric in their regulating instruments, forbidding wheat beer because its use led to sin, shame, and vice and grain spirits because they incited further drunkenness, were harmful to the health, or fooled the common man.[77] The correspondence between periods of rising prices and grain shortages and discourse addressing the wasteful use of grain on alcoholic drinks was also useful, for famine and inflation could be represented as God's punishment for sinful abuse of the products. Popular demand for the grain-based drinks was great, however, and control was difficult. During the financially troubled seventeenth century, the lure of additional tax revenues from the popular grain spirits came to outweigh the negative effects of wasting wheat.

The Regulation of 1590: A Case Study in City Legislation

In each of the above five areas of drinking control, the rules were initially presented in a moralizing tone. Limits on types of drinks and on the time and money that persons might spend in taverns were established in "praise and honor of God Almighty," in order to prevent the common man from falling into gluttony and leaving his wife and children in poverty.[78] Yet when we compare these norms with the realities of legal practice, we do not find a struggle for moral reform or even a struggle for control of the drinking lives of Augsburg's citizens. The struggle was rather for control over taxes and poor relief, concerns that are reflected openly in the ordinances of the seventeenth century. In the case of tavern closing times, we find no struggle at all—the reduced hours established during the Zwinglian-style phase of government were not enforced by the authorities, and the closing of taverns during the hours of darkness in the interest of public security met with no apparent resistance by the populace. Rather than a confrontation between discipline and disorder, we find evidence of a shared consensus on what an orderly society should be.

The reasons for the decisions of the city council in most of these cases, although possible to surmise, remain somewhat opaque. On occasion, however, we are fortunate to uncover direct evidence of the authorities' actual concerns and interests in making their decisions. We now turn to the analysis of a controversial drinking law of the late sixteenth century. Through the discovery of private correspondence between the city council and a secret government committee charged with examining the drink question, we are able to examine the history of this remarkable piece of legislation from the point of view of those who created it.

In December 1590 Augsburg's city council announced a regulation restricting tavern drinking for craftsmen to Sundays, Mondays, and holidays. The decree was met with considerable resistance by local tavern keepers. Six years later, the decree was rescinded; it reappeared, however, in the seventeenth century, with certain revisions. The debate that took place behind the scenes in connection with this rule tells us much more about the attitudes the authorities held toward tavern drinking, and their goals in establishing controls on the populace, than can be learned from any public laws and decrees against drunkenness. Rather than an attempt to discipline popular society or to suppress or regulate popular cultural practice, what is revealed is concession to that practice and an attempt to employ it in the interest of the city.

The restriction passed in 1590 applied to all "citizens and residents,"[79] who were forbidden to drink or to be seated in taverns on workdays. The rule was in fact specifically aimed at craftsmen, however, specifying that no "weavers or craftsmen [or] journeymen" should be seated in taverns other than on Sundays, holidays, Good Mondays, or for weddings. Exceptions were allowed for patricians, merchants, and civil employees (city council members, tax collectors, members of the court, and other bureaucrats), as well as visitors to Augsburg.[80] The decree, according to city leaders, was passed in the interest of the common man and his wife and children to discourage craftsmen from spending excess time and money in taverns at the expense of their households. A revision to the Police Ordinance of 1580 to reflect the new rule (added in 1591) included the clarification that those of lesser station than craftsmen, such as day laborers and vagrants, were also subject to the restriction.[81]

The implication that craftsmen, particularly single journeymen and the poorer weavers, needed protection against the temptation to spend money and time drinking when they should be working seems to support the view that the artisan class was by nature undisciplined and in need of the paternal correction of the city magistrates. A later version of the rule explained that it was passed in the interest of the "common poor craftsmen," so that they may better provide for their households and their "wives and children" — that is, for their own good.[82] It appears, then, that the purpose of the rule was to limit immoderate drinking among the craftsmen.

Nonetheless, the inclusion of Monday, also theoretically a workday, as legal for tavern visits was a concession to artisan tradition. The artisans were in the habit of allowing journeymen a drinking bout on Monday afternoon each work week, at times even paid for by the master.[83] The tradition, known as Good Monday (*Guter Montag*), is often taken as further evidence of the undisciplined nature of the preindustrial working classes, who were characterized as flaunting the work ethic by making a holiday of Mondays.[84] The persistence of the Good Monday tradition into the period of industrialization is something historians have understood as a type of resistance by the popular classes, who were "unaccustomed to a time sequencing that required planning" or to the rational discipline of industrial life.[85] Good Monday in this explanation is represented as a form of absenteeism, an inability to cease the weekend drinking binge in time to make it to work on Monday morning. As this legislation shows, however, artisans who drank in taverns on Monday afternoons in early modern Augsburg were not merely continuing their weekend binge but conforming to authoritative norms for social discipline. These norms supported the drinking traditions of the craftsmen. At work in the concession to Good Monday were unwritten ground rules of popular society, which often affected official policy.[86]

The sanction of Good Monday was not sufficient to appease the local tavern keepers, and their reaction was swift and vehement. A primary concern of the tavern keepers was that the craftsmen would not, as the city council hoped, cut back on their consumption of wine and beer; rather, they would simply leave the city and drink in the surrounding villages, where taverns were not regulated by Augsburg's laws. Hans Lang, one of numerous tavern keepers who opposed the rule, was arrested in 1591 for insulting the honor of the council members by making loud complaints that the rule would ruin him and wondering where the tavern guests in the neighboring villages of Oberhausen and Göggingen would find a place to sit.[87] Drinking in the villages, as noted above, was a major area of concern not only to the Augsburg tavern keepers but to the council as well; and Lang's complaint may have been calculated to appeal to the city leaders' apprehension over the budget.

The rule was initially passed on 4 December 1590, and it applied only to brewers. On 13 December, the leading masters of the brewers' craft petitioned against the decree on behalf of all of Augsburg's brewers. The brewers' argument was concerned primarily with their own economic health. The petition began by drawing attention to the high investment and running costs required to maintain a tavern. The new rule, the brewers complained, would lead to their financial ruin. They pointed out that it would mean not only the loss of drink sales to local craftsmen during the week but could cut in on their income from overnight guests, who might want to drink with local citizens. If visitors and local craftsmen could not drink together in the tavern, they would retire to the craftsmen's homes, which would endanger the brewers' livelihood. Since wine sellers were not included in the regulation, and craftsmen drank wine as well as beer, the brewers noted, the rule would not in any case prevent drinking bouts during the week.

In spite of the potential for disorder hinted at by the suggestion that visitors to the city might come to prefer private (and illegal) accommodations to public taverns, the brewers' arguments seemed to the city council to be self-serving, placing the interests of the brewers above those of the common good. The regulation for the brewers remained unchanged; however, in the interest of fair competition and the household economics of the craftsmen, the rule was made effective for wine sellers as well as brewers on 20 December 1590.[88]

In early 1591 a consortium of wine sellers led by Andreas Preiß filed another petition against the decree. Preiß and his colleagues used a more cautious approach than had the brewers, one calculated to appeal to the council's sense of responsibility to the city at large rather than to the livelihood of the tavern keepers alone. The craftsmen, the wine sellers argued, could suffer harm as a result of this rule. To begin with, the wine sellers pointed out that they recognized that the decision was made in the paternal interest of the poor craftsmen and their households and families. The petitioners conceded the correctness of this concern, their "own great loss notwithstanding."[89]

Drinking and Public Order

Certain points in the regulation, however, required clarification, otherwise the rule would do the craftsmen more harm than good. Preiß pointed out that when visitors of "high and low status" engaged in trade or other business with local citizens, they would naturally want to show their generosity "through food and drink." If the tavern keepers refused to allow them to uphold the tradition of the contract drink, Preiß maintained, they would be subject to inflammatory insults, an incitement to swearing, honor disputes, and other potentially disruptive behavior. Preiß then brought the reputation of the city of Augsburg into play, noting that when visitors to the "prestigious and renowned city" wanted to conclude their transactions, "as is the custom in all German lands," with a drink, they would find it "strange and unusual, that the citizens should be forbidden to eat and drink with them."[90]

Preiß's argument, linking German drinking tradition to the reputation of Augsburg, was an effective one. The wine sellers were basing their petition on cultural practice that was common to Germans at all levels of society and on the damage that could result to the city's reputation should this practice be forbidden. The city council reacted more sympathetically to this problem than they had to the economic woes of the brewers, and they decided to allow an exception to the rule for transactions with visitors. These business transactions, Augsburg's council conceded, could not always be postponed until a holiday, and a drink was necessary for the conclusion of legitimate business.[91]

In 1596, just six years after the council decreed that craftsmen should not waste their money drinking during the week, the rule was abolished. The Augsburg brewer Georg Siedeler recorded this event in his chronicle in connection with the death of the city mayor Hans Welser, immediately after which Welser's successors rescinded the rule. In 1614 it was reinstated, but this time it applied only to brewers. The clause excepting drinks with visitors to the city remained in effect.[92]

These decisions did not merely represent city leaders' changing attitudes toward tavern going. Rather, they were based on hard economic facts. In September 1596 a secret commission appointed to investigate city finances submitted a report of their findings to the Augsburg mayors and secret council (*Geheimer Rat*). The city had been beleaguered since 1591 with having to make contributions to the empire to support the war against the Turks, and it was suffering fiscally. The commission was charged with seeking a means to recoup these expenses without placing an undue burden on the citizens of Augsburg. Along with suggesting an increase in the tax on wine, the commission recommended suspending the rule restricting drinking during the week. The fears of the tavern keepers as expressed in the brewers' petition, according to this report, were valid, for those who were not responsible about their household finances were not deterred by the rule — rather, they simply went outside the city to drink. Worse, those who flaunted the rule by drinking within the city were then arrested and charged for the offense, so that they ended up spending more money on one drinking bout "than they would otherwise spend in three."[93] Drinkers, according to the commission's report, could not be discouraged from drinking by a regulation. The best solution, then, was to harness their drinking habits in the interest of city income.

The commission found the ordinance against drinking in the villages also to be more detrimental to city finances than helpful. Enforcement of the law was nearly impossible, so that a "good hundred" Augsburg citizens could be found at any one time drinking in one village alone.[94] Publishing ordinances against drinking outside the city, the commission suggested, only drew the artisans' attention to the fact that it would save them money in excise taxes. A more practical solution would be to legalize drinks (specifically, wheat beer)[95] and drinking times that were restricted in the city, which would both minimize competition and placate the citizens in the face of a rise in wine taxes.

The decision of Augsburg's citizens to drink outside the city, and the city council's disapproval of the habit, may not have been entirely a fiscal issue. Along with cheaper drinks, village drinking offered freedom from the cramped quarters and careful control that characterized tavern life in the city. Country taverns were likely to have tables outside where drinkers could enjoy fresh air or combine drinking with outdoor games. Augsburg citizens who drank in the villages were not only avoiding excise taxes, they were also drinking and possibly gambling or brawling away from the watchful eyes of the authorities. The special appeal of drinking in the country was not missed in the commission's report, which noted that the city craftsmen, having spent all week in their shops and close quarters often go to the villages just to get out where it is green and to enjoy some exercise and fresh air.[96] Another suggested incentive to drinking in the city, then, was allowing the construction of buildings with open spaces for drinking in the city's gardens (essentially, beer gardens) so that the craftsmen would not need to leave the city to enjoy fresh air and outdoor amusements.[97] In short, the commission was recommending that every possible measure be taken to encourage Augsburg's citizens to do their drinking in the city—through enticements rather than threats—to the advantage of the city coffers. While city leaders may have had real concerns about unregulated drinking bouts in the villages, the goals of the commission clearly did not include the curtailment of the craftsmen's drinking habits in general.

Faced with the recommendations of this secret commission, the Office of Excise Tax responded positively to raising the tax on wine and permitting drinking during the week, but it remained opposed to relaxing the law against drinking in the villages. This was a traditional law, the Excise Tax Lords pointed out, and they could not recommend changing it. Allowing drinking outside the city could possibly lead to even more village drinking and decreased income from excise taxes, whereas the result of relaxing the rule against drinking during the week would certainly be an increase in tax income. On 19 October 1596, the city council advised the Discipline Lords that drinking during the week was no longer punishable, and, according to Siedeler, the public rejoiced.[98]

Siedeler, based on his own account, ceased rejoicing eighteen years later when the rule against drinking during the week was reinstated. The 1614 decree, like the original decree of 1590, applied only to brewers and originally forbade them to seat guests at all. Beer sales under this law were legal exclusively for home consumption. Only after listening to the many complaints of the local brewers did the city council, in December 1615, allow visits to beer taverns on Sundays and holidays.[99] Mondays were not exempted in this regulation, nor were wine sellers included, but the exception for drinking with visitors to the city appears in the Police Ordinance of 1621. Also excepted from the 1614 rule, as in 1590, were city employees, members of the city court, city council members, and wedding guests. Specifically targeted in the ordinance were "weavers, other craftsmen, journeymen, day laborers and the like."[100]

The reason for restricting beer drinking in 1614, according to city council records, was because of the shortages of grain and the accompanying rise in grain prices.[101] The grain problem also appears in connection with the rule in Siedeler's chronicle. The entry describing the decree is followed by entries recording that wheat beer was again forbidden and the baking of the traditional All Saints' Day pretzels (*Seelenbrezen*) as well, because of the shortages of grain. Both were allowed in the autumn of 1615, just before the rule against brewers seating guests was relaxed to allow at least Sundays and holidays.[102] The purpose of the 1614 rule, then, was to cut back on beer sales in order to save grain during a period of shortage. Since wine was not made from grain, there was no reason to restrict wine sales. The regulation, however, again applied only to craftsmen and day laborers, and reference to the shortage of grain does not appear in the Police Ordinance of 1621. Rather, the rule as stated in 1614 was intended to prevent artisans and day laborers from engaging in drinking bouts during the week.

We have examined the association of the rule in 1614 with shortages of grain. A look at the agricultural picture during 1590 reveals that in the autumn of that year Augsburg was also experiencing high grain prices.[103] Why, then, did the 1590 decree include restrictions on wine sales, while the 1614 regulation did not? The documents left us by the city council do not explain this change in overt terms, but a clue to their motives can be found in the city's fiscal records. City income did indeed benefit from the 1596 decision to raise the excise tax on wine and open taverns during the week (see graph 3). The excise taxes on alcoholic beverages for the five years beginning in 1596 averaged 20 percent higher than the taxes collected during the previous five years, and they remained stable at the higher rate thereafter. By comparison, city revenues were not significantly affected by the reinstatement of the restriction in 1614. Beer taxes were not raised in 1596, as part of the campaign the Office of Excise Tax waged to placate the citizens in the face of the raise in wine taxes. Relaxing the rule against drinking during the week and leaving beer taxes alone, the Excise Tax Lords hoped, would suffice to keep the common man "content."[104] Even before the raise in wine taxes, revenues from beer sales were relatively minor compared to those from wine. Although city financial records do not list separate accounts for beer and wine taxes, a list of the total taxes collected on beer between 1583 and 1590 (prepared as evidence for the arrest of the beer inspector Balthasar Gausmeir) shows that taxes on beer accounted for less than 3.5 percent of the total excise taxes on alcoholic beverages.[105] In contrast, any move that cut back significantly on wine consumption would, by 1614, have been damaging to the city financially.

In addition, the combination of higher wine taxes and general inflation was making wine a luxury item that was no longer affordable to many craftsmen, who increasingly turned to beer as a less expensive alternative. In 1590,

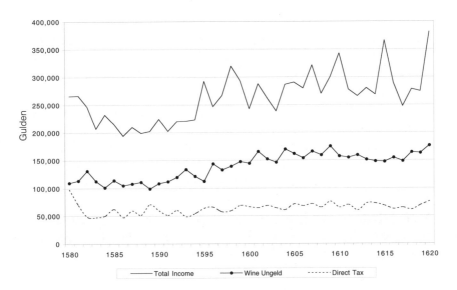

Graph 3. City Income, 1580–1620

however, city leaders may have believed that a restriction on the sale of beer
that did not apply to wine would lead to an unfair advantage on the part of
the wine sellers, a situation which, with wine still affordable to most craftsmen, could indeed have caused the economic ruin of the brewers.[106] Concern for the household expenses of the common man, too, as expressed in
the ordinances, would have been directed toward the control of beer more
than that of wine by 1614, although this was almost certainly not the driving force behind the restriction. In a period of grain shortages, beer became
a more valuable resource, and thus it was logical to restrict its use among
commoners. City elites, as we have noted, were not affected by the rule.

Social discipline in this case was aimed at regulating grain supplies, city expenditures, and excise tax revenues, with the drinking habits of craftsmen
providing the context not the focus of control. Although the decrees published in connection with this regulation were couched in moralizing tones
and were aimed at a particular "popular" group, the target of the authorities
was neither popular culture generally nor the specific cultural practice of
drinking excessively. The decisions of the city council suggest that they were
not only tolerant of cultural drinking practice but actively supported it. In

their initial negotiations with the tavern keepers in 1590, it is clear that the council viewed the cultural practice of the contract drink as inseparable from business transactions as well as from the city's greater image as a center of trade—both vital to Augsburg's economic health. And based on the documents associated with the 1596 decision to rescind the rule against drinking during the week, the authorities also did more than merely tolerate cultural practice. They courted and recruited the drinking habits of the populace in the interest of the city budget.

The Triumph of Carnival?

Drinking controls were relaxed just as other social controls were increasing because drinking, even drunkenness, was not viewed as disorderly either by the populace or authority. The purpose of controls on taverns and tavern drinking was not to limit the consumption of alcohol in general, for this would have caused the city budget to suffer. City legislation was calculated instead to maintain a vision of order in which certain persons could, and should, drink certain drinks in a prescribed way. What we see in the changes in legislation throughout the sixteenth and seventeenth centuries, then, is not so much a change in public attitudes toward drinking as a gradual adjustment of the norms of control to more closely match the norms of practice.

A similar trend is discernible in records of arrest for the same period. Comparing arrests for all infractions for the sample years 1540–1544, 1590–1594, and 1640–1644, it is possible to trace a decrease in arrests for moral crimes, such as adultery, prostitution, frivolous dancing, wasteful living, and disorderly drinking, and a relative increase in arrests for violence.[107] As we know from interrogation records, fights and disagreements were likely to have been related to social drinking, but punishments for violence did not target taverns, drinking, or drunkenness as the problem. Records of arrest and punishment, where interrogations are lacking, rarely note whether the offender was drunk, or had participated in tavern drinking, before committing the offense.

Conclusion

Aᴛ ᴛʜᴇ ʜᴇᴀʀᴛ of this study is the question of where early modern society established norms and how much these norms differed between elite and popular society. The norms that governed relationships within the early modern German city at large are reflected in the rules governing the use of alcohol within its taverns. These rules were as often the result of popular norms as of official regulation. Drinking partners were rarely randomly chosen, and drinking bouts, even when excessive, were seldom unbridled or without constraint.

We have examined many functions served by taverns and drinking bouts; yet at base, all of these functions served one greater purpose: the confirmation of the drinker's social identity. It was identity with each of the groups making up the urban commune that determined the norms of popular and elite culture and the relationship between them. Even the income from alcohol sales, which served an ultimately mundane economic purpose, at the same time contributed to the city leaders' identification with their vision of a wealthy and successful merchant city.

These norms were not obliterated by drunkenness. Drunkenness functioned neither as a legal defense nor as an acceptable excuse for socially unacceptable behavior. Immoderate drinking was always unacceptable when it interfered with the city council's vision of an orderly community. When the drinking habits of a head of a family threatened to intrude on his ability to provide for the household, for instance, the council stepped in and placed limits on his drinking behavior. Drunken and disorderly behavior, too, had its limits. Andreas Steiner discovered where the line between acceptable and unacceptable drunken behavior lay in 1544, when he lost his tongue for calling Augsburg a "Jew city"; so also did Simon Rayser, who was temporarily banished in 1593 for drunkenly expressing his wish that the free imperial city would fall to Bavaria.

The Culture of Drink in the Early Modern German City

The council's expectation that even drunkards respect their authority is further illustrated by the fact that fines for brawling, disorderly conduct, and other disturbances that occurred in areas representing civic authority, such as in front of the council house or around the city gates, were set at several times the normal rate, regardless of whether the perpetrators were drunk or sober. This vision of civic power found overt expression in the case of a drunken soldier who was arrested for disorderly behavior and resisting the guard in 1643. Members of the city council asked the soldier if he thought himself to be in "a village, where he might defy and brutalize people at will," rather than in a locality in which "better counsel" was appropriate.[1]

At the same time, even the term "drunkenness," embodying a notion of excess that might be seen as disorderly or sinful, could have a positive con-notation. Excess could be understood as a gift of plenty and an expression of joy. There is no contradiction at work when the authorities used the term "friendly drink" to describe a drinking bout that resulted in a drunken brawl or a mayor co-signed a line of illegal credit for an acquaintance to spend on drinks. City leaders allowed exceptions to tavern bans, closing times, and the ban on tax-free drinking in the surrounding villages for drinking bouts of an official nature, and in 1591, the tavern keeper Andreas Preiß was able to convince the authorities that Augsburg's reputation rested on the right of craftsmen to drink with visitors to their city. Drunkenness could also serve as a convenient legal excuse in cases in which city magistrates deemed it to be in the common interest. The line between acceptable and unacceptable drinking had nothing to do with the degree of excess consumption. Rather, it followed the line drawn between the council's view of responsible and ir-responsible citizenship.

Indispensable to responsible citizens was the maintenance of personal, professional, and corporate honor. Certainly, the orderly society that politi-cal and religious leaders envisioned in the early modern city was influenced by Christian values and the notion of a sacred hierarchy. Yet the ideal of per-sonal and corporate honor is not specific to Christianity. The pursuit of order and discipline within the godly city had a secular side, for religious belief was not the only vehicle through which the members of early modern society identified with their world. Tavern rituals were as much a part of their world-view as religious rituals. Early modern Germans found no conflict between the two, for as the sixteenth-century German preacher Johannes Matthesius,

Conclusion

"the Elder," noted in a sermon, "God can pardon an honorable German for an honorable tipsiness."[2] Indeed, the confessional issues that dominate the historiography on the sixteenth and seventeenth centuries hardly make an appearance in the everyday world of the tavern.

Among men the right to drink was a matter of honor at several levels. The capacity to maintain physical control in spite of consuming large amounts of alcohol was part of what defined manhood; the ability to pay for rounds defined economic viability; and participation in the drinking rituals of craft, guild, and commerce determined professional identity. Each of these definitions was necessary to personal honor, and it was the honor of the individual craftsman that defined his part in the civic corporation. This fact was commonly recognized at all social levels.

Society in the early modern German city, then, does not emerge as a simple two-part model of populace versus authority but as a complex collection of interest groups involved in a constant process of negotiation. The process included groups at every level of society, from beggars to city council members. This is not to imply that the system was free of social protest; but when protests occurred, the complaints of the perpetrators often did not so much attack social or economic differences as they appealed to shared notions of corporate identity and civic honor. The same process was at work when those interrogated for crimes developed their strategies of defense.

According to the theories of Elias and Oestreich, disciplining, or the acquiring of a new ethic, required first a change in elite norms and then the enforcement or passing on of the new norms to the populace. The discipline ordinances issued during the early modern period seemed to provide evidence of this process. The authorities, however, did not always enforce their own decrees. Many of the drinking controls issued during the sixteenth century, which concentrated on pledging healths, were in fact aimed at elite behavior; but if they resulted in a change in elite norms, there is no evidence before 1700 of a concentrated attempt to pass the new norms on to the populace.

Certainly, Augsburg's authorities saw the potential for disorder in the combination of social space and alcoholic drinks provided by the tavern, and their attempts at control do to some extent reflect their concern over this potential. Yet their instruments of regulation were not aimed at normal tavern comportment, for the disorderly element was the exception. As long as tavern

The Culture of Drink in the Early Modern German City

goers adhered to the shared norms of urban society, Augsburg's taverns were not seen as disorderly. Rather, they served as a means of defining and enforcing order. The drinking rooms associated with guilds, crafts, and elite societies underscored the social differences among the layers of the Society of Orders. Drinking traditions were viewed as a necessary part of urban professional life at all levels of society; and even more significant, drinking traditions helped shape and maintain social identity among the groups that made up the urban community. Taverns provided the authorities with public space for posting ordinances, for controlling the movements of strangers to the city, and for city craftsmen and wandering journeymen to establish professional networks. Financially, the city could not have survived without the income from taxes on alcoholic beverages consumed in taverns. The early modern German tavern bears little resemblance to Clark's description of sixteenth- and seventeenth-century English alehouses as establishments "run by the poor for the poor";[3] Augsburg's tavern keepers were anything but poor, and their establishments are better described as a haven away from the poor and disorderly elements of society than a shelter for beggars and thieves.

The imposition of drinking controls can be seen from two perspectives — either as benevolent reform, "inspired by visions of a new and better world for those to be reformed," or as repression, "inspired by the trouble that they (those being reformed) create for the controllers."[4] In the case of the culture of drink in the early modern German city, the drinkers, even when drunk, were simply not causing trouble for the authorities. They were acting according to the rules of a shared system. The popular and elite classes of sixteenth- and seventeenth-century Germany, the controllers and the controlled, lived in different social worlds, and the extent to which they could afford excess differed dramatically. Yet the mental world that shaped their attitudes and values remained united around a common vision of order and community. The tavern as well as the church had a part in fulfilling this vision, and it was one that could hardly have been opposed even by the defenders of the faith. After all, the Christian promise of salvation itself was concluded with a drink.

Notes

Abbreviations

Beruff 1541   StadtAA, Anschläge und Dekrete 1490–1649, Teil 1, no. 20, Beruff ains
Ersamen Rats . . . zu Pflantzung Christlichs / züchtigs vnd erbers
leben, 1541

CDS   *Die Chroniken der deutschen Städte*

HWA   Handwerkerakten

KA   Fürstlich und Gräflich Fuggerisches Familien- und Stiftungs-Archiv,
Kirchheim / Amtsrechnung

PO 1524   StadtAA, Anschläge und Dekrete 1490–1649, Teil 1, no. 5, Polizeiordnung 1524 (no title, 17 Jan.)

PO 1526   StadtAA, Ratserlasse 1507–1599, Polizeiordnung 1526 (no title, 21 Oct.)

PO 1528   StadtAA, Ratserlasse 1507–1599, Polizeiordnung 1528 (no title, second
Sunday in Lent)

PO 1530   StadtAA, Literalien, Polizeiordnung 1530 (no title, 24 Dec.)

PO 1683   StadtAA, Ratserlasse, Policey- Zierd- Kleider- Hochzeit- Kind
Tauf- und Leich-Ordnung 1683

PZS   Protokolle der Zucht- und Strafherren

StadtAA   Stadtarchiv Augsburg

SuStBA   Staats- und Stadt-Bibliothek Augsburg

Urg.   Urgichten

ZPO 1537   StadtAA, Ordnungen, Zucht- und Policeiordnung 1537

ZPO 1553   StadtAA, Schätze 36 / 8, Zucht- und Polizeiordnung 1553

ZPO 1580   StadtAA, Schätze ad 36 / 8, Zucht- und Polizeiordnung 1580

ZPO 1621   SuStBA, 4° Cod.Aug.132, Zucht- und Polizeiordnung 1621 (14 Jan.)

ZPO 1638   StadtAA, Anschläge und Dekrete 1522–1682, no. 21, Zucht- und
Polizeiordnung 1638

ZPO 1667   StadtAA, Anschläge und Dekrete 1522–1682, no. 52, Zucht- und
Polizeiordnung 1667

Introduction

1. "Er hab aber allweg sein gebürliche Zech bezalt." StadtAA, Urg., Lienhart Strobel, 28–29 July 1542.

2. The above cases are described in StadtAA, Urg., Georg Albrecht, 30 July 1590; Hainrich Frey, 20 March 1593; Lucas Fischer, 22 Nov. 1593; Michael Hurler, 22 March 1593; Andreas Stemmer, 7 March 1644; Rem, *Cronica*, 92.

3. Lyndal Roper coined this phrase in connection with Strobel's statement (*Holy Household*, 116–17).

4. Burke, *Popular Culture*, 207.

5. Clark, "Alehouse," 60.

6. Moryson, *Itinerary*, 290–91.

7. For an introduction to the drink literature, see Hauffen, "Trinklitteratur"; Austin, *Alcohol*, 138–42. Sermons against drunkenness and other temperance tracts are described in Janssen, *Geschichte* 8:274–300.

8. Austin, *Alcohol*, 138; Hauffen, "Trinklitteratur," 480; the critiques of Montaigne, John Owen, William Shakespeare, and others, quoted in Potthoff and Kossenhaschen, *Kulturgeschichte*, 140–43. For a more comprehensive list of sources on the "great German thirst" of the sixteenth century, see Spode, *Alkohol und Zivilisation*, 271.

9. Jellinek, "Specimen," 648.

10. The association of heavy alcohol consumption with anxiety has also been assumed by, for example, George, *London Life*, 20, 27, 36; Schivelbusch, *Tastes of Paradise*, 17–19, 149–53; Braudel, *Everyday Life*, 236–37; Jellinek, "Specimen," 654; Abel, *Ernährung*, 57; Stolleis, "Nachwort," 5; Hübner, *Durst*, 22. Peter Clark uses the same argument to explain tavern visits in early modern England ("Alehouse," 54, 58–59).

11. Thompson, *Working Class;* Thompson, "Work Discipline," 74–76; Burke, *Popular Culture*, 213; Walvin, *Leisure*, 2–4; Gusfield, "Benevolent Repression," 404–5.

12. K. Thomas, *Religion*, 19; Braudel, *Everyday Life*, 236–37.

13. "Das angestrebte Ziel des Trinkens." Legnaro, "Alkoholkonsum," 169.

14. Elias, *Zivilisation* 1:229–47; Spode, *Alkohol und Zivilisation*, 71–73.

15. Roberts, *Drink, Temperance*, esp. 130; Medick, "Plebejische Kultur," 157–204.

16. Stolleis, "Trinkverbote"; Dülmen, *Entstehung*, 208–9.

17. Stolleis, "Trinkverbote."

18. Austin, *Alcohol*, 123; Hauffen, "Trinklitteratur," 487–88.

19. For critique by contemporaries, see Tengler, *Layen Spiegel;* Welser, *Chronica*, 68; Schwarzenberg, *Gesatze*, D2–D3.

20. Austin, "Drogenkrise," 125–26.

21. Spode, *Alkohol und Zivilisation*, 18–47.

22. Gerhard Oestreich's basic thesis is outlined in "Strukturprobleme des europäischen Absolutismus," in his *Geist und Gestalt des frühmodernen Staates: Ausgewählte Aufsätze* (1969, 179–97), which in English is *Neostoicism and the Early Modern State.*

23. See, for example, Burke, *Popular Culture*, 205–44; on Germany, see Behringer, *Hexenverfolgung*, 111–20; Lehmann, "Witches," esp. 111–13.

24. Wrightson, "Alehouse," 12. This thesis is also developed in Clark, *English Alehouse.*

25. Smith, *Public House,* 5–6; Webb and Webb, *Liquor Licensing,* 2; Sharpe, "Enforcing the Law," 104.

26. Clark, *English Alehouse,* 145.

27. Curtis, "Quarter Sessions," 139.

28. N. Schindler, *Widerspenstige Leute,* 236–39; Stolleis, "Trinkverbote," 177–82, 188–89.

29. "Sie rufen und schreien des Nachts auf der Gassen wie junge Teufel aus der Hölle." Janssen, *Geschichte* 8:277.

30. Hans Sachs, *Werke* 3:45–60, 4:237–43, 12:539–40, 19:132–35, 19:328–32; [Schwarzenberg], *Zutrinken,* A3v; Franck, *Von dem greüwlichen laster,* D3–D4.

31. Herold, "Kartenspiel," 4:1015; K. Thomas, *Religion,* 121; Münch, *Lebensformen,* 360–61; Wrightson, "Alehouse," 12.

32. "Du machst inn summa mit eym wort, Armut, diebstal, ehbruch und mord." Sachs, *Werke* 4:252, 247–54.

33. "Schule aller irdischen und höllischen Laster." Albertinus, *Lucifers Königreich,* quoted in Janssen, *Geschichte* 8:279.

34. Ariès, *Childhood,* 391.

35. Wirth, "Acculturation Thesis"; Beik, "Popular Culture"; Lottes, "Volkskultur."

36. See, for example, Behringer, "Mörder;" Blauert and Schwerhoff, *Waffen der Justiz,* esp. "Vorbemerkung," 7–15; Schwerhoff, *Kreuzverhör;* Dinges, "Armenfürsorge."

37. Goode and Ben-Yehuda, *Moral Panics,* 124.

38. Cohen, *Folk Devils.*

39. See the study of youth violence by anthropologists Marsh, Rosser, and Harré, *Rules of Disorder.*

40. Darnton, *Cat Massacre,* 78.

41. "Saufen, schwelgen, [und] wild wüst Wesen." M. Volcius, *Sechs schöne Predigten von der Theuerung* (1615), quoted in Janssen, *Geschichte* 8:464.

42. This term was coined by Marsh, Rosser, and Harré in *Rules of Disorder.*

43. Goode and Ben-Yehuda, *Moral Panics,* 205–19; Marsh, Rosser, and Harré, *Rules of Disorder,* 2–10.

44. Moryson, *Itinerary,* 340.

45. Muchembled, *Popular Culture,* 33–40.

46. For general anthologies that examine the social and cultural uses of social drinking, see Pittman and Snyder, *Drinking Patterns;* Marshall, *Beliefs;* Völger and von Welck, *Rausch und Realität;* Douglas, *Constructive Drinking;* Barrows and Room, *Drinking.*

47. Some of the best major works in this genre include Bassermann-Jordan, *Geschichte des Weinbaus;* Potthoff and Kossenhaschen, *Kulturgeschichte;* Rauers, *Kulturgeschichte;* Schreiber, *Deutsche Weingeschichte.* (This posthumous 1980 publication was written during the decade preceding Schreiber's death in 1962 and was grounded in the folklorist tradition of the prewar years. See Gabriel Simons, "Vorwort des Herausgebers," *Deutsche Weingeschichte,* v–vi.) For a critical analysis of folklorist literature on drinking in Germany, see Hirschfelder, "Bemerkungen."

48. Brennan, *Public Drinking*, 227, 16–19; Rorabaugh, *Alcoholic Republic;* Lender and Martin, *Drinking in America;* Taylor, *Drinking, Homicide, and Rebellion.*

49. Early modern Germany is treated in passing in Völger and von Welck, *Rausch und Realität;* Spode, *Alkohol und Zivilization.*

50. See, for example, Schwerhoff, *Kreuzverhör,* 294–97; Roper, *Oedipus,* 145–67; N. Schindler, *Widerspenstige Leute,* esp. 231–35.

51. Taylor, *Drinking, Homicide, and Rebellion;* Brennan, *Public Drinking,* 16–19.

52. All statistics noted are based on this sample.

53. Davis, *Fiction,* 3–6.

54. "Wie aller orten Teutschen Lands gebreuchig." StadtAA, HWA, Weinwirte 6 1551–1704, 1591.

1. The City and Its Taverns

1. A popular poem (ca. 1500) reads as follows: "Hätt' ich Venedigs Macht, Augsburger Pracht, Nürnberger Witz, Strassburger Geschütz, und Ulmer Gelt, so wär' ich der Reichste von der Welt." (Had I the power of Venice, the splendor of Augsburg, the wit of Nürnberg, the defense of Strassburg, and the money of Ulm, I'd be the richest in the world.) Quoted in Zorn, *Augsburg,* 159.

2. Sehling, *Kirchenordnungen,* 18; Montaigne, *Works,* 897.

3. Bernd Roeck describes the construction of the new city council house and other improvements during the era of the Baumeister Elias Holl as a form of social politics, or social discipline via building design ("Sozialdisziplinierung durch Baukunst") (*Eine Stadt* 1:190–200).

4. Rogge, *Politisches Handeln,* 270–72; Roper, *Holy Household,* 15–20.

5. SuStBA, 2° S.141 Anschläge no. 6, 12 Aug. 1524.

6. StadtAA, Ratsbücher 15, fol. 14r, Straffherrn des Gotlesterns swerens vnd Zutrinkens.

7. "Papistisch[e] Abgötterei." Zorn, *Augsburg,* 182.

8. Roper, *Holy Household,* 21–27.

9. Rogge, *Politisches Handeln,* 270–72.

10. "Unordenliche[s] Regiment." Karolinische Regimentsordnung, 3 Aug. 1548, quoted in Bátori, *Reichsstadt,* 31.

11. Mair, *Chronik,* 115; Eberlein, "Entwicklung," 5.

12. The altercation was part of the period of unrest known as the Kalenderstreit, 1583–1591.

13. Immenkötter, "Kirche," 407. On the social identity of leaders and priority of maintenance of the status quo, see Mörke and Sieh, "Führungsgruppen," 310.

14. Based on tax and real estate holdings of the patricians and other members (*Mehrer*) of the Lords' Drinking Room Society, merchants, and doctors around 1600, their real property holdings increased to 30 percent by 1650 (Roeck, *Eine Stadt* 1:404, 502, 2:944).

15. The four gates listed for entry by outsiders were Rotes Tor, Gögginger Tor, Wertachbrucker Tor, and Jakober Tor (StadtAA, Ratserlasse 1684–1698, Ordinance of 1689).

16. StadtAA, Bauamt no. 215, Wasserzins-Register 1600–1629; Ruckdeschel, *Denkmale,* 21–25.

17. Officially the cathedral is named Mary's Visitation (Mariä Heimsuchung), but it is commonly called Our Lady.

18. StadtAA, Bauamt no. 215, Wasserzins-Register 1600–1629; StadtAA, Grundbuch-Auszüge G, H, J, no. 350.

19. Baer, *Stadtlexikon,* 31; "Geschichte der Brauerei," 27.

20. On the economic health of the quarter, see Roeck, *Eine Stadt* 1:309, 489–510.

21. StadtAA, Schätze 16, Eine Sammlung Städtischer Verordnungen und Erlässe, 1536–1633, 66v. The term "mayors' office" (*Bürgermeisteramt*) remained standard despite the change in title to "caretaker" (*Stadtpfleger*).

22. StadtAA, Ungeldamt, MMXVII, Carl Lindenmair, 1565. For tax breaks for innkeepers, see also SuStBA, 2° Cod.Aug.247, Bürgermeister-Instruktion, 241–43.

23. StadtAA, Ungeldamt, MMXVII, Carl Lindenmair, 1565. On the problems in finding lodging and stables during imperial diets, see A. Kohler, "Wohnen und Essen."

24. Wine clerks were high-level city bureaucrats responsible for taxing and recording sales at the Wine Market. See StadtAA, Schätze 194a, Eidbuch, 1583, 4v (Weinschreiber Eid).

25. "Von altershero mehr nit alß sechß Gastgeben . . . gewessen seind." StadtAA, HWA, Weinwirte 6 1551–1704, 1587. One of these "Sechs Gastgeben auff dem Weinmarkt" was located (as Mair pointed out) on a side street in the Lechviertel (see map 2).

26. "So haben sy sich . . . mehr zubedanckhen, alß zu beschwören." StadtAA, HWA, Weinwirte 6 1551–1704, 1562.

27. Montaigne, *Works,* 897–89, 903.

28. Roeck, *Eine Stadt* 1:497–501. On the wealth and exclusion of the city executioner, see Stuart, *Defiled Trades,* 69–93.

29. "Zu spielen und zu zechen, mit Meidung anderer Trinkstuben, allein denen, so hinauf geschrieben wurden, ihren Stand und Reputation also zu erhalten gebührt." Welser, *Chronica,* 151. The Lords' Drinking Room in Augsburg was also known as the Citizen's Room (*Bürgerstube*).

30. Stetten, *Geschichte* 1:144, 551, 556; Müller, "Über Trinkstuben," 249–50; Baer, *Stadtlexikon,* 162.

31. "Es war in einem Saale das Mal zugericht, der war mehr von Gold als Farben gesehen worden. Der Boden war von Marmelstein und so glatt, als wenn man auf einem Eise ging." Schweinichen, *Denkwürdigkeiten,* 77.

32. "Es ist auf der Trinkstuben allda ein feine Kurzweile. Man findet darauf Spieler, Säufer und andere Ritterspiel, wozu einer Lust hat." Ibid.

33. Montaigne, *Works,* 899.

34. See, for example, StadtAA, Strafbücher, Zuchtherren Ausgaben und Einkommen 1537–1557, 1558–1560, 1593–1603, 1603–1612, 1612–1623.

35. Rogge, *Politisches Handeln*, 186; Zorn, *Augsburg*, 184. Among the families given patrician status in 1538 were Peutinger, Baumgartner, von Stetten, and Fugger.

36. StadtAA, Evangelisches Wesensarchiv 1487, Bürgerstubenordnung. For example, Georg Vetter, a Bürgermeister's son, was banned from the Lords' Drinking Room for one year after he seriously injured another member of the society (Rem, *Cronica*, 92, 117).

37. Baer, *Stadtlexikon*, 198; Dirr, "Kaufleutezunft," 136, 142, 147; Hecker, "Herbrot," 47.

38. Roper, *Holy Household*, 23–24; Zorn, *Augsburg*, 185; Hecker, "Herbrot," 47.

39. Mair, *Chronik*, 178–79.

40. "Dern von beeden Trinkstuben," "gesellschaft der stuben." See, for example, StadtAA, Ratserlasse 1507–1599, Kleiderordnung 1582; Mair, *Chronik*, 180.

41. "Politische Standesvertretung des Kaufmannsstandes." Dirr, "Kaufleutezunft," 144.

42. See, for example, StadtAA, Chroniken 10, Chronik von Siedeler, 200.

43. Roeck, *Eine Stadt* 2:975–81.

44. StadtAA, HWA, Bierbrauer 6 1621–1639 (the incorrectly dated fascicle contains documents dated between 1621 and 1673), 1672.

45. Roeck, *Eine Stadt* 1:498, 2:910, 911.

46. This observation is based on lists of taverns operating in 1895 and 1903. See Boos, "Brauerei-Industrie"; Eberlein, *Hasenbrauerei*, 118–31.

2. Augsburg's Tavern Keepers

1. StadtAA, HWA, Bierbrauer 2 1577–1599, 24 Jan. 1604.

2. Mair, *Chronik*, 361; Stetten, *Geschichte* 1:553; Welser, *Chronica*, 108.

3. StadtAA, Chroniken 10, Chronik von Siedeler, 121r. It is not clear where the non-local beer originated.

4. Austin, *Alcohol*, 95, 96, 107, 124, 139; Eberlein, "Entwicklung."

5. StadtAA, Ungeldamt, Gesetze und Verordnungen des Ungeld-Amts, Bierbrauer-Ordnungen 1659, Article 54, 61–62.

6. The minimum apprenticeship was six months in 1549, but it was raised to two years in 1659, with brewers' sons excepted (StadtAA, HWA, Bierbrauer 24, Bierprewen-Ordnung 1549, Article 34, 1659, Article 3).

7. Baer, *Stadtlexikon*, 56; Reith, *Lexikon*, 30.

8. StadtAA, Chroniken 10, Chronik von Siedeler, 26–30, 136–40, 162–65, 205–10; Grundbücher Auszüge A–C, D–F, G–J. Estimates as high as 122 brewers for this period are based on a count of all members of the brewers guild, which included journeymen, city council representatives, and brewers' widows, who did not produce and sell beer (Baer, *Stadtlexikon*, 85, 56).

9. The "little ice age" refers to a period of lower average temperature; cool, wet summers; and long winters that began sometime in the 1560s–1570s and continued into the eighteenth century. For an introduction to the literature on this topic, see Lehmann, "Eiszeit," and the collection of articles on climate and history in *Journal of Interdisciplinary History* 10 (spring 1980).

10. Eberlein, *Hasenbrauerei*, 4–6; "Geschichte der Brauerei," 16–18.

11. StadtAA, HWA, Weinwirte 6 1551–1704, Andreas Preiß et al., 1591, Hans Heckel et al.

12. StadtAA, HWA, Weinwirte 6 1551–1704, 1656–1657; HWA, Bierbrauer 24, Bierbrauer-Ordnungen; SuStBA, 4° Cod.Aug.221, Bierprewen-Ordnung und Artikel, Article 63, 1657.

13. "Wie vor disem nur bey 20 Preuen, hingegen vf 100 Weinschenckhen waren, jetzt nur bey 20 Weinwürth vnnd entgegen 100 Preuen . . . sein." StadtAA, HWA, Weinwirte 6 1551–1704, 1657.

14. StadtAA, Ratserlasse, Policey- Zierd- Kleider- Hochzeit- Kind Tauf- und Leich-Ordnung 1683.

15. SuStBA, 2° Cod.Aug.449, Wirt- und Gastgeberordnung 1650–1753.

16. Austin, *Alcohol*, 156; French, *Fastnachtspiele*, 9, 26–27, 29, 34, 36, 56.

17. Kachel, *Herberge*, 142–43.

18. "Es ist der wirt gleych wie die gest / Es sindt die vögel wie das nest." Sachs, *Werke* 14:122.

19. Roeck, *Eine Stadt* 1:422, 2:938.

20. Only two wine sellers can be identified in the tax records for 1646. The analysis of these groups is based on taverns identified in the military musters' (Musterungs-bücher) for 1610 and 1646, together with real property records (Grundbücher) and brewery licensing records (Bierschenken-Gerechtigkeits-Buch). The total of 104 beer, wine, and mead sellers identified for 1610 and 88 for 1646 does not constitute a complete list of tavern keepers, but it represents the majority in business during these years and probably forms a fair representative sample. For a complete breakdown of tax payments for Augsburg tavern keepers by city quarter and profession, see Tlusty, "Devil's Altar," 94–96.

21. The mean tax that doctors paid was 27 gulden 41 kreuzer in 1618; compare this to merchants' payment at 76 gulden 52 kreuzer (Roeck, *Eine Stadt* 1:486).

22. In 1592 Martin Schopp purchased a tavern for 1,600 gulden (StadtAA, Urg., 5 May 1592); sales of eleven breweries with licenses recorded by the brewers craft between 1608 and 1646 show a price range from 2,000 to 7,000 gulden, with an average selling price of 4,181 (StadtAA, HWA, Bierbrauer 25, Bierschenken-Gerechtigkeits-Buch 1646, 4, 40, 41, 73, 87, 90, 94, 98, 120, 123).

23. Mair, *Chronik*, 151.

24. StadtAA, HWA, Bierbrauer 25, Bierschenken-Gerechtigkeits-Buch, 83.

25. "Einer die bierschenken gerechtigkeit nur in einen sack oder kretzen nemen darf, und dieselbige in der Statt herumb tragen, und seiner gefallens nider setzen, und in ein haus legen wo man will." StadtAA, Chroniken 10, Chronik von Siedeler, 302v. Those who inherited a franchise paid 1 gulden (StadtAA, HWA, Bierbrauer 24, Bierprewen-Ordnung 1549, Article 35, 1659, Article 15).

26. StadtAA, Chroniken 10, Chronik von Siedeler, 182r, 287v, 296r–97v; HWA, Bierbrauer 25; Grundbuch-Auszüge A–C, G–J.

27. StadtAA, HWA, Weinwirte 1 1520–1811, 1657, 1688.

28. The tavern mentioned in Paul Hegele's will was Fischzug Petri (St. Peter's Catch).

StadtAA, Urg., Joachim Pepfenhauser, 6 July 1641. Hegele paid 12 gulden in property taxes in 1604. This was 2½ gulden more than the 9½ average that all brewers paid in 1610 (StadtAA, Steuerbücher 1604, 1610). The testaments of other brewers also mention beds, linens, stables, and often a garden in addition to the brewing house, but they do not provide the monetary value of the estate (StadtAA, Stadtkanzlei, Urkundenkonzepte, Testamente 5.1, 1523–1571, 1573–1599).

29. StadtAA, Hochzeitsprotokolle 1563–1569; Stadtkanzlei, Heiratsbriefe 14.1, 1560–1599. Dowries of 1,000 gulden constituted a "definite social boundary" (Roper, *Holy Household*, 148).

30. Dülmen, *Entstehung*, 209.

31. Tlusty, "Devil's Altar," 101; Compare Roeck, *Eine Stadt* 1:486, table 56, 2:938, table 144. The mean tax payment of virtually every group in the city decreased between 1618 and 1646.

32. Kachel makes the point that country taverns were probably less economically stable (*Herberge*, 134). Potthoff and Kossenhaschen, *Kulturgeschichte*, 107–8; Glauser, "Wein, Wirt, Gewinn," 205–20.

33. See Stuart, *Defiled Trades*, 84–126.

34. StadtAA, Hochzeitsamt, Hochzeitsamtsprotokolle 1563–1593, 1618–1648.

35. Mair, *Chronik*, 159–69. The Large Council included 140 representatives from the commoners (among them were also two brandy sellers). In 1618 tavern keepers made up 1.5 percent of the city's taxpaying population and 2.4 percent in 1645 (Roeck, *Eine Stadt* 1:405, 2:898); the percentage would hardly have been higher in 1549.

36. StadtAA, Verzeichnis 39, "Besetzung aller Ämter in der Reichsstadt Augsburg, angefangen 1548," 24–28.

37. See, for example, StadtAA, Chroniken 10, Chronik von Siedeler (Siedeler commissioned a family coat of arms in 1601, 267); SuStBA, 4° Cod.S.10, Apolonia Hefelerin's Augsburger Chronik, 1554–1654; Potthoff and Kossenhaschen, *Kulturgeschichte*, 106, 123.

38. Sachs, *Werke* 9:3–11, 12–22, 120–35, 17:228–29, 21:76–90.

39. "Auch findt man manchen Gast der fragt / Ob der Wirt hab ein schöne Magdt / Ein Gast der soll benüget sein / Wenn er hat gute Speiß und Wein. / Wiewol eim Gast auch sehr wol thut / Wann das Bettgwand ist rein vnd gut." Mayr, *Wegbüchlein*, foreword.

40. StadtAA, Chroniken 10, Chronik von Siedeler, 128r; Schweinichen, *Denkwürdigkeiten*, 76–78; Seling, *Goldschmiede* 1:84–85, 113–15.

41. Emperor Maximilian I was a regular visitor at the house of the wealthy merchant Philipp Adler and was so fond of visiting Augsburg that he had a special gate constructed to allow him to come and go after the other city gates were closed (Eberlein, *Augsburg*, 85–86; Baer, *Stadtlexikon*, 8).

42. Peyer, *Gastfreundschaft*, 67–76, 205–19; Peyer, *Taverne*, x–xi.

43. Peyer, *Gastfreundschaft*, 34–51, 67.

44. StadtAA, Chroniken 10, Chronik von Siedeler, 98v; Schätze 16, Eine Sammlung Städtischer Verordnungen und Erlässe, 1536–1633, 296v–297r; PZS 1589–1594. The rules did not apply to the Lords' or Merchants' Drinking Rooms.

45. Peyer, *Gastfreundschaft*, 230–36.

46. Haupt, *Drei Mohren*.

47. StadtAA, HWA, Weinwirte 6 1551–1704, 1624; Evangelisches Wesensarchiv 458, 4 Sept. 1610, Tobias Wiedemann.

48. "Freundtlich[e] worten vnd geberden." StadtAA, Handwerker-Ordnungen A–Z, Ordnung / Wie sich die hierinn vermeldte Handtwercker vnd Handthierer . . . verhalten sollen, Heidelberg, 1579, C; Kachel, *Herberge*, 6–7.

3. The Drunken Body

1. Achilles Pirminius Gasser, "Warnungs Schlus Reden von der Trunckenheit, 1570, an die beede Stubens geselschafft zu Augsburg, gestelt," SuStBA 2° Cod.S.112, Abschriften von Privilegien in der Sammlung Paul von Stetten. I wish to thank Hans-Jörg Künast for this reference.

2. Norbert Haas provides numerous examples from this genre from popular literature as well as drinking songs in *Trinklieder*, 157–58.

3. Kienan, "Körper"; Sawday, *Body Emblazoned*, 20–23.

4. Mauss, "Techniques"; Paster, *Body Embarrassed*, 3. On the Enlightenment, see Duden, *Woman*.

5. Norbert Elias expresses this as a process of civilizing the human's fascination with natural functions, banning to the private sphere formerly acceptable activities such as urinating and farting. A related process might be identified in Michel Foucault's notion of confinement or Gerhard Oestreich's social discipline model. See Elias, *Zivilisation;* Foucault, *Sexuality;* Oestreich, *Neostoicism*.

6. Sawday, *Body Emblazoned*, 20.

7. Breitenberg, *Masculinity*, 29.

8. Sawday, *Body Emblazoned*, 32–36; Rubin, "Person," 115.

9. Bakhtin, *Rabelais*, 368.

10. According to Andrew Wear, at least 590 editions of Galen's works were published during the sixteenth century ("Medicine," 253).

11. *Regimen Sanitatis*, 28.

12. Ryff, *Spiegel*, 87; *Regimen Sanitatis*, 28; Avila, *Bancket*, 10v; Fries, *Spiegel der Arzney*, 23; Rau, *Gutachten*, 15, 27–28; StadtAA, HWA, Branntweinbrenner 2, 1552–1553.

13. Fries, *Spiegel der Arzney*, 6–7.

14. Avila, *Bancket*, chap. 7; Fries, *Spiegel der Arzney*, 23–26; Ryff, *Spiegel*, 62r, 66r, 87v.

15. Brunschwig, *Distilieren*, 2; Rau, *Gutachten*, 15; Zedler, *Universal-Lexicon*, "Brandt-wein" 4:1084.

16. StadtAA, HWA, Branntweinbrenner 2, 1631.

17. StadtAA, Ordnungen, Zucht- und Polizeiordnung 1537; StadtAA, HWA, Branntweinbrenner 2, Policey-Ordnung den prantt Weyn betreffentt, Oct. 1555, 1631.

18. StadtAA, Urg., Hans Block, 10 April 1544.

19. Ryff, *Spiegel*, 62–64.

20. *Regimen Sanitatis*, 20–21, 29; Pauli, *Schimpff und Ernst*, 45; Gasser, "Schlus Reden"; Ryff, *Spiegel*, 64; Schoen, *Eygenschafften;* Brunschwig, *Distilieren*, 41.

21. *Regimen Sanitatis*, 20–21.

22. Pauli, *Schimpff und Ernst*, 45. In Sachs's version of the fable, Noah nourishes his vines with the dung of the animals rather than the blood (*Werke* 4:237–45).

23. "Den kindern wein gebe[n] sey gleich als fewr zu fewr thun." Fries, *Spiegel der Arzney*, 24; Metlinger, *Regiment;* Magnus, *Der Weyber natürliche heymlichaiten*, 23.

24. Fries, *Spiegel der Arzney*, 26; Ryff, *Kochbuch*, 126v. Brandy was also used at least by the eighteenth century as an aphrodisiac (Zedler, *Universal-Lexicon*, "Brandtwein" 4:1084).

25. Ryff, *Spiegel*, 65; *Regimen Sanitatis*, 29. These assessments drew directly on classical sources; see similar recommendations in Plato, *Laws*, 666.

26. SuStBA, 4° Aug.1038, Occo *Pestilentz*, B4v, E4v; SuStBA, 4° Aug.1402, *Vnderricht von den Doctorn der Artzney daselbs / geordnet / Wie man sich in der kranckhait / Schwaißsucht genant / fürsehen vnd halten solle* (Augsburg, 1530), A5v.

27. Ryff, *Spiegel*, 62v; StadtAA, HWA, Branntweinbrenner 2, 1537–1698, 12 Jan. and 6 Feb. 1593.

28. "So doch der wein von Gott erschaffen ist / dar mit blöden vnd krancken armen leut zu erwermen vnd erfrewen." Ryff, *Spiegel*, 65v. Exceptions to regulations on drinking on credit applied to pregnant women also (SuStBA, 4° Cod.Aug.132, Zucht- und Polizeiordnung, 14 Jan. 1621, 38; SuStBA, 4° Cod.S.87, Unterschiedliche Ordnungen, "Berueff Zuegleich auch so wol die Würth als die Muessigenger betreffendt," 1581). The provision of wine for the destitute or the melancholy is supported by Scripture (Prov. 31:6).

29. Austin, *Alcohol*, 88, 97; Fries, *Spiegel der Arzney*, 24.

30. Ryff, *Spiegel*, 86.

31. Fries, *Spiegel der Arzney*, 24; Brunschwig, *Distilieren*, 39; *Regimen Sanitatis*, 28; Ryff, *Spiegel*, 65, 68; Gasser, "Schlus Reden"; Avila, *Bancket*, 10v.

32. "Das sie darum das leben haben, das sie sauffen sollen, vnd nicht darum trincken, das sie leben." Gasser, "Schlus Reden."

33. "In denen aber allen werden beede, die Zung vnnd füesse, so schwer, das sie weder reden noch gehen können." Gasser, "Schlus Reden."

34. Pansa, *Hauß-Apothecke*, 168–70.

35. Bontekoe, *Abhandlung*, 376, 390–95; Blankart, *Artzneyen*.

36. Zedler, *Universal-Lexicon*, "Brandtwein" 4:1086; Warner, "Old and in the Way."

37. Schorer, *Medicina;* Pansa, *Hauß-Apothecke*, 166–70; Bontekoe, *Abhandlung*, 450.

38. Although Jessica Warner suggests that sermons attacking drunkenness of the early seventeenth century already connote concepts of addiction, the language of these sources expresses a notion of spiritual addiction of the will rather than a concept of physical addiction (Warner, "'Resolv'd to Drink No More'").

39. Duden, *Woman.*

40. Die Ersten macht [Wein] frölich frydsam, / Gutwillig, milt, gütig vnd mitsam.

/ Die Andern rayzet er zu zorn, / Das sie wuten, zancken, rhumorn. / Die Dritten macht er alle sampt, / Groß wust kindisch vnd vnuerschampt. / Den Vierden ist der wein ein stewr / Zu fanttasey vnd abenthewr."

41. Schoen, *Eygenschafften*. On iconographic associations of animals, see Henkel and Schöne, *Emblemata*, 428–39, 539, 543–44, 548, 550–51; Kunzle, *Comic Strip*, 216–18.

42. For other examples of drunkards depicted as animals, see Harms, *Flugblätter*, "Der Trincker" 1:81; Eobarus, *De generibus Ebriosorum;* Bock, *Der vollen brüder orden.*

43. Suutala, *Tier und Mensch*, 129, 139.

44. "Wird ein stum unvernünfftigs thier . . . das nichts mer menschlichs an im ist." Franck, *Von dem greüwlichen laster,* H2v.

45. "Verstellung der Edlen Vernunfft / in vihische vnsinnigkait." StadtAA, ZPO 1537; "vichisch[es] lasster." StadtAA, Schätze 36/8, Zucht- und Polizeiordnung 1553, 6v, 7v.

46. Zentralbibliothek Zürich, EDR 16, Alkohol Ia.1.

47. Hans Weiditz, "The Winebag and His Wheelbarrow," Augsburg, 1521, in Geisberg, *Einblatt-Holzschnitt*, plate 18:32. Weiditz's Weinschlauch was imitated in later satirical prints; seventeenth-century examples with notes on parallel figures can be found in Harms, *Flugblätter,* "Des Bachi Bruderschafft" 1:75; "Marthin Lvther" 2:168.

48. Examples include StadtAA, Anschläge und Dekrete 1490–1649, no. 20, Beruff ains Ersamen Rats. . . zu Pflantzung Christlichs / züchtigs vnd erbers leben 1541; Anschläge und Dekrete 1522–1682, no. 21, Zucht- und Polizeiordnung 1638.

49. Roper, *Oedipus*, 23–24.

50. Ibid.

51. Fischart "winks at, and even appears to encourage, indulgence." Weinberg, *Gargantua*, 47–48.

52. This observation was also made in Osborn, *Teufelliteratur*, 74.

53. N. Schindler, *Widerspenstige Leute*, 160.

54. Haftlmeier-Seiffert, *Bauerndarstellungen*, 80–97; Schilling, *Bildpublizistik*, 209–10, 234, 244–45.

55. Stewart, "Paper Festivals," 304; Roper, *Oedipus*, 153.

56. "Der Wein wart also knollet druncken / Das jr vil vnther Penck suncken . . . Gantz fröhlich waren Jung vnd alt / Nit waiß ich wer die orten zalt." (The wine they did so grossly drink / that many under the bench did sink . . . young and old were very gay / and I don't know who was able to pay.) Geisberg, *Einblatt-Holzschnitt*, plate 16:1.

57. Sachs's comic intent in this poem is also analyzed in Roper, *Oedipus*, 157–58.

58. Schoen, *Eygenschafften;* Harms, *Flugblätter* 1:82.

59. Sachs, *Eygenschafft vnd würckung des Weins*, 8.

60. Aletheius, *Der Mässigkeit Wolleben*, 335; Harms, *Flugblätter* 1:81, 180; Zedler, *Universal-Lexicon* 30:1144.

61. Colerus, *Oeconomia*, 291.

62. Sawday, *Body Emblazoned*, 36.

63. Weinberg, *Gargantua*, 48.

4. The Drunken Spirit

1. "Sie saufen . . . als ob der Wein auf keinem anderen Weg als durch den menschlichen Körper ausgeschüttet und verloren werde könnte." Zwingli, *Schriften* 3:412.

2. For a list of biblical references to drinking, see Bassermann-Jordan, *Geschichte des Weinbaus* 2:1138–40.

3. Catholic theologians have concluded that there is "no absolutely compelling argument" that can be taken from the Scriptures to condemn "isolated acts of drunkenness, uncomplicated by association with other kinds of wicked action" as mortally sinful (*New Catholic Encyclopedia* 4:1069).

4. Hauffen, "Trinklitteratur," 483–85; Schauber and Schindler, *Heilige und Namenspatrone*, 251. See also the martyr Bibiana, who also serves as protector against drunkenness (Schauber and Schindler, *Heilige und Namenspatrone*, 620).

5. "[Er] fraget in wass saffts das [der Wein] wer . . . . Der wirt . . . sprach / es seind gottes trahen." Pauli, *Schimpff und Ernst*, 43v.

6. See, for example, Franck, *Von dem greüwlichen laster;* StadtAA, ZPO 1537; StadtAA, Strafbücher 1600–1650.

7. For example, the Frankfurt cleric Johannes Wolf's *Beichtbüchlein,* recorded in 1478, 4.

8. Alexander, "Deadly Sins." Some late medieval penitence manuals refer to the seven cardinal sins (pride, avarice, lust, envy, gluttony, anger, and sloth) as mortal sins (*Todsünden*) (for example, Landskron, *Hymel Straß,* 81–114). According to Morton W. Bloomfield, this designation is due to confusion on the part of theologians about the definitions of mortal and cardinal sins (*Deadly Sins,* 43).

9. See, for example, Wolf, *Beichtbüchlein,* 4, 27–28; *Spiegel des Sünders;* Landskron, *Hymel Straß; Beichtbüchlein;* Kaysersberg, *Das Buch Granatapfel,* "Die sieben Hauptsünden." The physician Heinrich Stromer, however, believed that many sorts of food could also cause "drunkenness" (*Verwarnung*).

10. "Das überessen vnd übertrincken tott mer menschen denn das schwert." Landskron, *Hymel Straß,* 114v.

11. Wolf, *Beichtbüchlein,* 28.

12. According to the theologian Godescalc Rosemondt (d. 1526), "there can be no sin without full consent" (Tentler, *Sin and Confession,* 149).

13. McNeill and Gamer, *Handbooks,* 172. Classification of sins as thought, word, or deed originated with Augustine (Alexander, "Deadly Sins," 11:427); and the difference among levels of sin in the case of drunkenness was described by Thomas Aquinas (Ebel, *Trunkenheitsdelikte,* 60–73). On willful consent separating mortal from venial sins ("The more rational and complete the consent, the more culpable the act"), see Tentler, *Sin and Confession,* 150.

14. Tentler, *Sin and Confession,* 101–2, 158, 272.

15. See especially Eph. 5:18 ("be not drunk with wine, wherein is excess").

16. McNeill and Gamer, *Handbooks,* 102, 184, 253–55, 272, 299.

17. Tentler, *Sin and Confession*, 138.

18. Franck, *Von dem greüwlichen laster*, A–B2.

19. Hans Schäuffelin's illustration is reproduced in *Hildener Museumsheft* 1 (1989): 37.

20. Roos, *Devil*, 28–30. Hasso Spode notes that this tract was written twenty years before its publication ("'Boozing Devil,'" 458).

21. Zedler, *Universal-Lexicon*, "Zutrinken" 64:915.

22. Römer, "Luther," 101. In the fifteenth-century tract *Des Teufels Netz* the tavern is described as "die Teufels Kapelle" (the devil's chapel) (Hauffen, "Trinklitteratur," 485; Franck, *Von dem greüwlichen laster*).

23. Roos, *Devil*, 62.

24. "Wan [der Teuffel] vns mit wein hat gefangen / aller sinn beraubt vnd zu narren gemacht / do treybt er seinen gespot / kurtzweil vn[d] faßnacht spil mit vns / treibt vns von einem laster in d[a]z ander." Franck, *Von dem greüwlichen laster*, A3.

25. See, for example, Wickram, *Werke*, "Die Siben Hauptlaster," 259–62, esp. 260; [Schwarzenberg], *Zutrinken*; Schwarzenberg, *Gesatze*.

26. "Unvernünfftig Sewisch leben"; "Ein Predig von Nüchterkait und Mässigkait," from 1539. Luther, *Werke* 47:762, 757–71.

27. Kobelt-Groch, "Unter Zechern," 116–17; Seifert, "Kampf."

28. Grisar, "Der 'gute Trunk,'" 495–500. "Ebriositas" in church Latin translates to the German word "Trunksucht," which implies habitual or addictive use, whereas "ebrietas" can be translated as "Rausch" or "Trunkenheit," mere inebriation (Sleumer, *Wörterbuch*, 290).

29. Luther, *Letters of Spiritual Counsel*, letter from 1530, 18:86.

30. Grisar, "Der 'gute Trunk,'" 501.

31. Ibid., 496.

32. Ibid., 497. See also Luther's statement "nam ebrietas, est ferenda, sed ebriositas, minime!" (intoxication is acceptable, drunkenness, never!). Luther, *Tischreden* 4:580.

33. One recurring image was a large drinking vessel labeled "Dr. M. Luther's Catechism" (Harms, *Flugblätter* 2:206–9).

34. *Ein Tractätlein*, 28–55; Fabricius, *Christlicher Schlafftrunck*, 13, 18–20.

35. Glassen, *Ebrietatis Infamia*, 9–10, 23–25.

36. Harms, *Flugblätter* 4:46.

37. For other examples of marvelous grapes, see Harms, *Flugblätter* 1:221, 220, 7:95.

38. Examples of such pictures can be found in A. Thomas, *Darstellung Christi*.

39. For an example of a giant wine barrel, see Harms, *Flugblätter*, "Vas Stvpendae Magnitvdinis" 3:230; on fruitful wine gardens or vines as a symbol of God's grace, see Schoen, "Klage Gottes über seinen Weinberg," 93, 125; Harms, *Flugblätter* "Friedens-Freude, Krieges-Leid" (1649) 4:260, "Der Geistliche Weinstock deß Herrn Jesu" 3:29, "Sancta Maria et omnes Sancti" 3:49. On an obese man as blessed by good wine, see SuStBA, 2°Lw Einblattdruck nach 1500, no. 164, "Abriß der gewohnlichen grösse Georg Sailer[s]" (Augsburg, 1612). For provision of wine as a symbol of secular power, see Harms, *Flugblätter*, "Kostenloser Weinausschank anläßlich des Friedensfestes in Nürnberg am 25. September 1649" 4:253.

40. Kobelt-Groch, "Unter Zechern," 119–20, 126; Clasen, *Anabaptism*, 142–43, 148; Schmidt, *Alkoholfrage*, 12–17. There is very little scholarship available on drinking among Anabaptists.

5. Drunkenness and the Law

1. Stafford, *Domesticating the Clergy*; Brady, "Godly City."

2. Jellinek, "Specimen," 654; Müller, "Über Trinkstuben," 721.

3. Midelfort, "Johann Weyer," 234; Watson, *Evolution of Law*, 66; Schaffstein, *Lehren vom Verbrechen*, 98–104.

4. Drunkenness does not appear as a punishable offense in the Augsburg Civic Code of 1276, nor is it mentioned in the *Schwabenspiegel* (Meyer, *Stadtbuch von Augsburg; Schwabenspiegel*).

5. Ebel, *Trunkenheitsdelikte*, 163; Schaffstein, *Lehren vom Verbrechen*, 103–4; Midelfort, "Johann Weyer," 255; Lubbers, *Zurechnungsfähigkeit*, 22.

6. The Carolina was completed and established as law during the imperial diets at Augsburg (1530) and Regensburg (1532), and it formed the basis for imperial law thereafter. The first printing was in 1533 (*Keyser Karls des fünfften vnd des heyligen Römischen Reichs peinlich gerichts ordnung;* J. Kohler, *Carolina*, 16–19).

7. Lubbers, *Zurechnungsfähigkeit,* 23; Bassermann-Jordan, *Geschichte des Weinbaus* 2:1175; Stolleis, "Trinkverbote," 185.

8. StadtAA, Römischer Kaiserlicher Majestät Ordnung und Reformation guter Polizei im Heiligen Römischen Reich, Augsburg, 1530; Zedler, *Universal-Lexicon*, "Zutrinken" 64:896–98.

9. StadtAA, Römischer Kaiserlicher Majestät Ordnung; Zedler, *Universal-Lexicon*, "Zutrinken" 64:896; Lubbers, *Zurechnungsfähigkeit*, 23.

10. Tengler, *Layen Spiegel*, "Vom Spül vnd zutrinken"; Tengler, *Der neu Layenspiegel*, 38–39.

11. Tengler, *Der neu Layenspiegel*, 227; Midelfort, "Johann Weyer," 236.

12. "Der trunckenheyte / die entschuldigen mag / alhie gesagt / solstu verstehen / daß es wahr seie / an der höchsten vnnd gar vbermässigen trunckenheyte / welche also häfftig ist / daß sie dem Menschen sinn vnnd Vernunfft hinwegnimbt / vnnd nicht an der schlechten geringen trunckenheyte / welche von der Straffe nicht entschuldigt." Damhouder, *Practica*, 154v. Other circumstances in this category included accidents, crimes committed while insane, acts carried out while sleeping, offenses by minor children, and various kinds of self-defense (Damhouder, *Practica*, 100).

13. "Vn[d] daher sagt man gemeynlich: Daß Trunckenheyt die schuld eynes theyls / vnnd doch nit allzumal entschuldigt." Damhouder, *Practica*, 104v; on moderating guilt in manslaughter cases, see also 154v.

14. Lubbers, *Zurechnungsfähigkeit*, 23–24. Carpzov's *Practica nova imperialis Saxonicae rerum criminalium* was first published in 1638, and it was a basic source for legalists throughout the German-speaking lands well into the eighteenth century (*Neue deutsche Biographie* 3:156–57). See Abele, *Metamorphosis* 2:232, which describes a case of a wealthy

widower who reportedly was held legally responsible for a marriage promise he made to a poor servant girl when he was drunk, unless he could prove he was sufficiently drunk to have lost his senses.

15. Midelfort, "Johann Weyer," 258; Austin, *Alcohol,* 222. Drunkenness differed from madness as a basis for diminished capacity because it was a state entered into voluntarily.

16. Binswanger, "Rechtsgeschichte," 15; Baer, *Stadtlexikon,* "Stadtrecht," 360.

17. City employees put together informal collections of these decrees and periodically updated them, apparently for reference use, but none of these collections was officially acknowledged as constituting a basic city law book (Binswanger, "Rechtsgeschichte," 16–19; Liedl, *Gerichtsverfassung,* 53, bib.). Examples include StadtAA, Schätze 16, Eine Sammlung Städtischer Verordnungen und Erlässe, 1536–1633; StadtAA, Strafamt, fasc. 6, Berichte und Dekrete, not indexed; SuStBA, 4° Cod.Aug.104, 122, 123; 2° Aug.10, 2° Cod.Aug.253, 254, 255, 256, 257, 290.

18. StadtAA, Schätze ad 36/3, ad 36/8, 16; Anschläge und Dekrete 1490–1649, Teil I, nos. 5, 15, 20; Anschläge und Dekrete 1522–1682, fol. 10; Ratserlasse 1507–1599, Polizeiordnung 1526 (no title); Literalien, Satzung 1529; ibid., Polizeiordnung 1530 (no title); StadtAA, ZPO 1537; SuStBA, 2° Aug.10, fol. 53.

19. StadtAA, PO 1526; StadtAA, Anschläge und Dekrete 1490–1649, Teil I, no. 5, Policeyordnung 1524 (no title); ibid., nos. 15, 20, Beruff 1541; StadtAA, Literalien, Satzung 1529; StadtAA, ZPO 1537; SuStBA, 2° Aug.10, fol. 53, "überige Beweinung" (excessive inebriation) or "mit wein beladen" (loaded with wine); SuStBA 2° Cod.Aug.275, 1553.

20. "Mercklich zaichen der Trunckenhait." StadtAA, ZPO 1537.

21. "Soll hinfüran noch fleissiger als vor . . . Anzaigung vnd Schein der Beweinung . . . gebürlich gestrafft werden." StadtAA, Beruff 1541.

22. Time in the tower could in some cases be bought off at rates ranging from ½ gulden to 2 guldens per day, thus ½ gulden was evidently a lesser penalty than two days in the tower (see StadtAA, Strafbuch 1539–1540, 95, Wolfgang Fugger; Strafbuch 1540–1543, 42, Wilhelm Artzt; SuStBA, 2° Cod.Aug 275, 12).

23. "Doch still vnd fridlich heimgehn, vnd niemand auf d[er] gassen nichts thun." StadtAA, ZPO 1580.

24. "Auf die jenigen welche sich ergerlich vnd lesterlich verhalten." StadtAA, Schätze ad 36/8, 28v–27r.

25. StadtAA, ZPO 1537; ZPO 1553.

26. McNeill and Gamer, *Handbooks,* 101–2, 158, 272; StadtAA, Literalien, Satzung 1529, PO 1524; ZPO 1537; ZPO 1553.

27. For example, in the ordinance of 1553, "verderbung der Seelen, Leibs, Lebens, Eeren, vnnd guets." StadtAA, ZPO 1553.

28. StadtAA, PO 1526; Literalien, Satzung 1529; ZPO 1537; Schätze 16, 36 (1538).

29. "Jemands bezechter, so mit boldern, geschrey, oder sonsten sich ärgerlich oder lästerlich verhalten." SuStBA, ZPO 1621.

30. StadtAA, PO 1526; Ratserlasse 1507–1599, Polizeiordnung 1528 (no title); Literalien, Satzung 1529; PO 1530; Beruff 1541.

31. Drunkenness does not appear as a punishable offense in the police ordinances of 1638, 1667, or 1683 (StadtAA, ZPO 1638; Anschläge und Dekrete 1522–1682, no. 52, Zucht- und Polizeiordnung 1667; StadtAA, PO 1683).

32. "Allen vnd yeden Burgern / Innwonern vnd verwandten diser Stat / Jung vnd Alt / Man vnd frawen / Reich vnd Armen." This terminology is used in the ordinances of 1537 and 1541, and it appears in a decree dated 1538 (StadtAA, ZPO 1537; Beruff 1541; Schätze 16, fol. 36).

33. "Geringerer Condition." StadtAA, HWA, Weinwirte 6 1551–1704, 1591; Schätze 36/8, 91.

34. StadtAA, Schätze 16, 113, 293.

35. StadtAA, Schätze 16, 296v–297. Norbert Schindler sees the growing popularity of late-night festivities among the elites during this period as a symbolic "colonization" of darkness, part of the growing separation of elite and popular culture (*Widerspenstige Leute*, 216–22).

36. Rajkay, "Bevölkerungsentwicklung."

37. StadtAA, Zuchtbücher 1539–1540, 1541–1542, 1542–1543, 1543–1544, 1544–1545. Offenses listed as Frevel included fights and other physical threats, such as drawing weapons, challenging to fights, or shooting guns within the city walls. An exchange of verbal insults was categorized as a Zucht offense, as were swearing, gambling, drinking in the villages, poor householding, tavern violations such as seating guests after hours or serving meat on Fridays, and illegal dancing and music. Fines for adultery were recorded in separate books.

38. Discipline books were not maintained between 1631 and 1646, probably because of the distractions of the Thirty Years' War. Records of sixty-six such brawls exist for 1640–1644, but they are not consistent in showing fines (StadtAA, Reichsstadtakten 818, 1640–1649, Frevelanzeigen for 1640–1644).

39. A total of 765 fines were collected for brawling between 10 July 1677 and 10 July 1682. Drunkenness as a separate fine was recorded in a separate book between 1646 and 1690 (StadtAA, Zuchtbücher 1646–1690).

40. StadtAA, Zuchtbücher 1646–1690, 46, 72, 74, 75, 118.

41. In thirty-four cases involving violence, thirty-one reported drinking socially before the incident, two reported having drunk with their wives, and only one claimed not to have drunk at all before the incident (StadtAA, Urg., 1540–1544).

42. Discipline fines collected in towns and villages outside Augsburg reflect similar attitudes. In Kirchheim, for example, lists of fines collected from brawlers show no variance whether or not the offenders were described as drunk (Fürstlich und Gräflich Fuggerisches Familien- und Stiftungs-Archiv, 78.1.4, KA 1592–1599; 78.1.17, KA 1642; 78.1.18, KA 1643; 78.1.19, KA 1644).

43. "Jetzt . . . wird die Trunkenheit, gemeinlich weder bei hohen noch niedern Standes Leuten für keine Schande mehr gehalten." Andreae, *Erinnerung*, quoted in Janssen, *Geschichte* 8:274.

44. "Überhaupt so viel, als zusammen oder in Gesellschaft trincken"; "Ein solches Sauff-Gelach . . . da ein Sauff- und Zech-Bruder oder Geselle den andern nothiget, eben

so viele und so grosse Humpen auszuleeren, als jener in seinen vollen Wanst hinein zu schütten vermag." Zedler, *Universal-Lexicon*, "Zutrinken" 64:890–91; Grimm, *Deutsches Wörterbuch*, "Zutrinken" 16:874.

45. "In Germanie, and in the low Countreyes to banquett and feast their friends often ys thought a great and magnificent thing, though not so in other places." Ashley, *Of Honour*, 53; Braudel, *Everyday Life*, 190–99; Schama, *Embarrassment of Riches*, 149–88.

46. Montaigne, *Works*, 892.

47. Opsopaeus, *De Arte Bibendi*, 686–700.

48. Blanke, "Alkoholismus," 77.

49. "Es solle auch nyemand . . . den andern / mit ernstlichen / oder gleichwol schimpflichen worten / noch in ander wege / zu freuenlichen vnd vnzymblichen zutrincken . . . weder müssen / nötten / tringen / manen / bedeüten / stupffen / noch in kainen andern wege / wie das menschen sinne erdenncken mag / bewegen." Stadt-AA, Literalien, Satzung 1529, no. 406, 5 Dec. 1529.

50. StadtAA, HWA, Fischer 1, 1429–1551 (1538).

51. "Ohne hohe übertrettung." StadtAA, Evangelisches Wesensarchiv 1487, Bürger-stubenordnung, 9. On elite pledging of healths, see the accounts of travelers in *Augsburg in alten und neuen Reisebeschreibungen;* Bates, *Touring*, 242, 255; Montaigne, quoted in Potthoff and Kossenhaschen, *Kulturgeschichte*, 140; and esp. Schweinichen, *Denkwürdigkeiten,* which describes drunkenness at court and patrician tables throughout Germany, 15, 50, 91–92, 314–16, 323, 326.

52. "Soll hinfüran kain Leykauff vmb ainicherlay Waar oder Kauff getruncken werden." StadtAA, Beruff 1541. "Leikauf," "Leykauf," "Leitkauf" (from Middle High German "lît," Early New High German "leit," "fruit wine"), also "Weinkauf." See Götze, *Glossar,* 149; Erler and Kaufmann, *Handwörterbuch* 1:1842–43; the present volume, chap. 6, n. 16.

53. "Ansingwein." Fischer, *Schwäbisches Wörterbuch* 5:262; Roper, *Holy Household*, 146. On consummation of the marriage as a point of legality, see Roper, "Church and Street," 66; StadtAA, Hochzeitsamt, Hochzeitsamtsprotokolle 1463–1729; Stadtkanzlei, Konzepte Heiratsbriefe 14.1, 1502–1559.

54. StadtAA, Anschläge und Dekrete 1522–1682, no. 4, Hochzeitsordnung 1540; Ratserlasse 1507–1599, Hochzeitsordnung 1536. Immoderate drinking of Ansing wine was forbidden as early as 1526; StadtAA, PO 1526; PO 1528.

55. "Leikauffen vnd anderen erlaubten ehrlichen Einladungen." SuStBA, ZPO 1621.

56. StadtAA, ZPO 1580.

57. StadtAA, Kaufmannschaft und Handel, fasc. 5, Kaufleutestube; StadtAA, Anschläge und Dekrete 1522–1682, no. 21, 1638. I have not found Zutrinken mentioned in any other documents of the seventeenth century.

58. StadtAA, Zuchtbücher 1539–1540, 96, Simon Flennder, "zusauffen"; Zuchtbücher 1540–1542, 15, Martin Weidenkranz, "zutrinken noten"; Zuchtbücher 1540–1542, 151, Georg von Burtenbach, "zusauffen." The name "von Burtenbach" and the lack of indication of any trade in all three cases suggest that these offenders may have been social elites.

59. Examples are provided in Basserman-Jordan, *Geschichte des Weinbaus* 2:1176–77; Bode, *Trinksitten*, 199; A. Kohler, "Wohnen und Essen," 251.

60. Franck, *Von dem greüwlichen laster*, J2; Opsopaeus, *De Arte Bibendi*, 678; Austin, *Alcohol*, 155; Janssen, *Geschichte*, 8:159–82; Zedler, *Universal-Lexicon*, "Zutrinken" 64: 912–13.

61. Mair, *Chronik*, 350–51; StadtAA, Schätze 13a, 178v.

62. "Welches aber [ist] nur für ein Gespott gehalten / vnd ein Sprichwort darauß gemacht worden." Welser, *Chronica*, 98.

63. "Es gilt dem Reichstagsabschied." Potthoff and Kossenhaschen, *Kulturgeschichte*, 140; Zedler, *Universal-Lexicon*, "Zutrinken" 64:898, "Es gilt dir auf des Reichs Abschied"; Schwarzenberg, *Gesatze*, B4v.

64. Spode, *Alkohol und Zivilisation*, 71–73.

65. SuStBA, ZPO 1621.

66. See, for example, Schwerhoff, *Kreuzverhör*, 294; Allen, "Crime and Punishment," 205–6. Both scholars claim that drunkenness served to reduce penalties, and, while regional variation is possible, neither of these works provides any evidence to support the assertion.

67. "On alle verursachung." StadtAA, Urg., 1543–1544, Veit Stöckle, 17 Dec. 1544; Stadt-AA, Strafbuch 1543–1553, 41; Urg., Hieronymus Schwab, 23 Jan. 1590.

68. "Freundliche abbitten [unverletzlich der ehren] mit gwohnliche[r] bietung der hand." SuStBA, ZPO 1621; StadtAA, Zuchtbücher 1540–1550, 1590–1600; PZS 1590–1600, which include hundreds of entries of persons released without fine, or with a reduced fine, after apologizing to one another before the Discipline Lords.

69. "Die Stat Augspurg wer ain Judenstat, unnd es muess sie . . . got in himel schen-den . . . der nechst der ime bekeme wolt er ain schlacht swerd in ine stossen, unnd der nechst wer ime der liebst darzu, er trueg gleich samet oder seiden an." "Dann er vom wein dismals so ubergangen, das er nit recht bei sich selbs gewest." StadtAA, Urg., Andreas Steiner, 14 May 1544. Steiner was exposed on the pillory and banished for life after his tongue was cut out.

70. StadtAA, Strafbuch 1509–1526, 88; Urg., Simon Rayser, 22 Jan. 1593.

71. The normal fine for brawling or causing a scene was 2 gulden, but any disorderly behavior (brawling, loud disputes, or exposed weapons) occurring in front of the city council house or at the city gates was fined at 7 gulden (StadtAA, PZS 1590–1594).

72. The fact that Hueber's name appeared in the records as "Herr S. Hueber" indicates that he belonged to the city elite. "Aufruherisch," "Schwedisch." StadtAA, Urg., Melchior Nershaimer, 20 Nov. 1642; StadtAA, Strafbuch 1633–1653, 260. Nershaimer was released with a warning. Examples of other such cases can be found in StadtAA, Straf-buch 1633–1653, 341, 344.

73. StadtAA, Strafamt, Ehebrecher-Strafbücher 1575–1591, 1591–1609, 1609–1620, 1620–1658, 1659–1704.

74. "Er [sei] gar kain man wann er truncken sei, welches er mit seim weib beweisen wöll." StadtAA, Urg., Hans Wagner, 20–24 Jan. 1592.

75. "Sie ime ein lust zumachen angerüete welches aber nichts gehofffen." Ibid.

76. "Ine vexiert . . . also wann er kain man were." Ibid.

77. "Das sein verbrechen höcher dann für ein *adulterium* zuhalten." StadtAA, Strafbuch 1588–1596, 136.

78. Ibid. For adultery fines, see StadtAA, Ehebrecher-Strafbücher 1575–1591, 1591–1609. Fines for a first offense ranged from 15 to 84 gulden, probably depending on the socio-economic status of the offender, and they could be commuted to time in the tower if the person charged was unable to pay. For repeat offenses, the fines were simply raised.

79. StadtAA, Ehebrecher-Strafbuch 1609–1620, 36; Ledigstand-Strafbuch 1636–1659, 40.

80. "Dieweiln dann dies werkh nit gäntzliche alß ein Ehebruch abzustraffen." Stadt-AA, Ledigestand-Strafbuch 1636–1659, 40; on Georg Reichlin, see Ehebrecher-Strafbuch 1609–1620, 36.

81. A total of seven women and six men associated with the prostitution ring were punished for prostitution, procuring, or incest (StadtAA, Strafbuch 1588–1596, 134v–136; StadtAA, Urg., 1592a, Sara Mair et al.).

82. "Der lei kurtzweil nirgends als zu Sodoma und Gomorra verstattet worden oder werden." StadtAA, Urg., Balthasar Weiss, 12–26 Feb. 1644.

83. Roper, *Holy Household*, 256–57; Brown, *Immodest Acts*, 14–20; Monter, *Ritual*, 116–17; Evans, "'Dangerous Classes,'" 6.

84. "Und sie beide wider zu gueten freunden gesprochen worden." StadtAA, Urg., Balthasar Weiss, 12–26 Feb. 1644.

85. "Offentliche schand." Ibid.

86. "Vnd ist allen fünf persohnen das *Silentium* auferlegt worden." Ibid. In none of the 2,181 other cases on which this sample is based did the interrogators issue similar instructions, but a comparison can be found in the 1535 case of the patrician's son Ulrich Hunold, who confessed incest with his sister (who became pregnant as a result), in which witnesses were also warned to remain silent (StadtAA, Personenselekt, Ulrich Hunold, 1535–1538).

87. Roger Kusch concludes that current German law still has not solved the problem of voluntary drunkenness serving to mitigate responsibility (*Vollrausch*).

88. These words ("dan man im trunckh gemainlich dasselbe heraußlasse, wessen d[a]z herz voll ist") were used by interrogators in the case of a craftsman who attempted to excuse with drunkenness his verbal attack on one of Augsburg's mayors (StadtAA, Urg., Matthäus Merkt, 25 July 1614).

6. The Contract Drink

1. StadtAA, HWA, Weinwirte 6 1551–1704, 1591.

2. StadtAA, Urg., Sixt Röting, 22 March 1542; Veit Bacher, 16 Dec. 1591; Jacob Ritter, 13 Aug. 1592; Jonas Schmid, 17 March 1593.

3. "Er wolt ehe im Thurn erfaulen, ehe er im die Wirtsheuser wolt verpieten lassen." StadtAA, Urg., Hainrich Frey, 20 March 1593. Whether Frey agreed to the tavern ban when he was finally released is not clear, but there is no mention of a ban in the punishment records.

4. To mention only a few of many examples from Greek literature, see Aeschines, *Against Ctesiphon*, 3.224; Aristophanes, *Lysistrata*, 229–30; Herodotus, *Histories*, 4.66, 4.70; Plato, *Critias*, 120a; Thucydides, *Histories*, 6.32. On the various drinking traditions of the Greek symposium, see Murray, *Sympotica*, esp. Oswyn Murray, "The Affair of the Mysteries: Democracy and the Drinking Group," 149–61, and Francois Lissarrague, "Around the Krater: An Aspect of Banquet Imagery," 197–209.

5. Kircher, *Bedeutung*, 66–67, 89. The Greek term for ritual intoxication was *"enthousiasmos,"* divine possession (Toussaint-Samat, *History of Food*, 253, 258).

6. These premodern examples include African, Semitic, and Egyptian cultures; see Kircher, *Bedeutung*, 82–90; Dillistone, *Christianity and Symbolism*, 224–27; Akyeoampong, "Alcohol," 54–60; Tegnaeus, *Blood-Brothers*, 19–27.

7. In Greek mythology, too, wine is represented by a twice-born god, as Dionysos is born once of his mother, the mortal Semele, and again from the thigh of his father, Zeus.

8. Matt. 26:28; 1 Cor. 11:21.

9. For a collection of these images with analysis, see A. Thomas, *Darstellung Christi*.

10. Dillistone, *Christianity and Symbolism*, 277; Huber, *Trankopfer*, 32–33. E. Huber theorized that wine as a sacrificial offering did not originate as a replacement for blood sacrifice; rather, wine had already independently developed a cultural meaning associated with sacrifices, and only then did it gradually replace blood in sacrificial rites.

11. Mauss, *Gift*, 60–61. Compare the rite of the treaty curse in ancient Greek, Roman, Trojan, and Babylonian traditions, in which wine represented the life of the participants and, according to Richard Onians, is the origin of the use of wine to conclude treaties (Onians, *Origins*, 217–18).

12. This may explain why blood rituals, including drinking blood as a sign of brotherhood, were not as prevalent among the Germans as they were among the wine-drinking cultures of the Mediterranean (Strack, *Jew and Human Sacrifice*, 43–47).

13. Spode, *Alkohol und Zivilisation*, 20–22; Huber, *Trankopfer*, 1–3.

14. See the comparisons in *International Handbook on Alcohol and Culture*, and esp. Heath, "Some Generalizations," 352.

15. "Also bracht der Rigler her Casper Wintzerers diener ain glaß mit wein, wie man dan zutringkt, der erst, der in kem auff der gassen, den wellten sie zu tod schlagen." Rem, *Cronica*, 6–7. Rem reported that Rigler met a just end two years later, when he died as the result of an accident while drunk (28).

16. "Leikauf," more archaic "Leitkauf" (Middle High German "lîtkouf"): combination of "Leit" (fruit wine) and "Kauf" (purchase); other combinations are "Leitgebe" (tavern keeper) and "Leithaus" (tavern). Assimilatory loss of the dental consonant in "Leikauf" and the vowel change to "Leut" (people), as in "Leuthaus" (public house), indicate that "Leit" had become obscure in later Early New High German. In the Augsburg documents of the sixteenth and seventeenth centuries, only the form "Leikauf" (also "Leykauf") appears (Lexer, *Handwörterbuch*, 1:1939–40; Grimm, *Deutsches Wörterbuch* 6:693–94, 849). On the term "Weinkauf" (and for a legal definition of the contract drink), see Erler and Kaufmann, *Handwörterbuch* 1:1842–43; Birlinger, *Volksthümliches*

3:58; Grimm, *Deutsches Wörterbuch* 14.1:944–48. The term "Weinkauf" did not imply that only wine could be used in the ritual, for symbolically, any beverage containing "spirits" was understood as a kind of wine.

17. Matter, "'Im Wein liegt Wahrheit,'" 43. A Weinkauf accepted as cash, without expenditure on drinks, was known as a "trockener [dry] Weinkauf" (Matter, 44).

18. Beier, *Handwerks-Lexicon*, "Leykauff machen," 252.

19. See, for example, StadtAA, Zuchtbücher 1540–1542, 64, 88, 132; Zuchtbücher 1542–1543, 83, 125. By the eighteenth century, concluding sales of real property with a Weinkauf in a public tavern was required by law in some parts of Germany (Schreiber, *Deutsche Weingeschichte*, 274).

20. StadtAA, Urg., Georg Allbrecht, July 30 1590; Samuel Lederer and Thomas Schießle, 26 July 1590. Other examples of city guards accused of accepting drinks as bribes include Urg., Christoph Seitz et al., 14 Dec. 1590; Hans Hainrich Keren, ca. 1593; Hans Franck, 11 March 1594.

21. StadtAA, Urg., Balthasar Gausmeir, Feb.–March 1591.

22. "Hatt ime ein trunck weins vill mehr als sein Aidt vnnd pflicht laßen angelegen sein." Stadtarchiv Nördlingen, Urfehdenbücher 1587–1592, 22r–23v.

23. Examples of oaths sworn before the city council can be found in StadAA, Strafamt, Urfehden. Those involved in a fight that broke out after a settlement were fined four times as much as participants in a normal fight. See StadtAA, PZS 1590–1594.

24. Examples include StadtAA, Urg., Elias Mair and Jacob Roth, 9 July 1590; Michael Eisenhuet, 9 Nov. 1592; Hans Bausch, 10 June 1592.

25. "Du hast . . . ein red gethon die mir nit gefällt, werst mir wol ein viertl Bier schuldig." StadtAA, Urg., Lorenz Greinwold et al., 7–17 July 1643.

26. This was the opinion of barber-surgeons who examined the victim (ibid.).

27. The city council suspected that the initial insults were of a confessional nature but none of the participants or witnesses confirmed this charge (ibid.).

28. StadtAA, Urg., Hans Bausch, 10 June 1592; Hans Stehele, 11 June 1592. This amount is based on prices for wine and beer in 1589 and 1602 (StadtAA, Chroniken 10, Chronik von Siedeler, 173, 284; Dirlmeier, *Untersuchungen*, 570).

29. Moryson's claim that "he that is wounded payes the wyne to all the rest who are partners of the quarell, or beholders of the fight" did not hold true in Augsburg, where the drinks were normally paid for by the first to offer the hand of peace, typically either the instigator or whoever inflicted physical injury (*Itinerary*, 347).

30. "Darauff sy beede sampt iren vertrags leuth, hingangen . . . ein guetten drunckh zur bestettigung d[er] sach, zu thun, vnd ein guetten Dampff zu hallten, Welliches nun geschech[en], vnd sein Also wid[er] guett gesellen worden . . . . Also ist widerumb ein Strudl fürübergangen." SuStBA, 2° Cod.S.41, Georg Kölderer Chronik, 3. Buch, 1584–1587, 57r–v, 79r–v. I wish to thank Benedikt Mauer for this reference.

31. The Einschank was enjoyed on arrival and the Ausschank (also known as the Weingang) on departure (Beier, *Handwerks-Lexicon*, 99, 104, 145, 473; Buff, "Ausgeschenk," 457–62).

32. StadtAA, Chroniken 10, Chronik von Siedeler, 200; Müller, "Über Trinkstuben," 725.

33. Schreiber, *Deutsche Weingeschichte,* 276.

34. StadtAA, Urg., Georg Schigner, 16 Feb. 1591; SuStBA, 4° Cod.S.10, Augsburger Chronik, 1554–1654, 1582, 1600.

35. Schreiber, *Deutsche Weingeschichte,* 239, 379, 382. According to tradition, John the Evangelist drank poison without injury, thus wine blessed on Johannistag had a protective quality (Grimm, *Deutsches Wörterbuch* 4.2:2333).

36. James, *Sacrifice,* 25.

37. Examples of such contrafacta can be seen in Steidel, *Zecher- und Schlemmerlieder,* 93–107.

38. Scribner, *Popular Culture,* 1–16.

7. Drinking and Gender Identity

1. "Von des zukünftigen Dursts wegen." Abele, *Metamorphosis* 2:676.

2. Koch, *Maior dignitas,* 233.

3. According to Agrippa von Nettesheim, the household serves as metaphor for the state ("Das Haus ist ein Bild des Staates") (*Eitelkeit,* 300).

4. Schuster, "Ehre und Recht," 40–66; Friedrich Zunkel, "Ehre, Reputation," in Brunner, *Grundbegriffe* 2:1–64.

5. His, *Geschichte,* 93.

6. See, for example, StadtAA, Urg., Hans Eisenhofer, 4 Oct. 1540; Jörg Fritz, 28 March 1542; StadtAA, Strafbuch 1540–1542, 1v, 4v, 21, 24v, 25, 31v, 37, 37, 39; Strafbuch 1543–1553, 1, 3v–4, 35.

7. "Und sey allain sein weib, welche ime zu haus und uber tisch kain ruehe lass, sonder stetiges zanck, an dism allem schuldig, das er ausgeen und ime anderer orten ruehe suechen muess." StadtAA, Urg., Hans Mair, 5 Feb. 1592.

8. StadtAA, Urg., Michael Alber, 8 June 1542. Alber undermined his own argument, however, by testifying that he had been drinking on the evening he beat his wife.

9. "Es hab jm daheim niemand kochen wollen, hab doch allein die nottruff gezert." StadtAA, Urg., Georg Bschorn, 29 Aug. 1590.

10. StadtAA, Urg., Bernhard Hartmann, 26 July 1544.

11. StadtAA, Urg., Ulrich Hemerle, 3 Sept. 1592; Strafbuch 1588–1596, 154v.

12. StadtAA, Schätze 16, 50v, 107r; StadtAA, HWA, Weinwirte 6 1551–1704, 1591; StadtAA, Schätze 36/8, 91; StadtAA, Chroniken 10, Chronik von Siedeler, 176r.

13. "Er sitz nur der Würtzheuser . . . zum welchen er dann nit nur für sich selbsten die zech, sondern für jederman auss zalt, und zugleich das gelt unnd die klaider in den würtzheusern gelassen." StadtAA, Urg., Jacob Ritter, Nov. 1591.

14. Steidel, *Zecher- und Schlemmerlieder,* 85–87; Haas, *Trinklieder,* 295.

15. StadtAA, Urg., Georg Balin, 18 Nov. 1592; Hans Mair, 5 Feb. 1592; Hans Waltmann, 7 Feb. 1592.

16. See, for example, StadtAA, Urg., Hans Lochner, 18 Nov. 1592; Georg Hartmann, 22 Sept. 1590.

17. StadtAA, Urg., Hans Bausch, 15–20 March 1591.

18. StadtAA, Urg., Hans Bausch, 10 June 1592; Barbara Weberin, 3 Oct. 1594, in which a baker's wife testified that she was willing to forgive her husband for meeting a lover in a tavern because she could not run the bakery without him.

19. StadtAA, Urg., Georg Bschorn, 29 Aug. 1590; Stafbuch 1588–1596, 81.

20. See, for example, StadtAA, Urg., Jonas Schmid, 17 March 1593; Ulrich Hemerle, 6 Sept. 1593.

21. Moryson, *Itinerary*, 340.

22. Crawley, "Drinks."

23. Brandes, *Power and Persuasion,* 176.

24. Ashley, *Of Honour,* 53; Zäh, "Hans Jakob Fugger."

25. These fines could be up to 10 gulden. StadtAA, Ratserlasse 1507–1599, Hochzeits-ordnung 1536; Hochzeitsordnung 1581; Anschläge und Dekrete 1522–1682, no. 4, Hoch-zeitsordnung 1540; no. 13, Hochzeitsordnung 1575; Anschläge und Dekrete 1490–1649, no. 51, Hochzeitsordnung 1599.

26. StadtAA, Urg., Caspar Aufschlager, 16 Aug. 1591; Philipp Schach, 19 May 1593; HWA, Weber 169, 17 Aug. 1669.

27. StadtAA, Urg., Lienhart Strobel, 28–29 July 1542; Roper, *Holy Household,* 116–17.

28. StadtAA, Ratsprotokolle 14, 1501–1520, 18, Bettelordnung 1519; StadtAA, Ratserlasse 1507–1599, Ordnung Almosenherren, 1522; StadtAA, Almosenamt, Almosen-Ordnungen, 1543, 1569.

29. "Warumb er am Samstag nitt langer bey jn bliben, er hette noch genug zutrincken gehabt, dann er vnd der Lederer haben dem thorwart 2 kantten bier auff dem tisch gelassen, . . . vnd sey er vnd der Lederer dermassen bezecht gewesen, Das er nitt wiß, wie sy auff der gassen von ainander komen." StadtAA, Urg., Georg Albrecht, 30 July 1590; Samuel Lederer and Thomas Schießle, 26 July 1590.

30. StadtAA, Urg., Hans Liepart, Hans Hohenberger, Barbara Hohenbergerin, 27–30 April 1542; Strafbuch 1540–1543, 46. Liepart subsequently admitted his sexual intention and was beaten, exposed on the pillory, and exiled from the city for two years; Hohen-berger was placed on house arrest for a few months. Hohenberger's wife was assumed innocent and left unpunished.

31. "Ehemals waren die Deutschen eine kriegerische Nation; jetzt suchen sie statt in Waffen ihre Mannhaftigkeit nur noch in Weingefechten; der größte Held ist, der am meisten vertragen kann." Giovanni Francesco Poggio Bracciolini, quoted in Potthoff and Kossenhaschen, *Kulturgeschichte,* 142.

32. Müller, "Über Trinkstuben," 622; Multibibus, *Zechrecht,* A2; Blanke, "Alkoholis-mus," 83; Franck, *Von dem greüwlichen laster,* B2, Anhang.

33. "Füllen vnd vnluterkeit [und] die groß vnküscheit / Hatt nider truckt alle man-heit." Zentralbibliothek Zürich, Wickianer Einblattdruck PAS 12/15.

34. A song from 1536 includes the verse, "Wir wollen sauffen zu halben vnd zu vollen / wer das nicht kan / er sol bey vns nicht bleyben / auss dem orden wollen wir jn schreiben / wir wollen jn bey vns nicht haben." (We want to guzzle half and full meas-ures / and who is not able / should not stay with us / we will kick him out of the order / we don't want to have him around.) See also the 1620 verse, "Vnd wilstu nicht auss

sauffen / so mustu mir entlauffen." (And if you don't want to drink up / see that you get away from me.) Steidel, *Zecher- und Schlemmerlieder*, 71.

35. Götze, *Glossar*, "Bescheid," 28.

36. Multibibus, *Zechrecht*, A8.

37. See, for example, StadtAA, HWA, Lodweber 157, 1550–1582, Hans Seidler, who was threatened with expulsion from his craft for drinking with a skinner. For the contaminating nature of dishonorable persons, see Stuart, *Defiled Trades*, 46–48, 194–97.

38. StadtAA, Urg., Lucas Fischer, 22 Nov. 1593.

39. Rem, *Cronica*, 92. Vetter was fined 10 gulden and banned from the Lords' Drinking Room for one year. For other examples of such disagreements, see StadtAA, Urg., Michael Hurler, 22 March 1593; Andreas Stemmer, 7 March 1644.

40. Compare Gerd Schwerhoff's evaluation of crime in Cologne, in which alcohol was involved in "well over half" of all violence cases (*Kreuzverhör*, 294).

41. Daß "er die Tag seines Lebens sich deß spihlens enthalten." StadtAA, Urg., Caspar Aufschlager, 16 Aug. 1591.

42. Grimm, *Deutsches Wörterbuch* 4.2:1934.

43. "Er hat dich nun hundsfud gehaissen, wilt Dus von im leiden, ich wolt dich selbs in das Angesicht schlagen, wan du woltest ein Landsknecht sein, und solliches gedulden." StadtAA, Urg., Caspar Aufschlager, 16 Aug. 1591.

44. "Kunde . . . weniger nit thun." Ibid.

45. "Der Rauner den Aufschlager, mit ehrnruerigen worten provociert." StadtAA, Strafbuch 1588–1596, 118. Aufschlager was expelled from the city for five years, a punishment that did not affect his honor, his property, or necessarily his livelihood, as he was a citizen of Nördlingen. Compare Aufschlager's penalty with the case of Thomas Mangmeister and Jörg Schmid, who were permanently banished for killing someone in a fight (StadtAA, Urg., 29 March 1541). Had the city council decided that Aufschlager's actions were necessary to defend his life, he would have been released without penalty.

46. Elias, *Zivilisation* 1:276–77; Bode, *Trinksitten*, 202–5; Ariès, *Childhood*, 391; Austin, *Alcohol*, 131–32, 140; N. Schindler, *Widerspenstige Leute*, 232–36.

47. A total of eighteen murders and manslaughters (excluding infanticide) were recorded during the fifteen years. Based on population estimates of 30,000 for 1540–1544, 40,000 for 1590–1594, and 21,000 for 1640–1644, the approximate per capita homicide rates were 1 per 15,000, 1 per 3,000, and 1 per 7,000, respectively. Richard van Dülmen sees in such numbers a level of violence decidedly higher than in modern times (*Kultur und Alltag* 2:254–55); Lawrence Stone comes to a similar conclusion about early modern England ("Violence," 32). Gerd Schwerhoff has shown, however, that such conclusions fail to take into consideration the higher rate of violent crime in modern cities. Augsburg's homicide rate was in any case much lower than that of contemporary Washington, D.C. (*Kreuzverhör*, 282–86).

48. "Auch die rauhe Wirtsstubengeselligkeit [beinhaltete] noch Formen wechselseitiger sozialer Kontrolle." N. Schindler, *Widerspenstige Leute*, 234; Bernhard Müller-Wirthmann, "Raufhändel." For a sociologist's view on the requirements to adhere to rules when responding to threats in company, see Paris and Sofsky, "Drohungen," 22.

49. This point is also made in Dinges, "Ehre," 421. For comparable anthropological perspectives on the fragile nature of male honor, see Gilmore, *Honor and Shame*, 2–21.

50. Müller-Wirthmann, "Raufhändel," 82.

51. Records of fines distinguish between blood fight (Blutfrevel) and bloodless scuffle (kleiner Frevel) (StadtAA, PZS 1590–1595).

52. StadtAA, Urg., Hans Bausch and Hans Stehele, 11 June 1592; Hans Jakob Eppelin and Veit Kesselbaur, 20 July 1594; Abraham Heberle, 1 Feb. 1590; Caspar Morhart, 31 May 1642.

53. Tengler, *Layen Spiegel*, Teil 3, n.f. According to Jost Damhouder, members of the nobility had a greater responsibility to defend their honor with the sword than did untitled persons (*Practica*, 139v).

54. StadtAA, PZS 1589–1595.

55. "Das er seiner Synn gar beraubt gewest." StadtAA, Urg., Hans Khrauer, 25 Oct. 1544.

56. StadtAA, Urg., Hans Lechmair, 6 March 1591; Caspar Wismüller, 12 Aug. 1591.

57. StadtAA, Urg., Philipp Zösching, 26 Feb. 1590.

58. "Weiln vihl leut ob der gasse waren, unnd er sich geschembtt da er sich nit wöhren soltt [habe er sich] feindschafft oder widerwillen wohl nit [sondern] not und schandt halber wöhren muessen." StadtAA, Urg., Caspar Morhart, 31 May 1642.

59. Austin, *Alcohol*, 156; Ariès, *Childhood*, 391.

60. The professions of the remaining 9 percent (thirteen defendants) cannot be identified. Of these defendants, two are identified as Augsburg citizens, indicating a minimum status of craftsman, and four as youth (*knap*), probably apprentices. The accused in the nine tavern incidents that ended with a killing included three guardsmen, four craftsmen, one barber-surgeon, and a group of butchers.

61. "Da ein frembden vom Adel, furstliche gestandten od[er] anndere ansehenliche leit alhie frevelten vnd sich nit anzeigten, d[a]z dieselben nit einzogen . . . damit man gemeiner Statt keinen anhang od[er] feindschafft mache." StadtAA, ZPO 1553, 23.

62. Häberlein, "Tod auf der Herrenstube"; Groebner, "Ratsinteressen," 289–90; Burghartz, *Leib, Ehre, und Gut*, 108–11, 116–18, 139–54; StadtAA, Urg., Matthes Neidhart, 22 Dec. 1644; Jeremias Weilbach, 5 June 1591; Hans Knopf, 18–22 Nov. 1591; Lucas Fischer, 22 Nov. 1593; Anton Weyler, 30 May 1640; Melchior Nershaimer, 20 Nov. 1642.

63. Muchembled, *Popular Culture*, 31.

64. Marsh, Rosser, and Harré, *Rules of Disorder*, 2–10.

65. An example from the 1590s can be found in Seling, *Goldschmiede* 1:85, 2:168; see also Lessing, "Wunderliches Trinkgerät."

66. Descriptions of charivaris directed against domineering women appear in Beattie, "Criminality of Women," 87; Dülmen, *Kultur und Alltag* 1:54–55.

67. Tuana, "Weaker Seed," 149–50.

68. These transmutations could occur as a result of vigorous physical activity, for example. See Wiesner, *Women and Gender*, 46; Schiebinger, *The Mind Has No Sex?* 163–64; Laqueur, *Making Sex*, 123, 126–29; Maclean, *Renaissance Notion of Women*, 38–39.

69. Schwarzenberg, *Gesatze*.

70. The image circulated during the seventeenth century in at least two versions, which can be found in Zentralbibliothek Zürich, Einblattdruck, Elsass, Ia, 2. The example reproduced here is from 1620.

71. See, for example, Hans Sachs's sixteenth-century tract "Die Zwelff Eygenschafft eines boszhafftigen verruchten weybs," reproduced in Strauss, *Illustrated Bartsch* 13:339; Franck, *Von dem greüwlichen laster,* D2. Additional literature addressing drunkenness among women is listed in Bassermann-Jordan, *Geschichte des Weinbaus* 2:1177; and Janssen, *Geschichte* 8:274–300.

72. "Wievil huren machet der weyn?" Franck, *Von dem greüwlichen laster,* D2.

73. Plummer, "Reforming the Family," 128–29, 139.

74. Behringer, *Hexen und Hexenprozesse,* 290, 292, 281; Bächtold-Stäubli, *Handwörterbuch* 8:1262–63.

75. See, for example, Accati, "Spirit of Fornication," 110–40; Roper, *Oedipus,* 171–98.

76. Roper, *Oedipus,* 176, 191, 199–225; Wiltenburg, *Disorderly Women,* 247–50.

77. Some witches reported eating and drinking at the sabbath but do not mention drunkenness. See StadtAA, Urg., Anna Wagnerin, 2 May 1690; Strafbuch 1633–1653, 337; Strafbuch 1654–1699, 159.

78. "Lumpen." StadtAA, Urg., Leonhart Wolfmüller, 9 Nov. 1594.

79. StadtAA, Urg., Matthäus Nate, 6 April 1541; Bernhart Jager, 3 Feb. 1542; Christoph Rörle, 29 April 1593; Hans Mehrer, 2 July 1640.

80. This is based on 4,576 fines collected for 1590–1594. StadtAA, PZS 1589–1591, 1591–1592, 1592–1593, 1593–1594, 1594–1595. Müller-Wirthmann's study of village violence suggests that women's resorting to physical violence was more common during the late sixteenth century than it was a century later ("Raufhändel," 81–91).

81. "Hab . . . dafür gehalten, weil es weiber handel gewest, hab es nicht zubedeuten, da er sy von einander helf bescheiden." StadtAA, Urg., David Bögle, 30 Oct. 1591.

82. During the late sixteenth century, men were fined 2 gulden for fighting, women ½ gulden. When the fine was split between a man and a woman who fought with one another, the man paid 1 gulden and the woman ¼ gulden (StadtAA, PZS 1590–1594). During the Reformation, fines for women were half those charged of men (Roper, *Oedipus,* 40).

83. See, for example, StadtAA, Urg., Jeremias Weilbach, 5 June 1591; Michael Schmid, 14 June 1593; Hans Ettlich, 17 May 1544; Hans Schuster, 24 Feb. 1541.

84. StadtAA, Urg., 1590b, Hans Pleig, 26 May 1590.

85. See, for example, StadtAA, Urg., Caspar Aufschlager, 16 Aug. 1591; Jeremias Weibach, 5 June 1591; Apollonia Möckin, 20 April 1594; Valentin Klay, 14 Oct. 1642.

86. StadtAA, Zuchtbücher 1540–1542, 82.

87. Daß "er weder steen noch geen . . . können." StadtAA, Urg., Niclaus Weber, 10 Jan. 1590.

88. StadtAA, Urg., Balthus Laimer, 23 July 1548.

89. Roper, "Discipline and Respectability."

90. StadtAA, Urg., Ursula Heckmairin, 10 Aug. 1541; Apollonia Saylerin, 21 June 1542; Ursula Müllerin, 8 Aug. 1542; Barbara Rugerin, 18 Jan. 1542; Ursula Paumaisterin, 28 Oct. 1542. On procuring, see Roper, "Mothers of Debauchery."

91. See, for example, StadtAA, Urg., Balthasar Eck, 17 Dec. 1590; Barbara Weberin, 3 Oct. 1594.

92. For example, see StadtAA, Urg., Anna Kienlerin, 9 Feb. 1591; Zacharias Prenner, 18 Sept. 1592; StadtAA, Strafbuch 1588–1596, 101.

93. "Beim hellen tag." "[O]b sie auch vermain d[a]z solches einer Erbarn frauen gebür oder wol ansthehe." StadtAA, Urg., Rosina Leinauer, 16 Aug. 1591.

94. StadtAA, Urg., 1541–1542, Agnes Axtin, 26 May 1542.

95. Two girls described as whores ("hurn") in 1593, for instance, refused to accompany customers to a tavern, insisting instead on sending out for beer to drink at home (StadtAA, Urg., Andreas Merckt, 14 Oct. 1593). For examples of suspicion for drinking together in a private home, see StadtAA, Urg., Jacob Frantz, 30 Sept. 1592; Felicitas Reischlerin, 30 Sept. and 1 Oct. 1592; Michael Eberhart, 1 April 1591.

96. Heegen, "Frauenrechtliches."

97. Karant-Nunn, *Reformation of Ritual*, 199.

98. A group of seven women gathered at a tavern for an unidentified invitation was described by a defendant in 1541 (StadtAA, Urg., Gerdraut Raumerin, 31 Aug. 1541). Tradition also has it that the Augsburg tavern known from the sixteenth century as the Weiberschule was so named because it was frequented by women after shopping at the city market (Potthoff and Kossenhaschen, *Kulturgeschichte*, 75).

99. Moryson, *Itinerary*, 230–91.

100. This statistic is based on two five-year samples of the records of the Discipline Lords during the sixteenth century (StadtAA, Zuchtbücher 1540–1544, 1590–1594), with a total of 549 fines, 3 from women; no drunkenness fines for women were recorded for the seventeenth century.

101. StadtAA, Urg., David Lutz, 24 Dec.1641; Anna Krug, 10 June 1541; Michael Dielen, 16 Nov. 1594.

102. "Darumb schlag er sy auch vbel . . . der Krug sey ain . . . armer gemarterter man . . . das weib sey ain verdrunckenes faß." StadtAA, Urg., Anna Krug, 10 June 1541.

103. For example, see StadtAA, Urg., Anna Krug, 10 June 1541; Anna Eytlerin, 10 April 1550; Anna Keppelin, 21 July 1574; Michael Dielen, 16 Nov. 1594; Sibilla Klausenburgerin, 27 April 1594.

104. StadtAA, Urg., Anna Krug, 10 June 1541.

105. "Wiwol di full / bringt nyemandt ehr / So schemt si doch die Weybsbild mehr." Schwarzenberg, *Teütsch Cicero*, "Ain Büchle wider das zutringken," 86.

8. Drinking and Social Identity

1. Heath, "Decade of Development," 46.

2. Barrows and Room, *Drinking*, 1.

3. "Mit dem Ernst Kratzer nit, sondern mit andern." StadtAA, Urg., Caspar Morhart, 31 May 1642.

4. StadtAA, Urg., Johannes Endriss, Jan. 1654. Hans Goff carried in the records the title "Herr," suggesting that he was a member of the city elite.

5. StadtAA, Urg., Georg Seidinger, 1 April 1591. The newcomer to the party was bragging about how many miles he had wandered.

6. StadtAA, Urg., Andreas Stemmer, 7 March 1644; Peter Gabler, 5 Oct. 1594.

7. "Het ain[er] mengl an mir, so sollt er mirs sagen, man werd kain kyend an ime fynden"; "er wolt ime seinen wein nit abschmoretz[en]." StadtAA, Urg., Balthus Laimer, 23 July 1548.

8. Stuart, *Defiled Trades*, 18.

9. "Was? [H]ab ich ein tode Sau geschunden, daß mir keiner kein [Wein] bringt?" Fischart, *Geschichtsklitterung*, 120.

10. "Darauf ich mit ihme gezecht, und vermaint, dieweil jeder besonders getrunken, es werde mir keinen Nachteil bringen." StadtAA, HWA, Lodweber 157, Hans Seidler, 1550–1582. Seidler was later allowed to reopen his shop, but members of his craft reprimanded him for his behavior. I wish to thank Kathy Stuart for drawing my attention to this case.

11. StadtAA, Strafbuch 1633–1653, 114–15. This case is also discussed in Stuart, *Defiled Trades*, 47.

12. Birlinger, *Volksthümliches* 2:445.

13. Unfortunately, the majority of drinkers in the 375 cases on which this study is based did not identify their drinking partners; or they identified them by name only, with no reference to profession or social status. The following discussion is based on a total of 543 identifiable customers divided into 175 drinking groups between 1540 and 1644. Forty of the groups, or 23 percent, are from 1540–1544; 115, or 66 percent, are from 1590–1594; and during the poorly documented years of 1640–1644, only 20 groups (totaling forty-seven customers), or 11 percent, could be positively identified as to profession and social status. The size of the drinking groups ranged from two to twenty participants.

14. See, for example, StadtAA, Urg., Jacob Haiser, April 1594; Lorentz Greinwold and Georg Fürst, 7–17 July 1643; Andreas Stemmer, 7 March 1644.

15. Breaking this down by period, 75 percent of groups in 1540–1544 and 1590–1594 included artisans and 85 percent in 1640–1644.

16. See, for example, StadtAA, Urg., Ulrich Gerst, 9 March 1594; Georg Hobel et al., Sept. 1591; Hans Fritz, 17 Feb. 1592; Caspar Lechner, 24 Oct. 1594; Hans Buechhofer, 28 May 1594.

17. Elites and officials did visit public taverns during the seventeenth century, but none were involved in the incidents making up this sample. See, for example, the case involving Johannes Endriss in 1646 (StadtAA, Urg., Johannes Endriss, 25 Oct. 1646), which describes the behavior of city council members, church officials, and city bureaucrats in the public tavern Weiberschule, and the case in 1654 (Johannes Endriss, Jan. 1654). In neither of these cases were elites drinking with commoners.

18. These practices are described in Moryson, *Itinerary*, 341; Schwarzenberg, *Gesatze*, C1; Seling, *Goldschmiede*, 1:85.

19. For example, "mit einem knappen welchen man den Schemel gehaissen." StadtAA, Urg., Hans Rochinger, 18 Nov. 1592.

20. "Andere mehr welche er nit kenne," or "kenne der andern keinen." For example,

see StadtAA, Urg., David Kaufmann, 21 Jan. 1591; Caspar Aufschlager, 16 Aug. 1591; Caspar Angerer et al., 6 Nov. 1591; Georg Seltmann, 26 June 1592.

21. "Hab kein gewisse gesellen, wann er in ein Würtshauss komme, so bekome er bald einen gesellen." StadtAA, Urg., Otmar Peter, 4 Jan. 1591.

22. Castiglione, *Courtier*, 140; Kavanagh, *Enlightenment*, 38–39.

23. StadtAA, ZPO 1537; Schätze 16, 34–35; Schätze ad 36/8; K. Thomas, *Religion*, 111, 121.

24. Brennan, *Public Drinking*, 250.

25. StadtAA, Schätze 36, Zuchtordnung 1472, 16; PO 1530.

26. "Verderblich," "teglich, oder gewonlich," "übermessig." StadtAA, ZPO 1537; ZPO 1553, 31, 38v–39; Anschläge und Dekrete 1490–1649, Teil 1, no. 20.

27. StadtAA, Schätze 16, 207v–208r; Evangelisches Wesensarchiv 138, Bürgerstubenordnung, 9. A clause in the Merchants' Drinking Room ordinances of 1541 and 1587 also forbade throwing cards or dice out of the window in anger (StadtAA, Kaufmanschafft und Handel, fasc. 5, nos. 5–9, Stubenordnung 1587).

28. K. Thomas, *Religion*, 20.

29. Brennan, *Public Drinking*, 254. Even when tavern gambling involved money, the winnings were normally used to pay for the drinks (See StadtAA, Urg., Georg Herlin, 21–28 Aug. 1592; compare Brennan, *Public Drinking*, 254–55).

30. For tolerance of gambling in other cities of Reformation Germany, see Smoller, "Playing Cards"; Ozment, *Reformation*, 98, 104.

31. StadtAA, Urg., Endres Kornmann, Aug. 1591; Michael Biler, 21 Oct. 1593; Hans Fischer, 8 Sept. 1593; Zuchtbücher 1539–1540, 81; Zuchtbücher 1540–1542, 84; Zuchtbücher 1542–1543, 22–23, 25, 27; Zuchtbücher 1543–1544, 114. Six tavern keepers were fined 1 to 2 gulden for allowing gambling between 1540 and 1544, and 13 gulden between 1590 and 1594 (StadtAA, PZS 1590–1594). No evidence of fines for tavern keepers exists for the seventeenth century.

32. "Hab nit vermaint, d[aß] vmb 1 halder oder pfennig zuspilen mangel soll bringen, hab zu einem armen mann nit solche gäst, die vil zuverspilen hab[en], sey . . . fro, wann er die zubezalen künd [vermögen]." StadtAA, Urg., Endres Kornmann, Aug. 1591.

33. A decree published in connection with the Imperial Diet of 1582 specifically allowed honest gaming ("ehrliche[s] Spil"), forbidding only false or fraudulent ("falsch oder betruglich") gambling (SuStBA, 2° S.14/1 Anschläge, no. 44).

34. These shooting grounds were also called Schießgarten. StadtAA, Schätze 16, 34–35; StadtAA, Urg., Michael Biler and Jacob Kegel, 4 Sept. 1591; Hans Herle, 30 Sept. 1591; Sixt Rauner, 16 Sept. 1591; Andreas Haid, 7 Dec. 1592; Jacob Kögler and Georg Nett, 18 Jan. 1593; Georg Mantz et al., 1 Nov. 1593; Georg Herlin, 21–28 Aug. 1592; Georg Herb, 17 Sept. 1593; Ulrich Reif, 8 July 1593; Strafbuch 1588–1596, 15, 18.

35. "Ich darzu mit glatten und herlen wortten gelockt unnd geraitzt worden bin." StadtAA, Urg., Georg Herlin, 21–28 Aug. 1592; Mair, *Chronik*, 242.

36. "Freundliche[r] Trunkh." StadtAA, Urg., Simon Bacher, 4–10 April 1590. Compare Urg., Ulrich Reif, 8 July 1593, in which an official let a prisoner out of jail in the village of Oberhausen to take part in a round of gambling for drinks.

37. StadtAA, Strafbuch 1540–1543, 1, iv, 5, 27, 33, 38; Urg., Lienhard Ritter, 1 July 1542.

38. Roeck, *Eine Stadt* 2:847–53.

39. Montaigne, *Works,* 899. Montaigne provided the example of the Catholic tavern keeper of the tavern in which he lodged, whose wife was Protestant, to illustrate his observation.

40. StadtAA, HWA, Bierbrauer 6 1621–1639 [1673]. A list of hostel fathers probably dating from between 1637 and 1660 is not divided by confession, whereas a list from 1672 identifies forty-four hostels as Protestant and nine as Catholic. Likewise, military musters of 1610 and 1615 do not specify confessions for tavern keepers; whereas in the muster of 1645, forty-six tavern keepers are listed as Protestant, six as Catholic, and four as Protestants heading a household of mixed confessions.

41. "Nicht allein in Bier vnd Würtshäusern / sonder auch auff offentlicher Gassen vnd Reichstraß." StadtAA, Anschläge und Dekrete 1522–1682, no. 24.

42. StadtAA, Urg., Melchior Nershaimer, 20 Nov. 1642, which describes a wedding at which Protestant and Catholic officials shared tables; Strafbuch 1654–1699, 83.

43. Mandelbaum, "Alcohol and Culture," 14.

44. Ibid., 17

45. Joseph Gusfield attributes the association of drinking with the "irrational, the impulsive, the 'free' side of life" to the assigning to the underclass a "romantic resistance to rationalization" ("Benevolent Repression," 418).

46. These words were used by the tavern keeper Andreas Preiß in his 1591 defense of the right of craftsmen to drink to conclude professional contracts (StadtAA, HWA, Weinwirte 6 1551–1704, Andreas Preiß et al., 1591).

9. The Social Functions of the Tavern

1. Lucian Hölscher, "Öffentlichkeit," in Brunner, *Grundbegriffe* 4:414–26; Roeck, *Eine Stadt* 1:365–84. The use of the term "public domain" here refers to spaces open to popular society and controlled by public authority, and it should not be confused with Habermas's concept of the development of a public sphere of opinion as a potential forum for social criticism in later centuries. Habermas noted that he was not concerned with the "plebeian" public sphere (Habermas, *Strukturwandel der Öffentlichkeit,* 8–21).

2. Grimm, *Deutsches Wörterbuch* 14.2:358, describes "Winkel" (corner or hidden spot) as "Gegensatz zum Begriff des Öffentlichen" (the antonym to the concept of public). Similarly, Hölscher, "Öffentlichkeit" 4:414–16, describes "geheim" (secret) as the opposite of "öffentlich" (public) during the sixteenth century, whereas "sonderlich" or "besunder" (private) was the antonym for "gemein" (public in the sense of common to all). Only in the seventeenth century did "öffentlich" take on the meaning of "staatlich" (public in the political sense, as in public office). See also Roeck, *Eine Stadt* 1:365, 378–79; Habermas, *Strukturwandel der Öffentlichkeit,* 12.

3. The word "Stube," often "grosse Stube," normally referred to the large, heated common room that was open to the public. The word probably derives from the same root as "stove," and in its most customary usage implied a room with an oven. Larger

taverns sometimes had more than one Stube (Grimm, *Deutsches Wörterbuch* 10.4:157–70; Fischer, *Schwäbisches Wörterbuch* 5:1888).

4. StadtAA, Urg., Endres Kornmann, Aug. 1591; Hans Fischer, 8 Sept. 1593; Maria Pretlerin, 8 Sept. 1593; Barbara Weberin, 3 Oct. 1594.

5. "In einer grossen Stuben . . . darinnen vil leut gesessen." StadtAA, Urg., Rosina Leinauer, 16 Aug. 1591.

6. StadtAA, Urg., Anna Catharina Millerin, 6 June 1641.

7. "Sey . . . inn keinen Winckhel nie, sonder inn offnen Würtsheusern." StadtAA, Urg., Christian Weber, 18 Dec. 1643.

8. StadtAA, Ratsbücher 16, 1529–1542, fol. 49; Schätze ad 36/8, 27; ZPO 1537, A4; SuStBA, 4° Cod.Aug.132, 38v; Peyer, *Gastfreundschaft,* 34–51, 67; N. Schindler, *Widerspenstige Leute,* 250; Erler and Kaufmann, *Handwörterbuch* 1:2022–23.

9. Unfortunately, nothing remains of this case but a fragment of the interrogation. StadtAA, Urg., "Pfeifenmann," 29 Nov. 1541.

10. "Hett vermeint, wenn es verbotten wer, der Würt solt es Inen verwörn." StadtAA, Urg., Hans Borst et al., 12 Dec. 1590; Strafbuch 1588–1596, 93v.

11. StadtAA, Urg., Andreas Stemmer, 7 March 1644; Leonhart Wolfmüller, 9 Nov. 1594; Hans Mehrer and Jeremias Flicker, 2 July 1640.

12. "Von frids wegen." StadtAA, Urg., Matthäus Nate, 6 April 1541.

13. StadtAA, Urg., Stefan Engelmair, 16 Feb. 1541; see also the similar case of Bernhart Jager, 3 Feb. 1542.

14. "So hatt er mir im meinem hauss weder mass noch ordnung zuegeben." StadtAA, Urg., David Bögle, 29 April 1592.

15. In 1597, for example, a collection of nineteen animal wonders (including a fish with two mouths, a living cow with six feet, half a dragon head) were displayed in Georg Siedeler's beer house (StadtAA, Chroniken 10, Chronik von Siedeler, 202).

16. StadtAA, Urg., Peter Siedler, 17 Nov. 1544; cases involving messages and letters include Urg., Simon Ment, 16 March, 1542; Wilhelm Schuchmacher and Stefan Vogel, 1518.

17. StadtAA, Urg., Georg Siedeler, March-Nov. 1590; Chroniken 10, Chronik von Siedeler, 174r–175v.

18. StadtAA, Urg., Margareta Fichtlin, 9 Jan. 1592.

19. Hans Zinder, for example, told his landlady in 1593 that he was attending school to learn to read and cipher so that he could get a position as a cellar boy (StadtAA, Urg., Hans Zinder, 13 Sept. 1593); Paulus Hett who attended St. Anna's school in order to become a beer cellar boy (Urg., 9 May 1590); Stefan Vogel, who employed a cellar boy to write letters (Urg., 1518).

20. Künast, *Getruckt zu Augspurg,* 116, 125–27.

21. StadtAA, HWA, Branntweinbrenner 2, 1537–1698, 1699–1732 (1698–1723).

22. A fur trader who set up shop in an Augsburg tavern, for example, faced charges by local tanners (StadtAA, HWA, Gerber 1548–1584, Jan.-Feb. 1581). For cases illustrating the other business transactions mentioned, see StadtAA, Urg., Endres Kornmann, Aug. 1591; Hans Knopf, 18–22 Nov. 1591; Friedrich Eberhart, 2 Dec. 1591; Georg Lempel,

21 March 1592; Christoph Schmied, 12 July 1593; Wilhelm de Nois, 22 April 1594; Christian Weber, 18 Dec. 1643; Christian Stainer, 4 April 1644. Although the last of these, a horse thief, was selling stolen horses in taverns, there is no indication that his customers or the tavern keepers knew the sales were illegal.

23. StadtAA, Literalien, Satzung 1529; ZPO 1537; SuStBA 2° Aug.10, fol. 53. A discussion of various arrests for the circulation of socially and politically critical pamphlets in Augsburg taverns can be found in Roeck, *Eine Stadt* 1:370–76. Examples of confiscated pornography are extant in StadtAA, Strafamt, Kriminalakten Beilagen.

24. Peyer, *Taverne*, xii.

25. Even representatives of the city council were restricted from entering private homes without just cause, for entering a house without the permission of the house father was a violation of the traditional right of household peace (N. Schindler, *Widerspenstige Leute*, 250).

26. StadtAA, ZPO 1537; ZPO 1580; Müller, "Über Trinkstuben," 720.

27. StadtAA, PO 1530.

28. "Verdechtlich." StadtAA, Schätze 16, Eine Sammlung städtischer Verordnungen und Erlässe, 1536–1633, 66v, Die Wirte betreffend, June 1541. This clause also appears in the 1530 ordinance (StadtAA, PO 1530).

29. StadtAA, Schätze 16, 90v, Fremde unnd hiesige Bettler belangend, 4 June 1544.

30. "Fremde mussigeheren und leichtfertige Personen." SuStBA, 2° Cod.Aug.247, Bürgermeister-Instruktion 1581–1653, 282. During the seventeenth century, the instructions were reissued in at least fifteen separate years, in some years on multiple dates (StadtAA, Ratserlasse 1579; Anschläge und Dekrete 1522–1682, Tom. 1, nos. 18, 37, 62, 65, 69, 78, 92, 95, ad 95; Anschläge und Dekrete 1490–1649, Teil 1, no. 69; Anschläge und Dekrete 1650–1711, Teil 2, no. 111; Schätze 16, 402; Ratserlasse 1669–1683, 1677, 1681, 1689, 1698; SuStBA, 2° Cod.Aug.247, 282; SuStBA, ZPO 1621).

31. "Er wurde sonst ain aignen Burgermeister brauchen." StadtAA, Urg., Hans Fischer, 8 Sept. 1593.

32. See, for example, StadtAA, Urg., Hans Fischer, 8 Sept. 1593; Christoph Schmied, 12 July 1593; Hans Lutz, 14 March 1594; Georg Remshart, 14 April 1640.

33. Tavern keepers outnumber guests as victims of tavern crime by nearly three to one; in 74 percent (23 out of 31) of the cases involving thefts in taverns occurring during the years covered by the sample, the tavern keeper was the victim. In no case in this sample was a tavern keeper found guilty of collaborating in theft. Examples of persons refused lodging include a pregnant serving girl (StadtAA, Urg., Catharina Kornmesserin, 18 March 1594) and a group of vagrants suspected of theft (Urg., Hans Hueber et al., 20 Dec. 1593).

34. StadtAA, Urg., Nikolaus du Ponchau von Tournay, 1640–1642. The tavern keeper complained that she had to provide beer for the prisoner, while her household was reduced to drinking only water. On the custom of keeping persons in the tower for debts at the creditor's expense, see Liedl, *Gerichtsverfassung*, 106.

35. Schweinichen, *Denkwürdigkeiten*, 79–80; StadtAA, HWA, Weinwirte 6 1551–1704, Hans Miller, 1624.

36. "Politten." Götze, *Glossar*, "bolet," 37.

37. StadtAA, Anschläge und Dekrete 1522–1682, Tom. 1, no. 69; ZPO 1537. The penalty for failure to register guests was 4 gulden for the first offense, 8 gulden for the second, and irons or worse for the third. On instructions for gatekeepers, see Anschläge und Dekrete 1650–1711, Teil 2, no. 111. The names and lodging plans of arriving nobles and elite bureaucrats also had to be noted by gatekeepers. Based on Montaigne's account, the purpose of this record keeping was to allow preparation of appropriate receptions (*Works*, 899).

38. Beier, *Handwerks–Lexicon*, "Vater auf der Herberge," 441; on the hostel father as representing authority and the hostel mother and household as pseudo-family, see also Wiesner, "Wandervogels," 773; Wissell, *Des alten Handwerks Recht* 2:59, 97; StadtAA, HWA, Müller 1583–1635, no. 347, Mühlknecht-Ordnung ("den Würth, Vatter, die Würthin, Mutter, auch deroselben Haußgesünd, Brüder vnd Schwester haissen").

39. Wissell, *Des alten Handwerks Recht* 1:151–52.

40. Beier, *Handwerks-Lexicon*, 441; Wissell, *Des alten Handwerks Recht* 1:344–45; StadtAA, Chroniken 10, Chronik von Siedeler, 200; HWA, Weber 185, Weberhaus-Ordnungen und Dekrete, 16 Aug. 1530.

41. Wissell, *Des alten Handwerks Recht* 1:157–58; Rauers, *Kulturgeschichte* 1:115–16; Schulz, "Gesellentrinkstuben," 236; Beier, *Handwerks-Lexicon*, 145; Buff, "Ausgeschenk." See also StadtAA, Chronik von Siedeler, in which the brewer Georg Siedeler describes the establishment of a craft hostel in his tavern in 1597 (200). Examples of the Willkommen cup can be seen in Seling, *Goldschmiede* 2:plates 111, 117, 387, 400, 408.

42. "Bix," "Buchs," "Büchß," "Laden," or "Zechtafel." See, for example, StadtAA, HWA, Müller 1583–1635, no. 347, Mühlknecht-Ordnung; Chroniken 10, Chronik von Siedeler, 200.

43. Adolf Buff describes ritual toasts that included the hostel mother in the bookbinder's hostel (459), although Merry Wiesner notes that she was unable to find evidence that the hostel mother attended the ceremonies ("Wandervogels," 771).

44. Wiesner, "Wandervogels," 771–73; Wiesner, "Guilds," 128–29.

45. StadtAA, HWA, Lodweber 158, 1583–1600, 1591.

46. These conditions were with the exception of recruitments for imperial forces, since Augsburg was officially under the emperor's jurisdiction (Kraus, *Militärwesen*, 96).

47. See, for example, StadtAA, Urg., Michael Jeckle, 30 Sept. 1591; Hans Mair, 6 Aug. 1592; Matthäus Naterer, 1592; Hans Büler, 25–26 Jan. 1594.

48. StadtAA, Militaria 53, Werbungen 1578–1716.

49. The Laufgeld was normally 1 gulden in the 1590s, but it was raised to 6 gulden during the Thirty Years' War (Kraus, *Militärwesen*, 188). For persons who enlisted while drunk and later returned the Laufgeld, see StadtAA, Urg., Hans Dietrich, 15 May 1590; Michael Jeckle, 30 Sept.–12 Oct. 1591; Matthäus Naterer, Sept. 1592; Georg Eberle, 10 Oct. 1594; Elias Köln, 9 May 1590.

50. StadtAA, Urg., Hans Dietrich, 15 May 1590; Hans Mair, 6 Aug. 1592; Matheus Funck, 5 Aug. 1594.

51. StadtAA, Militaria 55, Landquartierwesen 1518–1638, includes many complaints

from private homes about quartering soldiers during the earlier sixteenth century, but complaints from the period of the Thirty Years' War are mostly from tavern keepers. Exceptions occurred during the Swedish occupation of 1632–1635, when the city was so overburdened that private citizens were again forced to quarter soldiers.

52. StadtAA, Militaria 34, Werbungen 1624–1745, 1632; Militaria 55, 1561.

53. "Grosse hoche gefahr." StadtAA, HWA, Bierbrauer 6 1621–1639, 1635, Andreas Weber et al., 13–18 Aug. 1635, 3–8 Nov. 1635.

54. "Sünden [und] Gottslästern." StadtAA, Militaria 34, 1632.

55. "Sovill und was sy gelust ires gefallens geben." StadtAA, Militaria 55, 1551.

56. StadtAA, Militaria 55, 1619.

57. StadtAA, Militaria 55; Militaria 59, Landquartierwesen 1639–1647. Foods consumed are not itemized in any of the bills.

58. StadtAA, Militaria 34; Militaria 55; Militaria 59. One petitioner was still trying to get his payment six years after the fact (Militaria 59, 1638).

59. "Wann sy jar und tag bey mir legen, wolten sy mir kain haller geben, Kay. M. sey reich gnug." StadtAA, Militaria 55, 1561.

60. Kraus, *Militärwesen*, 198; Baer, *Stadtlexikon*, 426. The Zwinger was so named because of its location in the barbican, the area between the city's inner and outer fortifications.

61. "Inn betrachtung sie Bierschenckhen alle offne würthßheüser vnd stallungen auch pflicht vnd aydt halber haben müßen, dergleichen wie meniglich bewust bei andern burgern vnd handels leüthen nicht zu finden sein." StadtAA, Militaria 55, petitions from 1634.

62. Roper, *Holy Household*, 132–64.

63. These rituals are described in city wedding ordinances (StadtAA, Anschläge und Dekrete 1522–1682, Tom. 1, no. 4, Hochzeitsordnung 1540; no. 13, Hochzeitsordnung 1575; Anschläge und Dekrete 1490–1649; no. 51, Hochzeitsordnung 1599. See also SuStBA, 4° Cod.S.10, Augsburger Chronik, 1554–1654, 1582, 1600). On the authorities' demand for publicity in marriage arrangements, see Safley, *Let No Man Put Asunder*, 14, 31–32, 153–54, 183–86.

64. Roper, "Weddings," 66; Belmont, "Symbolic Function." For examples of such testimony, see StadtAA, Stadtkanzlei, Urkundenkonzepte, Geburtsbriefe 12.1, 1509–1619.

65. "Inn Hewsern oder winckeln / nit . . . sonder offentlich zu Kirche vnd strassen gehen." StadtAA, Anschläge und Dekrete 1522–1682, no. 4, Hochzeitsordnung 1540, 5; no. 13, Hochzeitsordnung 1575, 10; Anschläge und Dekrete 1490–1649, no. 51, Hochzeitsordnung 1599, B1.

66. StadtAA, StadtAA, Anschläge und Dekrete 1522–1682, no. 13, Hochzeitsordnung 1575, 18; 1490–1649, no. 51, 1599, fol. C; SuStBA, 2° Cod.Aug.247, Bürgermeister-Instruktion, xi.

67. StadtAA, Ordnungen, Hochzeitsordnung 1550, B1v; Hochzeitsordnung 1562, 6v; Hochzeitsordnung 1575, 10v.

68. "Der Gemeind." StadtAA, Anschläge und Dekrete 1522–1682, Tom. 1, no. 13, Hochzeitsordnung 1575, 1–2, 12–15, 18; Anschläge und Dekrete 1490–1649, no. 51,

Hochzeitsordnung 1599, A2–3, B3–4; Anschläge und Dekrete 1522–1682, Tom. 1, no. 4, Hochzeitsordnung 1540.

69. Roper, *Holy Household,* 154.

70. StadtAA, Ordnungen, no. 174, Instruktion an die Verordneten Hochzeitsherren, 7–10; Ratsbücher, 46, 1590–1592, 4 Dec. 1590.

71. SuStBA, 4° Cod.S.10, Augsburger Chronik, 1554–1654, 1582, 1600; StadtAA, Hochzeitsamt, Hochzeitsamtprotokolle 1563–1593, 1618–1648; StadtAA, Stadtkanzlei, Urkundenkonzepte, Geburtsbriefe 12.1, 1509–1619.

72. "Auf medt, win vnd pyer vnd bynamen auf allerhand trincken das man da schencken wirdet ain genant ungelt und gabe setczen und das selb . . . an der egenanten stat schulde, nutz vnd notturft wenden." "Das Ungeld in Augsburg," *Die Chroniken der Stadt Augsburg,* CDS 4, Beilage III, 158, 157–65.

73. Ibid., 157–58; StadtAA, Evangelisches Wesensarchiv 458.

74. Stetten, *Geschichte* 1:137; StadtAA, Chroniken 10, Chronik von Siedeler, 1r–2v; *Die Chroniken der Stadt Augsburg,* CDS 4, 109–10, 161–62; Zink, *Chronik:* 52; Welser, *Chronica,* 146. All accounts specifically note the basis for the protest as the excise tax on wine and beer. Other excise taxes, which were minimal in comparison, were not in question.

75. The income figures are drawn from StadtAA, Einnehmerbücher, 1550–1650, and were coordinated over periods of changing currency rates with the aid of Hans Georg Kopp (*Einnehmer- und das Baumeisteramt,* 68, 468–736). For figuring the income total, I have relied on Kopp's definition of real income, or laufende Einnahmen (excluding loans, repaid debts) (68).

76. Beer and mead taxes are not specifically mentioned in city finance books (Einnehmerbücher), but separate records of the Office of Excise Tax (Ungeldamt) list beer and mead taxes as part of the general Wein-Ungeld account (in the seventeenth century listed in finance books simply as Ungeldkonto). See their petitions to the city council in StadtAA, Urg., Balthasar Gausmeir, Feb.–March 1591; StadtAA, Ungeldamt, MMXVII, fasc. 2; Evangelisches Wesensarchiv 457, Acta das Ungeldamt betreffend 1592–1804, Tom. 1, Ungeldordnung 1597, 27. The term "Ungeld" was used for other excise tax accounts as well (wood, honey, grain, cloth, and other goods), but these taxes were collected by the Einnehmeramt not the Ungeldamt. The Ungeldamt was concerned only with Ungeld on alcoholic beverages (Evangelisches Wesensarchiv 458, "Extractus . . . ab Anno 1578 biß ad Annum 1718 das Ungelt-Amt betreffend," Protokoll 2, 105).

77. StadtAA, Schätze 179, Ungeldbuch 1459–1536; StadtAA, Urg., Michael Jacob and Michael Heisle, 19 Feb. 1594; StadtAA, Einnehmerbücher, 1500–1550; StadtAA, Evangelisches Wesensarchiv 457, Tom. 1, Ungeldordnung 1597, 33–34, 38–39. Between 1472 and 1543 the taxes on alcoholic beverages are listed as three separate accounts: Gross Wein-Ungeld (Large, probably wholesale, wine tax); Clain Wein-Ungeld (Small, or retail, wine tax); and brandy tax. Between 1543 and 1550 the three taxes are incorporated under one heading: Wein-Ungeld. Initially, the excise tax on salt (Salz-Ungeld) is also included in this total. The salt tax has been subtracted from the total for the years represented in graph 1.

78. The tax on wine was raised by 50 percent, so that nearly half the price of a glass of wine was for tax. Tax on beer and mead was also raised but at a lesser rate (Welser, *Chronica*, 68). In 1547, 85,619 gulden in Wein-Ungeld was collected, an increase of 87 percent over the previous year (StadtAA, Einnehmerbücher, 1546, 1547). Altogether the city had to pay 270,000 gulden to the emperor and his allies, most of which was financed by loans (Zorn, *Augsburg*, 189).

79. "Kein bequemer mittel." StadtAA, Schätze 16, 438, Verruf vnd Anschlag wegen Erhöhung des Ungelds, 15 Sept. 1633.

80. StadtAA, Ungeldamt, MMXVII.

81. Ibid; StadtAA, Schätze 16, 438, 448.

82. The city was blockaded by imperial and Bavarian troops in order to force the surrender of the (Protestant) Swedish troops of Gustavus Adolphus, who occupied the city between 1632 and 1635. (Adolphus died in battle in 1632, but his troops remained in Germany.) Augsburg's population dropped by two-thirds between 1618 and 1635, largely due to starvation and disease (Roeck, *Eine Stadt* 2:733–75; Zorn, *Augsburg*, 217–19).

83. The only other revenues that rivaled Wein-Ungeld during this period were special surtaxes placed on grain and other products, as a special measure to support the war effort. Although the grain surtax surpassed property taxes, the only source of income that ever exceeded the tax on alcohol was credit (StadtAA, Einnehmerbücher, 1624–1648; Roeck, *Bäcker*, 110–13, 126).

84. Mair, *Chronik*, 230.

85. Major roundups of brewers occurred in 1554, 1563, 1591, and 1635 (StadtAA, Chroniken 10, Chronik von Siedeler, 120v, 128v, 177; HWA, Bierbrauer 6 1621–1639).

86. StadtAA, Urg., Balthasar Gausmeir, Feb.–March 1591; Strafbuch 1588–1596, 105–8; Chroniken 10, Chronik von Siedeler, 177; HWA, Bierbrauer 2 1577–1599, 16 March 1591. The fines would represent 7.3 percent of the 111,889.5 gulden in Ungeld collected during fiscal year 1591, although it is possible that some brewers were unable to pay the fines immediately.

87. StadtAA, Ungeldamt, MMXVII, 1635; StadtAA, HWA, Bierbrauer 6 1621–1639, Andreas Weber et al., 13–18 Aug. 1635, 3–8 Nov. 1635.

88. "Gemainer Stat am Ungelt grosser abbruch und schaden," "wider sein burgerlich pflicht . . . betrogen." StadtAA, Urg., Matthäis Egk, 17 Dec. 1594; Georg Gall, 27 Sept. 1550; Balthasar Gausmeir, Feb.–March 1591; HWA, Bierbrauer 6 1621–1639, 1635; Mair, *Chronik*, 230.

89. "Der Cammer bey solchem vbermässigen Sauffen . . . täglich ein namhafften vnd grossen Gelt einträgt." Welser's remark was made in connection with the excise tax raise of 1547 (*Chronica*, 68).

90. StadtAA, Urg., 1524; on thieves and gamblers see, for example, Urg., Jacob Kögler and Georg Nett, 18 Jan. 1593; Michael Huber, 29 Dec. 1593–1 Feb. 1594.

91. StadtAA, Urg., Georg Gassteiger, 20 July 1592; Jacob Kögler and Georg Nett, 18 Jan. 1593; Hieronymus (Niedermair), March 1594; Hans Zinder, 17–19 Jan. 1594; Michael Huber, 29 Dec. 1593–1 Feb. 1594.

92. The Finstere Stube was supposedly frequented during the sixteenth century by many elite visitors, among them Emperors Maximilian I and Charles V ("Geschichte der Brauerei," 32). See also StadtAA, Urg., Johannes Endriss, Jan. 1654, which describes a visit to the Finstere Stube by the lawyer Johannes Endriss and a member of the city elite (Herr Hans Goff).

93. StadtAA, Urg., Hans Knopf, 18–22 Nov. 1591; Hans Schnegg, 29 Jan. 1592; Georg Rueff, 8–13 Sept. 1593; Georg Furtenbach, 3–6 Dec. 1593. Hans Schnegg was one of Augsburg's wealthier tavern keepers, reporting assets in 1592 at 6,655 gulden (StadtAA, Stadtkanzlei, Urkundenkonzepte, Testamente 5.1, 1523–1571).

94. See, for example, Clinard, "Public Drinking House," 279.

10. Drinking and Public Order

1. Burke, *Popular Culture*, 207–43.

2. This is the thesis Bátori explores in "Daily Life."

3. *Criminal Justice*, 229–303. Sumptuary laws (clothing ordinances), wedding ordinances, and tax controls were also sometimes published under the general heading Police Ordinances.

4. Roper, *Holy Household*, 27.

5. "So wöllen wir trincken die gantze Nacht, / biß an den hellen Morgen, / Hol Wein, schenck ein, wir wöllen frölich sein, / wer aber nicht will frölich sein, / der soll nicht bei vns bleiben."

6. Smith, *Public House*, 6, 40; Webb and Webb, *Liquor Licensing*, 2.

7. Stolleis, "Trinkverbote," 187; N. Schindler, *Widerspenstige Leute*, 237.

8. StadtAA, Schätze 36, Zuchtordnung 1472, 17; Anschläge und Dekrete 1490–1649, Teil 1, nos. 5, 20; Anschläge und Dekrete 1522–1682, no. 10; ZPO 1537; SuStBA, 2° Aug.10, fol. 53; Kachel, *Herberge*, 130–32.

9. "Weinglocke," "Bierglocke," "Trinkglocke," "Lumpenglocke." On Rothenburg, see *Criminal Justice*, 261; on Frankfurt, see SuStBA, 2° H.III, vol. 2, Florian, *Chronica*, 676; for other cities, see Müller, "Über Trinkstuben," 720, 728; Kachel, *Herberge*, 130–32.

10. People were not supposed to be in the streets after 9 P.M. in any case without a legitimate reason (StadtAA, PO 1530). On the earlier time of 7 P.M. in winter, see Mair, *Chronik*, 362, 1559; StadtAA, Ratserlasse, 16 Oct. 1579; StadtAA, Anschläge und Dekrete 1522–1682, no. 80, 1677.

11. StadtAA, Schätze 16, fols. 24, 38, 46, 287–88. "Mummerey" was specifically forbidden by separate ordinances issued in 1542, 1544, 1546, 1622, and 1631 (StadtAA, Schätze 16, 72v, 86v, 105v, 293, 370).

12. "Altem brauch nach." StadtAA, Beruff 1541.

13. StadtAA, Strafbuch 1540–1542, 97; StadtAA, PZS 1540–1544. Fines were inconsistent, ranging from 12 to 30 kreutzer for guests, and 30 kreutzer to 1 gulden for a total of eleven tavern keepers between October 1541 and March 1542 (30 kreutzer = ½ gulden).

14. StadtAA, Urg. 1540, 1541–1542, 1543–1544; StadtAA, Strafbücher 1540–1543, 1543–1553.

15. StadtAA, Schätze ad 36/8; StadtAA, HWA, Bierbrauer 24, Bierbrauerordnungen 32; SuStBA, 2° Aug.324, Anschläge, Verrufe, Dekrete und Verordnungen 1528–1735, 1665, 1667, 1723. This loosening of regulations during the early seventeenth century contradicts Norbert Schindler's claim that controls on tavern closing times tightened during the post-Reformation period (*Widerspenstige Leute,* 236–39).

16. Spode, *Alkohol und Zivilisation,* 62; Blanke, "Alkoholismus," 84–85; Schreiber, *Deutsche Weingeschichte,* 464.

17. Although Norbert Schindler argues that the issue of closing time was a major point of contention between authority and populace, he does not provide evidence of enforcement (*Widerspendige Leute,* 236–39).

18. Twenty tavern keepers and their guests were fined between 1540–1544, and 27 between 1590–1594. StadtAA, Zuchtbücher 1540–1544, 1590–1594; StadtAA PZS 1590–1594; Reichsstadtakten 818, 1640–1649. By comparison, 156 fines were levied for serving meat on Friday or Saturday between 1590–1594 and 203 fines for seating craftsmen during the week, which was illegal between 1590 and 1596 (PZS 1590–1594).

19. Achilles Pirminius Gasser, *Annales Augustani,* trans. Markus Welser, in *Chronica,* 108; Stetten, *Geschichte* 1:553.

20. StadtAA, Literalien, 8 Dec. 1528; Schätze 13c 102–3; Schätze 194a, Eidbuch, 19v–20r.

21. StadtAA, HWA, Branntweinbrenner 2, 1537–1698, 1553, 1555, 1557, 1580, 1614, 1623, 1627, 1631; StadtAA, Schätze 16, fol. 26, Gebrannten Wein betreffend; StadtAA, PZS 1589–1591, 1591–1592, 1592–1593; StadtAA, Evangelisches Wesensarchiv 457, Tom. 1, Ungeldordnung 1597, 32–33.

22. Numerous examples are provided in Stewart, "Paper Festivals," 310–21.

23. Gasser, in Welser, *Chronica,* 68.

24. StadtAA, Anschläge und Dekrete 1522–1682; StadtAA, Schätze 16, 239r, 286v, 299r, 329r, 359r–362v, 440r; SuStBA, 2° S.14/1 Anschläge, nos. 54, 63, 79, 82; SuStBA, ZPO 1621; StadtAA, PO 1683.

25. StadtAA, Schätze 16, 286–287; Anschläge und Dekrete 1522–1682 no. 20, 23 April 1630; PO 1683; StadtAA, Schätze ad 36/12, 82; StadtAA, Anschläge und Dekrete 1522–1682, no. 20; StadtAA, PZS 1589–1594 and Zuchtprotokolle 1595–1599. Although higher fines were established for repeat offenses, there is no indication that they were enforced during the 1590s. No fines for village drinking are recorded between 1540 and 1544, and protocols of fines do not exist for the seventeenth century; military records do provide evidence, however, of a soldier who was fined 15 gulden for village drinking in 1664 (StadtAA, Militaria 199, 9 Feb.–17 April 1664).

26. "Allein zechens halben hinaus gehen." StadtAA, Schätze 16, 239, 17 May 1607; SuStBA, 2° Cod.Aug. 275; SuStBA, 2° Cod.Aug.247, Bürgermeister-Instruktion, 6, this entry from 1641; also "Licenz-Zettel:" PO 1683, 41.

27. SuStBA, 2° Cod.Aug.275, 19 May 1577.

28. StadtAA, Anschläge und Dekrete 1522–1682, no. 20, 23 April 1630.

29. Metlinger, *Regiment;* Zentralbibliothek Zürich, GS, Einblattdruck AZZ 17.1, Tischzucht, 1645, which counsels children to mix their wine with water.

30. According to Ulf Dirlmeier, this meant between ½ and 1½ liters per day (*Untersuchungen*, 326–27). StadtAA, Urg., Valentin Mair, 31 Oct. 1544, who threatened the master of the poorhouse because his mother was not receiving her ration of wine.

31. See, for example, StadtAA, Urg. 1641–1642, Nikolaus du Ponchau von Tournay. Von Tournay was put in the tower at the expense of his creditor, a tavern keeper who complained about having to provide the prisoner with beer.

32. Pauli, *Schimpff und Ernst*, 19v.

33. Clasen, "Armenfürsorge."

34. Arrests for alms recipients in taverns totaled two in the period 1540–1544 and six between 1590 and 1594, with zero recorded during the 1640s (StadtAA, Strafbücher 1540–1644).

35. StadtAA, ZPO 1537; Urg., Michael Alber, 8 June 1542; "Ule" Schmid, 22 March 1542; Sixt Röting, 22 March 1542. It is worth noting, however, that repeated cases of wife beating could lead to banishment whether or not the offender used alcohol. See, for example, StadtAA, Urg., Caspar Mülich, 17 June 1542.

36. For examples of tavern bans extended for years, see StadtAA, Strafbuch 1588–1596, 19, 39v; Urg., Wilhelm Schöffler, 15 May 1542; Hans Hohenberger, 27 April 1542; Hans Eisenhofer, 4 Oct. 1540.

37. There were four bailiffs before 1537 (StadtAA, Chroniken 10, Chronik von Siedeler, 95r).

38. In Augsburg the official position of the authorities was that the bailiffs were honorable citizens, and every effort was made to shield them from dishonorable status. Nonetheless, their sons were often excluded from honorable crafts. For a discussion of the status of bailiffs and others living on the periphery of dishonor, see Stuart, *Defiled Trades*, 97–105, 135–39.

39. See, for example, StadtAA, Urg., Hans Bausch, 10 June 1592; Hans Bausch, 15–20 March 1591; and StadtAA, Strafbuch 1633–1653, 183–84, which describes two bailiffs in the company of four city guards who seriously injured a tavern keeper because he did not offer them the expected drink.

40. "Trinkgeld . . . dieweil sie an das täglich trunken weren." StadtAA, Ratsprotokolle 27, 1553, 32v; StadtAA, Geheime Ratsprotokolle 5, 210. I thank Kathy Stuart for this reference.

41. Keith Wrightson describes the English alehouse during this period as a source of friction between respectability and the "poorer sort" ("Alehouse," 12–20).

42. In the sixteenth century, the rule normally applied to anything over one drink or meal. SuStBA, 4° Cod.S.87, Unterschiedliche Ordnungen, Beruf zugleich auch sowohl die Wirte als die Müßigänger betreffend, 21; StadtAA, Anschläge und Dekrete 1490–1649, Teil 1, no. 43, 1574, 18–19.

43. SuStBA, 4° Cod.S.87, Feb. 1581, 27v–18r; SuStBA, 2° Cod.Aug.247, 308–9, 1596; StadtAA, Schätze 16, 50v, 175; Anschläge und Dekrete 1490–1649, Teil 1, no. 43, 18–19; StadtAA, Evangelisches Wesensarchiv 1487, Bügerstubenordnung; StadtAA, Kaufmannschaft und Handel, fasc. 5, Kaufleutestube, Stubenordnung 1587.

44. See, for example, StadtAA, Urg., Niclaus Baumaister, 21 April 1593; Philipp Schach,

19 May 1593. City guards apparently supported the tavern keepers' right to demand a marker. See, for example, StadtAA, Urg., Hans Ettlich and Felix Schweyer, 17 May 1544, in which a tavern keeper took knives from his customers by force at the suggestion of the night watchman.

45. Steidel, *Zecher- und Schlemmerlieder,* 85–90; Haas, *Trinklieder,* 295–96.

46. StadtAA, Urg., Daniel Schmied, 13 Feb. 1591.

47. "Welches dan auch dem vngelt zuo gueten keme." StadtAA, Militaria 196, Jonas Göttel, 1599–1603.

48. For a more comprehensive discussion of this process, see Tlusty, "Water of Life."

49. StadtAA, Gesetze und Verordnungen des Ungeld-Amts, Bierbrauer-Ordnung 1604–1659, Article 63.

50. Roeck, *Bäcker,* 129; SuStBA, 2° Cod.Aug.273 Stadtämter, Bierschenken-Artikel-Buch 1564–1782, 6, 19. Brewing was forbidden entirely during the grain shortage of 1534 (StadtAA, Chroniken 10, Chronik von Siedeler, 2–6).

51. StadtAA, Anschläge und Dekrete 1490–1649, Teil 1, "Ains Erbern Rats der Stat Augspurg ansehen / die Weingemacht belangend," 1528; SuStBA, 4° Cod.S. 87, Wein-Bier- und Ungeltordnung der Stadt Augsburg (sixteenth century, n.d.), 16; StadtAA, Evangelisches Wesensarchiv 457, Tom. 1, Ungeldordnung 1597, 20r–21v; StadtAA, HWA, Weinwirte 6 1551–1704, 1604: Maluesier, Muskatel, Rainfal, and other sweet wine.

52. The muster list for 1610 lists seventy-four brewers or beer tavern keepers, fifty-two wine tavern keepers, and only three mead tavern keepers (StadtAA, Musterungs-bücher 1610); mead also does not appear in records of arrest as the reason for drunkenness nearly as often as wine and beer.

53. StadtAA, HWA, Metschenken 1590–1640, 1591.

54. "Weilen vnser handtierung deß Metsiedens diser Zeit gantz zue boden ligen." StadtAA, HWA, Branntweinbrenner 2, 1637, 1642; StadtAA, HWA, Metschenken 1590–1640, 1636.

55. The first entry for excise tax on brandy was made in 1472 (StadtAA, Schätze 179, Ungeldbuch 1459–1536).

56. References to drinking brandy in the morning can be found in StadtAA, HWA, Branntweinbrenner 2, 1614, 1620, 1623; StadtAA, Urg., Jacob Schmalholtz, 29 March 1591; Militaria 59; Spode, *Alkohol und Zivilisation,* 70.

57. The restriction was relaxed to 2 pfennigs in 1580, 4 pfennigs in 1614, and to 12 kreutzer during the Thirty Years' War (in 1623) (StadtAA, HWA, Branntweinbrenner 2, 1537–1698, documents from 1580, 1614, 1623).

58. StadtAA, PZS 1590–1594.

59. StadtAA, Chroniken 10, Chronik von Siedeler, 145, 196, 212, 293; StadtAA, Ungeld-amt, MMXVII, 8 Sept. 1596. The Office of Excise Tax noted that the common man was particularly fond of wheat beer ("der gemein mann dem weissen bier gar sehr nach-laufft").

60. StadtAA, Chroniken 10, Chronik von Siedeler, 134, 184, 196v; StadtAA, Ungeld-amt, MMXVII, 1596.

61. Wheat beer was forbidden due to grain shortages from 1600 to 1602 and from 1614

to 1615, and it was blamed for outbreaks of plague in 1600 and 1607 (StadtAA, Chroniken 10, Chronik von Siedeler, 134, 145, 184, 196, 212, 284, 293, 304, 311).

62. Clasen, "Armenfürsorge im 16. Jahrhundert," 338–39; Stetten, *Geschichte* 1:595, 601.

63. "Pranntwein vß Waizen . . . zu trinckhen, an iren gesundt schedlich, auch der Waitzen dardurch vnnutzlich verschwendt wirdt." StadtAA, HWA, Branntweinbrenner 2, 1570.

64. Ibid. Distilling false brandy from beer yeast or other grains was forbidden in other cities at least as early as 1530 (Rau, *Gutachten*, 8).

65. StadtAA, HWA, Branntweinbrenner 2, 1589; Evangelisches Wesensarchiv 457, Tom. I, Ungeldordnung 1597, 35v. This presumably coveted position was also established in Nuremberg as early as 1567 (Stadtarchiv Nuremberg, B15/IV Branntwein-Ordnung, 1567).

66. This drink is also called Wacholderbeerwasser. Schrick, *Von allen geprenten wassern*, 10. Schrick's recipe appeared fifty years before the first recipe for juniper-flavored brandy in the Dutch language, which has been cited as the beginning of the history of gin (Austin, *Alcohol*, 168; Forbes, *Distillation*, 159).

67. StadtAA, HWA, Branntweinbrenner 2, 1613; StadtAA, Urg., Matthäus Egk, 17 Dec. 1594. On the use of juniper to mask the taste of grain alcohol, see Berton Roueché, "Alcohol," 173; Zedler, *Universal-Lexicon*, "Brandtwein" 4:1088–89. Roueché attributed the discovery of gin to the Dutch professor Franciscus Sylvius some fifty years later. Sylvius's major role in the growth of the gin industry was not its initiation but its introduction in Holland, from which it quickly spread to England.

68. StadtAA, HWA, Branntweinbrenner 2, 1537–1698, Conrad Ebling et al., 7 Sept. 1613; Evangelisches Wesensarchiv 457, Tom. 1, Ungeldordnung 1597, 47v–48, 1613.

69. StadtAA, Collegium Medicum, Destillatores et Chymici, Deputierte über die Apotheken, Dec. 1623. Distillers took exception to the claims of the apothecaries, insisting that their products were much too costly to be used for drinking bouts.

70. StadtAA, HWA, Branntweinbrenner 2, 1631.

71. Stadtarchiv Nuremberg, B15/I Ordnung des Branntweinbrennens 1648; A6/1655, Einschleichen des Branntweins 1655; Austin, *Alcohol*, 219; Forbes, *Distillation*, 103.

72. StadtAA, HWA, Branntweinbrenner 2, 13–22 Jan. 1637, Johann Schaur; on comparative prices, see Rau, *Gutachten*, 7.

73. StadtAA, HWA, Branntweinbrenner 2, Anna Thomain, 1643; Strafbuch 1633–1653, 271. No further arrests for production or sale of grain spirits are recorded in the punishment books between 1643 and 1700.

74. "Verkaufft sowohl öffentlich alß heimlich . . . sowohl in dem Weinstadel, als in denen Läden." StadtAA, HWA, Branntweinbrenner 2, 1674.

75. "Hierdurch gemainer Statt am Ungelt schaden . . . verursacht." StadtAA, Strafbuch 1633–1653, 271.

76. On the "gin epidemic" in Germany, see Medick, "Plebejische Kultur," 104–8.

77. SuStBA, 2° Cod.Aug. 273 Stadtämter, Bierschenken-Artikel-Buch 1565–1782, 4; StadtAA, HWA, Branntweinbrenner 2, 1570, 1631.

78. "Got dem Allmechtigen zu lob und Eere." StadtAA, Literalien, 24 Dec. 1530; HWA, Branntweinbrenner 2, Oct. 1555; SuStBA, 2° Cod.Aug.275.

79. "Burger und inwoner." Chroniken 10, Chronik von Siedeler, 176r.

80. "Ausser der gebotnen feierteg, keinen burgern von webern odern andern handtwerckern, gleich so wenig auch die handtwercks gesellen . . . ausser des guetten Montags, heuratsabend . . . vnd hochzeiten." StadtAA, Schätze 36/8, 91, 96; HWA, Weinwirte 6 1551–1704, 1591.

81. StadtAA, HWA, Weinwirte 6 1551–1704, 1590, 1595; StadtAA, Schätze 36/8, 91.

82. "Des Gemeinen Manß halben . . . wie Weib vnd Kindern." StadtAA, HWA, Weinwirte 6 1551–1704, 1615.

83. SuStBA, Landes- und Polizeiordnung der Fürstentümer Ober- und Niederbayern; StadtAA, HWA, Weinwirte 6 1551–1704.

84. Elsewhere, the day was called Blue Monday or Saint Monday; see Reulecke, "Vom blauen Montag zum Arbeiterurlaub"; Thompson, "Work Discipline," 74–76; Austin, *Alcohol*, 156, 278; Gusfield, "Benevolent Repression," 405.

85. Gusfield, "Benevolent Repression," 405; Roberts, "Industrial Work Discipline." According to Peter Clark, the tradition of Saint Monday was not established as a custom in England until the early eighteenth century (*English Alehouse*, 223).

86. This suggestion was advanced by Behringer, "Mörder," 125. The problem in reconciling control from the top with concession to popular tradition is ironically evident in the Bavarian Police Ordinance of 1616, in which craftsmen were, on the one hand, forbidden to celebrate Good Monday and, on the other hand, allowed to drink in taverns only on Sundays and Mondays (SuStBA, Landes- und Polizeiordnung der Fürstentümer Ober- und Niederbayern). Reulecke also describes Blue Monday in the preindustrial period as a "socially accepted phenomenon" ("Vom blauen Montag zum Arbeiterurlaub," 214).

87. StadtAA, Urg., Hans Lang, 9 Sept. 1591; StadtAA, HWA, Weinwirte 6 1551–1704, 1591, Hans Kuchler; StadtAA, Urg., Apollonia Negelerin, 25 Jan. 1591.

88. StadtAA, HWA, Weinwirte 6 1551–1704, 1590.

89. "Vnsers grossen schadens vngeachtet." StadtAA, HWA, Weinwirte 6 1551–1704, 1591, Andreas Preiß et al.

90. "Item wann . . . leutt Proviant, wahren, vnd andere notturfftige ding, in dise fürneme weit berumbte Statt herbringen . . . da ein Theil mit den andern zu erhaltung guten willens vnd kundtschafft, wie aller orten Teutschen Lands gebreuchig, ein trunck zuthun begert: So wer bey frembden seltzam vnd vngewonlich, daß den Burgern mit Ihnen zuessen vnd zutrincken solte . . . verbotten sein." Ibid.

91. Ibid.; StadtAA, Handwerksgerichtsprozessakten, not indexed, 6 April 1596.

92. StadtAA, Chroniken 10, Chronik von Siedeler, 193r, 614; SuStBA, ZPO 1621.

93. "Komen under ainst umb mehr gellts als sy sonst auff drei mal verzehren." StadtAA, Ungeldamt, MMXVII, 1596.

94. The village mentioned was Friedberg, a market town by 1596 (ibid.).

95. Wheat beer (Weißbier) was illegal at this time for tavern sales.

96. "Welcher die ganze wochen inn seiner werckstatt und seinem engen hauswesen sitzt, maist darumb auff die dörffer zughen begert, damit er . . . ain wenig in das grüen

kommen, ainen freyen lufft empfangen und sich erspazieren und ergözen möge." Stadt-AA, Ungeldamt, MMXVII, 1596.

97. The report cites the example of Nuremberg as support for the beauty and success of drinking gardens; I have not found evidence, however, that Augsburg went through with this plan.

98. StadtAA, Ungeldamt, MMXVII, 1596; StadtAA, HWA, Weinwirte 6 1551–1704, 1596; StadtAA, Chroniken 10, Chronik von Siedeler, 193v, "vnd die Gmain . . . erfröwet worden." Wheat beer was made legal the following year (Chronik von Siedeler, 196v).

99. StadtAA, Chroniken 10, Chronik von Siedeler, 306r–311v.

100. "Burger von webern, oder andern handwerkern, wie gleichfalls die allhie arbeitende handwerksgesellen, tagwerker v[nd] dergleich." SuStBA, 4° Cod.Aug.132, 38.

101. StadtAA, Schätze 26/12, 103v.

102. StadtAA, Chroniken 10, Chronik von Siedeler, 310v–311.

103. Grain prices rose throughout Europe beginning in 1590 (Abel, *Agrarkrisen,* 307, on Augsburg 308–9).

104. "Ganz wol zufriden." StadtAA, Ungeldamt, MMXVII.

105. StadtAA, Urg., Balthasar Gausmeir, Feb.–March 1591.

106. The years 1590–1596 were also years of low wine production (Bassermann-Jordan, *Geschichte des Weinbaus* 1:983).

107. By the 1640s, for example, arrests for fights and insults make up 60 percent of the total arrests, compared to less than 17 percent in the 1540s, and around 25 percent in the 1590s. Conversely, arrests for sexual crimes dwindle from 13.5 percent of the total in the 1540s to 3 percent by the seventeenth century, while arrests for gambling and illegal dancing disappear entirely. By comparison, the ratio of arrests for theft remains fairly constant at around 5 percent. For a complete statistical breakdown of arrests for these years, see Tlusty, "Devil's Altar," 355–57.

Conclusion

1. "Ob er villeicht vermain das er allhie in einem Dorff sei, allwo er die leuth nach seinem gefallen trutzen und bochen möge, oder ob er nit alberaith befinde, das er an einem sollichen orth sitze, allwo man . . . bessere rath . . . zuerwarten khönde?" Stadt-AA, Urg., Hans Schwarzenberg, 13 July 1643.

2. "Gott könne einem ehrlichen Deutschen ein ehrliches Räuschlein zu gute halten." Johannes Matthesius, quoted in Janssen, *Geschichte* 8:276.

3. Clark, "Alehouse," 53.

4. Gusfield, "Benevolent Repression," 400–401.

Bibliography

Unpublished sources

Stadtarchiv Augsburg

Almosenamt
    Almosen-Ordnungen 1543, 1569
Anschläge und Dekrete
    1490–1649
    1650–1711
    1522–1682
Bauamt no. 215, Wasserzins-Register 1600–1629
Chroniken
    10, Chronik von Siedeler
Collegium Medicum
    Destillatores et Chymici
Einnehmerbücher 1500–1650
Evangelisches Wesensarchiv
    138
    457
    458
    1487
Geheime Ratsprotokolle 5
Grundbuch-Auszüge
Handwerkerakten (HWA)
    Branntweinbrenner 2 1537–1698
    Branntweinbrenner 3 1699–1732
    Bier- und Weinwirte 1 1520–1811
    Bierbrauer 2 1577–1599
    Bierbrauer 6 1621–1639 (incorrectly dated; includes documents to 1673)
    Bierbrauer 24 Bierbrauer-Ordnungen
    Bierbrauer 25, Bierschenken-Gerechtigkeits-Buch 1646
    Fischer 1 1429–1551
    Gerber 1548–1584

Bibliography

Lodweber 157 1550–1582
Lodweber 158 1583–1600
Lodweber 1583–1600
Metschenken 1590–1640
Müller 1583–1635
Weber 169, 185
Weinwirte 1 1520–1811
Weinwirte 6 1551–1704
Handwerker-Ordnungen A-Z
Handwerksgerichtsprozessakten
Hochzeitsamt, Hochzeitsamtsprotokolle 1463–1729
Kaufmannschaft und Handel 5, Kaufleutestube
Literalien 1528–1530
Militaria
    34 Werbungen 1624–1745
    53 Werbungen 1578–1716
    55 Landquartierwesen 1518–1638
    59 Landquartierwesen 1639–1647
    196 Verschiedenes, die Stadtgarde betreffend 1556–1779
    199 Differenzen und Exzesse der Stadtgardeoffiziere 1604–1805
Musterungsbücher 1610, 1615, 1645
Ordnungen
    Zucht- und Policey-Ordnung 1537
    Hochzeitsordnung 1550
    Hochzeitsordnung 1562
    Hochzeitsordnung 1575
    Instruktion [an] die Verordneten Hochzeitsherren
Personenselekt
    Ulrich Hunold
Ratsprotokolle (Ratsbücher) 14, 15, 16, 27, 46
Ratserlasse
    1507–1599
    1684–1698
Reichsstadtakten
    818 1640–1649
Römischer Kaiserlicher Majestät Ordnung und Reformation guter Polizei im
    Heiligen Römischen Reich. Augsburg, 1530.
Schätze
    13a, 13c
    16, Eine Sammlung Städtischer Verordnungen und Erlässe
    26/12
    36, Zuchtordnung 1472

ad 36/3, Polizeiordnung
ad 36/7, Polizeiordnung
ad 36/8, Polizeiordnung
ad 36/12, Polizeiordnung
179, Ungeldbuch 1459–1536
194a, Eidbuch
Stadtkanzlei Urkundenkonzepte
Testamente 5.1
Geburtsbriefe 12.1
Heiratsbriefe 14.1
Steueramt, Steuerbücher
1604, 1610, 1646
Strafamt
Kriminalakten Beilagen
Fasc. 6, Berichte und Dekrete
Strafbücher:
Ehebrecher-Strafbücher 1575–1704
Ledigstand-Strafbücher 1636–1659
Protokolle der Zucht- und Strafherren (PZS) 1576–1631
Strafbücher 1509–1699
Zuchtbücher 1537–1700
Zuchtherren Ausgaben und Einkommen 1537–1623
Urfehden
Urgichten 1540–1644
Ungeldamt (these two fascicles do not appear in any archival indexes)
MMXVII
Gesetze und Verordnungen des Ungeld-Amts
Verzeichnis 39, "Besetzung aller Ämter in der Reichsstadt Augsburg, angefangen
1548"

Staats- und Stadtbibliothek Augsburg

2° Aug.10
2° Cod.Aug.253, 254, 255, 256, 257, 275, 290, 324
2° Cod.Aug.247, Bürgermeister-Instruktion
2° Cod.Aug.273 Stadtämter
2° Cod.Aug.449, Wirt- und Gastgeberordnung 1650–1753
2° Cod.S.41, Georg Kölderer, Chronik
2° Cod.S.112, Abschriften von Privilegien in der Sammlung Paul von Stetten
2° H.111, Gebbard Florian, Chronica der Stadt Frankfurt
2° S.14/1 Anschläge
4° Cod.Aug.104
4° Cod.Aug.122

Bibliography

4° Cod.Aug.123
4° Cod.Aug.132, Zucht- und Polizeiordnung 1621
4° Cod.Aug.221, Bierprewen-Ordnung und Artikel
4° Cod.S.10, Apolonia Hefelerin, Augsburger Chronik, 1554–1654
4° Cod.S.87, Underschiedliche Ordnungen

Fürstlich und Gräflich Fuggerisches Familien- und Stiftungsarchiv

Kirchheim/Amtsrechnung
    78.1.4, 1592–1599
    78.1.17, 1642
    78.1.18, 1643
    78.1.19, 1644

Stadtarchiv Nördlingen

Urfehdenbücher 1587–1592

Stadtarchiv Nuremberg

A6/1655, Einschleichen des Branntweins
B15/I Ordnung des Branntweinbrennens 1648
B15/IV Branntwein-Ordnung 1567

Zentralbibliothek Zürich

Wickianer Einblattdruck PAS 12/15
Einblattdruck Elsass, Ia., 2
Einblattdruck AZZ 17.1

Published Sources and Literature

Abel, Wilhelm. *Agrarkrisen und Agrarkonjunktur.* Berlin, 1978.
———. *Stufen der Ernährung.* Göttingen, 1981.
Abele, Matthias von und zu Lilienberg. *Metamorphosis telae iudiciariae. d. i. Seltsame Gerichts-Händel.* 2 vols. Nuremberg, 1668.
Accati, Luisa. "The Spirit of Fornication: Virtue of the Soul and Virtue of the Body in Friuli, 1600–1800." In *Sex and Gender in Historical Perspective,* edited by Edward Muir and Guido Ruggiero, 110–40. Baltimore, 1990.
Akyeoampong, Emmanuael Kwaku. "Alcohol, Social Conflict, and the Struggle for Power in Ghana, 1919 to Recent Times." Ph.D. diss., University of Virginia, 1993.
Albertinus, Ägidius. *Lucifers Königreich und Seelengejaidt.* Augsburg, 1617.
Aletheius, Hygiophilus [Georg Phillipp Harsdörffer]. *Der Mässigkeit Wolleben und Der Trunckenheit Selbstmord.* Ulm, 1653.

Bibliography

Alexander, Archibald B. D. "Seven Deadly Sins." In *Encyclopaedia of Religion and Ethics*, 13 vols., edited by James Hastings, 11:426–28. New York, 1920.

Allen, Richard Martin. "Crime and Punishment in Sixteenth-Century Reutlingen." Ph.D. diss., University of Virginia, 1974.

Andreae, Jakob d. Ä. *Christliche/ notwendige vnd ernstliche Erinnerung nach dem Lauf der jrdischen Planeten gestellt . . . in fünff Predigten verfasset.* Tübingen, 1567.

Ariès, Phillip. *Centuries of Childhood: A Social History of Family Life.* Translated by Robert Baldick. New York, 1962.

Ashley, Robert. *Of Honour.* Edited by Virgil Heltzel. San Marino, Calif., 1947.

Augsburg in alten und neuen Reisebeschreibungen. Düsseldorf, 1992.

Austin, Gregory. *Alcohol in Western Society from Antiquity to 1800.* Santa Barbara, Calif., 1985.

———. "Die europäische Drogenkrise des 16. und 17. Jahrhunderts." In *Rausch und Realität: Drogen im Kulturvergleich,* edited by Gisela Völger and Karin von Welck, 115–32. Reinbek, 1982.

Avila, Luis Lobera de. *Bancket der Höfe und Edelleut.* Frankfurt, 1551.

Bächtold-Stäubli, Hanns. *Handwörterbuch des deutschen Aberglaubens.* Edited by E. Hoffmann-Krayer. 10 vols. Berlin, 1927–1942.

Backmann, Sibylle, et al., eds. *Ehrkonzepte in der Frühen Neuzeit. Identitäten und Abgrenzungen.* Berlin, 1998.

Baer, Wolfram, et al., *Augsburger Stadtlexikon.* Augsburg, 1985.

Bakhtin, Mikhail. *Rabelais and His World.* Cambridge, Mass., 1968.

Barrows, Susanna, and Robin Room. *Drinking: Behavior and Belief in Modern History.* Los Angeles, 1991.

Bassermann-Jordan, Friedrich von. *Geschichte des Weinbaus.* 2 vols. Frankfurt, 1923.

Bates, Stuart. *Touring in 1600: A Study in the Development of Travel as a Means of Education.* Boston, 1911.

Bátori, Ingrid. "Daily Life and Culture of an Urban Elite: The Imperial City of Nördlingen in the 15th and 16th Century." *History of European Ideas.* Special Issue, *Turning Points in History* 11 (1989): 621–27.

———. *Die Reichsstadt Augsburg im 18. Jahrhundert: Verfassung, Finanzen und Reformversuche.* Göttingen, 1969.

Beattie, John M. "The Criminality of Women." *Journal of Social History* 8 (1975): 80–116.

Behringer, Wolfgang. *Hexenverfolgung in Bayern.* Munich, 1987.

———. "Mörder, Diebe, Ehebrecher. Verbrechen und Strafen in Kurbayern vom 16. bis 18. Jahrhundert." In *Verbrechen, Strafen, und soziale Kontrolle. Studien zur historischen Kulturforschung,* edited by Richard van Dülmen, 85–132. Frankfurt, 1990.

———, ed. *Hexen und Hexenprozesse in Deutschland.* Munich, 1988.

Beichtbüchlein. Augsburg, 1491.

Bibliography

Beier, Adrien. *Handlungs- Kunst- Berg- und Handwerks-Lexicon.* Jena, 1722.

Beik, William. "Popular Culture and Elite Repression in Early Modern Europe." *Journal of Interdisciplinary History* 11 (summer 1980): 97–103.

Belmont, N. "The Symbolic Function of the Wedding Procession in the Popular Rituals of Marriage." In *Ritual, Religion, and the Sacred,* edited by Robert Forster and O. Ranum, 1–7. Baltimore, 1982.

Binswanger, J. "Zur äusseren Rechtsgeschichte der Stadt Augsburg." In *Festschrift zum 22. Deutschen Juristentag,* 15–20. Augsburg, 1893.

Birlinger, Anton. *Volksthümliches aus Schwaben.* 3 vols. Freiburg im Breisgau, 1861.

Blankart, Stephan. *Von Würckungen deren Artzneyen in dem Menschlichen Leibe.* Leipzig, 1690.

Blanke, Fritz. "Reformation und Alkoholismus." *Zwingliana* 9 (1953): 75–89.

Blauert, Andreas, and Gerd Schwerhoff, eds. *Mit den Waffen der Justiz: zur Kriminalitätsgeschichte des späten Mittelalters und der Frühen Neuzeit.* Frankfurt, 1993.

Bloomfield, Morton W. *The Seven Deadly Sins.* Ann Arbor, 1952.

Bock, Hieronymus. *Der vollen brüder orden.* N.p., 1552.

Bode, Wilhelm. *Kurze Geschichte der Trinksitten und Mäßigkeitsbestrebungen in Deutschland.* Munich, 1896.

Bontekoe, Cornelius. *Kurtze Abhandlung von dem Menschlichen Leben.* N.p., 1685.

Boos, Anton. "Zur Geschichte unserer Brauerei-Industrie." *Neueste Nachrichten,* 8 May 1895.

Brady, Thomas. "In Search of the Godly City: The Domestication of Religion in the German Urban Reformation." In *The German People and the Reformation,* edited by R. Po-Chia Hsia, 14–31. Ithaca, N.Y., 1988.

Brandes, Stanley. *Power and Persuasion: Fiestas and Social Control in Rural Mexico.* Philadelphia, 1988.

Brant, Sebastian. *The Ship of Fools.* 1494. Translated by E. Zeydel. New York, 1944.

Braudel, Fernand. *Civilization and Capitalism, 15th–18th Century.* Vol. 1, *The Structures of Everyday Life: The Limits of the Possible.* Translated by Siân Reynolds. New York, 1981.

Breitenberg, Mark. *Anxious Masculinity in Early Modern England.* Cambridge, 1996.

Brennan, Thomas. *Public Drinking and Popular Culture in Eighteenth-Century Paris.* Princeton, 1988.

Brown, Judith. *Immodest Acts: The Life of a Lesbian Nun in Renaissance Italy.* New York, 1986.

Brunner, Otto, Werner Conze, and Reinhart Koselleck, eds. *Geschichtliche Grundbegriffe: Historisches Lexikon zur politisch-sozialen Sprache in Deutschland.* 8 vols. Stuttgart, 1972–1997.

Brunschwig, Hieronymus. *Das Buch zu Distilieren.* Strasbourg, 1532.

Buff, Adolf. "Das Ausgeschenk der Augsburger Buchbinder." *Der Grenzbote* 3 (1981): 457–62.

Burghartz, Susanna. *Leib, Ehre, und Gut: Delinquenz in Zürich Ende des 14. Jahrhunderts.* Zürich, 1991.

Burke, Peter. *Popular Culture in Early Modern Europe.* New York, 1978.

Castiglione, Baldesar. *The Book of the Courtier.* Translated by George Bull. London, 1967.

Clark, Peter. "The Alehouse and the Alternative Society." In *Puritans and Revolutionaries: Essays in Seventeenth-Century History Presented to Christopher Hill,* edited by Donald Pennington and Keith Thomas, 47–72. Oxford, 1978.

———. *The English Alehouse: A Social History, 1200–1830.* London, 1983.

Clasen, Claus-Peter. *Anabaptism: A Social History, 1525–1618. Switzerland, Austria, Moravia, and South and Central Germany.* Ithaca, N.Y., 1972.

———. "Armenfürsorge im 16. Jahrhundert." In *Geschichte der Stadt Augsburg von der Römerzeit bis zur Gegenwart,* edited by Gunther Gottlieb et al., 337–42. Stuttgart, 1985.

———. "Armenfürsorge in Augsburg vor dem Dreißigjährigen Kriege." *Zeitschrift des historischen Vereins für Schwaben* 78 (1984): 64–115.

Clinard, Marshall. "The Public Drinking House and Society." In *Society, Culture, and Drinking Patterns,* edited by David Pittman and Charles Snyder, 270–95. New York, 1962.

Cockburn, James S., ed. *Crime in England, 1550–1800.* London, 1977.

Cohen, Stan. *Folk Devils and Moral Panics.* London, 1972.

Colerus, Johannes. *Oeconomia Ruralis et domestica.* Mainz, 1665.

Crawley, Alfred E. "Drinks, Drinking." In *Encyclopaedia of Religion and Ethics,* 13 vols., edited by James Hastings, 5:72–82. New York, 1912.

Criminal Justice through the Ages: From Divine Judgment to Modern German Legislation: Schriftenreihe des mittelalterlichen Kriminalmuseums 4. Rothenburg ob der Tauber, 1981.

Curtis, T. C. "Quarter Sessions Appearances and Their Background: A Seventeenth-Century Regional Study." In *Crime in England, 1550–1800,* edited by James S. Cockburn, 135–54. London, 1977.

Damhouder, Jost. *Practica Gerichtlicher vbunge.* Translated by Michael Beuther von Carlstatt. Frankfurt, 1565.

Darnton, Robert. *The Great Cat Massacre and Other Episodes in French Cultural History.* New York, 1985.

Davis, Natalie. *Fiction in the Archives: Pardon Tales and Their Tellers in Sixteenth-Century France.* Stanford, 1987.

Deutsches Wörterbuch von Jacob und Wilhelm Grimm. 16 vols. in 32 parts. Leipzig, 1854–1971.

Die Chroniken der Stadt Augsburg. Die Chroniken der deutschen Städte vom 14. bis 16. Jahrhundert. Edited by the Historischen Commission bei der königlichen Akademie der Wissenschaften. Vol. 4. Leipzig, 1865.

Dillistone, Frederick. *Christianity and Symbolism.* London, 1955.

Dinges, Martin. "Die Ehre als Thema der Stadtgeschichte: Eine Semantik im Übergang vom Ancien Régime zur Moderne." *Zeitschrift für historische Forschung* 16 (1989): 409–40.

Bibliography

———. "Frühneuzeitliche Armenfürsorge als Sozialdisciplinierung? Probleme mit einem Konzept." *Geschichte und Gesellschaft* 17 (1991): 5–29.

Dirlmeier, Ulf. *Untersuchungen zu Einkommenverhältnissen und Lebenshaltungskosten in oberdeutschen Städten des Spätmittelalters (Mitte 14. bis Anfang 16. Jahrhundert).* Heidelberg, 1978.

Dirr, Pius. "Kaufleutezunft und Kaufleutestube zur Zeit des Zunftregiments." *Zeitschrift des Historischen Vereins für Schwaben* 35 (1909): 133–51.

Douglas, Mary, ed. *Constructive Drinking: Perspectives on Drink from Anthropology.* New York, 1987.

Duden, Barbara. *The Woman beneath the Skin: A Doctor's Patients in Eighteenth-Century Germany.* Princeton, 1991.

Dülmen, Richard van. *Entstehung des frühneuzeitlichen Europa, 1550–1648.* Frankfurt, 1982.

———. *Kultur und Alltag in der Frühen Neuzeit.* 3 vols. Munich, 1992.

———. *Verbrechen, Strafen, und soziale Kontrolle. Studien zur historischen Kulturforschung.* Frankfurt, 1990.

Ebel, Klaus. *Die strafrechtliche Bewertung der Trunkenheitsdelikte in der italienischen Wissenschaft bis zum ausgehenden 16. Jahrhundert.* Ph.D. diss., University of Marburg, 1968.

Eberlein, Hans. *Augsburg.* Berlin, 1939.

———. "Die Entwicklung des Brauwesens in Augsburg." *Der Brauer und Mälzer* 6:14 (1953): 3–13.

———. *350 Jahre Hasenbrauerei Augsburg 1589–1939.* Augsburg, 1939.

Elias, Norbert. *Über den Prozeß der Zivilisation.* 13th ed. 2 vols. Frankfurt, 1988.

Eobarus, Helius, *De generibus Ebriosorum.* Nuremberg, 1516.

Erler, Adalbert, and Ekkehard Kaufmann, eds. *Handwörterbuch zur deutschen Rechtsgeschichte.* 8 vols. Berlin, 1967.

Evans, Richard. "The 'Dangerous Classes' in Germany from the Middle Ages to the Twentieth Century." In *The German Underworld,* edited by Richard Evans, 1–28. New York, 1988.

———, ed. *The German Underworld.* New York, 1988.

Fabricius, Guilielmus. *Christlicher Schlafftrunck.* Frankfurt, 1624.

Fischart, Johann. *Geschichtsklitterung (Gargantua).* Edited by Ute Nyssen. Darmstadt, 1967.

Fischer, Hermann. *Schwäbisches Wörterbuch.* 6 vols. Tübingen, 1920–1942.

Florian, Gebhard. *Chronica der Stadt Franckfurt.* Frankfurt, 1706.

Forbes, Robert James. *A Short History of the Art of Distillation from the Beginnings up to the Death of Cellier Blumenthal.* Leiden, 1970.

Foucault, Michel. *The History of Sexuality.* London, 1990.

Franck, Sebastian. *Von dem greüwlichen laster der trunckenheyt.* [Justenfelden], ca. 1531.

French, Walter. *Medieval Civilization as Illustrated by the Fastnachtspiele of Hans Sachs.* Baltimore, 1925.

Bibliography

Fries, Lorenz. *Spiegel der Arzney*. Strasbourg, 1546.

Geisberg, Max. *Der Deutsche Einblatt-Holzschnitt in der ersten Hälfte des XVI. Jahrhunderts*. 43 plates. Munich, 1923–1930.

George, Dorothy. *London Life in the Eighteenth Century*. New York, 1965.

"Geschichte der Brauerei in Augsburg." In *Festschrift für den III. Bayerischen Brauertag in Augsburg am 19. 20. und 21. Juli 1903*, 11–39. Augsburg, 1903.

Gilmore, David D., ed. *Honor and Shame and the Unity of the Mediterranean*. Washington, D.C., 1987.

Glassen, Salomon. *Ebrietatis Infamia*. Gotha, 1645.

Glauser, Fritz. "Wein, Wirt, Gewinn, 1580: Wirteeinkommen am Beispiel der schweizerischen Kleinstadt Sursee." In *Gastfreundschaft, Taverne, und Gasthaus im Mittelalter*, edited by Conrad Peyer, 105–220. Munich, 1983.

Goode, Erich, and Nachman Ben-Yehuda. *Moral Panics: The Social Construction of Deviance*. Oxford, 1994.

Gottlieb, Gunther, et al., eds. *Geschichte der Stadt Augsburg von der Römerzeit bis zur Gegenwart*. Stuttgart, 1985.

Götze, Alfred. *Frühneuhochdeutsches Glossar*. 7th ed. Berlin, 1967.

Greyerz, Kaspar von. *Religion and Society in Early Modern Europe*. London, 1984.

Grisar, S. J. "Der 'gute Trunk' in den Lutheranklagen: Eine Revision." *Historisches Jahrbuch* 26 (1905): 479–507.

Groebner, Valentin. "Ratsinteressen, Familieninteressen: Patrizische Konflikte in Nürnberg um 1500." In *Stadtregiment und Bürgerfreiheit: Handlungsspielräume in deutschen und italienischen Städten des Späten Mittelalters und der Frühen Neuzeit*, edited by Klaus Schreiner and Ulrich Meier, 278–308. Göttingen, 1994.

Gusfield, Joseph. "Benevolent Repression: Popular Culture, Social Structure, and the Control of Drinking." In *Drinking: Behavior and Belief in Modern History*, edited by Susanna Barrows and Robin Room, 399–424. Los Angeles, 1991.

Haas, Norbert. *Trinklieder des deutschen Spätmittelalters*. Göppingen, 1991.

Häberlein, Mark. "Tod auf der Herrenstube: Ehre und Gewalt in der Augsburger Führungsschicht, 1500–1620." In *Ehrkonzepte in der Frühen Neuzeit. Identitäten und Abgrenzungen*, edited by Sibylle Backmann et al., 148–69. Berlin, 1998.

Habermas, Jürgen. *Strukturwandel der Öffentlichkeit*. 4th ed. Neuwied and Berlin, 1969.

Haftlmeier-Seiffert, Renate. *Bauerndarstellungen auf deutschen illustrierten Flugblättern des 17. Jahrhunderts*. Frankfurt, 1991.

Harms, Wolfgang. *Deutsche illustrierte Flugblätter des 16. und 17. Jahrhunderts*. 7 vols. Munich and Tübingen, 1980–1997.

Hastings, James, ed. *Encyclopaedia of Religion and Ethics*. 13 vols. New York, 1912–1920.

Hauffen, Adolf. "Die Trinklitteratur in Deutschland bis zum Ausgang des sechszehnten Jahrhunderts." *Vierteljahrsschrift für Literaturgeschichte* 2 (1889): 481–516.

Bibliography

Haupt, Karl. *Die Drei Mohren zu Augsburg.* Augsburg, 1956.

Heath, Dwight. "A Decade of Development in the Anthropological Study of Alcohol Use, 1970–1980." In *Constructive Drinking: Perspectives on Drink from Anthropology,* edited by Mary Douglas, 16–69. New York, 1987.

———. "Some Generalizations about Alcohol and Culture." In *International Handbook on Alcohol and Culture,* edited by Dwight Heath, 348–61. Westport, Conn., 1995.

———, ed. *International Handbook on Alcohol and Culture.* Westport, Conn., 1995.

Hecker, Paul. "Der Augsburger Bürgermeister Jakob Herbrot und der Sturz des zünftigen Regiments in Augsburg." *Zeitschrift des Historischen Vereins für Schwaben* 1 (1874): 34–98.

Heegen, Fritz. "Frauenrechtliches im fränkischen Brauchtum." *Bayerisches Jahrbuch für Volkskunde* 14 (1963): 133–43.

Henkel, Arthur, and Albrecht Schöne. *Emblemata: Handbuch zur Sinnbildkunst des XVI. und XVII. Jahrhunderts.* Stuttgart, 1967.

Herold, Ludwig. "Kartenspiel." In *Handwörterbuch des deutschen Aberglaubens,* by Hanns Bächtold-Stäubli, edited by E. Hoffmann-Krayer, 4:1014–23. Berlin, 1932.

Hildener Museumsheft 1 (1989): 37.

Hirschfelder, Gunther. "Bemerkungen zu Stand und Aufgaben volkskundlich-historischer Alkoholfourschung der Neuzeit." *Rheinisch-westfälische Zeitschrift für Volkskunde* 39 (1994): 87–127.

His, Rudolph. *Geschichte des deutschen Strafrechts bis zur Karolina.* Munich, 1928.

Hölscher, Lucian. "Öffentlichkeit." In *Geschichtliche Grundbegriffe: Historisches Lexikon zur politisch-sozialen Sprache in Deutschland,* edited by Otto Brunner, Werner Conze, and Reinhart Koselleck, 4:414–26. Stuttgart, 1978.

Huber, E. *Das Trankopfer im Kulte der Völker.* Hannover, 1900.

Hübner, Regina, and Manfred Hübner. *Der deutsche Durst.* Leipzig, 1994.

Immenkötter, Herbert. "Kirche zwischen Reformation und Parität." In *Geschichte der Stadt Augsburg von der Römerzeit bis zur Gegenwart,* edited by Gunther Gottlieb et al., 391–412. Stuttgart, 1985.

James, Edwin Oliver. *Origins of Sacrifice.* Port Washington, N.Y., 1971.

Janssen, Johannes. *Geschichte des deutschen Volkes seit dem Ausgang des Mittelalters.* Edited by Ludwig von Pastor. 15th ed. 8 vols. Freiburg, 1924.

Jellinek, Elvin Morton. "A Specimen of the Sixteenth-Century German Drink Literature: Obsopoeus's Art of Drinking." *Quarterly Journal of Studies on Alcohol* 5 (1945): 647–700.

Kachel, Johanna. *Herberge und Gastwirtschaft in Deutschland bis zum 17. Jahrhundert.* Stuttgart, 1924.

Karant-Nunn, Susan. *Reformation of Ritual: An Interpretation of Early Modern Germany.* New York, 1997.

Kavanagh, Thomas. *Enlightenment and the Shadows of Chance: The Novel and the Culture of Gambling in Eighteenth-Century France.* Baltimore, 1993.

Bibliography

Kay, Sarah, and Miri Rubin, eds. *Framing Medieval Bodies*. Manchester, 1994.

Kaysersberg, Johann Geiler von. *Das Buch Granatapfel*. Strasbourg, 1511.

Keyser Karls des fünfften vnd des heyligen Römischen Reichs peinlich gerichts ordnung. Mainz, 1543.

Kienan, Christian. "Der Körper der Humanisten." *Zeitschrift für Germanistik* 8:2 (1998): 302–16.

Kircher, Karl. *Die sakrale Bedeutung des Weines im Altertum*. Giessen, 1910.

Kobelt-Groch, Marion. "Unter Zechern, Spielern, und Häschern. Täufer im Wirtshaus." In *Aussenseiter zwischen Mittelalter und Neuzeit. Festschrift für Has-Jürgen Goertz zum 60. Geburtstag*, edited by Norbert Fischer and Marion Kobelt-Groch, 111–26. Leiden, 1997.

Koch, Elisabeth. *Maior dignitas est in sexu virili. Das weibliche Geschlecht im Normensystem des 16. Jahrhunderts*. Frankfurt, 1991.

Kohler, Alfred. "Wohnen und Essen auf den Reichstagen des 16. Jahrunderts." In *Alltag im 16. Jahrhundert. Studien zu Lebensformen in mitteleuropäischen Städten*, edited by Alfred Kohler and Heinrich Lutz, 222–57. Vienna, 1987.

Kohler, J., ed. *Die Carolina und ihre Vorgängerinnen*. Halle, 1900.

Kopp, Hans Georg. *Das Einnehmer- und das Baumeisteramt Augsburgs im 16. Jahrhundert. Studien zum Haushalt der freien Reichsstadt*. Ph.D. diss., University of Augsburg, 1994.

Kraus, Jürgen. *Das Militärwesen der Reichsstadt Augsburg, 1548–1806*. Augsburg, 1980.

Künast, Hans-Jörg. *"Getruckt zu Augspurg." Buchdruck und Buchhandel in Augsburg zwischen 1468 und 1555*. Tübingen, 1997.

Kunzle, David. *The Early Comic Strip: European Broadsheet from ca. 1450 to 1825*. Berkeley, 1973.

Kusch, Roger. *Der Vollrausch: § 323 a StGB in teleologischer Auslegung*. Berlin, 1984.

Landskron, Stephan von. *Die Hymel Straß*. Augsburg, 1484.

Laqueur, Thomas. *Making Sex: Body and Gender from the Greeks to Freud*. Cambridge, Mass., 1990.

Legnaro, Aldo. "Alkoholkonsum und Verhaltenskontrolle: Bedeutungswandel zwischen Mittelalter und Neuzeit in Europa." In *Rausch und Realität: Drogen im Kulturvergleich*, edited by Gisela Völger and Karin von Welck, 153–75. Reinbek, 1982.

Lehmann, Hartmut. "Frömmigkeitsgeschichtliche Auswirkungen der 'kleinen Eiszeit.'" *Volksreligiosität in der modernen Sozialgeschichte: Geschichte und Gesellschaft*, Sonderheft 11, edited by Wolfgang Schieder, 31–50. Göttingen, 1986.

———. "The Persecution of Witches as Restoration of Order: The Case of Germany, 1590s–1650s." *Central European History* 21:2 (1988): 107–21.

Lender, Marx, and James Martin. *Drinking in America*. New York, 1982, 1987.

Lessing, J. "Wunderliches Trinkgerät." *Westermanns illustrierte deutsche Monatshefte* 63 (1887–1888): 438.

Bibliography

Lexer, Matthias. *Mittelhochdeutsches Handwörterbuch.* 3 vols. 1872–1887. Reprint, Stuttgart, 1974.

Liedl, Eugen. *Gerichtsverfassung und Zivilprozeß der freien Reichsstadt Augsburg.* Augsburg, 1958.

Lottes, Günther. "Volkskultur im Absolutismus—Zerstörte oder eigenständige Lebensweise?" *Sozialwissenschaftliche Information für Unterricht und Studium* 12:4 (1983): 238–45.

Lubbers, Franz. *Die Geschichte der Zurechnungsfähigkeit von Carpzow bis zur Gegenwart.* Breslau-Neukirch, 1938.

Luther, Martin. *Letters of Spiritual Counsel.* The Library of Christian Classics. Vol. 18. Translated and edited by Theodore Tappert. London, 1955.

———. *Tischreden.* Vol. 4. Weimar, 1916.

———. *Werke.* Vol. 47. Weimar, 1912.

Maclean, Ian. *The Renaissance Notion of Women: A Study in the Fortunes of Scholasticism and Medical Science in European Intellectual Life.* Cambridge, 1980.

Magnus, Albertus. *Der Weyber natürliche heymlichaiten vnd zugehör.* Augsburg, 1531.

Mair, Paul Hektor. *Chronik, 1517–1579. Chroniken der deutschen Städte* 32. Leipzig, 1917.

Mandelbaum, David G. "Alcohol and Culture." In *Beliefs, Behaviors, and Alcoholic Beverages: A Cross-Cultural Study,* edited by Mac Marshall, 14–30. Ann Arbor, 1979.

Marsh, Peter, Elisabeth Rosser, and Rom Harré. *The Rules of Disorder.* London, 1978.

Marshall, Mac, ed. *Beliefs, Behaviors, and Alcoholic Beverages: A Cross-Cultural Study.* Ann Arbor, 1979.

Matter, Max. "'Im Wein liegt Wahrheit.' Zur symbolischen Bedeutung gemeinsamen Trinkens." *Hessissche Blätter für Volks- und Kultureforschung* 20. Alkohol im Volksleben, 37–54. Marburg, 1987.

Mauss, Marcel, *The Gift: Forms and Functions of Exchange in Archaic Societies.* Translated by Ian Cunnison. Glencoe, Ill., 1954.

———. "Techniques of the Body." *Economy and Society* 2 (1973): 70–88.

Mayr, Georg. *Wegbüchlein.* 3rd ed. Augsburg, 1612.

McNeill, John T., and Helena M. Gamer. *Medieval Handbooks of Penance.* New York, 1979.

Medick, Hans. "Plebejische Kultur, plebejische Öffentlichkeit, plebejische Ökonomie: Über Erfahrungen und Verhaltensweisen Besitzarmer und Besitzloser in der Übergangsphase zum Kapitalismus." In *Sozialanthropologische Perspekten in der Geschichtsschreibung,* edited by Robert M. Berdahl et al., 157–204. Frankfurt, 1982.

Metlinger, Bartholomaeus. *Ein Regiment der jungen Kinder.* Augsburg, 1497.

Meyer, Christian, ed. *Stadtbuch von Augsburg.* Augsburg, 1872.

Midelfort, H. C. Erik. "Johann Weyer and the Transformation of the Insanity Defense." In *The German People and the Reformation,* edited by R. Po-Chia Hsia, 234–61. Ithaca, N.Y., 1988.

Bibliography

Montaigne, Michel de. *Complete Works: Essays, Travel Journal, Letters.* Translated by Donald Frame. Stanford, 1957.

Monter, William. *Ritual, Myth, and Magic in Early Modern Europe.* Norfolk, 1983.

Mörke, Olaf, and Katarina Sieh. "Gesellschaftliche Führungsgruppen." In *Geschichte der Stadt Augsburg von der Römerzeit bis zur Gegenwart,* edited by Gunther Gottlieb et al., 301–11. Stuttgart, 1985.

Moryson, Fynes. *Shakespeare's Europe: A Survey of the condition of Europe at the end of the 16th century. Being unpublished chapters of Fynes Moryson's Itinerary.* 1617. Edited by Charles Hughes. London, 1903.

Muchembled, Robert. *Popular Culture and Elite Culture in France, 1400–1750.* Baton Rouge, 1985.

Müller, J. "Über Trinkstuben." *Zeitschrift für deutsche Kulturgeschichte* 2 (1857): 239–66, 619–42, 719–32, 777–805.

Müller-Wirthmann, Bernhard. "Raufhändel: Gewalt und Ehre im Dorf." In *Kultur der einfachen Leute,* edited by Richard van Dülmen, 79–111. Munich, 1983.

Multibibus, Blasius [pseud.]. *Jus Potandi oder Zechrecht.* 1616. Edited by Michael Stolleis. Frankfurt, 1984.

Münch, Paul. *Lebensformen in der frühen Neuzeit, 1500 bis 1800.* Frankfurt, 1992.

Murray, Oswyn, ed. *Sympotica: A Symposium on the Symposium.* Oxford, 1994.

Nettesheim, Agrippa von. *Die Eitelkeit und Unsicherheit der Wissenschaften.* Edited by Fritz Mauthner. Munich, 1913.

New Catholic Encyclopedia. 15 vols. New York, 1967.

Occo, Adolph, et al., *Was die Pestilentz an ir selbs sey.* Augsburg, 1535.

Oestreich, Gerhard. *Neostoicism and the Early Modern State.* Translated by David McLintock. Cambridge, 1982.

Onians, Richard. *The Origins of European Thought about the Body, the Mind, the Soul, the World, Time, and Fate.* Cambridge, 1951.

Opsopaeus, Vincentius. *De Arte Bibendi Libri tres.* 1536. Translated by Elvin Morton Jellinek in "A Specimen of the Sixteenth-Century German Drink Literature—Obsopoeus's Art of Drinking," *Quarterly Journal of Studies on Alcohol* 5 (1945): 647–700.

Osborn, Max. *Die Teufelliteratur des XVI. Jahrhunderts.* Hildesheim, 1965.

Ozment, Steven. *The Reformation in the Cities: The Appeal of Protestantism to Sixteenth-Century Germany and Switzerland.* New Haven, 1975.

Pansa, Martin. *Köstliche und Nützliche Hauß-Apothecke.* Frankfurt and Leipzig, 1673.

Paris, R., and W. Sofsky. "Drohungen: Über eine Methode der Interaktionsmacht." *Kölner Zeitschrift für Soziologie und Sozialpsychologie* 39 (1987): 16–39.

Paster, Gail Kern. *The Body Embarrassed: Drama and the Disciplines of Shame in Early Modern England.* Ithaca, N.Y., 1993.

Pauli, Johannes. *Schimpff und Ernst.* Augsburg, 1534.

Peyer, Conrad, ed. *Gastfreundschaft, Taverne, und Gasthaus im Mittelalter.* Munich, 1983.

Bibliography

————. *Von der Gastfreundschaft zum Gasthaus: Studien zur Gastlichkeit im Mittelalter.* Hannover, 1986.

Pilz, Georg, ed. *Ein Sack voll Ablaß. Bildsatiren der Reformationszeit.* Berlin, 1983.

Pittman, David, and Charles Snyder, eds. *Society, Culture, and Drinking Patterns.* New York, 1962.

Plummer, Marjorie Elizabeth. "Reforming the Family: Marriage, Gender, and the Lutheran Household in Early Modern Germany, 1500–1620." Ph.D. diss., University of Virginia, 1996.

Potthoff, O. D., and Georg Kossenhaschen. *Kulturgeschichte der deutschen Gaststätte.* Berlin, ca. 1932.

Rajkay, Barbara. "Die Bevölkerungsentwicklung von 1500 bis 1648." In *Geschichte der Stadt Augsburg von der Römerzeit bis zur Gegenwart,* edited by Gunther Gottlieb et al., 252–58. Stuttgart, 1985.

Rau, Erich Johannes. *Ärtzliche Gutachten und Polizeivorschriften über den Branntwein im Mittelalter.* M.D. diss., University of Leipzig, 1914.

Rauers, F. *Kulturgeschichte der Gaststätte.* 2 vols. Berlin, 1942.

Regimen Sanitatis. Augsburg, 1474.

Reith, Reinhold. *Lexikon des alten Handwerks vom späten Mittelalter bis ins 20. Jahrhundert.* Munich, 1990.

Rem, Wilhelm. *Cronica newer geschichten, 1512–1527. Die Chroniken der deutschen Städte* 25. Leipzig, 1896.

Reulecke, Jürgen. "Vom blauen Montag zum Arbeiterurlaub: Vorgeschichte und Entstehung des Erholungsurlaubs für Arbeiter vor dem Ersten Weltkrieg." *Archiv für Sozialgeschichte* 16 (1976): 205–48.

Roberts, James. "Drink and Industrial Work Discipline in Nineteenth-Century Germany." *Journal of Social History* 15 (1982): 25–38.

————. *Drink, Temperance, and the Working Class in Nineteenth-Century Germany.* Boston, 1984.

Roeck, Bernd. *Bäcker, Brot, und Getreide in Augsburg. Zur Geschichte des Bäckerhandwerks und zur Versorgungspolitik der Reichsstadt im Zeitalter des Dreißigjährigen Krieges.* Sigmaringen, 1987.

————. *Eine Stadt in Krieg und Frieden. Studien zur Geschichte der Reichsstadt Augsburg zwischen Kalenderstreit und Parität.* 2 vols. Göttingen, 1989.

Rogge, Jörg. *Für den gemeinen Nutzen: Politisches Handeln und Politikverständnis von Rat und Bürgerschaft in Augsburg im Spätmittelalter.* Tübingen, 1996.

Römer, A. "Luther und die Trinksitten." *Die Alkoholfrage* 13 (1917): 100–114.

Roos, Keith L. *The Devil in Sixteenth-Century German Literature: The Teufelsbücher.* Bern, 1972.

Roper, Lyndal. "Discipline and Respectability: Prostitution and the Reformation in Augsburg." *History Workshop* 19 (spring 1985): 3–28.

————. "Going to Church and Street: Weddings in Reformation Augsburg." *Past and Present* 106 (1985): 62–101.

————. *The Holy Household: Women and Morals in Reformation Augsburg*. Oxford, 1989.

————. "Mothers of Debauchery: Procuresses in Reformation Augsburg." *German History* 6 (April 1988): 1–19.

————. *Oedipus and the Devil: Witchcraft, Sexuality, and Religion in Early Modern Europe*. London, 1994.

Rorabaugh, W. J. *The Alcoholic Republic: An American Tradition*. Oxford, 1979.

Roueché, Berton. "Alcohol in Human Culture. In *Alcohol and Civilization*, edited by Salvatore Lucia, 167–83. New York, 1963.

Rubin, Miri. "The Person in the Form: Medieval Challenges to Bodily 'Order.'" In *Framing Medieval Bodies*, edited by Sarah Kay and Miri Rubin, 100–122. Manchester, 1994.

Ruckdeschel, Wilhelm. *Technische Denkmale in Augsburg*. Augsburg, 1984.

Ryff, Walter. *New Kochbuch für die Krancken*. Frankfurt, 1545.

————. *Spiegel und Regiment der Gesundheit*. Frankfurt, 1544.

Sachs, Hans. *Die vier wunderberlichen Eygenschafft vnd würckung des Weins*. 1528. Translated by Peter Schäffer in *Hans Sachs: Two Poems*, 1–24. Davis, Calif., 1990.

————. *Werke*. Edited by Adelbert von Keller and Edmund Goetze. 26 vols. 1870–1908. Reprint, Hildesheim, 1964.

Safley, Thomas. *Let No Man Put Asunder: The Control of Marriage in the German Southwest: A Comparative Study, 1550–1600*. Kirksville, Mo., 1984.

Sawday, Jonathan. *The Body Emblazoned: Dissection and the Human Body in Renaissance Culture*. New York, 1995.

Schaffstein, Friedrich. *Die allgemeinen Lehren vom Verbrechen in ihrer Entwicklung durch die Wissenschaft des Gemeinen Strafrechts. Beiträge zur Strafrechtsentwicklung von der Carolina bis Carpzov*. Aalen, 1973.

Schama, Simon. *The Embarrassment of Riches: An Interpretation of Dutch Culture in the Golden Age*. London, 1987.

Schauber, Vera, and Hans Michael Schindler. *Heilige und Namenspatrone im Jahreslauf*. Augsburg, 1992.

Schiebinger, Londa. *The Mind Has No Sex? Women in the Origins of Modern Science*. Cambridge, Mass., 1989.

Schilling, Michael. *Bildpublizistik in der frühen Neuzeit. Aufgaben und Leistungen des illustrierten Flugblatts in Deutschland bis um 1700*. Tübingen, 1990.

Schindler, Norbert. *Widerspenstige Leute. Studien zur Volkskultur in der frühen Neuzeit*. Frankfurt, 1992.

Schivelbusch, Wolfgang. *Tastes of Paradise: A Social History of Spices, Stimulants, and Intoxicants*. New York, 1992.

Schmidt, Kurt Dietrich. *Die Alkoholfrage in Orthodoxie, Pietismus, und Rationalismus*. Berlin, 1927.

Schoen, Erhard. "Klage Gottes über seinen Weinberg." 1532. In *Ein Sack voll Ablaß. Bildsatiren der Reformationszeit*, edited by Georg Pilz, 93. Berlin, 1983.

————. *Die Vier Eygenschafften des Weins.* Ca. 1528. In *Der Deutsche Einblatt-Holzschnitt in der ersten Hälfte des XVI. Jahrhunderts,* edited by Max Geisberg, 30. Munich, 1923–1930.

Schorer, Christoph. *Medicina Peregrinantium.* Ulm, 1667.

Schreiber, Georg. *Deutsche Weingeschichte: Der Wein in Volksleben, Kult, und Wirtschaft.* Cologne, 1980.

Schrick, Michael Puff von. *Von allen geprenten wassern.* Nuremberg, 1518.

Schulz, Knut. "Gesellentrinkstuben und Gesellenherbergen im 14., 15., und 16. Jahrhundert." In *Gastfreundschaft, Taverne, und Gasthaus im Mittelalter,* edited by Conrad Peyer, 221–42. Munich, 1983.

Schuster, Peter. "Ehre und Recht. Überlegungen zu einer Begriffs- und Sozialgeschichte zweier Grundbegriffe der mittelalterlichen Gesellschaft." In *Ehrkonzepte in der Frühen Neuzeit. Identitäten und Abgrenzungen,* edited by Sibylle Backmann et al., 40–66. Berlin, 1998.

Schwabenspiegel. Edited by Wilhelm Wackernagel. Zurich, 1840.

Schwarzenberg, Johannes von. *Der Teütsch Cicero.* Augsburg, 1535.

————. *Der Zudrincker vnd Prasser Gesatze, Ordenung, vnd Instruction.* Oppenheim, ca. 1512.

[————]. *Vom Zutrinken.* Bamberg, 1523.

Schweinichen, Hans von. *Denkwürdigkeiten.* Edited by Hermann Oesterley. Breslau, 1878.

Schwerhoff, Gerd. *Köln in Kreuzverhör. Kriminalität, Herrschaft, und Gesellschaft in einer frühneuzeitlichen Stadt.* Bonn, 1991.

Scribner, Robert. *Popular Culture and Popular Movements in Reformation Germany.* London, 1987.

Sehling, Emil. *Die evangelischen Kirchenordnungen des XVI Jahrhunderts.* Vol. 12, *Bayern.* Part 2, *Schwaben.* Tübingen, 1963.

Seifert, Eckhart. "Der Kampf um des Priesters Rausch. Eine Quellenstudie." In *Ferdinandina (Festschrift für Ferdinand Elsener),* edited by Friedrich Ebel et al., 81–92. Tübingen, 1973.

Seling, Helmut. *Die Kunst der Augsburger Goldschmiede, 1529–1868.* 2 vols. Munich, 1980.

Sharpe, James Anthony. "Enforcing the Law in the Seventeenth-Century English Village." In *Crime and the Law: The Social History of Crime in Western Europe since 1500,* edited by V. A. C. Gatrell, Bruce Lenman, and Geoffrey Parker, 97–119. London, 1980.

Sleumer, Albert. *Kirchenlateinisches Wörterbuch.* Limburg a. d. Lahn, 1926.

Smith, Michael. *The Public House, Leisure and Social Control.* Salford, 1981.

Smoller, Laura A. "Playing Cards and Popular Culture in Sixteenth-Century Nuremberg." *The Sixteenth Century Journal* 17:2 (1986): 183–214.

Spiegel des Sünders. Augsburg, ca. 1476.

Bibliography

Spode, Hasso. *Alkohol und Zivilisation. Berauschung, Ernüchterung, und Tischsitten in Deutschland bis zum Beginn des 20. Jahrhundert.* Berlin, 1991.

———. "The First Step toward Sobriety: The 'Boozing Devil' in Sixteenth-Century Germany." *Contemporary Drug Problems* 21 (fall 1994): 453–83.

Stafford, William S. *Domesticating the Clergy: The Inception of the Reformation in Strasbourg.* Ann Arbor, 1974.

Steidel, Max. *Die Zecher- und Schlemmerlieder im deutschen Volksliede bis zum Dreissigjährigen Kriege.* Karlsruhe, 1914.

Stetten, Paul von. *Geschichte der Heil. Röm. Reichs Freyen Stadt Augspurg aus Bewährten Jahr-Büchern und Tüchtigen Urkunden gezogen.* 2 vols. Frankfurt, 1743.

Stewart, Alison. "Paper Festivals and Popular Entertainment: The Kermis Woodcuts of Sebald Beham in Reformation Nuermberg." *Sixteenth Century Journal* 24:2 (1993): 301–50.

Neue deutsche Biographie. Edited by Otto Graf zu Stolberg-Wernigerode et al. Vol. 3. Berlin, 1971.

Stolleis, Michael. "Nachwort." In *Jus Potandi oder Zechrecht,* by Blasius Multibibus [pseud.]. Frankfurt, 1984.

———. "'Von dem grewlichen Laster der Trunckenheit.' Trinkverbote im 16. und 17. Jahrhundert." In *Rausch und Realität: Drogen im Kulturvergleich,* edited by Gisela Völger and Karin von Welck, 177–91. Reinbek, 1982.

Stone, Lawrence. "Interpersonal Violence in English Society, 1300–1980." *Past and Present* 101 (1983): 22–33.

Strack, Hermann. *The Jew and Human Sacrifice: Human Blood and Jewish Ritual.* New York, 1971.

Strauss, Walter, ed. *Erhard Schoen–Niklas Stoer: The Illustrated Bartsch: German Masters of the Sixteenth Century.* Vol. 13. New York, 1984.

Stromer, Heinrich. *Ein getrewe, vleissige, und ehrliche Verwarnung Widder das hesliche laster der Trunckenheit.* Wittemberg, 1531.

Stuart, Kathy. *Defiled Trades and Social Outcasts: Honor and Ritual Pollution in Early Modern Germany.* Cambridge, 1999.

Suutala, Maria. *Tier und Mensch im Denken der deutschen Renaissance.* Helsinki, 1990.

Taylor, William. *Drinking, Homicide, and Rebellion in Colonial Mexican Villages.* Stanford, 1979.

Tegnaeus, Harry. *Blood-Brothers.* New York, 1952.

Tengler, Ulrich. *Layen Spiegel: Von rechtmässigen Ordungen in burgerlichen und peinlichen Regimenten.* Augsburg, 1509.

———. *Der neu Layenspiegel.* Augsburg, 1511, 1512.

Tentler, Thomas N. *Sin and Confession on the Eve of the Reformation.* Princeton, 1977.

Thomas, Alois. *Die Darstellung Christi in der Kelter.* Düsseldorf, 1936.

Thomas, Keith. *Religion and the Decline of Magic: Studies in Popular Beliefs in Sixteenth- and Seventeenth-Century England.* London, 1971.

Bibliography

Thompson, Edward Palmer. *The Making of the English Working Class*. London, 1963.
———. "Time, Work Discipline, and Industrial Capitalism." *Past and Present* 38 (1967): 56–97.
Tlusty, B. Ann. "The Devil's Altar: The Tavern and Society in Early Modern Augsburg." Ph.D. diss., University of Maryland, 1994.
———. "Water of Life, Water of Death: The Controversy over Brandy and Gin in Early Modern Augsburg." *Central European History* 31 (fall 1998): 1–30.
Toussaint-Samat, Maguelonne. *History of Food*. Translated by Anthea Bell. Cambridge, Mass., 1992.
Ein Tractätlein/ genannt Zäch-Bruder Spiegel. N.p., 1654.
Tuana, Nancy. "The Weaker Seed: The Sexist Bias of Reproductive Theory." In *Feminism and Science*, edited by Nancy Tuana, 147–71. Bloomington, 1989.
Vnderricht von den Doctorn der Artzney daselbs/ geordnet/ Wie man sich in der kranckhait/ Schwaißsucht genant/ fürsehen vnd halten solle. Augsburg, 1530.
Völger, Gisela, and Karin von Welck, eds. *Rausch und Realität: Drogen im Kulturvergleich*. Reinbek, 1982.
Vom Zutrincken. Neun laster unnd mißbreuch die Erfolge[n] auß dem . . . zutrinckenn. Bamberg, 1523.
Walvin, James. *Leisure and Society, 1830–1950*. New York, 1978.
Warner, Jessica. "Old and in the Way: Widows, Witches, and Spontaneous Combustion in the Age of Reason." *Contemporary Drug Problems* 23 (summer 1996): 197–220.
———. "'Resolved to Drink No More': Addiction as a Preindustrial Construct." *Journal of Studies on Alcohol* 55 (1994): 685–91.
Watson, Alan. *The Evolution of Law*. Oxford, 1985.
Wear, Andrew. "Medicine in Early Modern Europe, 1500–1700." In *The Western Medical Tradition 800 B.C. to A.D. 1800*, edited by Lawrence Conrad et al., 215–361. Cambridge, 1995.
Webb, S., and B. Webb. *The History of Liquor Licensing in England*. London, 1903.
Weinberg, Florence. *Gargantua in a Convex Mirror: Fischart's View of Rabelais*. New York, 1986.
Welser, Markus. *Chronica der weitberuhmten Kaiserlichen freien und des H. Reichs Stadt Augsburg in Schwaben*. 1595. Reprint, Augsburg, 1984.
Wickram, Georg. *Werke*. Edited by Johannes Bolte. Tübingen, 1903.
Wiesner, Merry. "Guilds, Male Bonding, and Women's Work in Early Modern Germany." *Gender & History* 1:2 (1989): 125–37.
———. "Wandervogels and Women: Journeymen's Concepts of Masculinity in Early Modern Germany." *Journal of Social History* 24:4 (1990–1991): 767–82.
———. *Women and Gender in Early Modern Europe*. Cambridge, Mass., 1993.
Wiltenburg, Joy. *Disorderly Women and Female Power in the Street Literature of Early Modern Germany*. Charlottesville, 1992.
Wirth, Jean. "Against the Acculturation Thesis." In *Religion and Society in Early*

Bibliography

Modern Europe, edited by Kaspar von Greyerz, 66–78. London, 1984.

Wissell, Rodolf. *Des alten Handwerks Recht und Gewohnheit.* 2 vols. Berlin, 1929.

Wolf, Johannes. *Beichtbüchlein.* Edited by F. W. Battenberg. Gießen, 1907.

Wrightson, Keith. "Alehouse, Order, and Reformation in Rural England, 1590–1660." In *Popular Culture and Class Conflict, 1590–1914: Explorations in the History of Labour and Leisure,* edited by Eileen Yeo and Stephen Yeo, 1–27. Brighton, 1981.

Yeo, Eileen, and Stephen Yeo. *Popular Culture and Class Conflict, 1590–1914: Explorations in the History of Labour and Leisure.* Brighton, 1981.

Zäh, Helmut. "Hans Jakob Fugger, der 'Wassermann' in der Korrespondenz Hans Fuggers." In *Die Welt des Hans Fugger, Materialen zur Fuggergeschichte* 1. Augsburg, 2001.

Zedler, Johann Heinrich. *Grosses Universal-Lexicon aller Wissenschafften und Künste.* 64 vols. Leipzig and Halle, 1732–1750.

Zink, Burkard. *Chronik 1368–1468. Die Chroniken der deutschen Städte* 5. Leipzig, 1866.

Zorn, Wolfgang. *Augsburg: Geschichte einer deutschen Stadt.* Augsburg, 1972.

Zwingli, Ulrich. *Schriften.* Edited by Thomas Brunnschweiler and Samuel Lutz. 4 vols. Zurich, 1995.

Index

Index

Index

Index

Studies in Early Modern German History

H. C. Erik Midelfort, *Mad Princes of Renaissance Germany*

Arthur E. Imhof, *Lost Worlds: How Our European Ancestors Coped with Everyday Life and Why Life Is So Hard Today,* translated by Thomas Robisheaux

Peter Blickle, *Obedient Germans? A Rebuttal: A New View of German History,* translated by Thomas A. Brady, Jr.

Wolfgang Behringer, *Shaman of Oberstdorf: Chonrad Stoeckhlin and the Phantoms of the Night,* translated by H. C. Erik Midelfort

B. Ann Tlusty, *Bacchus and Civic Order: The Culture of Drink in Early Modern Germany*